Sheffield Hallam University
Learning and IT Services
Collegiate Learning Centre
Collegiate Crescent Campus
Sheffield S10 2BP

102 101 455

Sheffield Hallam University
Learning and Information Services
Withdrawn From Stock

THE PRINCIP
COMMERCIA

SE(

The Principles and Practice of International Commercial Arbitration provides the reader with immediate access to understanding the world of international arbitration. Arbitration has become the dispute resolution method of choice in international transactions. This book explains how and why arbitration works. It provides the legal and regulatory framework for international arbitration, as well as practical strategies to follow and pitfalls to avoid. It is short and readable, but comprehensive in its coverage of the basic requirements, including the most recent changes in arbitration laws, rules, and guidelines. The second edition includes updates on rules and guidelines, such as the arbitration rules of the ICC, the SCC, the ACICA, and UNCITRAL, as well as the 2010 IBA Rules on the Taking of Evidence in International Arbitration. In this book, the author includes insights from numerous international arbitrators and counsel, who tell firsthand about their own experiences with arbitration and their views of the best arbitration practices. Throughout the book, the principles of arbitration are supported and explained by the practice, providing a concrete approach to an important means of resolving disputes.

Margaret L. Moses is Professor of Law at Loyola University Chicago School of Law. She teaches international commercial arbitration, international business transactions, European community law, international trade finance, and contracts. Professor Moses is also the Director of the International Program at Loyola and coaches the Vis Moot International Arbitration teams, which compete in Vienna and Hong Kong.

Sheffield Hallam University
Learning and Information Services
Withdrawn From Stock

The Principles and Practice of International Commercial Arbitration

Second Edition

Margaret L. Moses
Loyola University Chicago School of Law

CAMBRIDGE
UNIVERSITY PRESS

CAMBRIDGE UNIVERSITY PRESS
Cambridge, New York, Melbourne, Madrid, Cape Town,
Singapore, São Paulo, Delhi, Mexico City

Cambridge University Press
32 Avenue of the Americas, New York, NY 10013-2473, USA

www.cambridge.org
Information on this title: www.cambridge.org/9781107401334

© Margaret L. Moses 2008, 2012

This publication is in copyright. Subject to statutory exception
and to the provisions of relevant collective licensing agreements,
no reproduction of any part may take place without the written
permission of Cambridge University Press.

First edition published 2008
Second edition published 2012

Printed in the United States of America

A catalog record for this publication is available from the British Library.

Library of Congress Cataloging in Publication data

Moses, Margaret L.
The principles and practice of international commercial
arbitration / Margaret L. Moses. – 2nd ed.
   p.   cm.
Includes bibliographical references and index.
ISBN 978-1-107-00878-6 (hardback) – ISBN 978-1-107-40133-4 (pbk.)
1. Arbitration and award, International.   I. Title.
K2400.M65 2012
341.5'22–dc23   2011044158

ISBN 978-1-107-00878-6 Hardback
ISBN 978-1-107-40133-4 Paperback

Cambridge University Press has no responsibility for the persistence or accuracy of URLs for
external or third-party Internet websites referred to in this publication and does not guarantee
that any content on such websites is, or will remain, accurate or appropriate.

Contents

APPENDICES

Preface to the Second Edition

The purpose of this book is to provide an overview of the world of international commercial arbitration. It is a world that needs to be understood by both legal practitioners and their clients, as well as by students and others who may participate in resolving disputes privately, outside a national court system.

This book is designed to help the reader obtain an understanding of international commercial arbitration quickly but comprehensively. Although there are many fine treatises available on international commercial arbitration, there are few that are short. This book is compact and readable, but comprehensive in its coverage of the basic requirements, including the most recent changes in arbitration laws, rules, and guidelines. In writing the book, I have had input from many practitioners and arbitrators, who took time to meet with me to share their insights and experience. The resulting benefit is that the principles of arbitration are supported by the practice. Thus, the book provides not only the legal and regulatory framework, but also a practical sense of how international arbitration works, and how some of the better strategies and practices can lead to both procedurally efficient and substantively reasonable resolutions.

Topics range from drafting an arbitration agreement to enforcing an award. There is specific advice from arbitrators and practitioners relating to choosing arbitrators, selecting the chair of the tribunal, interviewing experts, managing hearings, cross-examining witnesses, and a host of other issues. In addition to dealing with pertinent laws and the interaction of arbitration and the courts, the book contains a final chapter on investment arbitration. Arbitrations growing out of foreign investments, whether based on a contract or on a treaty, have increased significantly in the past decade. Finally, there are Appendices containing important laws, rules, ethics codes, model clauses, and useful websites.

In talking with friends and colleagues, I have learned that this book has proved very useful to professors teaching arbitration, to students trying to gain a grasp of arbitration, and to practitioners and arbitrators new to the field. As international commercial arbitration grows, so does the need to bring new people, both legal professionals and arbitrators, into the field. Clients also need to know the parameters of international commercial arbitration, which today is the dispute resolution method of choice in international transactions. This book provides a practitioner, student, professor, or businessperson with immediate access to understanding the world of international commercial arbitration. This second edition updates important sets of rules and guidelines, such as the arbitration rules of the ICC, the SCC, the ACICA, and UNCITRAL, as well as the 2010 IBA Rules on the Taking of Evidence in International Arbitration.

I very much appreciate the helpful comments and insight of the following international practitioners, arbitrators, and professors: Louise Barrington, Guido Carducci, Jack Coe, Diana Droulers, Hew Dundas, Sarah François-Poncet, Claudia Kälin-Nauer, Pierre Karrer, Gillian Lemaire, Pierre Mayer, Sylwester Pieckowski, Ryan Reetz, Jose Rosell, Mauro Rubino-Sammartano, Claudia Salomon, Larry Schaner, Eric Schwartz, Ingeborg Schwenzer, Christopher Seppälä, Nicholas Simon, Jingzhou Tao, and David Wagoner. A special thank-you to Professor Michael Zimmer, whose encouragement and support were essential.

My research was supported by a grant from the Loyola University Chicago School of Law. I am grateful to Loyola and to my student research assistants, Ben Boroski, Paul Hage, Jean LaViolette, Anna Woodworth, and Aaron Siebert-Llera. For research on the second edition, I am most appreciative of the work of Brittany Kubes and Matthew Levitt. The errors that remain are my own.

Foreword to the First Edition

Professor Moses' book is appearing at an auspicious time. The year 2008 marks the fiftieth anniversary of the 1958 Convention on the Recognition and Enforcement of Foreign Arbitral Awards (New York Convention), the keystone on which the entire edifice of international commercial arbitration is built. The anniversary will be celebrated in arbitration circles by events around the world.

It is little remarked, but 2008 is also the eighty-fifth anniversary of the 1923 Protocol on Arbitration Clauses. Although the New York Convention is currently by far the more important, the 1923 Protocol was the more revolutionary. It marked the first occasion on which the international community through the League of Nations agreed upon a multilateral text in the field of arbitration. It was followed four years later by the 1927 Convention for the Execution of Foreign Arbitral Awards. The Protocol and the Convention were highly successful, but both were flawed. At the instance of the International Chamber of Commerce, the United Nations undertook the revision that resulted in the New York Convention.

For the modern student, scholar, and practitioner, this may all be ancient history. However, it is important to remember just how recent the development of international commercial arbitration is. Arbitration has, of course, a long history. Depending on how it is defined, one can find examples going back to Roman times and even before. However, once the modern nation-state asserted the monopoly of law creation in the late eighteenth and early nineteenth centuries, it was only natural that there would be a concomitant assertion of a monopoly (or something akin to it) of dispute settlement by the courts. The manifestation was a common rule that predispute arbitration agreements were not enforceable as such. The refusal by the respondent to enter into the arbitration might be treated as a breach of contract leading to a claim for damages. However, because it was normally impossible to show that any damages had arisen, a claim for damages was of no value.

The 1923 Protocol and the 1925 Federal Arbitration Act, both designed to allow for the enforcement of predispute arbitration agreements, date from the same period. During the inter-war years, there was a growth in the use of arbitration, but there was still little that could be considered to be international commercial arbitration as it is understood today. Any arbitration of an international commercial dispute was conducted under national rules that seldom took the international aspect of the dispute into consideration. That began to change with the adoption of the New York Convention in 1958. This change was quickly followed by the European Convention on International Commercial Arbitration of 1961, which was the first international text to use the words "international commercial arbitration." There was further progress in 1966 with the European Convention Providing a Uniform Law on Arbitration, unsuccessful though it was, and the Arbitration Rules of the United Nations Economic Commission for Europe, which have been widely used.

To this observer's eyes, the final breakthrough came with the adoption of the UNCITRAL Arbitration Rules in 1976 and the UNCITRAL Model Law on International Commercial Arbitration in 1985. The UNCITRAL Arbitration Rules were the first to reconcile some of the procedural differences between the civil law and the common law. The Model Law introduced the idea that it would be appropriate to have separate rules for domestic arbitrations and for international arbitrations, thereby liberating international arbitration from many of the policy constraints that continue to be thought appropriate for domestic arbitration in many countries. Those two related texts have provided the template for modern institutional arbitration rules and for national legislation on arbitration, both international and domestic.

The institutional changes brought about by the various texts had another important effect that was more in the nature of a change in attitude. Although "international commercial arbitration" as a distinct area of law was first announced in 1961 in the European Convention, the past thirty years has seen the development of a body of rules and procedures unique to it that are generally recognized in much of the world. There is by now general agreement on basic procedures to follow in international commercial arbitration.

It has become common to describe arbitration as the preferred method for resolving international commercial disputes. There are a number of ways in which it is preferable to litigation, of which only a few of the more salient need to be mentioned. Arbitration is certainly better than litigating a dispute in the other party's courts, which would otherwise be the usual result for one of the parties. Even if one could feel confident that those courts were unbiased, they might operate in a different language and with a civil procedure that was unfamiliar. Under modern arbitration laws, the dispute can be arbitrated in a neutral third country to which neither party belongs. Because of the New York Convention, an arbitral award is more easily enforced throughout the world than are decisions of foreign courts.

The most significant of those advantages of arbitration over litigation of international commercial disputes relevant to this book is that it is easily possible to pick a seat for the arbitration that allows the parties to be represented by their regular counsel, which is not possible when litigating in a foreign court. Local counsel must be engaged to handle the dispute. Although local counsel may be expert in local procedure and may be highly competent, it may be estranged from the client and perhaps from regular counsel, with all the possibilities of misunderstanding the relevant business culture and legal dynamics that motivated the client. It is far preferable that counsel familiar with the client be able to handle the dispute to completion.

This recital of developments makes it seem all too easy. It appears as though international commercial arbitration was a single subject with a clearly defined body of law. As compared to a half century ago, it is. In absolute terms, it is not. Although there has been a large convergence of rules and procedures and the specialists in the field speak a common language, those rules and procedures remain specific to each arbitral organization and to the individual national laws governing arbitration. Even the New York Convention is subject to the varied interpretations given to it by the national courts.

Furthermore, the increased popularity of arbitrating international commercial disputes has brought many new players to the game. It is no longer just a field for the Grand Old Men as it was a half century ago. There are a large number of arbitrators, counsel, and parties who come to international arbitration knowing little about the subject. Those who are new to it undoubtedly expect that an international arbitration will be conducted the way that arbitration is conducted in their own country, and that probably means in a manner similar to litigation in the national courts. They are apt to have an unhappy experience as a result.

Traditionally, lawyers have entered the field by working with a senior lawyer who is already engaged in arbitration. The apprenticeship approach may still be the major mode of entry. Until the last few years, very few law schools in any country have offered courses that have gone into international arbitration in any depth, if they had courses that mentioned it at all. That is beginning to change, particularly at the graduate level. There are currently several excellent LL.M. programs specifically in international arbitration, particularly in Sweden, the United Kingdom, and the United States, and these have begun to feed a certain number of academically trained young lawyers into the field. The Chartered Institute of Arbitrators has long had courses for those new to the field. I would be remiss if I did not mention the Willem C. Vis International Commercial Arbitration Moot, which introduces more than a thousand law students to the subject every year. However, an introduction is just that. They need more.

There are many books on arbitration and more arrive every year. Most of them are directed at the specialist, but are often limited to the law in a given country. There are several excellent books that treat the subject from an international perspective and in depth. They may, however, treat the subject in too much depth for the newcomer, whether a senior lawyer without experience in this field, the young lawyer newly entering the field, or the student. What they need is a short, concise discussion of the issues with enough detail to explain what is involved and with reference to sources that treat the individual issues in more depth.

Professor Moses has undertaken to fulfill this need. She has succeeded. If you are reading this Foreword, then you have probably already purchased the book, and I congratulate you on your choice. If you have not yet purchased it, I urge you to do so. Even a person knowledgeable in the field will find much in it of interest. I did.

Eric E. Bergsten

CHAPTER ONE

Introduction to International Commercial Arbitration[1]

A. PURPOSE

Arbitration is a private system of adjudication. Parties who arbitrate have decided to resolve their disputes outside any judicial system. In most instances, arbitration involves a final and binding decision, producing an award that is enforceable in a national court. The decision makers (the arbitrators), usually one or three, are generally chosen by the parties. Parties also decide whether the arbitration will be administered by an international arbitral institution, or will be ad hoc, which means no institution is involved. The rules that apply are the rules of the arbitral institution, or other rules chosen by the parties. In addition to choosing the arbitrators and the rules, parties can choose the place of arbitration and the language of arbitration.

Arbitration thus gives the parties substantial autonomy and control over the process that will be used to resolve their disputes. This is particularly important in international commercial arbitration because parties do not want to be subject to the jurisdiction of the other party's court system. Each party fears the other party's "home court advantage." Arbitration offers a more neutral forum, where each side believes it will have a fair hearing. Moreover, the flexibility of being able to tailor the dispute resolution process to the needs of the parties, and the opportunity to select arbitrators who are knowledgeable in the subject matter of the dispute, make arbitration particularly attractive. Today, international commercial arbitration has become the norm for dispute resolution in most international business transactions.

---

[1] This chapter presents a brief overview of some of the basic characteristics of arbitration and how it works. Specific points mentioned in this chapter will be developed in greater detail in subsequent chapters.

B. DEFINING CHARACTERISTICS

1. Consent

The parties' consent provides the underpinning for the power of the arbitrators to decide the dispute. The parties' consent also limits an arbitrator's power because an arbitrator can decide only issues within the scope of the parties' agreement. Arbitrators are also expected to apply rules, procedures, and laws chosen by the parties. Normally, the parties express their consent to submit any future dispute to arbitration in a written agreement that is a clause in the commercial contract between them. If they do not have an arbitration clause in their contract, however, they can still enter into an agreement after a dispute has arisen. This is known as a *submission agreement*.

2. Nongovernmental Decision Makers

Arbitrators are private citizens. They do not belong to any government hierarchy. Compared with judges, they will probably weigh less heavily any questions of public policy or public interest, because they see their primary responsibility as deciding the one dispute the parties chose them to decide. Also, unlike some judges, arbitrators tend to be very thoughtful of the parties and considerate in their interactions with them. Arbitrators are chosen by the parties and, of course, they would like to be chosen again. It is in their interest to be perceived as even-tempered, thoughtful, fair-minded, and reasonable.

Arbitrators do not have to be lawyers. In some industries, the technical skills of architects and engineers cause them to be chosen as arbitrators. When there are three arbitrators, quite often each party will choose one arbitrator, and the third, who will be the chair, will be chosen by the two party-appointed arbitrators. International arbitrators, however, are all expected to be independent and impartial. They can be challenged, either before the arbitral institution or a court, if there is evidence that they are not independent and impartial.

3. A Final and Binding Award

One of the reasons parties choose to arbitrate is that arbitration results in a final and binding award that generally cannot be appealed to a higher-level court. Although there are occasional opportunities to appeal in some jurisdictions,[2] for the most part, a party can challenge an award only if there is some defect in the process. A party can try to vacate the award in the court

---

[2] Under the English Arbitration Act, for example, in certain limited circumstances, unless the parties have agreed otherwise, a party to an arbitral proceeding may appeal to the court on a question of law. English Arbitration Act of 1996, art. 69(1).

of the country where the arbitration was held (the seat of the arbitration). However, under most arbitration laws, the only grounds for setting aside an award will be quite narrow, such as a defect in the procedure, or an instance where the arbitrators exceeded their powers and decided an issue that was not before them.

Once the arbitrators render an award, the losing party may voluntarily comply with the terms of the award. If it does not, the prevailing party will try to have the award recognized and enforced by a court in a jurisdiction where the losing party has assets. In the enforcing court, the losing party can also challenge the award but, again, only on very narrow grounds. Basically, the award cannot be challenged on the merits; that is, even if the arbitrators made mistakes of law or mistakes of fact, these are not grounds for nonenforcement, and the award will still be enforced. Once a party's award is recognized in the enforcing jurisdiction, it is generally considered to have the same legal effect as a court judgment, and can be enforced in the same way that a judgment would be enforced in that jurisdiction.

C. ADVANTAGES OF ARBITRATION

The benefits of international commercial arbitration are substantial. An empirical study of why parties choose international arbitration to resolve disputes found that the two most significant reasons were (1) the neutrality of the forum (that is, being able to stay out of the other party's court) and (2) the likelihood of obtaining enforcement,[3] by virtue of the New York Convention, a treaty to which more than 145 countries are parties.[4] An arbitration award is generally easier to enforce internationally than a national court judgment because under the New York Convention, courts are required to enforce an award unless there are serious procedural irregularities, or problems that go to the integrity of the process. The New York Convention is considered to have a pro-enforcement bias, and most courts will interpret the permissible grounds for nonenforcement quite narrowly, leading to the enforcement of the vast majority of awards.

Other advantages include the ability to keep the procedure and the resulting award confidential. Confidentiality is provided in some institutional rules, and can be expanded (to cover witnesses and experts, for example) by

---

[3] *See* Christian Bühring-Uhle, *A Survey on Arbitration and Settlement in International Business Disputes*, in Christopher R. Drahozal & Richard W. Naimark, TOWARDS A SCIENCE OF INTERNATIONAL ARBITRATION, p. 31 (2005).

[4] United Nations Convention on the Recognition and Enforcement of Foreign Arbitral Awards, 1958, UN DOC/E/CONF.26/8/Rev.1 ("New York Convention"). Available at www.uncitral.org. *See also* Appendix A for the text of the New York Convention.

the parties' agreement to require those parties to be bound by a confidentiality agreement. Many companies want confidential procedures because they do not want information disclosed about the company and its business operations, or the kinds of disputes in which it is engaged, nor do they want a potentially negative outcome of a dispute to become public.

Parties also like being able to choose arbitrators with particular subject-matter expertise. In addition, they like the fact that there is less discovery in arbitration, thereby generally resulting in a shorter process than in a full-scale litigation, or at least shorter than is found in U.S.-style litigation. The lack of opportunity for multiple appeals of the decision on the merits is also an attractive aspect. For businesspeople, there is great value in finishing a dispute so they can get on with their business.

Although one advantage that has been touted in the past is that arbitration is less expensive than litigation, many companies today do not think that advantage actually exists.[5] As commercial arbitrations have grown in number and in the amount of money at stake,[6] parties have increasingly incorporated many litigation tactics into arbitration. These tactics tend to raise the costs, create delays, and increase the adversarial nature of the process. Nonetheless, even if the arbitration process has begun to resemble litigation in a number of ways, parties tend to find that arbitration is still worth the cost, because of the other advantages it provides.

D. DISADVANTAGES OF ARBITRATION

To an extent, some of the disadvantages of arbitration are the same as the advantages, just viewed from a different perspective. For example, less discovery may be generally viewed as an advantage. Nonetheless, certain kinds of disputes that typically involve extensive discovery, such as antitrust disputes, are increasingly arbitrated. These kinds of disputes often require the aggrieved party to prove a violation that it can prove only if it has sufficient access to documents under the control of the offending party. Less discovery in this kind of case means less of a chance for a claimant to meet its burden of proof.

Moreover, the lack of any significant right of appeal in most arbitrations may be a benefit in terms of ending the dispute, but if an arbitrator has rendered a decision that is clearly wrong on the law or the facts, the lack of

---

[5] *See* Bühring-Uhle, *supra* note 3, at 33 ("More than half [51%] of the respondents thought that the cost advantage did not exist.").

[6] For example, for contract arbitrations active in 2007–2008, the ten largest amounts in controversy ranged from U.S. $4 billion to U.S. $28 billion. *The American Lawyer/Arbitration Scorecard: Contracts*, July 1, 2009. Available at http://www.law .com/jsp/tal/PubArticleFriendlyTAL.jsp?id=1202431683613.

ability to vacate an award on those grounds can be frustrating to a party. For this reason, some parties in the United States had included in their arbitration clauses an agreement that any award would be subject to review on the merits in court. However, in 2008, the U.S. Supreme Court ruled that parties cannot contract for judicial review of the merits of an award.[7] Rather, the exclusive grounds for review are those listed in the Federal Arbitration Act.[8] Those grounds provide for judicial review of issues concerning an unfair process or problems of arbitral bias or misconduct, but do not permit review for arbitrator errors of law or fact.[9]

Another disadvantage is that arbitrators have no coercive powers – that is, they do not have the power to make a party do something by being able to penalize it if it does not. A court, for example, can impose a fine for contempt if a party does not comply with a court order. Arbitrators, on the other hand, cannot impose penalties, although they can draw adverse inferences if a party does not comply with an order of the tribunal. However, with respect to nonparties, arbitrators generally have no power at all. Thus, it may be necessary at times for the parties or the tribunal to seek court assistance when coercive powers are necessary to ensure compliance with the orders of the tribunal.

Moreover, in multiparty disputes, an arbitral tribunal frequently does not have the power to join all relevant parties, even though all may be involved in some aspect of the same dispute. Because the tribunal's power derives from the consent of the parties, if a party has not agreed to arbitrate, usually it cannot be joined in the arbitration. A tribunal generally does not have the right to consolidate similar claims of different parties, even if it would be more efficient for all concerned to do so.

Finally, it could be viewed as a disadvantage that the pool of experienced international arbitrators lacks both gender and ethnic diversity. Although some institutions and a few individual members of this group have made efforts to broaden that pool, on the whole there has been little change.

E. THE REGULATORY FRAMEWORK

The various laws, rules, and guidelines governing the arbitral process will be dealt with extensively in later chapters, but a brief overview is in order. One way to envision the regulatory framework of arbitration is in the form

---

[7] Hall Street Associates, L.L.C. v. Mattel, Inc., 552 U.S. 576 (2008). The Court did leave open, however, the possibility that parties could contract for judicial review of the merits of an award under state statutory or common law. *Id.* at 590.

[8] 9 U.S.C. §§ 1–16,

[9] 9 U.S.C. § 10.

of an inverted pyramid. The point is facing down, and at that point is the arbitration agreement, which affects only the parties to it.

International Treaties
International Arbitration Practice
National Laws
Arbitration Rules

Arbitration Agreement

The arbitration agreement is the underpinning for the regulatory framework governing the private dispute resolution process. If the arbitration agreement is not valid, then there is no legal basis for arbitration.

On the pyramid above the arbitration agreement, the framework expands in terms of scope and applicability beyond the immediate parties. At one step above the arbitration agreement are the arbitration rules chosen by the parties. These rules, which apply to the arbitrations of all the parties that choose them, may be varied in a particular case by the arbitration agreement. Frequently, a rule will contain a provision that says, "unless otherwise agreed in writing by the parties." This means that the rule is not mandatory, but rather is a default rule that will apply if the parties have not reached their own agreement on the particular topic.[10] Therefore, if the parties have agreed on a particular matter, their agreement will trump the arbitration rules, unless the particular rule is considered mandatory by the arbitral institution.

At the next level of the pyramid are the national laws. Both the arbitration law of the seat of the arbitration (the *lex arbitri*) and substantive laws will come into play, and they are likely to be different national laws. Many countries have adopted as their arbitration law the UNCITRAL Model Law on International Commercial Arbitration.[11] The Model Law is meant to

[10] *See, e.g.*, LCIA Rules, art. 17.1 ("The initial language of the arbitration shall be the language of the Arbitration Agreement, unless the parties have agreed in writing otherwise.").

[11] UNCITRAL is the United Nations Commission on International Trade Law. Its mandate is to further the progressive harmonization and unification of the law of international trade. The following countries, territories, or states within the United States have adopted the UNCITRAL Model Law on International Commercial Arbitration: Armenia, Australia, Austria, Azerbaijan, Bahrain, Bangladesh, Belarus, Bulgaria, Cambodia, Canada, Chile, in China: Hong Kong Special Administrative Region, Macau Special Administrative Region; Croatia, Cyprus, Denmark, Dominican Republic, Egypt, Estonia, Georgia, Germany, Greece, Guatemala, Honduras, Hungary, India, Iran (Islamic

work in conjunction with the various arbitration rules, not to conflict with them. Thus, the Model Law also has many provisions that are essentially default provisions: that is, they apply "unless the parties have agreed otherwise." If the parties have chosen arbitration rules that provide for a process or rule that is different from the Model Law, normally the arbitration rules will govern, because they represent the parties' choice of how to carry out the arbitration, that is, they indicate how the parties have "otherwise agreed."

The substantive law chosen by the parties is the national law that will be used to interpret the contract, to determine the merits of the dispute, and to decide any other substantive issues. If the parties have not chosen a substantive law, then the tribunal will determine the applicable substantive law.

At the next step above the national laws in the regulatory pyramid is international arbitration practice, which tends to be utilized to various degrees in all arbitrations. This includes various practices that have developed in international arbitration, some of which have been codified as additional rules or guidelines. There are, for example, rules that have been developed by the International Bar Association on the Taking of Evidence (see Appendix E), and on Rules of Ethics (see Appendix F). The IBA has also produced Guidelines on Conflicts of Interest for Arbitrators (see Appendix G). The American Arbitration and the American Bar Association have also produced A Code of Ethics for Arbitrators (see Appendix H). The ICC has added Case Management Techniques in Appendix IV of its new Arbitration Rules. UNCITRAL has produced Notes on Organizing Arbitral Proceedings "to assist arbitration practitioners by providing an annotated list of matters on which an arbitral tribunal may wish to formulate decisions during the course of arbitral proceedings."[12] Although the Notes do not impose any obligation on the parties or the tribunal, they potentially contribute to harmonizing arbitration practice.

Republic of), Ireland, Japan, Jordan, Kenya, Lithuania, Madagascar, Malta, Mauritius, Mexico, New Zealand, Nicaragua, Nigeria, Norway, Oman, Paraguay, Peru, the Philippines, Poland, Republic of Korea, Russian Federation, Rwanda, Serbia, Singapore, Slovenia, Spain, Sri Lanka, Thailand, Tunisia, Turkey, Uganda, Ukraine, within the United Kingdom of Great Britain and Northern Ireland: Scotland; Bermuda, an overseas territory of the United Kingdom; within the United States of America: the states of California, Connecticut, Florida, Illinois, Louisiana, Oregon, and Texas; Venezuela, Zambia, and Zimbabwe. Available at http://www.uncitral.org/uncitral/en/uncitral_texts/arbitration/1985Model_arbitration_status.html. *See* Appendix B for text of the 1985 UNCITRAL Model Law and Appendix C for the text of the 2006 amendments, which have been adopted in twelve jurisdictions.

[12] Available at www.uncitral.org.

Arbitrators and parties may agree that some of these international practices will be followed, or arbitrators may simply use them as guidelines. International arbitrators are a relatively small group, and international practices – both those that are codified by various international organizations or institutions and those that are merely known and shared in the arbitration community as good practices – tend to create a relatively coherent system of procedures.

Finally, at the top of the inverted pyramid are any pertinent international treaties.

For most international commercial arbitrations, the New York Convention will be the relevant treaty because it governs the enforcement of both arbitration agreements and awards, and because so many countries are parties to the Convention.[13] In addition to the New York Convention, three other important conventions are the Inter-American Convention on International Commercial Arbitration (the "Panama Convention"),[14] the European Convention on International Commercial Arbitration,[15] and the Convention on the Settlement of Investment Disputes between States and Nationals of other States (the "Washington Convention" or the "ICSID Convention").[16]

The Panama Convention, which has been ratified or adopted by seventeen South or Central American countries and by the United States and Mexico, is similar in intent and effect to the New York Convention. It has been influential in making arbitration much more acceptable in Latin American countries.

The European Convention supplements the New York Convention in the contracting states. It provides for a number of general issues concerning party's rights in arbitration and provides specific limited reasons for when the setting aside of an award under the national law of one Contracting State can constitute a ground for refusing to recognize or enforce an award in another Contracting State.[17] The European Convention's effect on awards that have been set aside will be discussed more fully in Chapter 10.[18]

The Washington Convention on the Settlement of Investment Disputes between States and Nationals of other States is also known as the ICSID Convention because the Convention created the International Center for

---

[13] *See supra*, text accompanying note 4.
[14] O.A.S. Ser. A20 (S.E.P.E.F.), 14 I.L.M. 336 (1975).
[15] 484 U.N.T.S. 349 (1961).
[16] 575 U.N.T.S. 159, T.I.A.S. 6090, 17 U.S.T.1270 (1965).
[17] European Convention on International Commercial Arbitration (1961), 484 U.N.T.S. 349, art. IX. Not all EU countries are parties to the Convention, and some distinctly non-European countries are parties, such as Cuba and Burkina Faso. List of countries available at http://untreaty.un.org/sample/EnglishInternetBible/partI/chapterXXII/treaty2.htm.
[18] *See infra*, Chapter 10, Section 10(D)(5)(f).

the Settlement of Investment Disputes (ICSID). The ICSID Convention was promoted by the World Bank, which wanted to encourage investors to make investments in developing countries. Historically, investors could not bring any kind of action against a government, and had to depend on their own government to take up their cases against a foreign government. The ICSID Convention provides the opportunity for the country and the investor to arbitrate any dispute directly, either pursuant to an arbitration agreement in a state contract, or by virtue of a bilateral investment treaty that includes a clause whereby the state consents to arbitrate with investors covered by the treaty. The ICSID Convention, and treaty arbitrations generally, will be discussed more fully in Chapter 11.

Thus, as seen above, the regulatory framework for international commercial arbitration includes private agreements, agreed-upon rules, and international practice, as well as national laws and international conventions. Although parties have substantial autonomy to control the arbitration process, the supplementation and reinforcement of the process by both national and international laws help ensure that the process functions in a fair and effective manner. The regulatory framework also gives parties confidence that they will have a reasonable method of recourse when problems develop in their international business transactions.

F. INSTITUTIONAL ARBITRATION V. AD HOC ARBITRATION

One of the choices parties must make when they decide to arbitrate is whether they want their arbitration to be administered by an arbitral institution, or whether they want the arbitration to be ad hoc.[19] There are advantages and disadvantages for each choice. With an institutional arbitration, the institution's performance of important administrative functions is considered advantageous. It makes sure the arbitrators are appointed in a timely way, that the arbitration moves along in a reasonable manner, and that fees and expenses are paid in advance. From the arbitrators' point of view, it is an advantage not to have to deal with the parties about fees. The arbitral institution handles any issues of fees or payment. Moreover, the arbitration rules of the institution are time-tested and are usually quite effective to deal with most situations that arise. Another advantage is that an award rendered under the auspices of a well-known institution may have more credibility in the international community and the courts. This may encourage the losing

---

[19] Ad hoc arbitration is not an option in China. *See* Jingzhou Tao & Clarisse von Wunschheim, *Article 16 and 18 of the PRC Arbitration Law – The Great Wall of China for Foreign Arbitration Institutions*, 23 Arb. Int. 309, 324 (2007).

party not to challenge an award, and possibly to voluntarily pay the amount awarded.

With an ad hoc arbitration, there is no administering institution. One resulting advantage is that the parties are not paying the fees and expenses of the administering institution. The parties also have more opportunity to craft a procedure very carefully tailored to the particular kind of dispute. They may draft their own rules, or they may choose the UNCITRAL Arbitration Rules, which are frequently used in ad hoc arbitrations.[20] (UNCITRAL itself does not administer arbitrations and is not an arbitral institution.) Ad hoc arbitrations are sometimes particularly useful when one of the parties is a state, and there may be a need for more flexibility in the proceedings. It can be decided, for example, that neither party is the respondent, because both sides have claims against each other. Then each party will simply have the burden of proof of the claims it raises against the other party. An ad hoc proceeding can be disadvantageous, however, if either of the parties engages in deliberate obstruction of the process. In that situation, without an administering institution, the parties may have to seek the assistance of the court to move the arbitration forward.

G. ARBITRAL INSTITUTIONS

As international commercial arbitration has grown and expanded with the growth of international business,[21] arbitral institutions have also grown and changed. The American Arbitration Association, for example, has created an international division – the International Centre for Dispute Resolution (ICDR) – just to deal with international disputes. Arbitral institutions continually update their rules to present an international arbitration-friendly format, and to improve their ability to deal with certain issues.

Institutions vary in cost and quality of administration. Many companies prefer to work with the older, better-established institutions, even if the cost may be somewhat higher. Parties are concerned that if they go with a brand-new arbitral institution, that institution might not be in business a few years down the road when a dispute might arise. Listed in the following section are brief descriptions of a few of the major international arbitration institutions.

---

[20] The UNCITRAL Arbitration Rules have been updated, effective August 15, 2010. Available at http://www.uncitral.org/uncitral/en/uncitral_texts/arbitration/2010Arbitration_rules.html.

[21] The international caseload of major arbitral institutions nearly doubled between 1993 and 2003 and, during the same period, more than tripled before the American Arbitration Association and its International Centre for Dispute Resolution. *See* Christopher R. Drahozal & Richard W. Naimark, TOWARDS A SCIENCE OF INTERNATIONAL ARBITRATION: COLLECTED EMPIRICAL RESEARCH, 341, app.1 (2005).

1. The International Chamber of Commerce (ICC) International Court of Arbitration

The ICC International Court of Arbitration is one of the better-known and most prestigious arbitral institutions. The International Court of Arbitration is not a court in the ordinary sense of the word; it is not part of any judicial system. Rather the Court of Arbitration is the administrative body that is responsible for overseeing the arbitration process. Its members consist of legal professionals from all over the world. In addition, the ICC has a Secretariat, which is a permanent, professional administrative staff. The ICC's latest Arbitration Rules went into effect on January 1, 2012.

A few features distinguish the ICC as an arbitral institution. First, every ICC arbitral award is scrutinized by the Court of Arbitration, meaning the award is not provided to the parties until it has been reviewed by the Court.[22] Although the Court does not have the power to change the award substantively, if it finds anything amiss, it sends the award back to the arbitrators with its comments. Second, another requirement of the ICC is that at the outset of the arbitration, the parties are asked to complete and sign a document called the "Terms of Reference," which lists a summary of the claims and relief sought, all the parties, the place of arbitration, the rules, and sometimes other information pertaining to discovery or scheduling.[23] This ensures that everyone knows at the beginning of the process what the parameters of the arbitration will be. In addition, practitioners before the ICC like the fact that the actual case administrators, who are part of the Secretariat staff, are lawyers. Although the seat of the ICC International Court of Arbitration is in Paris, it administers arbitrations all over the world.[24]

2. The American Arbitration Association's (AAA) International Center for Dispute Resolution (ICDR)

The ICDR has greatly expanded the number of arbitrations it handles yearly. The number of international arbitration cases filed with the AAA or the ICDR in 2010 was 888, a 6 percent increase over 2009 and a 26 percent increase over 2008.[25] Moreover, the ICDR has opened offices in other countries: Mexico City in 2006, Singapore in 2006, and Bahrain in 2010.[26] In Mexico, the ICDR has a cooperative agreement with the Mediation and Arbitration Commission of the Mexico City National Chamber of Commerce (CANACO). In Singapore, the ICDR has entered into a joint venture

---

[22] *See* ICC Rules, art. 33.

[23] *See* ICC Rules, art. 23.

[24] In 2004, the place of arbitration for various ICC arbitrations included 49 different countries. *See* Yves Derain & Eric Schwartz, A GUIDE TO THE ICC RULES OF ARBITRATION, 427, app. 6 (2d ed. 2005).

[25] Information on file with the ICDR in its New York office.

[26] *See* The ICDR International Arbitration Reporter, Issue 1, p. 3.

with the Singapore International Arbitration Centre (SIAC) to establish a dispute resolution center. This step is expected to help make Singapore a leading arbitration center in Asia. In Bahrain, the AAA and Bahrain's Ministry of Justice and Islamic Affairs have established the Bahrain Chamber for Dispute Resolution (BCDR-AAA). The ICDR has reached Cooperative Agreements with sixty-six institutions in at least forty-six countries.[27] The ICDR also administers cases on behalf of the Inter-American Commercial Arbitration Commission (IACAC).

3. The London Court of International Arbitration (LCIA)

The LCIA is also not a "court" in the judicial sense, but rather the responsible supervising body of the arbitration institution. The LCIA Arbitration Court, made up of thirty-five members, is the final authority for the proper application of the LCIA Rules. It also has the responsibility of appointing tribunals, determining challenges to arbitrators, and controlling costs. The LCIA is the oldest international arbitration institution, having been founded in the late nineteenth century. Its Secretariat is headed by a Registrar, and is responsible for the administration of disputes referred to the LCIA. The LCIA will administer cases and apply its rules at any location the parties choose. In 2009 and 2010, the number of cases filed with the LCIA increased by 9 percent over the previous twenty-four-month period.[28] In addition to the organization in London, the LCIA has established LCIA India, an independent arbitral institution based in New Delhi, with rules closely modeled on the LCIA rules. It has also created the DIFC-LCIA Arbitration Center in Dubai.

4. Other Arbitral Institutions

A number of other arbitral centers actively conduct international arbitrations. The Arbitration Institute of the Stockholm Chamber of Commerce (SCC) became particularly well-known for handling East–West arbitrations. Its latest arbitration rules came into force on January 1, 2010. Other European institutions include the European Court of Arbitration, the German Institute of Arbitration (DIS), the Netherlands Arbitration Institute (NAI), the Vienna International Arbitration Centre (VIAC), and the Permanent Court of Arbitration in the Hague (PCA). The PCA is an intergovernmental organization that provides dispute resolution services to states and handles some international commercial arbitrations between private parties. The China International Economic Trade Arbitration Commission (CIETAC) adopted new arbitration rules in 2012, and has moved toward a more

---

[27] *See* www.adr.org/icdr (use the "search" feature for specific information about the various ICDR offices worldwide).

[28] *See* Director General's Report, 2010, available at the LCIA website www.lcia.org.

mainstream approach to international arbitration. The World Intellectual Property Organization (WIPO) Arbitration and Mediation Center has rules on mediation and arbitration considered particularly appropriate for technology, entertainment, and other disputes involving intellectual property. International arbitrations are handled by institutions in Hong Kong, Switzerland, Cairo, Venezuela, Mexico, and many other cities and countries.

U.S. dispute resolution organizations, such as JAMS and the Institute for Conflict Prevention and Resolution (CPR), have adopted international arbitration and mediation rules, and are increasingly handling international arbitrations and mediations. In addition, there are some specialized arbitral institutions such as the Grain and Feed Trade Association (GAFTA), the London Maritime Arbitration Association (LMAA), the Federation of Oils, Seeds and Fats Association (FOSFA), and the London Metal Exchange (LME), all of which have industry-based rules and procedures for resolving disputes of their members.

H. ARBITRATIONS INVOLVING STATES

1. ICSID Arbitrations

State or state-owned entities are generally immune from suits by individuals or companies. However, if the state or state entity engages in a commercial deal, and particularly if it enters into an arbitration agreement, normally it will be considered to have waived immunity. Moreover, it may be obliged to arbitrate under the provisions of a bilateral investment treaty. For Contracting States that agree to arbitration under the ICSID Rules of Arbitration, any resulting award is not appealable to a court, and national laws are not applicable to the process. Under the ICSID Rules, however, the award can be reviewed by an ad hoc committee of three arbitrators and, if annulled, may be arbitrated again by yet another tribunal. A monetary award is enforceable in a Contracting State as though it were a final judgment in the court of that state. Treaty arbitrations will be discussed further in Chapter 11.

2. The Permanent Court of Arbitration

The PCA, located in the Hague, provides a variety of arbitration, conciliation, and fact-finding services. It is primarily known for arbitrating disputes between states and state entities, including disputes arising out of various treaties. However, international commercial arbitration can also be conducted by the PCA. The organization also plays an important role under the UNCITRAL Rules of Arbitration. When parties to an ad hoc arbitration have not agreed on selecting an arbitrator, or an appointing authority, either party may request the Secretary-General of the PCA to designate an appointing authority.[29] In addition, the Editorial Staff of the International Council for Commercial Arbitration (ICCA) is located on the premises of the PCA in the Peace Palace. ICCA publishes the YEARBOOK COMMERCIAL ARBI-TRATION, the INTERNATIONAL HANDBOOK ON COMMERCIAL ARBITRATION, and the ICCA Congress Series, which are important sources of arbitration cases, laws and practice, and scholarly papers in the field.

I. OTHER DISPUTE RESOLUTION METHODS

Other dispute resolution methods, aside from litigation and arbitration, may be used to try to resolve international disputes. These other methods, which are often nonbinding, are sometimes combined with arbitration. For example, parties may agree that they will first try to resolve their dispute by negotiation, and if unsuccessful, they will engage in mediation. If that does not work, then they will commence binding arbitration. The other dispute resolution mechanisms are sometimes referred to under the term *alternative dispute resolution* (ADR). However, the term ADR does not mean the same thing to all people. In Europe and much of the rest of the world, ADR refers to dispute resolution methods that exclude both litigation and arbitration. Although many of these methods are nonbinding, such as mediation and conciliation, some kinds of ADR can be binding, such as expert determination and baseball arbitration. In the United States, on the other hand, ADR is understood to mean all kinds of dispute resolution methods other than litigation, so the term ADR would include arbitration. Parties should be clear that when they discuss resolving disputes by ADR that they understand what the other party means by ADR.

The methods described in the following sections are dispute resolution mechanisms that can be used either in conjunction with an arbitration or independently. Good lawyers will always try to help a client explore ways of resolving disputes that might avoid the lengthy and costly procedures of either arbitration or litigation.

1. Mediation

Mediation differs from arbitration because it is nonbinding. An arbitral institution is likely to have rules for mediation as well as rules for arbitration. A mediator will try to make sure each party understands the other's point of view, will meet with each party privately and listen to the parties' respective viewpoints, stress common interests, and try to help them reach a settlement.

Mediation is confidential. There is usually a provision in the chosen rules that no disclosure made during the mediation can be used at the next level

---

[29] UNCITRAL Arbitration Rules, art. 6.

of the dispute, whether arbitration or litigation. If the rules do not provide for this, there should be an agreement in writing to the effect that anything disclosed in the mediation process cannot be used at the next level, except to the extent it comes in through documents not created for the mediation.

Mediation can occur at any time in the dispute. If parties get to a point in litigation or in arbitration, where they want to settle, and need some help, they can get a mediator. Mediators are also sometimes used in the negotiation stage of a contract, when negotiations have reached an impasse but both parties actually want the deal to go through. Because mediators try to understand and reconcile the interests of the parties, mediation is sometimes referred to as an *interest-based* procedure, while arbitration is referred to as a *rights-based* procedure.

2. Conciliation

What is the difference between conciliation and mediation? Often, the terms are used interchangeably. The UNCITRAL Model Law on International Commercial Conciliation[30] takes a very broad view. It essentially considers conciliation as different from negotiation because it involves a third party who will impartially and independently help the parties resolve their dispute. It is different from arbitration because it is nonbinding. However, from UNCITRAL's perspective, conciliation is not substantially different from mediation, although in its Guide to Enactment, it acknowledges that practitioners may distinguish between the two based on the amount of involvement of the neutral third party.[31] Traditionally, mediators have been viewed as more facilitative, and conciliators more directed, but these differences do not necessarily hold true today.

3. Neutral Evaluation

An institution can arrange for a neutral party, or the parties can find and agree on a neutral party, who will listen to each side, and then give a nonbinding opinion about an issue of fact, an issue of law, or perhaps a technical issue. The neutral party typically assesses the strengths and weaknesses of the case, which may help parties be more realistic about their claims in subsequent settlement discussions.

4. Expert Determination

When an issue in the arbitration involves a highly technical question, parties can agree that an expert may determine that question. Frequently, the

---

[30] Available at www.uncitral.org.
[31] Guide to Enactment, para.7. The Guide to Enactment and Use is included as Part Two of the UNCITRAL Model Law on International Commercial Conciliation. Available at www.uncitral.org.

decision of the expert is binding, but parties can agree to use an expert under rules that permit a nonbinding opinion.[32]

5. Mini-Trials

A number of arbitral institutions have rules for mini-trials. In a mini-trial, usually there is a panel composed of one neutral decision maker and one executive from each of the companies involved in the dispute. The executives should be at a high level in the company, have decision-making authority, and should not be employees who were personally involved in the issues leading to the dispute. A mini-trial usually lasts only one or two days, there is limited exchange of documents, each side puts forth its best case, and the panel (the neutral and the two executives) tries to reach a settlement. The proceedings are generally confidential, so that disclosures at the mini-trial generally cannot be used at a subsequent trial or arbitration. The proceeding is nonbinding, but serves the purpose of letting high-level executives know what is at stake, and provides the opportunity for them to resolve the dispute at an early stage to avoid expensive arbitration or litigation.

6. Last-Offer Arbitration (Baseball Arbitration)

This is a technique within an arbitration to try to bring both parties closer together in terms of what the amount awarded should be. Each party states its best offer as to the amount it thinks should be awarded, and the arbitrator has only the ability to choose either one proposal or the other. Thus, each side has an incentive to be reasonable, because if one side is too extreme, the other side's number will be chosen. This is sometimes called "baseball arbitration" because it has on occasion been used in establishing players' contracts in Major League Baseball in the United States.

J. CONCLUSION

Any dispute resolution method has its problems and its downsides. International commercial arbitration is sometimes referred to as the "least ineffective" method of resolving international disputes. But many participants express a more positive view. Ingeborg Schwenzer, a professor and arbitrator in Switzerland, finds the atmosphere in arbitration to be very different from litigation – "more professional, less nasty."[33] David Wagoner, a U.S. arbitrator, says that what he likes about arbitration is that "you can take

---

[32] *See, e.g.*, ICC Rules for Expertise, art.12(3) ("Unless otherwise agreed by all of the parties, the findings of the expert shall not be binding on the parties.").

[33] Interview with Ingeborg Schwenzer, March 2007. Notes of interview on file with author.

the best practices from civil and common law, use them in arbitration, and keep improving the process."[34] Certainly, the goal in international arbitration is to permit people from different countries and cultures to resolve their differences in ways that leave all parties feeling that the private system of dispute resolution serves a shared sense of justice.

[34] Interview with David Wagoner, March 2007. Notes of interview on file with author.

CHAPTER TWO

The Arbitration Agreement

A. FUNCTION AND PURPOSE

When parties agree to arbitrate their disputes, they give up the right to have those disputes decided by a national court. Instead, they agree that their disputes will be resolved privately, outside any court system. The arbitration agreement thus constitutes the relinquishment of an important right – to have the dispute resolved judicially – and creates other rights. The rights it creates are the rights to establish the process for resolving the dispute. In their arbitration agreement, the parties can select the rules that will govern the procedure, the location of the arbitration, the language of the arbitration, the law governing the arbitration, and frequently, the decision makers, whom the parties may choose because of their particular expertise in the subject matter of the parties' dispute. The parties' arbitration agreement gives the arbitrators the power to decide the dispute and defines the scope of that power. In essence, the parties create their own private system of justice.

1. Arbitration Clauses and Submission Agreements

The parties' arbitration agreement is frequently contained in a clause or clauses that are embedded in the parties' commercial contract. The agreement to arbitrate is thus entered into before any dispute has arisen, and is intended to provide a method of resolution in the event that a dispute does arise. However, if there is no arbitration clause in the parties' contract, and a dispute arises, at that time the parties can nonetheless enter into an agreement to arbitrate, if both sides agree. Such an agreement is generally referred to as a *submission agreement*. However, submission agreements are much less common than arbitration clauses in contracts, because once a dispute arises, the parties often cannot agree on anything. For that reason, it is generally better for the parties to agree to arbitrate at the beginning of the relationship, when they are still on good terms.

2. Separability

Even though the arbitration clause is most often contained within the contract between the parties, under most laws and rules it is nonetheless considered a separate agreement. It thus may continue to be valid, even if the main agreement – that is, the contract in which the arbitration agreement is found – may be potentially invalid. In most jurisdictions, this doctrine of separability permits the arbitrators to hear and decide the dispute even if one side claims, for example, that the contract is terminated, or is invalid because it was fraudulently induced. Such claims would not deprive the arbitrators of jurisdiction because they pertain to the main contract and not specifically to the arbitration clause.[1] Because the arbitration clause is considered a separate and distinct agreement, it is not affected by claims of invalidity of the main contract, and still confers jurisdiction on the arbitrators to decide the dispute.[2] The separability doctrine is embodied in numerous arbitration laws and rules.[3]

B. VALIDITY

In light of the important rights that are extinguished when the parties agree to arbitrate, the question of the arbitration agreement's validity is critical. Arbitration is a creature of consent, and that consent should be freely, knowingly, and competently given.[4] Therefore, to establish that parties have actually consented, many national laws, as well as the New York Convention, require that an arbitration agreement be in writing.[5] In addition, the

---

[1] When such claims are directed at the arbitration clause itself, the question of the arbitrators' jurisdiction is more murky, and may in some countries have to be resolved by the national court rather than by the arbitrator. *See, e.g.*, Prima Paint Co. v. Flood & Conklin Manufacturing Corp., 388 U.S. 395, 404–05 (1967) ("[I]f the claim is fraud in the inducement of the arbitration clause itself . . . the federal court may proceed to adjudicate it."); Harbour Assurance Co. (UK) Ltd. v. Kansa General International Assurance Co. Ltd. [1993] 3 All ER 897, QB 701 (English Court of Appeal) ("[A]n arbitrator [could] determine a dispute over the initial validity or invalidity of the written contract provided that the arbitration clause itself was not directly impeached.").

[2] The arbitrators' ability to determine their own jurisdiction, known as the competence-competence doctrine, is discussed *infra* Chapter 5(A)(2).

[3] *See, e.g.*, UNCITRAL Model Law, art. 16; English Arbitration Act, § 30; UNCITRAL Rules, art. 23(1); LCIA Rules, art. 23(1). *See also* Buckeye Check Cashing v. Cardegna, 546 U.S. 440, 445 (2006) ("[A]s a matter of substantive federal arbitration law, an arbitration provision is severable from the remainder of the contract.").

[4] *See* Volt Information Sciences, Inc., v. Stanford, 489 U.S. 468, 479 (1989) ("Arbitration under the Act is a matter of consent, not coercion, and parties are generally free to structure their arbitration agreements as they see fit.").

[5] *See, e.g.*, New York Convention, art. II, UNCITRAL Model Law, art. 7 (Option 1, as amended); Swiss PILA, art. 178(1); English Arbitration Act, § 5; French Code of Civil Procedure, art. 1443; U.S. Federal Arbitration Act, § 2.

Convention requires that in some circumstances, the written agreement be signed by both parties.[6]

The issue of whether the agreement was in writing, signed, and therefore valid, is likely to arise when one party seeks to renege on its agreement to arbitrate. Although the party may have agreed to arbitrate, after a dispute arises it may decide that it would rather go to court, and will therefore commence litigation. In addition, the issue of the arbitration agreement's applicability to specific parties may arise when, for example, one party asserts that it never signed the agreement, or when a nonsignatory tries to enforce the agreement against a signatory. In these situations, a party may call on the court for assistance.

International arbitration agreements are enforceable under the New York Convention. Even though the title of the Convention does not mention agreements – it is called the Convention on the Recognition and Enforcement of Foreign Arbitral Awards – nonetheless, the Convention deals with arbitration agreements in Article II. In accordance with Article II, Contracting States must recognize arbitration agreements in writing. If the court is seized of a matter that is in fact the subject matter of a binding arbitration agreement, the court must stay the proceedings and refer the parties to arbitration.[7]

NEW YORK CONVENTION

Article II

1. Each Contracting State shall recognize an agreement in writing under which the parties undertake to submit to arbitration all or any differences which have arisen or which may arise between them in respect of a defined legal relationship, whether contractual or not, concerning a subject matter capable of settlement by arbitration.

2. The term "agreement in writing" shall include an arbitral clause in a contract or an arbitration agreement, signed by the parties or contained in an exchange of letters or telegrams.

3. The court of a Contracting State, when seized of an action in a matter in respect of which the parties have made an agreement within the meaning of this article, shall, at the request of one of the parties, refer the parties to arbitration, unless it finds that the said agreement is null and void, inoperative or incapable of being performed.

---

[6] *See* New York Convention, art. II(2).

[7] *See* Albert Van Jan den Berg, THE NEW YORK ARBITRATION CONVENTION OF 1958, at 129 (1981) ("If the court refers the parties to arbitration... it implies automatically that the court proceedings are stayed."). *See also* Domenico Di Pietro & Martin Platte,

From Article II, a number of the requirements for the validity of an arbitration agreement are derived. Paragraph one provides that to be enforced, the agreement must be in writing, the dispute that arises must be "in respect of a defined legal relationship," and the subject matter must be capable of being settled by arbitration. Paragraph two defines "agreement in writing," including, in some circumstances, a signature requirement by the parties. Paragraph three requires the court to refer the parties to arbitration, unless the agreement is null and void, inoperative, or incapable of being performed. These requirements will be discussed in the following sections.

1. The Writing Requirement

Today, contracts are frequently entered into orally or by emails or faxes, without much attention to formalities. In many countries, such contracts are valid. If an arbitration agreement is valid under the pertinent national law, should it not be enforceable under the New York Convention? In some cases, courts have strictly enforced the writing requirement, invalidating arbitration agreements even though parties may have reached agreement by conduct or trade practice. When this happens, the Convention becomes a less effective means of enforcing parties' arbitration agreements. Although an amendment to make the writing requirement less rigid may be in order, it is difficult to amend an international convention that has more than 145 adherents, and impossible to ensure that it would be amended uniformly. However, there are some other ways, which will be discussed in the subsections immediately following, of trying to ensure that the purpose of the Convention – to provide for prompt enforcement of arbitration agreements and awards – is not undermined by an insistence upon formalities that appears inconsistent with the realities of today's transactions.

First, it is necessary to understand what the Convention requires with respect to a writing. Whereas Article II(1) sets forth the writing requirement, Article II(2) defines what "in writing" means. The writing requirement may be met either by a clause in the contract or a separate agreement to arbitrate (a submission agreement), "signed by the parties," or it can be satisfied by an exchange of letters or telegrams.[8] A number of interpretive issues are presented by the language of paragraph 2. First, does the signature requirement apply to both the contract containing the clause, as well as to the submission agreement, or only to the submission agreement? Second, does the signature requirement also apply to the exchange of letters or telegrams? Different courts have taken different positions. The U.S. Fifth

---

ENFORCEMENT OF INTERNATIONAL ARBITRATION AWARDS, 66 (2001) (explaining that "refer the parties to arbitration" in Article II(3) of the New York Convention "means that the Court becomes incompetent to entertain the case and must stay proceedings").

[8] New York Convention, art. II(2).

Circuit Court of Appeals has suggested that only the separate agreement must be signed, and not the contract containing the arbitration clause.[9] On the other hand, the U.S. Second and Third Circuits have disagreed with this interpretation,[10] stating that the signature requirement applies to both. With respect to the exchange of letters and telegrams, a Swiss court has held that if the parties expressed their intention to enter into an arbitration agreement by an exchange of documents, signatures were not necessary.[11] Similarly, the U.S. Third Circuit has held that the arbitral agreement "may be unsigned if it is exchanged in a series of letters."[12] It is generally the rule today in most jurisdictions that the contract containing the arbitration clause, or the submission agreement, must be signed, but there is no signature requirement for the exchange of documents.[13]

Courts differ, however, on how strictly they will interpret the Convention's writing requirement to invalidate an arbitration agreement. Some are quite strict in following the letter of the law: the arbitration agreement is valid only if it is in a contract or in a separate agreement signed by the parties, or in an exchange of documents.[14] In some instances, courts have strictly required express written acceptance, even if denying validity appeared contrary to principles of good faith.[15] The question of the arbitration agreement's validity normally arises when one party is trying to enforce an agreement to arbitrate. However, the issue may come up again at the award enforcement stage, when one party tries to prevent enforcement by asserting that the agreement to arbitrate was invalid.[16]

---

[9] *See* Sphere Drake Ins. PLC v. Marine Towing 16 F.3d 666, 669–70 (1994), *cert. denied*, Marine Towing v. Sphere Drake Ins. P.L.C., 513 U.S. 871 (1994).

[10] *See, e.g.*, Kahn Lucas Lancaster, Inc., v. Lark International Ltd. 186 F.3d 210, 217–18 (2d Cir. 1999); Standard Bent Glass Corp. v. Glassrobots OY, 333 F.3d 440, 449 (2003).

[11] Compagnie de Navigation et Transports S.A. v. MSC (Mediterranean Shipping Company) S.A. (Swiss Federal Tribunal, January 16, 1995), YEARBOOK COMMERCIAL ARBITRATION XXI (1996).

[12] Standard Bent Glass Corp. v. Glassrobots OY, 333 F.3d 440, 449 (2003).

[13] With respect to an arbitral clause in a contract, the clause itself does not have to be signed separately. It is sufficient for the parties to sign the contract as a whole. *See* van den Berg, *supra* note 7, at 192 (1981).

[14] *See, e.g.*, the Netherlands, Court of First Instance of Dordrecht, North American Soccer League Marketing, Inc. (USA), v. Admiral International Marketing and Trading BV (Netherlands) and Frisol Eurosport BV (Netherlands), August 18, 1982 (YEARBOOK COMMERCIAL ARBITRATION X at 490 (1985)); Germany, Brandenburg Court of Appeal, June 13, 2002 (No. 8, Sch 2/01); Spain, Supreme Court, Delta Cereales Espana SL (Spain) v. Barredo Hermanos S.A., October 6, 1998 (YEARBOOK COMMERCIAL ARBITRATION XXVI, at 854 (2001)).

[15] *See, e.g.*, Italy, Supreme Court, Robobar Limited (UK) v. Finncold sas (Italy) October 28, 1993, YEARBOOK COMMERCIAL ARBITRATION XX at 739 (1995) (formal requirements cannot be derogated from, even where contesting arbitration agreement's validity is contrary to good faith).

[16] *See* discussion *infra* in Chapter 10(D)(1).

Perhaps the most common situation that produces a divergent judicial response occurs when there is clearly a contract, but the arbitration clause within that contract does not meet the form requirements of the Convention. For example, assume that parties reach an oral agreement by telephone. One of the parties sends a written confirmation, which contains an arbitration clause. The other party performs under the contract – for example, it ships goods, but it never sends a written response to the first party's written confirmation. Most courts would have no difficulty finding that a contract was formed. But quite a few would say that the arbitration clause was not valid.[17] There was no "exchange" of documents, because only one document was sent. Some commentators believe that tacitly concluded agreements to arbitrate are simply not enforceable under the New York Convention.[18]

On the other hand, some courts will find a way to interpret such an arbitration agreement as valid, frequently by using domestic law. Assuming the agreement falls under the Convention, Article II should supersede domestic law regarding the proper form of an arbitration agreement.[19] However, State courts have not always viewed the Convention as superseding their domestic law.[20] Moreover, even when a court applies the New York Convention, its interpretation may be influenced by its national law. For example, the domestic law could affect a national court's interpretation to the extent that a judge perceives the Convention to be silent, ambiguous, or out of date. As commentators have noted, "Many national courts...interpret[] Article II(2) in the light of Article 7(2) of the Model Law and their more liberal national arbitration laws."[21]

Nonetheless, although acceptance of a more lenient definition of "agreement in writing" under national law makes sense in terms of the purpose and language of the Convention and in terms of accommodating more modern means of communication than letters and telegrams, there still are courts that will not enforce an award if the underlying agreement does not meet Article II(2) requirements.[22] Thus, different courts, interpreting the Convention differently, can cause a nonuniform application of the Convention.

To promote harmonious interpretation by amending an international convention when there are more than 145 Contracting States would be

---

[17] See Frey et al. v. Cucaro e Figli, Italy, YEARBOOK COMMERCIAL ARBITRATION I, at 193 (1976) (Of four contracts that were performed, court only enforced arbitration agreements in two, because only two were signed and returned).

[18] See Di Pietro & Platt, *supra* note 7, at 75–78.

[19] See Van den Berg, *supra* note 7, at 170.

[20] See, *e.g.*, France, Court of Appeal, Paris, France, Société Abilio Rodriguez v. Société Vigelor (1990) (Rev. Arb. 1990), at 691.

[21] DiPietro & Platte, *supra* note 7, at 82.

[22] See *id*. at 76–77.

difficult, if not impossible. The likelihood would be that some States would amend and others would not, thereby diminishing rather than increasing harmonization. To encourage courts to apply a less rigid interpretation of Article II of the Convention, the United Nations Commission on International Trade Law (UNCITRAL) began in 1999 to consider "the means through which modernization of the New York Convention could be sought."[23] Two of the more propitious means that UNCITRAL considered were (1) to develop declarations addressing the interpretation of the New York Convention that would reflect a broad understanding of the form requirement and would permit the application of more lenient national law, and (2) to revise Article 7 of the UNCITRAL Model Law on Arbitration. These two steps are related, as will be discussed in the next two sections.

a. Recommended Interpretation of Articles II and VII

In July 2006, UNCITRAL adopted recommendations regarding the interpretation of Articles II(2) and VII(1) of the Convention, as well as revised provisions on the form of the arbitration agreement in Article 7 of the UNCITRAL Model Law on Arbitration. The recommendation as to Article II is that it should be applied "recognizing that the circumstances described therein are not exhaustive."[24] UNCITRAL is suggesting that there can be additional bases for meeting the writing requirement outside of those specified in the Convention (presumably, bases found in domestic law), and that courts should apply the Article II writing requirement less rigidly.

UNCITRAL has also recommended that Article VII(1), which by its terms only applies to arbitration awards, be interpreted to apply to arbitration agreements as well.[25] Article VII(1) provides as follows:

> The provisions of the present Convention shall not ... deprive any interested party of any right he may have to avail himself of an arbitral award in the manner and to the extent allowed by the law or the treaties of the country where such award is sought to be relied upon.[26]

Article VII(1) is sometimes referred to as "the more favorable right" provision because it permits a party who is attempting to enforce an award ("the award creditor") to take advantage of any more favorable law in the

---

[23] *See* Note by the Secretariat, Article II (2) of the Convention on the Recognition and Enforcement of Foreign Arbitral Awards (New York, 1958), A/CN.9/WG.II/WP.139, at 3, ¶ 2, available at www.uncitral.org

[24] Report of the Working Group on Arbitration and Conciliation on the work of its forty-fourth session (New York, January 23–27, 2006) Annex III, A/CN.9/592. Available at www.uncitral.org. For text of recommendation, *see* Appendix D.

[25] *See id.*

[26] New York Convention, art. VII(1).

enforcing jurisdiction, thereby making enforcement easier. The UNCITRAL recommendation is as follows:

> [UNCITRAL] [r]ecommends that article VII, paragraph (1), of the Convention . . . should be applied to allow any interested party to avail itself of rights it may have, under the law or treaties of the country where an arbitration agreement is sought to be relied upon, to seek recognition of the validity of such an arbitration agreement.[27]

If Article VII(1) is read to apply not just to awards but also to agreements, it would provide a party with "a more favorable right" to enforcement of its agreement, based on the local law in the court that was ruling on the agreement's validity. In other words, to the extent that any local laws would be more favorable to a party than the Convention with respect to enforcement of the arbitration agreement, the party would be entitled to the protection of those laws.[28] Thus, if the jurisdiction of the court considering the agreement had adopted a modern version of a writing requirement, the court would not have to strictly enforce the Convention's requirement of a writing.

This, of course, leads to the second step taken by UNCITRAL in July 2006 – to amend Article 7 of the Model Law on Arbitration. An amended Article 7 would provide states in Model Law jurisdictions with a modern statute on the writing requirement. That statute would make it easier for an arbitration agreement to be valid under a domestic "writing" requirement. Then, for courts in a Model Law jurisdiction that were willing to interpret the more favorable right provision of Article VII as applicable to arbitration agreements, the arbitration agreement would be more easily enforced. It would not be undermined by the formalistic requirements of Article II of the Convention.

b. Amendment to Article 7 of UNCITRAL Model Law

UNCITRAL amended Article 7 of the Model Law on International Commercial Arbitration to try to align the Model Law with current practices

---

[27] See Report, supra note 24.

[28] Interpreting Article VII(1) to apply to arbitration agreements as well as awards is not a new idea. Albert Jan van den Berg, in his classic work on the New York Convention, suggested in 1981 that "[t]he omission of an express mention of the arbitration agreement in Article VII(1) must be deemed unintentional as the provisions concerning the agreement were inserted in the Convention at a very late stage of the New York Conference of 1958. . . . [I]t would seem contrary to the pro-enforcement bias of the Convention that the [most favorable right] provision, which aims at making enforcement of awards possible in the greatest number of cases possible, would not apply also to the enforcement of the arbitration agreement." (THE NEW YORK ARBITRATION CONVENTION OF 1958, at 86–87.)

in international trade.[29] The UNCITRAL amendment, of course, will not be the law anywhere until it is adopted by one of the seventy countries, states, administrative regions, or territories that have already adopted the Model Law, or unless the Model Law, as amended, is adopted by a new jurisdiction.[30] UNCITRAL does not expect that its proposed law will be adopted uniformly, because it provides alternative versions of the amendment. However, even if not adopted uniformly, the UNCITRAL amendment should help provide guidelines for interpreting what constitutes a valid arbitration agreement for purposes of today's international transactions.

Article 7 of the Model Law is entitled "Definition and form of arbitration agreement." UNCITRAL provides two different versions of amended Article 7 that a country can adopt. Option 1 requires an arbitral agreement to be in writing, and spells out what a "writing" means, but Option 2 does not require a writing. Option 1 defines an agreement "in writing" as one having its content recorded in any form, even if the arbitration agreement or contract was concluded orally.[31] There is no signature requirement. Thus, as long as there is some record of the arbitration agreement, the agreement is valid. This should take care of the situation in which the parties reached an agreement over the telephone and only one confirmation was sent. Even though the other party might have responded by shipping goods, and not by sending back a written form, under the Model Law's amended Article 7, section 3, the confirmation would appear to be a record that would satisfy the writing requirement. Thus, this section may in some situations make tacitly concluded arbitration agreements valid.

Option 2, on the other hand, defines an arbitration agreement as "an agreement by the parties to submit to arbitration all or certain disputes which have arisen or which may arise between them in respect of a defined legal relationship, whether contractual or not."[32] A writing is not required. Thus, if a country has adopted this option containing no writing requirement, an enforcing court in that country should be able to enforce an oral arbitration agreement under the New York Convention, assuming that the court applies the "more favorable right" provision of Article VII(1) to arbitration agreements.

---

[29] *See* Press Release, UNCITRAL website, UNIS/L/102, July 7, 2006. ("The main achievements of the [UNCITRAL 39th annual] session were the...adoption of revised legislative provisions on interim measures of protection and the form of the arbitration agreement."). The text is available on the UNCITRAL website, www.uncitral.org.

[30] For list of jurisdictions that have adopted the UNCITRAL Model Law on International Commercial Arbitration, see Chapter 1, note 11. *See also* UNCITRAL website at www.uncitral.org.

[31] UNCITRAL Model Law, art. 7(3) (amended 2006) available at www.uncitral.org. *See also* Appendix C.

[32] UNCITRAL Model Law, art. 7, option 2 (amended 2006), available at www.uncitral .org.

Further, the UNCITRAL Working Group wanted to clarify that the term "writing" included "modern means of communication that might not be considered, in some countries, as meeting the writing requirement."[33] Article 7(4) provides that the writing requirement is met by an electronic communication, as long as the information can be used for subsequent reference.

ARTICLE 7

4. The requirement that an arbitration agreement be in writing is met by an electronic communication if the information contained therein is accessible so as to be useable for subsequent reference; "electronic communication" means any communication that the parties make by means of data messages; "data message" means information generated, sent, received or stored by electronic, magnetic, optical or similar means, including, but not limited to, electronic data interchange (EDI), electronic mail, telegram, telex or telecopy.[34]

Electronic communication is defined in the same way that it is defined in the United Nations Convention on the Use of Electronic Communications in International Contracts.[35] The definition of "data message" is also identical to that of the UNCITRAL Model Law on Electronic Commerce.[36]

Although the New York Convention provides that an agreement in writing can be contained in an exchange of "letters or telegrams,"[37] in our modern times, other means of communication, such as faxes and emails, are also used to form contracts. Although most courts have rather broadly accepted newer modes of communication,[38] there has been some

---

[33] Report of the Working Group on Arbitration and Conciliation on the work of its forty-fourth session (New York, January 23–27, 2006), A/CN.9/592, at 10, para. 50.

[34] UNCITRAL Model Law on Commercial Arbitration, art. 7(4) (amended 2006). For text of the Model Law 2006 amendments, *see* Appendix C.

[35] Available at www.UNCITRAL.org. As of December 2011, this Convention was not yet in force. See *infra* note 43.

[36] The UNCITRAL Model Law on Electronic Commerce, adopted in 1996, attempts to facilitate use of electronic commerce, in part by developing functional electronic equivalents or terms such as "writing" or "signature." Available at www.uncitral.org.

[37] New York Convention, art. II(2).

[38] *See, e.g.*, Chloe Z Fishing Co., Inc., v. Odyssey re (London) Limited, 109 F. Supp. 2d 1236 (D.C. CA 2000) ("[T]he Court finds that Article II section 2 of the Convention could not have intended to exclude all other forms of written communications regularly utilized to conduct commerce in the various signatory nations by failing to provide an exhaustive list of 'letters' or 'telegrams.'"). *See also* Di Pietro & Platt, *supra* note 7, at 72 ("[T]here is common agreement that writing now does not only mean what it meant in 1958.").

resistance.[39] By making the definition of "writing" in amended Article 7 consistent with both its Convention on Electronic Commerce and its Model Law on Electronic Commerce, UNCITRAL is attempting to create an internationally accepted definition of "writing" that includes electronic commerce, and to bring the Model Law's concept of writing in line with the most modern international practices.

Moreover, by eliminating the signature requirement, amended Article 7 removes a formality that has caused some courts to deny enforcement of arbitral agreements. An unsigned contract containing an arbitration clause, or an unsigned submission agreement, would be enforceable under the New York Convention, assuming the enforcing country had adopted both Article 7 of the amended Model Law and UNCITRAL's recommended interpretation of Article VII(1) of the New York Convention, which applies the "more favorable right" provision to arbitration agreements.

c. U.N. Convention on Use of Electronic Communications

UNCITRAL is also trying to use the United Nations Convention on the Use of Electronic Communications in International Contracts (CUECIC) to update other, less modern conventions. Article 20 of CUECIC provides that when a Contracting State for CUECIC is also a Contracting State for other conventions, such as the New York Convention and the Convention on Contracts for the International Sale of Goods, the CUECIC provisions will apply to the use of electronic communications in connection with the formation or performance of a contract covered by the other conventions (unless the Contracting State opts out of this obligation).[40] The Explanatory Note by the Secretariat states that Article 20 is not meant to amend any convention, or to provide an authentic interpretation.[41] Rather, the drafters intended this article, combined with scope provisions in Article 1 of CUECIC (making the Convention applicable to international contracts), "to provide a domestic solution for a problem originating in international instruments.... [The provisions] are based on the recognition that domestic courts already interpret international commercial law instruments."[42] Thus, UNCITRAL is trying to develop a uniform approach for domestic courts to use in applying modern practices to older conventions. A court could use

---

[39] An exchange of emails was found not to satisfy the Convention's writing requirement by the Norwegian Court of Appeal. *See* Decision of the Halogaland Court of Appeal, August 16, 1999, YEARBOOK COMMERCIAL ARBITRATION XXVII, at 519 (2002).

[40] CUECIC, art. 20(2).

[41] Explanatory note by the UNCITRAL Secretariat on the United Nations Convention on the Use of Electronic Communications in International Contracts, available as an attachment to the Convention's text on the UNCITRAL website, at 91, para. 289 http://www.uncitral.org/pdf/english/texts/electcom/06–57452_Ebook.pdf.

[42] *Id*. at 92, para. 290.

the definition of a "writing" from the CUECIC to update the New York Convention's definition of "writing," because it provides an international definition of electronic commerce that would satisfy a writing requirement. If a country was not a party to CUECIC (and so far CUECIC is not in force in any jurisdiction),[43] courts could nonetheless refer to it as guidance – or refer to the Model Law on International Arbitration, the Model Law on Electronic Commerce, or all three – to note that there is a widely accepted international definition of writing that includes electronic communication. These various texts demonstrate UNCITRAL's efforts to encourage an interpretation of the Convention's writing requirement that would reflect actual practices, and be more uniform across national borders.

d. Other Article 7 Issues

Two other issues in connection with the writing requirement are dealt with in the amended Article 7 of the Model Law. These same issues are included in existing Article 7 and are not substantially different in the amended version. Section 5 provides that if parties have exchanged statements of claims and defenses in which one party alleges an arbitration agreement and the other party does not deny it, then the writing requirement is met. This prevents parties from trying to assert a technical defense at a later point after the parties have essentially admitted there was an agreement to arbitrate.

Finally, in Section 6, a reference in a contract to another document containing an arbitration clause satisfies the writing requirement as long as the reference makes the clause in the other document part of the contract. This is an area that comes up regularly in practice, but is not dealt with specifically in the New York Convention. As a result, courts in different jurisdictions have reached different conclusions about when an arbitration agreement can be incorporated by reference, and how it must be done. Section 6 simply requires that the reference in a contract to another document containing an arbitration clause must establish that the arbitration clause becomes part of the contract.

e. Effect of the More Favorable Right Provision

There is clearly a trend today to support prompt enforcement of arbitration agreements and awards. In recommending that the "more favorable right" provision be applied to arbitration agreements as well as to awards, UNCITRAL is recommending a solution already followed by some courts.[44] When

---

[43] As of December 2011, two countries, Singapore and Honduras, had ratified CUECIC, but there must be actions by three countries before the treaty will enter into force. *See* http://www.uncitral.org/pdf/english/texts/electcom/06-57452-Ebook.pdf.

[44] *See* Supreme Court, Germany, May 25, 1970, YEARBOOK COMMERCIAL ARBITRATION 1977 at 237 ("European Convention, being of younger date than the New York Convention, prevails." Under the European Convention, "any arbitration agreement

a party can take advantage of domestic laws in the enforcing court that are not as limited as the writing requirement of Article II of the Convention, the parties' expectations will more likely be met. A more modern approach to the writing requirement means that parties that agreed to arbitrate are much less likely to be thwarted because of a failure to meet formalistic requirements.

Parties can benefit from the application of the more favorable right provision in Article VII(1) of the Convention even if they are not in a Model Law State. A party bringing an enforcement action in any State that has more favorable laws regarding the writing requirement of an arbitration agreement will benefit. For example, in the United States, a claimant would benefit from the adoption by the U.S. Congress of a law known as E-Sign.

ELECTRONIC SIGNATURES IN GLOBAL AND NATIONAL COMMERCE ACT[45] ("E-SIGN")

Notwithstanding any statute, regulation, or other rule of law ... with respect to any transaction in or affecting interstate or foreign commerce –

(1) a signature, contract, or other record relating to such transaction may not be denied legal effect, validity, or enforceability solely because it is in electronic form; and

(2) a contract relating to such transaction may not be denied legal effect, validity, or enforceability solely because an electronic signature or electronic record was used in its formation.

Circuit courts in the United States[46] have found that E-Sign provides that an email agreement to arbitrate is enforceable under the Federal Arbitration Act (FAA) because it satisfies the FAA's "written provision" requirement.[47] Although to date research has not revealed a U.S. case interpreting E-Sign in

---

concluded in form authorized by [local] laws suffices."); The Netherlands, Court of Appeal, The Hague, Owerri Commercial Inc. (Panama), v. Dielle Srl. (Italy), YEARBOOK COMMERCIAL ARBITRATION XIX 703 (1993) (Arbitration clause valid under English law, therefore valid under the New York Convention).

[45] 15 U.S.C. § 7001(a).

[46] *See, e.g.*, Campbell v. General Dynamics Government Systems Corporation, 407 F.3d 546 (1st Cir. 2005); Specht v. Netscape Communications Corp., 306 F.3d 17, 26 n.11 (2d Cir. 2002) ("[T]he agreement is a 'written provision' despite being provided to users in a downloadable electronic form. The latter point has been settled by the Electronic Signatures in Global and National Commerce Act ('E-Sign Act'.)").

[47] 9 U.S.C. § 2.

relation to the New York Convention's writing requirement, there is little doubt that a U.S. court would apply E-Sign and find that an arbitration agreement could not be denied legal effect or validity simply because it was in electronic form.[48]

2. A Defined Legal Relationship

Under the New York Convention, the dispute between the parties must be "in respect of a defined legal relationship, whether contractual or not."[49] Most arbitration agreements are by their nature contractual. But the defined legal relationship could be a noncontractual one. A noncontractual relationship could be based, for example, on tort laws. As will be discussed further in Chapter 3 on Drafting the Arbitration Agreement, it is prudent to draft an arbitration clause broadly, so it includes not only disputes arising out of the contract, but also other disputes that might be based on tortious acts or unfair business practices. For this reason, most drafters of arbitration clauses will not only provide that the parties agree to resolve "all disputes *arising out of* the contract," but will also make the arbitration clause more broad by saying "all disputes arising out of *or related to* the contract." Usually a party's tortious claims or claims of unfair business practices will be related to the contract, even though not necessarily arising out of it.

Assume, for example, that a supplier decided to terminate an international distribution agreement. Without the knowledge of the distributor, the supplier hired some of the distributor's key employees to work for a new distribution company that would be owned by the supplier. The termination of the distribution agreement would not take place for a few months, and during that time, the key employees continued to work for the first company, but solicited customers of that company to switch to the new company once it would be in operation. The dispute that was related to this unfair business practice could be arbitrated under a broad arbitration clause. The dispute did not arise out of the contract, because there was no term in the contract that said that the supplier could not hire the distributor's key employees nor encourage them to solicit the distributor's customers. That kind of

---

[48] In the United States, however, even without "the more favorable right" provision of the Convention, E-Sign displaces any interpretation of the Convention's writing requirement that is inconsistent with this law. Because treaties and statutes in the U.S. are considered to be on equal footing, under a last-in-time rule, if E-Sign conflicted with the Convention, the provisions of E-Sign, being later in time, would govern. *See* Breard v. Greene, 523 U.S. 371, 376 (1998) ("[A]n Act of Congress . . . is on full parity with a treaty, and . . . when a statute which is subsequent in time is inconsistent with a treaty, the statute, to the extent of conflict, renders the treaty null."). The interpretation of the more favorable right provision as applicable to arbitration agreements would mean, however, that the United States would not be seen as being in violation of its obligations under the Convention.

[49] New York Convention, art. II.

conduct is against the law in most jurisdictions, and a term prohibiting such unlawful conduct would not be expected to be included in a contract. Because the parties' relationship and mutual obligations with respect to fair or unfair business practices were defined and governed by laws that were not contract laws, the dispute did not arise out of the contract. Nonetheless, the tortious conduct was related to the contract. By having a clause that referred to *disputes arising out of or related to the contract*, the parties could arbitrate both the disputes about the termination of the agreement, which arose out of the contract, and the unfair business practices, which were related to the contract. Although the dispute over the unfair business practices was not a contractual dispute, the arbitration agreement would still be enforceable under the New York Convention, because the clause was broad enough to cover this kind of legal relationship, which was defined under other laws.

3. Capable of Being Settled by Arbitration

For an arbitration agreement to be enforceable, the subject matter must be arbitrable – that is, it must be a subject that the State considers appropriate to be arbitrated. In most jurisdictions, for example, issues such as criminal matters, child custody, family matters, and bankruptcy are not arbitrable. It would be against the law or the public policy of the local jurisdiction to try to arbitrate disputes in these areas. In addition, in patent law, the validity of the patent will generally not be arbitrable because that is considered to be an issue for a local regulatory agency or for a court. On the other hand, disputes arising out of an agreement *to license* a patent normally would be arbitrable, because those disputes are basically contract disputes.

Increasingly, disputes involving antitrust laws, which were formerly considered inappropriate for arbitration, are being arbitrated.[50] Securities issues are also arbitrable, at least in the United States.[51] Some tribunals have held that issues of bribery are not arbitrable,[52] but more recently, commentators and courts have taken the position that a mere allegation of illegality should not relieve a tribunal of jurisdiction to determine the dispute, including the question of illegality.[53] In sum, most disputes today are considered to be

---

[50] *See, e.g.*, Mitsubishi Motors v. Soler Chrysler-Plymouth, 473 U.S. 614 (1985); Eco Swiss China Time Ltd. v. Benetton International N.V., Case C-126/97[1999] ECR 1–3055; Decision of the Swiss Tribunal Fédéral (April 28, 1992) Rev. Arb. (1993); A.S.A. Bull 368 (1992), aff'd A.S.A. Bull. Vol. 18, no. 2, at 421–26.

[51] *See* Scherk v. Alberto-Culver, 417 U.S. 506 (1974); Shearson v. McMahon, 482 U.S. 220 (1987).

[52] *See* ICC arbitration No. 1110 (1963); *see also* J. Gillis Wetter, *Issues of Corruption before International Arbitral Tribunals*, 10 Arb. Int. 277 (1994).

[53] *See, e.g.*, R. Kreindler, *Aspects of Illegality in the Formation and Performance of Contracts*, Int. Arb. L. Rev. 2003, 6(1), 1–24. *See also* Fiona Trust v. Yuri Privalov

arbitrable, except for those that fall within clearly defined areas such as criminal law, family law, and patent law.

4. Null and Void, Inoperable, or Incapable of Being Performed

In addition to the conditions required for enforceability – a writing, a legal relationship, and a subject matter capable of being arbitrated – the New York Convention provides certain defenses to enforcement of an arbitration agreement. In Article II(3), the Convention states that when an arbitration agreement meets the conditions of Article II(1), a court, at the request of a party, must refer the matter to arbitration unless the agreement is "null and void, inoperable, or incapable of being performed."[54] Even though these terms appear similar or at least overlapping, commentators and courts have attempted to distinguish them.[55]

a. Null and Void

An arbitration agreement could be considered null and void if there was lack of actual consent because of fraud, duress, misrepresentation, undue influence, or waiver.[56] In addition, a lack of capacity by a party could render the agreement null and void. Capacity issues may come up when a party – for example, a state agency – did not have authority or necessary approvals to enter into an arbitration agreement.[57]

An arbitration agreement may also be considered a nullity because the language of the clause is so vague that the parties' intent cannot be determined. Defective arbitration clauses, referred to as "pathological," may nonetheless be interpreted by a court in some instances to preserve the parties' intent to arbitrate, even if the choice of an arbitral institution or rules was unclear. In other instances, however, the clause may be viewed as so vague that it simply nullifies the agreement.[58]

[2007] EWCA Civ. 20 (Even in cases in which bribery is alleged, arbitration clause is still valid.).

[54] New York Convention, art. II(3).

[55] *See, e.g.*, Albert Jan van den Berg, THE NEW YORK ARBITRATION CONVENTION OF 1958, at 154–61 (1981); Domenico Di Pietro & Martin Platte, *supra* note 7, at 104–19. *See also* Bautista v. Star Cruises, 396 F.3d 1289, 1301–02 (11th Cir. 2005) (differentiating "null and void" from "incapable of being performed").

[56] *See* Apple & Eve, LLC v. Yantai North Andre Juice Co. Ltd. 610 F. Supp. 2d 226, 228–29 (E.D.N.Y. 2009); Bautista v. Star Cruises, 396 F. 3d 1289, 1302 (11th Cir. 2005) ("Null and void" encompasses "those situations – such as fraud, mistake, duress and waiver – that can be applied neutrally on an international scale.").

[57] *See* Alan Redfern & Martin Hunter et al., REDFERN AND HUNTER ON INTERNATIONAL ARBITRATION, § 2.34–38, at 97–99 (2009).

[58] *See, e.g.*, Germany, Court of Appeal, Hamm, YEARBOOK COMMERCIAL ARBITRATION, XXII (1997) at 707, 709 ("[A]n arbitration agreement is null and void when the competent arbitral tribunal is neither unambiguously determined nor unambiguously determinable."). *Citations omitted. See also* Teck Guan SDN BHD v. Beow Guan

b. Inoperable

An arbitration agreement may be inoperable as to a particular dispute if it is barred by *res judicata*, because the identical issues between the same parties have previously been decided in another legal forum. It could become inoperable because the parties revoked it or entered into an agreement to settle the dispute. Another possibility would be that a required time limit had expired. If, for example, a party had a limited time after the termination of a contract to make a demand for arbitration, and that time period had expired, the agreement would be considered inoperable.

c. Incapable of Being Performed

An arbitration agreement that is incapable of being performed may also be inoperable, and a nullity, so in some cases the overlap of terms may make them seem synonymous. An arbitration agreement could be incapable of being performed if, for example, there was contradictory language in the main contract indicating the parties intended to litigate. Moreover, if the parties had chosen a specific arbitrator in the agreement, who was, at the time of the dispute, deceased or unavailable, the arbitration agreement could not be effectuated unless, of course, the parties could agree on a new arbitrator. This would depend on whether both parties still wanted to arbitrate. In addition, if the place of arbitration was no longer available because of political upheaval, this could render the arbitration agreement incapable of being performed. If the arbitration agreement was itself too vague, confusing, or contradictory, it could prevent the arbitration from taking place.

C. BINDING NONSIGNATORIES

Although there is a trend today toward finding an arbitration agreement enforceable even if not all formalities are strictly met, courts still have justifiable concerns about requiring a party to arbitrate if it appears that the party did not agree to do so.[59] The question of whether a party signed a contract containing an arbitration clause can raise issues of intent as well as formal contract validity. Moreover, in some instances, a question may arise about a third party who did not sign a contract that was valid between at least two other parties. In this case, validity of the contract is not an issue; rather the question is whether a particular party – a nonsignatory – can

---

Enterprises PTE Ltd. 4 SLR 276 [2003] (Arbitration clause was vague and did not make clear that parties had agreed to resolve disputes by arbitration.).

[59] *See* Grigson v. Creative Artists Agency, 210 F.3d 524, 528 (5th Cir. 2000) ("[A]rbitration is a matter of contract and cannot, in general, be required for a matter involving [a] . . . nonsignatory.").

be required to arbitrate, or whether a nonsignatory can compel arbitration with a signatory.

Because consent to arbitration is fundamental, courts have asserted that "[a]rbitration agreements apply to nonsignatories only in rare circumstances."[60] Increasingly, however, there appears to be a trend among tribunals and courts to extend the obligation to arbitrate to nonsignatories.[61] The issue arises in many different contexts. Frequently, there is an attempt to bind a parent company of a subsidiary that is a signatory, or a State, when a company or other entity appears to be State-controlled.[62] Sometimes the attempt is to bind a related or affiliated company, a successor corporation, or a manufacturer.

A body of jurisprudence has developed concerning when a nonsignatory can be required to arbitrate or compel arbitration, although it is not uniform across national borders or within them. Normally, the question of who is a party to an arbitration agreement, or who should be estopped from asserting nonadherence to the agreement, is determined by applying principles of contract and agency.[63] U.S. federal cases have set forth six theories for binding nonsignatories: incorporation by reference, assumption, agency, veil-piercing/alter ego, estoppel, and third-party beneficiary.[64] Additional

[60] The Rice Company (Suisse), S.A. v. Precious Flowers Ltd. 523 F. 3d 528, 536 (5th Cir. 2008), *citing* Bridas SAPIC v. Turkmenistan, 345 F.3d 347, 358 (5th Cir. 2003).

[61] *See* Carolyn B. Lamm & Jocelyn A. Aqua, *Defining the Party – Who Is a Proper Party in an International Arbitration before the American Arbitration Association and Other International Institutions*, 34 Geo. Wash. Int'l L. Rev. 711, 713 (2003).

[62] *See, e.g.*, Dallah Real Estate and Tourism Holding Company v. Ministry of Religious Affairs, Government of Pakistan, [2010] UKSC 46 (Nov. 3, 2010) (Deciding in the negative the question of whether the Pakistani government was a signatory, the UK Supreme Court denied enforcement of a French arbitration award. Nonetheless, the French Cour d'appel subsequently reached a different decision, upholding the award.).

[63] In the United States, courts have stated that both state and federal law may apply in deciding whether a party may be compelled to arbitrate a dispute. *See, e.g.*, R. J. Griffin & Co. v. Beach Club II Homeowners Assoc., 384 F.3d 157 (4th Cir. 2004) ("In deciding whether a party may be compelled to arbitrate a dispute, we 'apply ordinary state law principles that govern the formation of contracts' (*citing* First Options of Chicago v. Kaplan, 514 U.S. 938 (1995)), and 'the federal substantive law of arbitrability' (*citing* Moses H. Cone Mem'l Hosp. v. Mercury Constr. Corp., 460 U.S. 1, 24 (1983)."). *See also* International Paper Company v. Schwabedissen, 206 F.3d 411, 417, n. 4 (4th Cir. 2000). ("[S]tate law determines questions 'concerning the validity, revocability, or enforceability of contracts generally,' *citing* Perry v. Thomas, 482 U.S. 483, 493, n. 9, *but* where there are no issues of the contract's formation or validity, the question of whether a nonsignatory is bound to a contract that exists between other individuals is governed by the 'federal substantive law of arbitrability.'"). This means that in many situations, federal common law, based on federal cases interpreting the Federal Arbitration Act and the New York Convention, will be used to determine whether to compel arbitration.

[64] The Rice Company (Suisse), S.A. v. Precious Flowers Ltd. 523 F. 3d 528, 536–37 (5th Cir. 2008), *citing* Hellenic Inv. Fund, Inc., v. Det Norke Veritas, 464 F.3d 514, 517

theories, such as implied consent, assignment, novation, guarantee clauses, succession by operation of law, subrogation, and the "group of companies" doctrine, have also served as underpinnings for court and tribunal analyses concerning rights and obligations of nonsignatories.[65] Some of these theories overlap, and a discussion of each of them is beyond the scope of this chapter. Nonetheless, it may be useful to consider a few in more detail.

1. Agency

Although typically an arbitration agreement binds only those who are parties to it, a party need not physically negotiate or physically sign the contract to be bound, because an agent may act to bind the party. Under agency laws of most jurisdictions, an agent who signs an agreement acting on behalf of a principal binds that principal to the agreement.[66] The agent must act within the scope of his or her authority, and generally, there must be proof that the agent had actual authority to act for the principal.[67] In certain circumstances, however, a principal may be bound if the agent had "apparent authority." For a tribunal to find apparent authority, the principal, not the agent, must have created the impression with the third party that the agent was authorized to act for the principal.[68] Somewhat similarly, the French doctrine of *mandat apparent* provides that a principal may be bound by the action of an agent without authority if the apparent principal and the apparent agent created a belief in third parties that such authority existed. The third parties' reliance interest must outweigh the principal's interest in avoiding responsibility based on a lack of actual authority.[69]

2. Equitable Estoppel

Equitable estoppel is applied to parties rather often in the United States, but rarely in civil law countries. However, the concept of good faith, or abuse of right, is sometimes used to the same effect in non–common law

---

(5th Cir. 2006) and Bridas S.A.P.I.C. v. Turkmenistan, 345 F.3d 347, 358 (5th Cir. 2003).

[65] *See, e.g.*, Bernard Hanotiau, COMPLEX ARBITRATIONS, pp. 49–99 (2005). James M. Hosking, *The Third Party Non-Signatory's Ability to Compel International Commercial Arbitration: Doing Justice without Destroying Consent*, 4 Pepp. Disp. Resol. L.J. 469, 483–84 (2004).

[66] *See* FOUCHARD, GAILLARD & GOLDMAN ON INTERNATIONAL COMMERCIAL ARBITRATION § 498 (Emmanuel Gaillard & John Savage, eds., 1999).
   See also Thomson-CSF S.A. v. Am. Arb. Ass'n, 64 F. 3d 773,776 (2d Cir. 1995) ("[A] nonsignatory party may be bound to an arbitration agreement if so dictated by the 'ordinary principles of contract and agency.'").

[67] *See, e.g.*, Bridas S.A.P.I.C. v. Govt. of Turkmenistan, 345 F. 3d 347, 356 (5th Cir. 2003).

[68] *See id.*

[69] *See., e.g.*, Otto Sandrock, *Arbitration Agreements and Groups of Companies*, 27 Int'l Law. 941 (1993).

countries.[70] The doctrine of estoppel serves to preclude a party from enjoying rights and benefits under a contract while at the same time avoiding its burdens and obligations.[71] There are basically two forms of estoppel that courts consider in these circumstances. One is based on a theory of intertwined issues, and the other is based on a theory of direct benefits.

First, with respect to the intertwined issues, it matters whether the party that is seeking to bind the other party to arbitrate is a signatory or a nonsignatory. When a nonsignatory seeks to bind a signatory, the courts are much more willing to bind the signatory when claims that involve the nonsignatory are inextricably intertwined with the contract obligations under the agreement signed by the signatory. Because the signatory had expressly agreed to arbitrate claims of the very type that involve the nonsignatory, the signatory cannot refuse to arbitrate with the nonsignatory.[72] On the other hand, the fact that claims are inextricably intertwined is insufficient, standing alone, to bind a resisting nonsignatory that is not otherwise subject to the tribunal's jurisdiction.[73]

However, a nonsignatory can be estopped from denying the obligation to arbitrate if it has received direct benefits by "knowingly exploiting the agreement [which contained the arbitration clause]."[74] In these cases, a nonsignatory has typically embraced the agreement, benefited from its provisions, and then, once a dispute arises, has repudiated the arbitration clause. Courts are not pleased with this kind of conduct, stating, "To allow [a plaintiff] to claim the benefit of the contract and simultaneously avoid its burdens would both disregard equity and contravene the purposes underlying enactment of the Arbitration Act."[75] Thus, under this theory, if a nonsignatory has directly benefited from the provisions of a contract, it will likely be held to the arbitration clause.

3. Implied Consent

A nonsignatory may be bound to arbitrate if, under principles of contract law, it appeared that the nonsignatory intended to be bound, and the other

---

[70] *See, e.g.,* Philippe Pinsolle, *Distinction entre le principe de l'estoppel et le principe de bonne foi dans le droit du commerce international,* 125 J.D.I. (Clunet) 905 (1998). *See also* Gary B. Born, INTERNATIONAL ARBITRATION, Vol. 1 (2009) at 1197–98, notes 284–87 and accompanying text.

[71] *See* Sourcing Unlimited, Inc., v. Asimco Intern., Inc., 526 F. 3d 38, 47 (1st Cir. 2008) *citing* Intergen N.V. v. Grina, 344 F.3d 134, 145 (1st Cir. 2003).

[72] *See, e.g.,* Sunkist Soft Drinks, Inc., v. Sunkist Growers, Inc., 10 F.3d 753, 757–58 (11th Cir. 1993), *cert. denied,* 513 U.S. 869 (1994); McBro Planning & Devl. Co. v. Trinagle Elc. Constr. Co., 741 F.2d 342, 344 (7th Cir. 1984).

[73] *See* Bridas, *supra* note 60, 345 F.3d at 361.

[74] *See* Thomson-CSF, *supra* note 66, 64 F.3d at 778.

[75] *See* International Paper Co. v. Schwabedissen Maschinen & Anlagen GMBH, 206 F.3d 411, 418 (4th Cir. 2000).

parties intended to accept that intent. Such implied consent might arise, for example, if a nonsignatory to a contract performed certain obligations under the contract.[76] Questions of implied consent are heavily fact-based and will be determined on a case-by-case basis.

A question may arise over whether the nonsignatory intended to be bound by the arbitration clause as well as by the contract. Under the doctrine of separability, this may require two separate analyses. However, tribunals and courts have found that a party's performance of obligations under a contract can bind it not just to the contract generally, but also to the arbitration clause.[77]

4. Group of Companies

The "group of companies" doctrine has been used to find arbitration obligations in situations in which a number of affiliated companies, not all of which are signatories of the particular contracts that contain an arbitration clause, have been involved with various contracts. Usually, the companies are all involved in various aspects of a project, and their obligations and responsibilities are interrelated. In an ad hoc arbitration involving four defendants, only one of which was a signatory, a tribunal found that the other three defendants were also bound to arbitrate.[78] The three other companies controlled and financed the signatory corporation and were the only ones that were solvent.[79] Although in this case, the nonsignatories – all related companies – were deemed to be bound to the arbitration clause, the "group of companies" doctrine has been criticized as being insufficiently grounded in legal reasoning, and simply too vague a basis on which to bind a nonsignatory.[80] When a number of affiliated or related companies are involved in a situation in which not all are signatories, some jurisdictions use more traditional bases – such as alter ego, agency, estoppel, and third-party beneficiaries – to determine whether the nonsignatories should be bound.[81]

---

[76] *See, e.g.*, Lamm & Aqua, *supra* note 61, at 88 (Party's conduct may indicate that it has accepted obligation to arbitrate).

[77] *See, e.g.*, Judgment of November 28, 1989, 1990 Rev. Arb. 675 (Paris Cour d'appel) (Party bound to both contract and arbitration clause when it performed contract obligations of another entity.).

[78] *See* Hanotiau, *supra* note 65, at 42, § 87.

[79] *See id.*

[80] *See, e.g.*, Redfern & Hunter et al., *supra* note 57, § 2.45 at 102 (noting that Switzerland has refused to recognize the doctrine, that an English court found the doctrine nonexistent under English law, and that it is not a doctrine generally relied on by courts in France, England, and the United States, even though they may at times permit piercing of the corporate veil to bind nonsignatory affiliates).

[81] *See id.*

5. Veil Piercing/Alter Ego

As a general matter, a corporate relationship, such as a parent–subsidiary relationship, is not sufficient to bind a nonsignatory to an arbitration agreement. However, a court will "pierce the corporate veil" when it no longer treats a parent company and a subsidiary as separate legal entities, but rather finds that one is the "alter ego" of the other. The theory is also sometimes used to bind a government when the contract containing an arbitration clause is signed by a government-controlled entity, but not by the government itself. Two affiliated entities may lose their distinct juridical identities when their conduct demonstrates an abandonment of separateness.[82] This could occur, for example, if they operate in ways such as sharing a common office and staff, managing both entities by the same officers and directors, intermingling funds, or paying all bills from only one account. Generally, courts do not readily pierce the corporate veil. However, they may hold that one entity is the alter ego of the other with respect to the obligations of an arbitration agreement if:

1. the owner [parent] exercised complete control over the [subsidiary] corporation with respect to the transaction at issue; and
2. such control was used to commit a fraud or wrong that injured the party seeking to pierce the corporate veil.[83]

In Bridas S.A.P.I.C. v. Government of Turkmenistan, Bridas, an Argentine company, was awarded U.S. $495 million against the Government of Turkmenistan and the state-controlled company, Turkmeneft.[84] Turkmeneft had entered a joint venture with Bridas, and the arbitral tribunal had found that the Government of Turkmenistan, although a nonsignatory to the joint venture agreement, was bound by the arbitration agreement. The award against both Turkmeneft and the Government was confirmed by a U.S. district court. On appeal, the Fifth Circuit refused to find the Government was bound to the arbitration agreement under theories of agency, estoppel, or third-party beneficiary, but remanded the case for a fuller determination by the lower court of whether the Government of Turkmenistan was the alter ego of Turkmeneft.[85]

The appellate court instructed the lower court to consider a number of factors focused on establishing the extent to which Turkmeneft was controlled by the Government or was independent from it. The appellate court also wanted the district court to focus on factors that U.S. courts take into account when determining whether a state agency is the "alter ego"

---

[82] See Thomson-CSF, *supra* note 66, 64 F.3d at 777–78.
[83] See Bridas, *supra* note 60, 345 F.3d at 359.
[84] See *id*. at 352.
[85] See *id*.

of a state for purposes of establishing whether it is entitled to sovereign immunity:

> (1) whether state statutes and case law view the entity as an arm of the state; (2) the source of the entity's funding; (3) the entity's degree of local autonomy; (4) whether the entity is concerned primarily with local, as opposed to statewide problems; (5) whether the entity has the authority to sue and be sued in its own name; and (6) whether the entity has the right to hold and use property.[86]

The district court concluded that the Government did not "exercise complete domination or extensive control" over Turkmeneft and that the Government was therefore not an alter ego of Turkmeneft.[87] The Fifth Circuit disagreed. It reversed on the ground that the undercapitalization of Turkmeneft and various acts of the Government made it impossible for the objectives of the joint venture to be carried out. These governmental acts constituted sufficient evidence of the lack of separateness of the two parties. The court noted that

> [d]espite some indicia of separateness, the reality was that when the Government's export ban forced Bridas out of the joint venture, the Government then exercised its power as a parent entity to deprive Bridas of a contractual remedy. Intentionally bleeding a subsidiary to thwart creditors is a classic ground for piercing the corporate veil.[88]

Although the court indicated a general reluctance to use the alter ego theory to bind a nonsignatory to an arbitration agreement, it nonetheless found that in this case, circumstances warranted such a finding.

A recent case also involving an alter ego theory is Dallah Real Estate and Tourism Holding Company v. Ministry of Religious Affairs, Government of Pakistan ("the Government").[89] In this case, Dallah and the Government signed a Memorandum of Understanding to the effect that Dallah would provide for construction of housing for Pakistani pilgrims to Mecca. The Government then established a Trust, which entered into a contract with Dallah that contained an arbitration clause. Dallah and the Trust were the only two signatories of the contract. When the Trust ceased to exist shortly thereafter, Dallah commenced an arbitration in France against the Government for breach of contract. The award, which was in Dallah's favor, was refused enforcement in the U.K. on the grounds that the Government

---

[86] *See id.*
[87] *See* Bridas S.A.P.I.C. v. Government of Turkmenistan, 447 F.3d 411, 414, 418 (5th Cir. 2006).
[88] *See id.* at 420.
[89] [2010] UKSC 46 (Nov. 3, 2010).

was not a signatory to the contract. Subsequently, in France, the Cour d'appel found that the award was enforceable.[90]

The diametrically opposite results of the English and French courts are somewhat ironic, because the U.K. Supreme Court thought it was applying French law in determining that the Government was not bound to arbitrate. The U.K. Court accepted the French view that international law, including recognition and enforcement of international arbitration awards, is governed by "transnational principles,"[91] rather than any particular national law. However, the U.K. Court noted that this did not mean it was excluding French law, but rather that "the arbitration agreement is no longer affected by the idiosyncrasies of local law."[92] The Court further noted, relying on expert testimony about French law, that according to "customary practices of international trade," to determine whether a nonsignatory can be bound, arbitrators must look to the common intent of the parties.[93] Once the Court determined that common intent was the proper test, it had no difficulty finding that the Government was not bound to arbitrate, because the contract with the Trust had been deliberately structured in order for the Government not to be a party.[94]

The French Cour d'appel took a very different approach.[95] It looked not to common intent, but rather to conduct indicating control, including conduct by Government officials that occurred both before and after the conclusion of the contract. It followed a much more typical alter ego analysis and found that the creation of the Trust was purely formal because the Government always acted as if it were the true party.

The differences in the approaches of the two courts will play out over time on the international stage. The U.K. decision places great weight on the content and structure of the agreement in determining the parties' intent. Such an interpretation would make it easier for sovereigns to shield themselves from liability.[96] The French Court, on the other hand, followed the more typical alter ego analysis, similar to the court in *Bridas*, of considering indicia of control and domination by the State over the underlying transaction in determining that a nonsignatory State was bound to arbitrate.

---

[90] Gouvernement de Pakistan, Ministère des Affaires Religieuses v. Société Dallah Real Estate and Tourism Holding Co., joined cases 09/28533, 09/28541 (Ct. App. Paris, Feb. 17, 2011).

[91] Dallah, *supra* note 62, ¶¶ 14–16. See George A. Bermann, *The U.K Supreme Court Speaks to International Arbitration: Learning from the Dallah Case*, 22 Am. Rev. Int'l Arb. 1, 4 (2011).

[92] Dallah, ¶ 115.

[93] *See id.* ¶¶ 13, 18.

[94] *See id.* ¶ 66.

[95] The approach was different in style as well as substance. The French opinion was seven pages; the U.K. opinion was sixty-two pages.

[96] See Bermann, *supra* note 91 at 19–20.

6. Timing of Objections

In sum, although requiring arbitration between a signatory and a nonsignatory is not something courts or tribunals are eager to do, they will in some instances compel a party to arbitrate by applying ordinary contract and agency principles. A signatory or nonsignatory that is opposing arbitration should always raise its objections at the earliest possible time, because it is much more likely to succeed if its claims are heard before an award is rendered. Once the parties have completed the arbitral process, a court is not nearly as likely to find that the original arbitration agreement did not bind the parties. Although the decisions do not always appear consistent, a party seems more likely to be bound if the failure to hold it to the arbitration agreement would be contrary to the reasonable expectations of the parties.

CHAPTER THREE

Drafting the Arbitration Agreement

The arbitration agreement serves the critical function of creating a framework for the parties' own private dispute resolution system outside of national courts. To ensure proper functioning of the system, the agreement should be drafted with great care. A well-drafted arbitration clause has a significant impact on how well the parties resolve the dispute – how efficiently, how fairly, and how successfully. Unfortunately, in negotiating and drafting a contract, attorneys and parties too often do not focus on drafting the arbitration clause. This can result in a "pathological clause"[1] – one that is defective in some way. It may be so defective that it invalidates the arbitration agreement. At the very least, the defect may create a basis for extensive disputes over the meaning of the clause and over how the arbitration will proceed.

Many kinds of defects can render a clause pathological. For example, the clause may be ambiguous or equivocal, or it may contain mistaken information. The clause may use the wrong name for an arbitral institution or its rules, resulting in the choice of a nonexistent institution. Clauses may provide for choosing a specific arbitrator, who may be deceased by the time an arbitration commences. Parties may state in one clause that disputes will be resolved by arbitration, and in another clause in the same contract may state that a particular court will have exclusive jurisdiction of any dispute. Even if not pathological, the clause may not provide a process that is efficient or beneficial to the parties.

There are several reasons for the sad neglect of the arbitration clause. First, the clause is frequently left until the end of the negotiations, after the major issues have been resolved. At that point, parties may think they

---

[1] Frederic Eisemann, former Secretary General of the ICC Court of Arbitration, is believed to be the creator of the expression, "pathological clause." *See* W. Laurence Craig, William W. Park, & Jan Paulsson, INTERNATIONAL CHAMBER OF COMMERCE ARBITRATION, 127, n. 1 (2000).

do not have sufficient energy or resources to engage in more negotiations over this provision. Second, the lawyers who draft arbitration clauses tend to be transactional lawyers, who may have little understanding or knowledge about the arbitration process or the significance of the arbitration clause.[2] And third, parties simply may not believe they will encounter disputes that would be worth the transaction costs of researching, understanding, and negotiating an arbitration clause that is anything more than boilerplate.

Increasingly, however, lawyers are recognizing that the stakes in arbitration may be high, and that a well-drafted clause can make an enormous difference in the ability of the parties to resolve a dispute efficiently and effectively. Help is available for drafting. The International Bar Association has recently promulgated the IBA Guidelines for Drafting International Arbitration Clauses.[3] These guidelines not only discuss the essential elements involved in drafting an effective arbitration clause, but also give examples of actual clauses to accomplish the desired result. In addition, the American Arbitration Association has available on its website "Drafting Dispute Resolution Clauses: A Practical Guide," which also provides drafting advice and recommends specific clauses,[4] and the ICDR has published its "ICDR Guide to Drafting International Dispute Resolution Clauses."[5] These drafting guides make clear that parties have many choices about how to draft a specific clause.

Even among experienced lawyers who have some understanding of arbitration, there can be disagreement about whether the client is better served by a short and simple clause or by a more extensive and complex clause. Much depends on the kind of transaction at issue, the likelihood that a dispute may develop, and the ultimate value that a potential dispute would likely have. This chapter considers the arbitration clause on a continuum, from the very basic clause to the more extensive and complex clause, to see what kinds of elements may provide added value, without turning toward the pathological.

---

[2] *See* Thomas Stipanowich, *Contract and Conflict Management*, 2001 Wis. L. Rev. 831, 834 (2001). As one litigation partner in a large law firm noted, "I found one of the problems was that many of these [arbitration] issues were addressed by my transactional corporate partners, who didn't like me tinkering with the [arbitration] provisions at the end of deals so they couldn't close the transaction. Unfortunately, the clauses they used were often taken out of form books and not really discussed between the parties." *Id.* at 834, n. 18.

[3] Available at the IBA website, http://www.ibanet.org/Default.aspx.

[4] Available at http://www.adr.org/si.asp?id=4125.

[5] Available at http://www.adr.org/si.asp?id=4945.

A. ESSENTIAL REQUIREMENTS

A fair amount of conventional wisdom holds that a short and simple arbitration clause is sufficient, and that there is no need for an elaborate or
complex clause.[6] Moreover, the extensive writings on pathological clauses,
which suggest that even simple clauses can go badly astray, provide a caveat
for drafters of more complex clauses.[7] For many arbitrations, the simple
model clause, proposed by the arbitral institution chosen by the parties to
administer the arbitration, will be sufficient. In addition, such a clause has
stood the test of time, and is clear and familiar to the parties and the arbitral
institution's administrators.

On the other hand, if the parties choose to have an ad hoc arbitration,
they may need to spell out more specifics in their arbitration clause. If
there is no administering institution, and the parties do not agree on how
to proceed, they may have to resort to the court. For example, if they
do not agree on the appointment of an arbitrator, a court may be asked to
make the appointment. However, in many ad hoc arbitrations, parties adopt
the UNCITRAL Arbitration Rules.[8] Those rules provide that if the parties
have not agreed on the appointment of the arbitrator, and if they have not
agreed on an appointing authority, either party may request the Secretary-
General of the Permanent Court of Arbitration at the Hague to designate an
appointing authority.[9] Once a tribunal is in place, there is less danger that
the parties will have to resort to a court to ensure that the arbitration goes
forward.

Whether the arbitration agreement is for an ad hoc arbitration or an
institutional arbitration, it is important for the agreement to be in writing.
As noted in the previous chapter, a writing is generally required for enforcement purposes under the New York Convention, and is also required by
many arbitration laws, such as the UNCITRAL Model Law, which has
been adopted as the law of many countries. Although, as discussed previously, UNCITRAL has proposed amendments to the Model Law and recommended interpretations of certain provisions of the New York Convention
that would render the writing requirement less critical,[10] for the present,
prudent counsel should ensure that an arbitration agreement is in writing.

---

[6] *See* Julian D. M. Lew, Loukas A. Mistelis, & Stefan M. Kroll, COMPARATIVE INTER-
NATIONAL COMMERCIAL ARBITRATION, 166 § 8-5 (2003) ("Whilst some lawyers draft
lengthy special form arbitration provisions, this is not generally necessary.").

[7] *See* Craig, Park & Paulsson, *supra* note 1 at 127–35 (2000).

[8] Available at http://www.uncitral.org/pdf/english/texts/arbitration/arb-rules/arb-rules
.pdf.

[9] *See id.* art. 6.2.

[10] *See* Chapter 2 *supra* Section B(1) (a–b).

Parties who choose an institution to administer their arbitration are well advised to use the institution's model arbitration clause in their contract. A fairly typical model clause is the one recommended by the London Court of International Arbitration (LCIA):

> Any dispute arising out of or in connection with this contract, including any question regarding its existence, validity or termination, shall be referred to and finally resolved by arbitration under the LCIA Rules, which Rules are deemed to be incorporated by reference into this clause.

> The number of arbitrators shall be [one/three].
> The seat, or legal place, of arbitration shall be [City and/or Country].
> The language to be used in the arbitral proceedings shall be [ ].
> The governing law of the contract shall be the substantive law of [ ].[11]

Parties who use such a clause, with the blank areas appropriately filled in, will be generally assured that if challenged, this clause will be upheld, and the arbitration will go forward according to its terms. Therefore, for many arbitrations, such a clause will suffice. The institution's arbitration rules, which are chosen in this clause, will deal with the formation of the arbitral tribunal, the conduct of the hearings, and other details in connection with the arbitral process.

The scope of the clause above is broad, because it does not just apply to contract interpretation issues, but to any issue in a dispute that *arises out of or in connection with* the contract. As noted in Chapter 2, the broad language means that both contract issues, which arise out of the contract, and tort issues, which are related to the contract, can be determined in the arbitration. The tort issues will not have to be decided in a separate litigation. The last thing most parties want is to have some issues decided in arbitration while related issues are decided in litigation because the arbitration clause was too narrow to cover the parties' various claims against each other.

1. Choice of Arbitrators

In filling in the blanks of the model clause in the listing above, parties will need to make some important decisions. In determining whether to have one

---

[11] Available at http://www.lcia-arbitration.com/. This clause anticipates application to a dispute that might arise sometime in the future. Slightly different language is generally used when there is no arbitration clause in the contract, but parties wish to submit an existing dispute to arbitration (a submission agreement). For a submission agreement triggering an arbitration under the LCIA rules, the first paragraph of this clause is changed to read as follows: "A dispute having arisen between the parties concerning [], the parties hereby agree that the dispute shall be referred to and finally resolved by arbitration under the LCIA Rules." The remaining language is the same as in the basic LCIA clause.

or three arbitrators, for example, a party should consider how complicated the transaction is, the likelihood that a dispute will arise, and the estimated value of the potential dispute. In a dispute involving contract interpretation issues, in which the amount at stake is around U.S. $500,000 to U.S. $1,000,000 or less, one arbitrator is probably adequate, although in any given case, needs and requirements may be different. With one arbitrator, it should be easier to schedule hearings, the costs would be lower, and the proceedings and award should move forward more quickly, because there would be no need for members of a tribunal to confer and debate over various points.

On the other hand, in complex, high-value disputes, parties generally prefer to have three arbitrators. Although having three arbitrators is much more expensive than having one, and organizing the schedules for hearings can be difficult, most parties feel more comfortable with three arbitrators when substantial amounts of money are at stake. With respect to the complexity of the issues, three minds are generally better than one at absorbing all the necessary information, and arriving at a reasonable resolution. In addition, when the parties are from different cultural or legal backgrounds, a party may want at least one arbitrator to have some knowledge and understanding of its own culture and legal system. In such a case, the parties may agree, and may put in their arbitration clause that each party will appoint one arbitrator,[12] and the two party-appointed arbitrators will choose the third arbitrator, who will serve as chair. If the parties do not agree on a method of choosing the arbitrators, selection will occur in accordance with the rules of the administering institution.

Parties also may want to set forth specific qualifications that the arbitrators should have, such as experience or expertise in a particular field, or the ability to speak a particular language. One should be careful, however, not to specify so many characteristics that it becomes impossible to find arbitrators who meet all the qualifications. This could possibly result in invalidating the arbitration clause.

2. Seat of the Arbitration

Choosing the seat of the arbitration is important because generally the arbitration law of the arbitral situs will be the law that governs the arbitration (the *lex arbitri*). Parties want an "arbitration-friendly" regime – that is, one that will not unduly interfere with the arbitral process. If any court intervention is needed or occurs during or after the arbitration, the local law governing arbitrations will have an impact on the proceedings.

---

[12] Even if appointed by one of the parties, an arbitrator must be independent and impartial, as will be discussed *infra* in Chapter 6.

Typically, parties in an arbitration want to select a venue where the court will not interfere with the arbitral process. At the same time, they need to view the court's potential assistance as another tool in the toolbox for achieving the client's objective.[13]

Claudia Salomon
New York

Parties will also tend to choose a country that is not the place of business of either party, so they will be in a "neutral" forum. In addition, it is important to choose a situs within a country that is a party to the New York Convention (a "Contracting State"). Many countries have declared they will enforce only arbitration awards that were made in another Contracting State.[14] Thus, if the seat of arbitration was not within a Contracting State, the award might not be enforceable in the jurisdiction where the losing party's assets are located.

In addition, the arbitration should be held in a place where the infrastructure is sufficiently developed to permit reasonable transportation to and from the location, where basic technology is available (phones, faxes, Internet access), and where the political and economic structure is stable. One rule of thumb: Do not hold an arbitration in a place where you would not go on vacation.

3. Language of the Arbitration

Parties should state the language of the arbitration in the arbitration clause. Although some parties assume the language of the contract will be the language of the arbitration, that may not necessarily be the case. The tribunal could decide differently, unless the parties have specifically agreed on a language. A client that had to assume unexpected costs of translating documents and witness testimony because the lawyers had never specified the language in the arbitration clause would not be a happy client.

4. Substantive Law

The substantive law governing the contract does not necessarily have to be in the arbitration clause, but it is not a bad idea to put it there. Its location within the arbitration clause should prevent one side from arguing that the substantive law governing the contract may not necessarily be the substantive law governing the arbitration agreement. No matter where they

---

[13] Interview with Claudia Salomon, July 2011. Notes of interview on file with author.

[14] New York Convention, art. I(3) ("[A]ny state may on the basis of reciprocity declare that it will apply the Convention to the recognition and enforcement of awards made only in the territory of another Contracting State."). Available at www.uncitral.org.

put it, however, the parties should definitely specify the substantive law on which they have agreed, in order to avoid unnecessary disputes at the time of the arbitration.

B. ADDITIONAL PROVISIONS

Although the preceding elements should be included in every arbitration agreement, additional clauses can give more control to parties that want to go beyond the basics. Before adding additional clauses, however, a lawyer should be very familiar with the rules that the parties have chosen to govern the arbitration. There is no need to add provisions that are already adequately covered by an institution's rules, and it is not a good idea to contradict institutional rules that appear to be mandatory. There have been instances when the International Chamber of Commerce (ICC), for example, has refused to administer an arbitration in which the parties chose its rules, but then tried to vary them in ways that the ICC did not consider permissible.[15] There will be many times, however, in any arbitral organization's list of rules when a rule will be required "unless otherwise agreed by the parties." That is a green light for the parties to "agree otherwise." On the other hand, if that proviso is not present, one should hesitate to include a provision that would contradict the institutional rule.

1. International Bar Association Rules on Taking Evidence

One fairly simple way of adding value without risk of pathology is to incorporate various rules developed by the International Bar Association (IBA). For example, because most arbitral rules do not deal in detail with issues of evidence, the arbitration clause could include an agreement that the arbitration be conducted according to the IBA Rules on the Taking of Evidence in International Arbitration, which were first published in 1999, and revised effective May 29, 2010.[16] These rules provide a good harmonization of civil and common law approaches to taking evidence, and provide parties with a fair amount of certainty about how the tribunal will deal with

---

[15] *See* Yves Derains & Eric Schwartz, A GUIDE TO THE ICC RULES OF ARBITRATION, at 8 (2005) ("[T]he ICC has, from time to time, refused to administer arbitrations where the parties have agreed to alterations of its Rules that the Rules do not themselves contemplate.").

[16] Available at http://www.ibanet.org.; click on "IBA guidelines, rules and other free materials." In the Foreword to these Rules, the drafters recommend adding the following clause if parties wish to adopt the IBA Rules of Evidence in their arbitration clause: "[In addition to the institutional, ad hoc, or other rules chosen by the parties], [t]he parties agree that the arbitration shall be conducted according to the IBA Rules of Evidence as current on the date of [this agreement/the commencement of the arbitration]."

documents, witnesses, and experts. Many practitioners, however, prefer that the IBA Rules on the Taking of Evidence be used as guidelines, rather than be imposed by party agreement.[17]

If, however, parties wanted more discovery than the IBA Rules provide, they would need to specifically provide for it in the arbitration clause. First, parties should negotiate in advance if they want rights to specific kinds of discovery, such as depositions or interrogatories, which are otherwise unlikely to be permitted in the arbitral proceedings. The clause might set forth a specific number of depositions permitted for each party, as well as other kinds of discovery devices that the parties can agree on, such as interrogatories and document requests, the extent of expert discovery, and possibly a timetable for completing discovery. However, most parties do not want this level of discovery in arbitration because they generally do not want to lengthen the proceedings and increase the cost. If the parties want more than the limited discovery normally provided in international arbitration, however, they should agree on the scope of discovery in the arbitration clause.

2. Preliminary Relief

Parties may also want to consider including a provision for preliminary or interim relief. Parties may need urgent relief, perhaps even before an arbitral tribunal can be constituted. However, many major arbitral institutions now include emergency arbitrator procedures that make it unnecessary to include a provision for interim relief in the arbitration clause.

For example, the American Arbitration Association International Centre for Dispute Resolution (ICDR) has adopted a procedure, titled "Emergency Measures of Protection," which it has included as Article 37 of its International Arbitration Rules.[18] Under the ICDR Rules, the provision on emergency measures will apply unless the parties have agreed otherwise. If the ICDR rules are chosen, therefore, there is no need for parties to specifically reference such interim relief in their arbitration clause. The Emergency Measure of Protection will be available to the parties, as long as they did not specifically opt out of Article 37. The emergency arbitrator appointed pursuant to the ICDR rules has the power "to order or award any interim or conservancy measure the emergency arbitrator deems necessary, including injunctive relief and measures for the protection or conservation of property."[19] The arbitration rules of the Netherlands Arbitration Institute (NAI) contain similar procedures.[20]

---

[17] *See* Chapter 7 *infra* Section E.
[18] ICDR International Arbitration Rules are available at its website, under International Dispute Resolution Procedures, International Arbitration Rules, http://www.adr.org/icdr.
[19] ICDR Rules, art. 37.
[20] *See* NAI Arbitration Rules, Section 4A – Summary Arbitral Proceedings, Article 42a–o.

Rules providing for an emergency arbitrator may portend a trend for the future. The new ICC rules, effective January 2012, provide rules for an emergency arbitrator in Appendix V.[21] The SCC has provided for an emergency arbitrator in its latest rules, effective January 2010.[22] In addition, the Australian Centre for International Commercial Arbitration (ACICA) has also amended its rules to include an emergency arbitrator, effective August 1, 2011.[23]

3. Technical Expertise

If there is likely to be a dispute about technical issues, parties can provide in their arbitration clause for the dispute to be resolved by an expert. The clause can provide that the expert will render either a binding or a nonbinding decision. If the decision is nonbinding, the parties can provide that if they cannot settle the dispute after the expert has rendered an opinion, a binding arbitration will follow. The ICC International Centre for Expertise, for example, provides experts to assist in technical, financial, or contractual matters. It suggests the following clause for a situation in which an expert's opinion will be nonbinding:

> In the event of any dispute arising out of or in connection with clause [X] of the present contract, the parties agree to submit the matter, in the first instance, to administered expertise proceedings in accordance with the Rules for Expertise of the International Chamber of Commerce. If the dispute has not been resolved through such administered expertise proceedings it shall, after the Centre's notification of the termination of the expertise proceedings, be finally settled under the Rules of Arbitration of the International Chamber of Commerce by one or more arbitrators appointed in accordance with the said Rules of Arbitration.[24]

4. Multistep Dispute Resolution Clauses

Another form of clause to consider is a multistep clause. This clause provides that when a dispute arises, the parties will first attempt to resolve it by negotiation. If they are unsuccessful, they will then engage in mediation, and, if they still cannot reach a resolution, they will commence the process of a binding arbitration. Many arbitral institutions propose clauses

---

[21] *See*, ICC Rules, art. 29, and Appendix V.

[22] Available at http://www.sccinstitute.com/skiljeforfarande-2/emergency-arbitrator. aspx. The provisions governing the Emergency Arbitrator are found in Appendix II to the Arbitration Rules and are incorporated into the Rules pursuant to Article 32 (4). *Id.*

[23] *See* http://www.acica.org.au. The Emergency Arbitrator Rules are contained in Schedule 2 of the Australian Arbitration Rules. *See* http://www.kluwerarbitrationblog.com, August 4, 2011.

[24] Available at http://www.iccwbo.org/court/expertise/id4461/index.html.

to accomplish this multistep procedure.[25] Some practitioners, however, refer to the multistep clause as "the courtesy trap." The problem with requiring parties to negotiate and mediate before going to arbitration is that if the relationship has broken down, one or both parties may have no real interest in negotiation or mediation, and having to go through the steps may simply delay the process. On the other hand, mediators will say that some very hostile parties have been able to resolve issues through mediation. Moreover, short time frames for each stage, with the possibility that parties can agree to extend the time frames, will help prevent unnecessary delay if the parties are not serious about resolving the dispute in the nonbinding stages.

If one uses a multistep clause, one should consider providing that executives at a certain high level in the company – generally, a level at which they have authority to negotiate and reach a settlement – are required to participate in the first (nonbinding) stages. A corporate executive who is at a level above the employees directly involved in the fray will have more business incentive to resolve the dispute, and less concern about posturing or saving face, than employees close to the dispute.

5. Dispositive Motions

Parties may also want to make dispositive motions – that is, motions that will summarily dispose of a claim or issue, sometimes without the need for a hearing. Institutional rules deal differently with the issue of whether a party has the right to a hearing. The Swiss Rules provide that "[a]fter consulting with the parties, the arbitral tribunal may . . . decide to conduct the proceedings on the basis of documents and other materials."[26] Thus, the decision whether to have a hearing is ultimately within the discretion of the tribunal. The LCIA Rules, on the other hand, establish a right to

---

[25] Multistep clauses are also sometimes referred to as "Step Clauses for Negotiation–Mediation–Arbitration." A step clause recommended by the ICDR is as follows:

> In the event of any controversy or claim arising out of or relating to this contract, the parties hereto shall consult and negotiate with each other and, recognizing their mutual interests, attempt to reach a solution satisfactory to both parties. If they do not reach settlement within a period of 60 days, then either party may, by notice to the other party and the International Centre for Dispute Resolution, demand mediation under the International Mediation Rules of the International Centre for Dispute Resolution. If settlement is not reached within 60 days after service of a written demand for mediation, any unresolved controversy or claim arising out of or relating to this contract shall be settled by arbitration administered by the International Centre for Dispute Resolution in accordance with its International Arbitration Rules.

> *See* ICDR Guide to Drafting International Dispute Resolution Clauses, available at http://www.adr.org/si.asp?id=4945.

[26] Swiss Rules, art. 15, § 2, available at https://http://www.sccam.org/sa/download/SRIA_english.pdf.

a hearing, if any party requests it. Article 19.1 provides that "[a]ny party which expresses a desire to that effect has the right to be heard orally before the Arbitral Tribunal on the merits of the dispute, unless the parties have agreed in writing on documents-only arbitration."[27]

The American Arbitration Association Commercial Rules and the ICDR Arbitration Rules provide that at the hearing, the arbitrator has the discretion to "direct the parties to focus their presentations on issues the decision of which could dispose of all or part of the case."[28] The JAMS International Arbitration Rules contain an identical provision.[29]

Parties participating in a complex commercial case could view the dispositive motion as an important cost-saving device, and may want to create in the arbitration clause a procedure for the filing and determining of such motions. Presumably, such a provision would override any institutional rule to the contrary that provided, for example, the right to a hearing if requested by either party. However, as noted earlier, in some instances an arbitral tribunal has refused to administer an arbitration because the parties agreed in the arbitration clause to changes in the rules not specifically permitted by the rules themselves.[30]

6. Legal Fees and Costs

When parties to arbitration agreements engage in increased discovery and other litigation devices within the arbitration framework, the inevitable result is additional legal fees and related costs. Parties should negotiate exactly how the issue of fees and costs will be handled – that is, whether the arbitrators will have complete discretion in determining who pays the costs and legal fees, whether the losing party will automatically bear all costs of the arbitration as well as the legal fees of the prevailing party, or whether each party will bear its own costs and fees. An economically stronger party may think it advantageous to require the losing party to bear all administrative and legal costs, reasoning that this may be a disincentive to the smaller party to commence arbitration. Between two relatively equal parties, there may be a preference for each party to bear its own costs (including legal fees), because costs in major arbitrations can be quite substantial. In any case, to avoid surprise, parties should consider including in the arbitration clause an agreement as to how costs will be allocated.

[27] LCIA Rule 19.1, available at http://www.lcia-arbitration.com/.

[28] American Arbitration Association Commercial Arbitration Rules, R-30(b), available at http://www.adr.org/sp.asp?id=22440#R30; ICDR Rules, art.16(3), available at http://www.adr.org/sp.asp?id=33994.

[29] JAMS International Arbitration Rules, Rule 20.3, available at http://www.jamsadr.com.

[30] See Derains & Schwartz, *supra* note 15.

7. Confidentiality

Another issue parties may wish to deal with in their arbitration clause is confidentiality. Although confidentiality is touted as one of the advantages of arbitration, some arbitral rules place obligations only on the administrators and arbitrators, but not on the parties.[31] Moreover, fact witnesses are not bound by confidentiality, nor are experts, unless they sign separate confidentiality agreements. Even if the parties agree on confidentiality provisions, these provisions may be overridden if there is a court challenge. Although some courts, particularly in England, have found an implied obligation of confidentiality, Australian and U.S. courts tend to only enforce parties' express agreements.[32] Even with an express agreement, however, it is difficult, if not impossible, to prove breach when information leaks out.[33] Nonetheless, a confidentiality clause may at least provide some disincentive to parties to talk freely about the process or results of an arbitration. If parties are concerned about keeping their arbitration proceedings and results confidential, and if the institutional rules do not sufficiently provide for confidentiality, they might consider using the following clause recommended by the American Arbitration Association:

> Except as may be required by law, neither a party nor an arbitrator may disclose the existence, content, or results of any arbitration hereunder without the prior written consent of both parties.[34]

The clause could also provide that any fact witness or expert witness testifying on behalf of a party will be required by that party to enter into a written confidentiality agreement.

---

[31] For example, the confidentiality provision of the ICDR, in Article 34, applies only to arbitrators and administrators, not to parties:

> Confidential information disclosed during the proceedings by the parties or by witnesses shall not be divulged by an arbitrator or by the administrator. Except as provided in Article 27, unless otherwise agreed by the parties, or required by applicable law, the members of the tribunal and the administrator shall keep confidential all matters relating to the arbitration or the award.

Available at http://www.adr.org/sp.asp?id=33994#Confidentiality.

The ICC Rules place no specific obligation of confidentiality on the parties, but provide in Article 22(3) that "Upon the request of any party, [t]he Arbitral Tribunal may make orders concerning the confidentiality of the arbitration proceedings . . . and may take measures for protecting trade secrets and confidential information."

[32] For a discussion of various cases dealing with this issue, *see* Craig, Park, & Paulsson, *supra* note 1, at 311–18. *See also* Alexis C. Brown, *Presumption Meets Reality: An Exploration of the Confidentiality Obligation in International Commercial Arbitration*, 16 Am. U. Int'l L. Rev. 969 (2001).

[33] *See* Brown, *supra* note 32, at 1014–17.

[34] Available in the AAA's Drafting Dispute Resolution Clauses – A Practical Guide, at 36 (amended and effective September 1, 2007), http://www.adr.org/si.asp?id=4125.

8. Expanded Judicial Review

Whenever parties add to an arbitration clause provisions that potentially conflict with the local law, they risk invalidating the arbitration agreement or the arbitration award. An example of a provision that might cause an arbitration award to be invalidated in some jurisdictions is a clause that provides for expanded judicial review of an arbitration award. In France, for example, the Paris Cour d'Appel annulled an international arbitration award because the parties had provided for an appeal of the arbitrators' award, which was not permissible under French law.[35] France permits an appeal of a domestic award, but not of an international award.[36]

In the United States, circuit courts were divided for a number of years over whether to enforce a clause in the parties' arbitration agreement providing for expanded judicial review.[37] However, in 2008, the U.S. Supreme Court held that the Federal Arbitration Act (FAA) does not permit an arbitration agreement to expand judicial review of an arbitration award.[38] According to the Supreme Court, the narrow grounds set forth in the FAA are the exclusive grounds that an appellate court may consider in an action to vacate an award.[39] Those grounds deal with procedural fairness and arbitrator conduct, and do not permit review by a court of a tribunal's mistakes of fact or law.[40] Although the Court left open the possibility that more extensive judicial review could be obtained under state statutory or common law,[41] parties to an international arbitration should not include such a clause, even if they asserted that state law governed, because such a provision would probably not be enforced under the New York Convention.

If the arbitration law applicable to the proceedings is English law, and if the parties are sure they do not want judicial review on questions of law, they may need to include a provision in their arbitration clause that there will be no appeal of questions of law. The English Arbitration Act provides that "unless otherwise agreed by the parties, a party to arbitral proceedings may...appeal to the court on a question of law arising out of an award made in the proceedings."[42] Even though such an appeal cannot be brought

---

[35] Société de Diseno v. Société Mendes, Cour d'Appel, Paris, October 27, 1994. Rev. Arb. at 263 (1995).

[36] Derains & Schwartz, *supra* note 15, at 110. England permits review on points of law in certain circumstances unless the parties opt out. English Arbitration Act of 1996, Article 69(1).

[37] For a discussion of these issues, *see* Margaret L. Moses, *Can Parties Tell Courts What to Do? Expanded Judicial Review of Arbitral Awards*, 52 Kans. L. Rev. 429 (2004).

[38] Hall Street Assoc. v. Mattel, Inc., 552 U.S. 576, 583–84 (2008).

[39] *See id.* at 586.

[40] *See* 9 U.S.C. § 10.

[41] See Hall Street v. Mattel at 590.

[42] English Arbitration Act 1996, art. 69(1).

without the leave of the court or the agreement of all the parties,[43] it is still possible that an appeal of legal issues decided by the tribunal in the award could occur unless the parties have specifically agreed otherwise in the arbitration clause. If, however, there is a waiver of the right of appeal in the arbitration rules chosen by the parties, courts have held that this constitutes an effective agreement not to appeal on the point of law.[44] A further limitation is that a "question of law" is defined in the Act as meaning a question of English law, and thus does not appear to include a question of foreign law.[45]

9. Waiver of State Immunity

When one party to a contract is a State or State entity, there is a risk that it will claim sovereign or State immunity from the jurisdiction of another State. However, if a State has agreed to an arbitration clause in its contract, that agreement is generally considered a waiver of its immunity, so that it should be bound to arbitrate under the rules and laws that govern the arbitration. This may not, however, be true in all jurisdictions.

A further risk is that the State entity will assert immunity from enforcement of an award against its assets. In some countries, the forum State will allow execution only against the *commercial* assets of a foreign sovereign. Moreover, courts are likely to defer to a foreign State's declaration that certain assets are not commercial assets.[46] For these reasons, it may be wise for parties dealing with a State entity to include in an arbitration clause a provision such as the following, if they can persuade the State entity to agree:

> The obligations and performance by the Purchaser as required under this Agreement constitute commercial acts rather than public or governmental acts. Neither the Purchaser nor its agents or representatives are entitled to or will claim any right of immunity in any jurisdiction from arbitration, suit, jurisdiction, judgment, attachment, set-off,

[43] *See id.* art 69(2).

[44] *See, e.g.*, Sanghi Polyesters Ltd. (India) v. International Investor (KCFC) (Kuwait) (2000), 1 Lloyd's Rep. 480 ("When parties agree to ICC arbitration they undertake by art. 24 to waive their right to appeal insofar as that can validly be done."). *See also* Marine Contractors, Inc., v. Shell Petroleum Development Co. of Nigeria Ltd. [1984] 2 Lloyd's Rep 77, CA.

[45] *See* English Arbitration Act 1996, art. 82(1).

[46] *See* Alcom Ltd. v. Republic of Columbia and others [1984] A.C. 580, where an English court accepted a foreign ambassador's declaration that a particular account was not used for commercial purposes. *See also* AIG Capital Partners, Inc., and another v. Republic of Kazakhstan and others [2005] EWHC 2239 (Comm) (Assets in London that were part of a National Fund managed by the National Bank of Kazakhstan were immune from enforcement proceedings with respect to arbitration award against Republic of Kazakhstan.).

enforcement or execution of an award against its assets, or from any other legal procedure or remedy relating to its obligations under this Agreement.

10. Multiparty Agreements

When a dispute is likely to involve more than two parties, some additional considerations need to be addressed in the arbitration clause.[47] Two kinds of situations represent the most common multiparty relationships. First, there might be several related contracts, such as in an owner–contractor–subcontractor dispute, or a supplier–distributor–bank financing dispute. Second, more than two parties could all be parties to one contract, such as in a consortium, a joint venture, or a partnership. In the first situation, in which there is more than one contract, one efficient way to handle the arbitration agreement is to have an identical arbitration clause in all contracts, which consolidates the dispute process.[48] In the second case, in which the parties are all parties to the same contract, one clause should suffice. However, it is often the case that individual parties to a multiparty contract may have reason to engage subcontractors, who might need to be joined in an arbitration procedure. Therefore, the arbitration clause should require any party that enters into a subcontract with a person not party to the main agreement to include in its subcontract that the subcontractor is bound by the dispute resolution provisions of the main contract.[49]

In either the case of multiple contracts or the case in which all the parties are parties to the same contract, the arbitration clause should make clear how the arbitrators are to be chosen. Complications may arise when two or more parties on a side have to choose a single arbitrator, and they cannot agree, or when parties represent more than two different viewpoints, but each cannot nominate its own arbitrator.

This kind of issue arose in the case of Siemens AG v. Dutco, in which the respondents were not able to agree on an arbitrator, so the ICC Court of Arbitration appointed that arbitrator.[50] The claimant, on the other hand,

---

[47] Bernard Hanotiau, COMPLEX ARBITRATIONS: MULTIPARTY, MULTICONTRACT, MULTI-ISSUE AND CLASS ACTIONS (2005) is very good source of information about multiparty agreements. It includes an Appendix with a number of model complex arbitration clauses.

[48] The AAA, in its online guide, DRAFTING DISPUTE RESOLUTION CLAUSES-A PRACTICAL GUIDE, provides at 29–30 an example of a clause for consolidating disputes among a number of parties. Available at http://www.adr.org/si.asp?id=4125.

[49] See, e.g., Hanotiau, supra note 47, at 314 ("[N]o Party shall enter into a contract relating to the Project with a person not a party to this Agreement . . . unless . . . a clause is included in such contract stating that any Dispute arising thereunder shall be exclusively and finally resolved pursuant to the provisions of the Agreement and that all Parties to any such contract expressly consent to be bound by this Agreement as if signatories hereto.").

[50] See Cour de Cassation, January 7, 1992, Rev. Arb. 470 (1992).

was able to appoint the arbitrator it wanted.[51] The French Cour de Cassation found that the parties were not treated equally, and invalidated the arbitration award.[52]

The ICC, the LCIA, and the DIS have since revised their rules so that if multiple parties on one side cannot agree on an arbitrator, the arbitral institution will appoint the arbitrators for both sides.[53] If the parties have chosen an ad hoc proceeding, or have selected an arbitral institution without a rule dealing with this kind of situation, they should consider drafting a provision in the arbitration clause permitting, in the absence of agreement of all the parties, a neutral third party to appoint all of the arbitrators.

C. CONCLUSION

Parties to an arbitration agreement enjoy substantial autonomy to determine the parameters of the legal regime in which their disputes will be resolved. In international agreements, counsel who draft arbitration clauses need to be well informed and educated about creating a legal framework that works well – that permits the procedures they desire, that minimizes the need for disputes about the framework itself, that does not risk violating institutional or legal mandatory rules, and that does not create the kind of ambiguities and uncertainties that can invalidate the agreement to arbitrate. Clear and knowledgeable drafting of an arbitration agreement can have a significant impact on an international transaction by providing for efficient resolution of disputes. Moreover, a well-drafted clause may even contribute to the ongoing business relationship by deterring parties from actually bringing a claim. When the arbitration clause is clearly valid, and sets forth a process that will work smoothly and efficiently, parties should have less incentive to resort to delaying tactics involving the courts, and more incentive to avoid both litigation and arbitration by simply settling their dispute informally.

[51] *See id.*
[52] *See id.*
[53] *See* ICC Rules, art. 12(8); LCIA Rules, art. 8.1; DIS Rules, Section 13(2).

CHAPTER FOUR

Applicable Laws and Rules

A. IMPORTANCE OF THE LAW

How important is the law in international commercial arbitration? That may depend on the particular case. In some arbitrations, the arbitrators' task will be primarily to understand the facts and to apply the contract terms to the facts. Procedural issues will be resolved in accordance with the rules chosen by the parties. Legal questions may not be raised or argued. In other arbitrations, difficult or technical legal questions may be at the core of the dispute.

Although party autonomy is an important element of arbitration, nonetheless, the parties' contract, and their dispute, do not exist in a legal vacuum. Layers of laws and rules may be applicable,[1] and complications may increase when more than one national law may properly apply to the arbitration. Typically, the parties will choose a law to govern the contract. This law, which is the substantive law, is likely to be the national law of one of the parties. Or, in a contract for the sale of goods, it could be an international law such as the United Nations Convention on Contracts for the International Sale of Goods (CISG).

The law applicable to the arbitration procedure is usually a different national law – the arbitration law at the seat of the arbitration. In addition to these two laws, other laws may come into play. This chapter will discuss the various laws, as well as what happens when parties have not chosen a governing law or a seat for the arbitration.

Today, the role of the various laws and their application to international arbitration is the subject of ongoing debate. Some of the debate focuses on the extent to which an international arbitration can detach itself from

---

[1] The term "applicable law" is used here to mean all laws applicable to international commercial arbitration, not simply the substantive law.

national law, how the new *lex mercatoria*[2] can or should be properly used in international arbitration, the amount of discretion arbitrators have to choose an applicable law and what methodology they should employ, and the duty of the arbitrator to apply the law. These and other issues will be discussed in the following sections.

B. DELOCALIZATION V. TERRITORIALITY

1. Arguments Favoring Delocalization

A number of years ago, primarily in the 1980s, some rather passionate arguments were made in favor of delocalization of international arbitration.[3] Delocalization is also referred to as *stateless, floating,* or *a-national arbitration.* It is based on a theory that international arbitration should not be fettered by the local law of the place where the arbitration occurs. Parties frequently choose a seat of arbitration in a country where neither party's business interests are located. In addition, the seat may be chosen simply because it is convenient to both parties. The concern is that the local peculiarities of a law and a court system, which might impede the effectiveness of the arbitration proceedings, should not be imposed on an international arbitration just because the proceedings happen to be located in that jurisdiction. A matter of particular concern is that the local court might find a way to vacate the arbitral award under its local law when a party moves to set aside the award, possibly rendering the process a waste of the parties' time and resources.

The proponents of delocalization argued that a State should not have any concern about a dispute between two parties who are not its citizens over a matter that has no connection to the State. They viewed international arbitration as self-regulating, and they opposed court interference with the arbitration process. From their perspective, international arbitration should be detached from the law of the seat; there was no reason, for example, that the conflicts of law rules of the seat of arbitration should necessarily be the ones applied when an arbitrator had to choose the governing law. Under the proponents' view, there should not be two legal systems supervising the arbitration process – first at the place of arbitration and then at the place of enforcement (i.e., the place where the losing party's assets are located). Rather, the only pertinent law should be the law applied by the court at the place of enforcement of the award.

---

[2] The *lex mercatoria,* or the law merchant, is generally described as including transnational legal rules, principles, and standards, as well as trade usages. *See infra* Section C.

[3] *See, e.g.,* Jan Paulsson, *Delocalisation of International Commercial Arbitration: When and Why It Matters,* 32 ICLQ 53 (1983).

2. Arguments Opposing Delocalization

The counterargument to delocalization is that every arbitration takes place in a specific territory, and must conform to the laws – at a minimum, to the mandatory laws – of that territory. Moreover, at times the assistance of the court is needed during the arbitral process – for example, to appoint arbitrators, for emergency relief, for preserving evidence, or for enforcing arbitral orders. Most States also want to exercise a supervisory function to ensure that the private system of dispute resolution in their territory is not being used to defraud, and is not tainted by corruption. When a party moves to set aside an award, the State where the arbitration takes place can exercise this supervisory function.

One response to the delocalization movement was a law passed in Belgium in 1985.[4] It provided that parties to an arbitration in Belgium who were not Belgian citizens and did not have a business located in Belgium would not be permitted to apply to a Belgian court to set aside an arbitral award. There would thus be no judicial review of the award in Belgium. It was believed at the time that this would increase the number of arbitrations in Belgium. In fact, however, the law had the opposite effect. Businesses were not drawn to a system with no possible court review. It appeared instead that businesses were avoiding Belgium as a place of arbitration. As a result, Belgium amended its law in 1998 to provide that parties lacking a Belgian link could enter into an agreement opting out of court review, but otherwise, the court would accept an application from a party to set aside an award.[5]

3. Some Modern Approaches to Delocalization

The Belgian experience suggests that parties are not very interested in completely delocalized arbitrations, and that they prefer having the possibility of court supervision at the place of arbitration. Today, the territorial approach prevails over delocalization, largely because it is easy to comprehend and apply, and because it promotes certainty. Some commentators have referred to the movement toward delocalization as having "run into the ground,"[6] whereas others have viewed it as a partial failure and partial success.[7] No matter how the trend may be characterized, today a number of developments deal in a new way with some of the issues raised in the delocalization debate. Moreover, as more modern kinds of arbitration take place, such as

[4] Belgian Judicial Code, Article 1717(4).
[5] Switzerland has a similar provision, permitting foreign parties arbitrating in Switzerland to opt out of any court review. Swiss Private International Law Act of 1987, ch. 12, art. 192.
[6] Alan Redfern & Martin Hunter et al., REDFERN AND HUNTER ON INTERNATIONAL ARBITRATION, § 3.85 at 192 (2009).
[7] Andrew Tweeddale & Karen Tweeddale, ARBITRATION OF COMMERCIAL DISPUTES, 248, § 7.77 (2005).

sports arbitration and online arbitration, the role of the law at the place of arbitration is likely to become less significant.

a. Sports Arbitrations

The Court of Arbitration for Sport (CAS), which operates under the aegis of the International Council of Arbitration for Sport,[8] conducts arbitrations in many areas related to sports, including arbitration related to commercial sponsorship contracts, disciplinary actions of athletes by sports organizations, and other complaints, such as complaints of unfair treatment or lack of due process by athletes against sports organizations. CAS has ad hoc divisions that provide for arbitrations at various international sports competitions, including the Olympics. The Code of Sports-related Arbitration (the Code) provides that the seat of the arbitration is Lausanne, Switzerland, although hearings may be held elsewhere. At the Olympic Games, for example, the hearings are held at the site of the games, but the "seat" is nonetheless Lausanne.[9] The law of the seat applies to procedural issues, to the extent they are not dealt with by the Code. Because the seat is always Lausanne, regardless of where the arbitration hearings are actually held, the arbitration to some extent is a delocalized arbitration, detached from the procedural law at the actual place of arbitration. If a party wishes to apply to a court to set aside the arbitration, it must do so before the court of the seat in Switzerland. The seat of the arbitration is thus in some ways a mere fiction, because hearings do not, and are not even expected to, occur there. Rather, declaring the seat to be Lausanne is a way of ensuring that a uniform law will be applied to all sports arbitrations conducted by the CAS, and that this arbitration-friendly regime is not likely to overturn an arbitration award.

b. Online Arbitrations

Increasingly, as more business is conducted electronically, there is more interest in also conducting arbitrations electronically. With online dispute resolution (ODR), it is indeed difficult to say where the "seat" of the arbitration is found. ODR has had some setbacks,[10] but is continuing to present opportunities for dispute resolution. UNCITRAL, for example, has a Working

---

[8] *See, e.g.,* www.tas-cas.org.

[9] *See* Gabrielle Kaufmann-Kohler, *Arbitration and the Games or The First Experience of the Olympic Division of the Court of Arbitration for Sport,* 12–2 Mealey's Int'l Arbitration Report (Feb. 1997).

[10] "Virtual Magistrate," begun by the American Arbitration Association, the Cyberspace Law Institute, the Villanova Center for Information Law and Policy, and the National Center for Automated Information Research, which was an early forum for online arbitration and fact-finding, became dormant after a short period of operation. "Online Resolution," one of the first ODR providers in the United States, ceased operations in 2003.

Group exploring online dispute resolution options.[11] In addition, a number of organizations offer online arbitration, or at least an arbitration procedure that is predominantly online.[12] Under the Electronic Transaction Arbitration Rules of the Hong Kong International Arbitration Centre, for example,[13] hearings may be conducted "by video link, by telephone, or online (by email or by other electronic or computer communication),"[14] but in-person hearings are permitted if the parties agree or if the arbitrator thinks it necessary.[15] As for the "seat" of the arbitration, the Hong Kong Rules are similar to the sports arbitration rules of CAS in that they name the seat in the Rules. The seat of every arbitration conducted under the Electronic Transaction Arbitration Rules is the Hong Kong Special Administrative Region (SAR).[16] Hong Kong remains the seat even if the hearings are online or held outside Hong Kong.

Thus, in both sports arbitrations and in some online arbitrations, the seat of the arbitration is a fiction, at least as a place where the hearings occur. The actual venue of the arbitration hearings (and there may be no real venue in online arbitration) does not impose its laws and rules, and any challenge to the arbitration award must be before courts in the specified "seat" of the arbitration. In these instances, the arbitration is "delocalized," but only up to a point, because the territory of the named seat nonetheless provides a place for recourse if there is a problem with the arbitration process. The selection of one seat for all arbitrations, however, ensures that the seat will be a place with arbitration-friendly laws and courts that will not obstruct or unnecessarily intrude on the arbitration process.

Outside these newer forms of arbitration, however, the doctrine of territoriality has, for the most part, prevailed over the doctrine of delocalization. The law of the seat of the arbitration remains an important source of the law governing an arbitration.[17] Nonetheless, international commercial

---

[11] Working Group documents available at http://www.uncitral.org/uncitral/commission/working_groups/3Online_Dispute_Resolution.html.

[12] *See, e.g.*, (1) the four providers approved by ICANN (Internet Corporation for Assigned Names and Numbers): (a) WIPO (http://www.wipo.int/portal/index.html.en; (b) the National Arbitration Forum (http://domains.adrforum.com/); (c) the Asian Domain Name Dispute Resolution Center (https://www.adndrc.org/index.html); and (d) the Czech Arbitration Court Arbitration Center for Internet Disputes (http://www.adr.eu/index.php; (2) Ciber Tribunal Peruano (www.cibertribunalperuano.org); and (3) Resolution Forum (www.resolutionforum.com). For more information, *see* the National Center for Technology and Dispute Resolution, www.odr.info.

[13] *See* Hong Kong Electronic Transaction Arbitration Rules. Available at http://www.hkiac.org/documents/Arbitration/Arbitration%20Rules/en_ETArbRules.pdf.

[14] *See id.* art. 9.1.

[15] *See id.* art. 7.1.

[16] *See id.* art. 14.

[17] The arbitration law of the seat of arbitration, or the *lex arbitri*, will be discussed more fully below in Section D.

arbitration is increasingly finding ways to become more international, and less local, as will be seen in the following sections.

C. THE *LEX MERCATORIA*

The delocalization movement focused on the law governing the arbitration proceedings, which is normally the arbitration law of the seat of the arbitration. A similar debate focuses on the substantive law governing the contract or the legal relationship between the parties. The arguments in the debate may sound familiar. Why should parties to an international arbitration be required to choose a substantive law of a particular nation, one that is probably more suited to domestic transactions than international transactions? Why shouldn't party autonomy mean that parties can choose to have their substantive rights governed by customary commercial law or general principles of law, or transnational rules of law? These may include nonlegal standards that are generally considered part of the *lex mercatoria*, or the law merchant.[18] For those who favor delocalization and the application of the *lex mercatoria*, the ideal international commercial arbitration would have an a-national arbitration procedure governed by a transnational nonlegal standard.[19]

Today, however, most arbitrations are still anchored in the law of the seat of the arbitration, and governed by a national substantive law. Nonetheless, just as there are types of arbitration where the actual place of arbitration has a less important role, so too there are occasions when the *lex mercatoria* can properly replace or supplement a national substantive law.

1. Definition of the *Lex Mercatoria*
Many practitioners and commentators have criticized the *lex mercatoria* on a number of grounds, but especially on the ground that it is a concept too vague and uncertain to apply.[20] Although agreement is increasing about

---

[18] Historically, the law merchant grew out of a system of customary law, developed in Europe during medieval times. It pertained to dealings between merchants. In the seventeenth century in England, it gradually became incorporated into the common law.

[19] *See* Roy Goode, *The Role of the Lex Loci Arbitri in International Commercial Arbitration*, 17 Arb. Int. 19, 21–22 (2001). ("[T]he drive for freedom of arbitral procedure from national laws was paralleled by a move towards resurrection in modern form of the medieval *lex mercatoria* as a supposedly free-floating, autonomous body of law, which . . . obviated the need to resort to national legal systems.")

[20] "[Critics have objected that] the *lex mercatoria* does not provide a complete legal system, that the principles and rules are too vague and lack the necessary certainty and predictability." *See* Klaus Peter Berger, Holger Dubberstein, Sascha Lehmann, and

what the *lex mercatoria* is, the definition is not uniformly agreed on. Here are some characteristic definitions:

- A loosely organized system of transnational legal principles, rules, and standards derived from the usages, customs, and practice of international commerce.[21]
- General principles of law, transnational rules, a method of decision making.[22]
- Customary commercial law.[23]
- "Transnational substantive rules of law and trade usages and the method of their application to international economic transactions."[24]
- A set of substantive rules developed to regulate international trade in the business community, which are derived "not only from international commercial dealings, standard clauses, international conventions and arbitral awards but also from various sets of legal rules issued by the International Chamber of Commerce (ICC) or other international organizations."[25]

From these various definitions, some common themes emerge. The *lex mercatoria* is not based on any one legal system, but incorporates international commercial rules, general principles of law, standards, and trade usages. An example of today's *lex mercatoria* is the UNIDROIT Principles of International Commercial Contracts.[26] These principles are not law as such, because they are not adopted as law by any jurisdiction. Rather, they are a restatement of the law of international commercial contracts. In the preamble, the principles are said to apply when the parties choose them, or "when the parties have agreed that their contract be governed by general principles of law, the *lex mercatoria* or the like."[27] The *lex mercatoria* is also thought

---

Viktoria Petzold, *The Central Enquiry on the Use of Transnational Law in International Contract Law and Arbitration*, 227, n. 81 and accompanying text in TOWARDS A SCIENCE OF INTERNATIONAL ARBITRATION, COLLECTED EMPIRICAL RESEARCH (Drahozal & Naimark, eds., 2005).

[21] L. Yves Fortier, *The New, New Lex Mercatoria, or, Back to the Future*, 17 Arb. Int. 121, 128 (2001).

[22] Emmanuel Gaillard, *Transnational Law: A Legal System or a Method of Decision Making?* 17 Arb. Int. 59, 59–61 (2001).

[23] Roy Goode, *The Role of the Lex Loci Arbitri in International Commercial Arbitration*, 17 Arb. Int. 19, 21 (2001).

[24] Antonis Patrikios, *Resolution of Cross-Border E-Business Disputes by Arbitration Tribunals: The Emergence of the Lex Informatica*, 38 U. Tol. L. Rev. 271, 273 (2006).

[25] Dr. Beda Wortmann, *Choice of Law by Arbitrators: The Applicable Conflict of Laws System*, 14 Arb. Int. 97, 101 (1998).

[26] UNIDROIT (the International Institute for the Unification of Private Law) is an independent intergovernmental organization with its seat in Rome. Its goals include drafting conventions, model laws, and other legal guides to help harmonize international commercial law. The UNIDROIT Principles of International Commercial Contracts are available at http://www.unidroit.org.

[27] *See id.*

to include other kinds of rules, such as the ICC's Uniform Customs and Practice for Documentary Credits (UCP 600),[28] which are the rules that govern virtually all letters of credit, and the ICC's INCOTERMS,[29] which are international commercial terms, such as FOB and CIF. Some commentators also include in the *lex mercatoria* international arbitration awards, as well as principles derived from international conventions or international public law. Moreover, there have been attempts to make the *lex mercatoria* more concrete by collecting lists of principles that can be regularly updated to conform to the best and most current international practices.[30] Grasping a reasonable understanding of the meaning of *lex mercatoria* is important for considering the purposes for which it can be used.

2. Application of the *Lex Mercatoria*

As noted earlier, many practitioners resist any reference to the *lex mercatoria*. In drafting a contract, they want a law that is accessible, is clear, and has an established jurisprudence that can provide some amount of certainty. Arbitrators, as well, even when using some transnational rules to reach a decision, have sometimes been reluctant to say they are relying on the *lex mercatoria*.[31] In some situations, however, the *lex mercatoria* can be quite useful.

a. Contracts between States

Assume there is a commercial contract between two States or State-controlled entities. Neither sovereign wants to be subject to the laws of any other sovereign. In such a situation, the parties may well decide that they want the contract to be governed by general principles of international law, or the *lex mercatoria*. They could also specify that the UNIDROIT Principles apply, as well as general principles of international law.

---

[28] ICC Publication No. 600, revised and in force as of July 1, 2007.

[29] *See* INCOTERMS 2010, International Chamber of Commerce Publication No. 715, which constitute the ICC Official Rules for the Interpretation of Trade Terms. The trade or commercial terms are a way of allocating responsibilities between buyer and seller. For example, "FOB," which means "free on board," indicates the responsibility for the goods passes to buyer when goods are delivered on board the carrier. "CIF" or "cost, insurance, freight," means the seller's invoice price will include the cost of goods, the insurance, and the freight. The seller arranges the freight and the insurance, but the buyer will ultimately pay for both, because they will be included in the invoiced price along with the cost of goods.

[30] *See, e.g.*, Trans-Lex Principles, available at www.trans-lex.org.

[31] One arbitration counsel noted: "According to my experience, most of the distinguished arbitrators I have been dealing with preferred to invoke 'general principles of law' or 'legal principles common to the parties' ... rather than [rules of transnational law or *lex mercatoria*.]" *See* Berger et al., *supra* note 20, at 223.

b. Contracts between a State and a Private Company

A State that is dealing with a private company may well have the leverage to insist that its domestic laws apply to the contract. Sometimes the private company will be able to persuade the State to include a clause that "freezes" the law, by providing that the law as it exists at the time of the formation of the contract will be the governing law. The private company wants to prevent the State from undermining various terms of the contract by enacting new legislation. Similarly, parties try to deal with potential changes in the law by including a stabilization clause, which provides that the State will not amend the contract by legislation without the consent of the other party. Nonetheless, during the effective period of a long-term economic development contract, laws may change; these changes may affect the private party, and may be viewed by an arbitral tribunal as a legitimate act by the government. Thus, parties may try to control some of the impact of State legislation by asking the State to agree that not only the State's domestic law, but also general principles of international law, will apply. Thus, while giving proper recognition to the State's interest in applying its own law, such a choice could act as a restraint on the State's ability to change or enforce the law arbitrarily, to the detriment of the private company.[32]

The *lex mercatoria* may also come into play when two parties choose it as the law governing their contract, or when no choice of law is made and the arbitral tribunal decides to apply the *lex mercatoria*. These two ways of applying the *lex mercatoria* will be considered in Sections D and E of this chapter.

D. THE PARTIES' CHOICE OF LAW

Against the background of the debate focusing on resistance to applying national laws and favoring an international approach, this section examines what parties usually do. Most parties choose a national substantive law to govern their contract and a place of arbitration whose *lex arbitri* will govern the arbitral proceedings. Typically, when the parties have chosen a law, the arbitrators will apply that law. To ignore that choice could cause an award rendered by the arbitrators to be set aside on the grounds that the arbitrators exceeded their authority, or that the arbitral procedure was not in accordance with the agreement of the parties.[33] Moreover, although

---

[32] Redfern & Hunter note the restraining impact of principles of international law when an act of nationalization is valid under local law, but "would not be valid under international law unless it was shown to be nondiscriminatory and to serve a public purpose, with proper compensation being offered." *See supra* note 6, § 3.144 at 210.

[33] *See, e.g.*, New York Convention, art. V(1)(c–d).

parties typically do not specifically choose a procedural law, they do usually choose the seat of the arbitration, and almost inevitably, the procedural law governing the arbitration will be the arbitration law of the seat. This section deals with issues affecting the laws when the parties have made a choice as to a governing law or a seat of arbitration. The next section, Section E, will deal with issues that arise when parties did not make a choice.

1. The Law Governing the Arbitral Proceedings

The *lex arbitri*, which governs the arbitral proceedings, is almost always the law of the place of arbitration. It is sometimes referred to as the *procedural law*, or as the *curial law*. In fact, the *lex arbitri* is mostly a procedural law, but it also has some substantive elements. In any event, the line between substance and procedure is not always clear, and is not always viewed the same way in different countries. What is important to understand is the type of issues that are governed by the *lex arbitri*, and how this law interacts with the rules chosen by the parties and with the substantive law governing the main contract.

A good example of a country's *lex arbitri* is the UNCITRAL Model Law on International Commercial Arbitration. Although it has been adopted in at least seventy countries, regions, and states, it has not always been adopted uniformly. Nevertheless, in most jurisdictions that have enacted it as their international arbitration law, the major elements are the same. The Model Law covers the formal validity of the arbitration agreement and the obligation for a court to refer parties to arbitration, unless the agreement is void. It limits interference of the court in arbitration matters and permits parties to seek interim relief from a court without losing the right to arbitrate. It deals with the composition of the arbitral tribunal, challenges to arbitrators, jurisdiction of the tribunal, and the tribunal's powers to order interim measures. It regulates the arbitral proceedings, basically providing that the parties can agree on how the proceedings will take place. It also provides that, if the parties do not agree, then the tribunal can determine how the arbitration will proceed. It has rules pertaining to the award, settlement, recourse against the award, and recognition and enforcement of the award.

Countries that have not adopted the Model Law nonetheless may have very detailed arbitration laws. In England, for example, the English Arbitration Act of 1996 is an extensive, well-developed *lex arbitri*. In contrast, the United States' Federal Arbitration Act, which was adopted in 1925 and has not been updated, is a much shorter and more limited law, although it has been greatly expanded by case law and interpretation by the courts.[34]

---

[34] *See, e.g.*, Margaret L. Moses, *Statutory Misconstruction: How the Supreme Court Created a Federal Arbitration Law Never Enacted by Congress*, 34 Fla. St. U.L. Rev. 99 (2006).

2. The Rules Governing the Arbitral Proceedings

Very few, if any, of the procedural requirements of the *lex arbitri* are mandatory, so if the parties have chosen arbitration rules – for either an ad hoc arbitration or an institutional arbitration – those rules will prevail. The choice of the arbitration rules represents the agreement of the parties as to how the proceedings should be conducted. These rules will probably be the most important guide for conducting the proceedings. Prudent counsel should be very familiar with the differences in the various arbitration rules before choosing a set for the arbitration.

No matter which rules are chosen, however, they are not detailed in some areas. For example, they do not usually spell out what kind of disclosure can be compelled, or what kind of evidence can be admitted. In most instances, this is left to the discretion of the arbitrator (unless the parties reach an agreement on a particular method or procedure). If parties want more specificity, they may agree to adopt or refer to other rules, such as the International Bar Association's Rules on the Taking of Evidence in International Arbitration.[35]

3. The Law Governing the Arbitration Agreement

Although the *lex arbitri* usually deals with the formal validity of the arbitration agreement,[36] the law governing the arbitration agreement's substantive validity could be any of a number of laws.[37] It will, however, most likely be either the law of the seat of the arbitration, or the substantive law chosen by the parties. Validity of an arbitration agreement is for the most part a question of consent, and whether there is consent is governed by ordinary principles of contract law. The two most likely stages where the question of the arbitration agreement's validity arise are at the beginning of the proceeding, when one party resists arbitration, and at the award stage, when the losing party has two tries to defeat the arbitration award. A losing party can first try to set aside the award at the seat of arbitration. Second, it can challenge enforcement of the award in the enforcing jurisdiction.[38] The question of what law applies can be raised at any time.

Suppose, for example, that State A is the seat of arbitration. Assume that under State A's law, the arbitration agreement is not valid, but the

---

[35] Available at http://www.ibanet.org/Publications/publications IBA guides and free materials.aspx.

[36] The writing requirement is discussed *supra* in Chapter 2, Section B(1).

[37] *See* Marc Blessing, The Law Applicable to the Arbitration Clause, ICCA Congress series no. 9 (Paris/1999), at 169–79, identifying various conflicts of laws approaches and ultimately suggesting nine different laws or rules of law that could govern the arbitration agreement.

[38] The grounds for vacating an award are quite narrow. *See* Chapter 9 *infra*. Similarly, grounds for refusing to enforce an award under the Convention are also very narrow, and do not include any review of the merits. *See* Chapter 10 *infra*.

parties have chosen the law of State B as the substantive law governing their contract. Under the law of State B, the arbitration agreement is valid. If the arbitrators proceed to an award, will the losing party be able to vacate the award on the ground that the arbitration agreement is invalid under the law of State A, which is the seat of the arbitration? Which law governs the substantive validity of the arbitration agreement – the law of State A or that of State B? Additionally, how will State C, the enforcing jurisdiction, decide a challenge to enforcement on the ground that the arbitration agreement was not valid under the law of the seat of arbitration?

Different tribunals and courts answer these questions differently. In one case, when a determination of validity was sought at an early stage of the arbitration, an arbitral tribunal was faced with the argument that the arbitral agreement was invalid under the law chosen by the parties to govern the contract. The arbitration agreement was valid, however, under the law of the seat of arbitration. The tribunal concluded that the question of validity of the arbitration agreement was subject to the law of the seat, not the law applicable to the merits, and ruled that the agreement was valid.[39]

Switzerland has a very broad concept of which law applies to the substantive validity of an arbitration agreement. Article 178(2) of the Swiss Private International Law Act provides:

> As to the substance, the arbitration agreement shall be valid if it complies with the requirements of the law chosen by the parties, or the law governing the object of the dispute, and, in particular, the law applicable to the principal contract, or with Swiss law.[40]

Thus, when an arbitration takes place in Switzerland, if the arbitration agreement is valid under either the law chosen to govern it, the substantive law governing the contract, or the law of the forum, it would be found valid by a court or tribunal.

Under the Model Law, an award may be set aside if the arbitration agreement was "not valid under the law to which the parties [had] subjected it,"[41] or, if no law was chosen, then invalidity would be determined under the law of the seat of arbitration.[42] Because parties rarely choose a law that specifically governs the arbitration agreement, under the Model Law, the plain meaning of the provision indicates that invalidity will most likely be determined by the law of the seat of arbitration. Thus, the court in a

---

[39] ICC Award in Case No. 6162, Consultant (France) v. Egyptian Local Authority (1992) XVII YEARBOOK COMMERCIAL ARBITRATION 153.

[40] Moreover, the Swiss Private International Law Act provides in art. 177(1) that "[a]ny dispute involving property may be the subject-matter of an arbitration."

[41] See UNCITRAL Model Law on Arbitration, art. 34(2).The language is very similar to that of the New York Convention, art. V(1)(a).

[42] See id.

Model Law State, in an action to set aside an arbitral award on grounds of invalidity of the arbitration agreement, should first determine whether the parties chose a law to govern the arbitration agreement, and if no choice by the parties can be determined, it should apply its own law to determine the agreement's validity.[43] Under this scenario, it would appear that in Model Law States, the law of the place of arbitration would generally govern the validity of the arbitration agreement.

However, some tribunals and courts hold that the substantive law of the contract should apply to determine the validity of the arbitration clause. One arbitral tribunal stated that "it is commonly accepted that the choice of law applicable to the principal contract also tacitly governs the situation of the arbitration clause, in the absence of a specific provision."[44] If a Model Law court were to construe the language of article 34(2)(a)(i) – "the law to which the parties have subjected [the agreement]" – to mean that when the parties chose the substantive law of the contract they had also implicitly chosen the law of the arbitration agreement, then the parties' substantive choice of law would govern. It makes sense at some levels to have the same law apply to both agreements, because otherwise certain difficulties could arise. Professor Pierre Mayer has pointed out, for example, that there might be different statutes of limitations that could cause one agreement, but not the other, to be time-barred.[45]

The counterargument is that if a court does not accept the theory that the parties' choice of a governing law is a tacit decision to make the law that governs the contract also govern the arbitration clause, and if the agreement is invalid under the law of the seat of arbitration, an award may not survive in an action to set it aside either in the seat of arbitration or in an action to enforce it in the place of enforcement. In an action to vacate the award, a court at the seat of arbitration could decide that because the arbitration agreement was not valid under its own law, then the award was not valid. A court in an enforcing State could determine, pursuant to the New York Convention, that the award could not be enforced, because the arbitration agreement was not valid under the law of the country where the award was made.[46]

Thus, various tribunals and courts take different positions as to what law applies to the validity and construction of the arbitration agreement.

---

[43] Even if the agreement is considered to be invalid under the law, the Model Law permits the court some discretion, by providing that an arbitral award *may* be set aside if the arbitration agreement is not valid. Art. 34(2).

[44] ICC Award in Case No. 2626, S. Jarvin and Y. Derains, COLLECTION OF ICC ARBITRAL AWARDS, 1974–1985 (1990), 316.

[45] Pierre Mayer, The Limits of Severability of the Arbitration Clause, ICCA Congress series no. 9, at 267 (Paris, 1999).

[46] *See* New York Convention, art. V(1)(a).

In France, for example, courts have held that the existence and validity of the arbitration agreement depend on the intent of the parties, and not on provisions of any national law.[47] This seems reasonable when one considers that even when the parties have chosen both the substantive law and the seat of the arbitration, as in the hypothetical situation described earlier, if the laws conflict, the tribunal may become involved in a possibly lengthy analytical effort to determine which law will govern the validity of the arbitration agreement. A simple "intent of the parties" test would probably be easier to apply and no less likely to meet the parties' expectations.

The question of what law applies to the arbitration agreement can be complicated. It becomes even more complicated when parties have not chosen a seat of arbitration or a governing law. These issues will be further discussed in Section E of this chapter, which deals with conflicts of laws.

4. The Law Governing Arbitrability

The parties' choice of the seat of arbitration not only determines the law governing the proceedings, and sometimes the law governing the arbitration agreement, but also generally governs the question of arbitrability, that is, whether the subject matter can be arbitrated or whether the particular dispute must be resolved in court.[48] As noted earlier, some issues such as family matters, patent regulation, criminal law, and sometimes issues of bankruptcy are generally not permitted by law to be arbitrated. Because different jurisdictions may have different approaches to arbitrability, a tribunal faced with an arbitrability question must decide whether to apply the law of the seat, the law chosen by the parties, the law of the enforcing jurisdiction, or another law.

Most tribunals in this instance will apply the law of the seat of arbitration. If the award is not considered arbitrable in the seat of arbitration, it is quite likely that an award would be vacated by the court in that jurisdiction. The Model Law, for example, provides as a basis for vacating an award that

---

[47] *See, e.g.*, Cour de cassation, December 20, 1993, Comité populaire de la municipalité de Khoms El Mergeb v. Dalico Contractors, 121 Clunet 432 (1994).

[48] This is the usual definition of arbitrability. In the United States, however, the term *arbitrability* is also used to describe the question of who determines the arbitrator's jurisdiction – the arbitrator or the court. In other words, when is an issue of the arbitrator's jurisdiction arbitrable (decided by the arbitrator), as opposed to being decided by the court? The U.S. Supreme Court has said that the "question of arbitrability" is "an issue for judicial determination unless the parties clearly and unmistakably provide otherwise." Howsam v. Dean Witter Reynolds, 537 U.S. 79, 83 (2002) (*internal citations omitted*). In the United States, absent a clear agreement by the parties that the arbitrator should decide whether she has jurisdiction, the presumption is that the court will make that determination. This presumption is, however, so riddled with exceptions that, for the most part, the arbitrator in the United States will determine whether she has jurisdiction. *See infra* discussion of the competence-competence doctrine in the United States, Chapter 5(A)(2).

"the subject-matter of the dispute is not capable of settlement by arbitration under the law of this State."[49] Thus, for example, in a jurisdiction where issues of bankruptcy were not considered to be arbitrable, if an arbitration of bankruptcy issues were held within that jurisdiction, and an arbitral award rendered, the losing party would probably be able to have the award set aside by the court in that jurisdiction.

Should the arbitrator also consider whether the subject matter is arbitrable in the enforcing court's jurisdiction? The New York Convention, like the Model Law, provides for nonenforcement if the dispute is not arbitrable under the laws of the enforcing State.[50] Arbitrators have generally not wanted to refuse to arbitrate because the dispute was not considered arbitrable in the enforcing State. After all, in many cases, parties voluntarily agree to pay the award once it is rendered. In addition, an award can be enforced in more than one State, if assets can be found in more than one. Nonetheless, an award may well be challenged if the dispute is not arbitrable in all the relevant jurisdictions. For the most part, however, if the dispute is arbitrable at the seat of arbitration, it is probably reasonable for the arbitral tribunal to place the risk of nonenforcement in the enforcing jurisdiction on the parties (generally the claimant).[51]

5. The Law Governing the Contract

a. National or International Law
When the parties choose a law to govern construction and interpretation of the contract, and any disputes arising out of or in connection with the contract, normally they choose the substantive national law of one of the parties. If neither party has leverage to force the other party to accept its law, and if the contract involves sales of goods, sometimes the parties will choose the United Nations Convention on Contracts for the International Sale of Goods ("CISG") as the substantive law of the contract. Even if they agree on the CISG, however, they should choose a national law to cover areas that are not covered by the CISG, such as questions of validity of the contract, or the "effect which the contract may have on the property in the

---

[49] UNCITRAL Model Law of Arbitration, art. 34(2)(b)(i).

[50] See New York Convention, art. V(2)(a) (Court in country of enforcement can refuse to enforce if "[t]he subject matter of the difference is not capable of settlement by arbitration under the law of that country.").

[51] See Homayoon Arfazadeh, *Arbitrability under the New York Convention: The Lex Fori Revisited*, 17 Arb. Int. 73, 83 (2001). Mr. Arfazadeh's view is that the enforcing court under the Convention, art. V(2)(a), should refuse to enforce "only if, under the laws of the forum, the subject matter of the dispute is expressly reserved to the mandatory jurisdiction of [the] ... court ..., to the exclusion of arbitration." *Id.* at 87.

goods sold,"[52] that is, any effect on a security interest in the goods. Because these issues are left for national law, it would be advisable for the parties to agree on a national law that would apply not only to these issues, but also to any other issues that might not be covered by the CISG.

b. *Lex Mercatoria*

If parties are unable to reach agreement on a choice of national or international law, or if they simply do not want either of these choices, they can theoretically choose the *lex mercatoria* to govern their contract, *e.g.*, general principles of international law, the UNIDROIT Principles of International Commercial Contracts, or transnational commercial law.[53] This is not the usual choice for two private parties, however. As noted above, in contracts between States, or between States and private parties, parties sometimes choose these kinds of standards. On the other hand, when private parties enter into a contract with other private parties, they are generally more interested in having a specific governing law with a developed jurisprudence that they know is enforceable.[54] For the most part, they want a sense of certainty as to how this known law will be interpreted.

Parties may, however, use aspects of the *lex mercatoria* to assist them in contract negotiations or to supplement the law of their contract. For example, a study of the use of transnational law found that 59 percent of the respondents said they had used the UNIDROIT Principles as guidelines in contract negotiation, and another 13.1 percent had referred to the Principles in connection with a solution adopted in an arbitration award.[55] Moreover, the parties might refer in their contracts to other international rules or standards, such as INCOTERMS 2010, which are the commercial terms published by the International Chamber of Commerce.

c. Unrelated National Law

If parties cannot agree to choose the national law of one of them, and they do not want to choose general principles of law, another option is to choose

---

[52] United Nations Convention on Contracts for the International Sale of Goods, art. 4 (a-b). The UN-certified English text is published in 52 Federal Register 6262, 6264–80 (March 2, 1987); United States Code Annotated, Title 15, Appendix (Supp. 1987). Available at http://cisg.law.pace.edu.

[53] Some commentators suggest that the term *lex mercatoria* should be abandoned in favor of the "broader terminology, transnational commercial law." *See, e.g.*, Klaus Peter Berger et al., *supra* note 20, at 223.

[54] Although awards have been made on the basis of the *lex mercatoria*, and have survived challenges to enforcement, most parties continue to prefer application of a national law. *See* Derains & Schwartz, A Guide to ICC Rules of Arbitration, 236–37 (2005) ("[T]he application of [the *lex mercatoria*] in ICC arbitration has been increasing in recent years, although parties more often refer to a national law when contracting, as do most ICC arbitrators."). *Citations omitted*.

[55] *See id.* at 224.

a national law of a neutral country, that is, a country with no particular relationship to any party. In most jurisdictions, the strong concept of party autonomy will permit parties to choose an unrelated national law.[56] Parties might want to choose a law that is well developed in a particular sector, or simply a law of a country where many international transactions occur. A number of international conventions support the free choice by parties of a law to govern their contract.[57] Party autonomy is limited, however, by mandatory law (a law that cannot be excluded by a contract term) and by the public policy of a country.

In the United States, parties are not free to choose any law. Under the Restatement (Second) of Conflicts of Laws, there must be either a substantial relationship between the party or the transaction and the law that is chosen, or a reasonable basis for the parties' choice.[58] Therefore, a United States court might not honor a choice of Florida law if the transaction was between a German and a Japanese company, and the transaction had no connection to Florida.[59]

New York, on the other hand, is a special case. New York will enforce the parties' choice of New York law under certain conditions even if there is no reasonable relationship to the state. The contract must not involve personal, family or household services, or labor, and the amount involved must be at least U.S. $250,000.[60] Moreover, New York will enforce the choice of a New York forum when a foreign party has agreed to submit to the jurisdiction of the courts of New York and has stipulated that New York law is the law of the contract. In that case, New York provides for personal jurisdiction and its courts may not dismiss for *forum non conveniens* if the

---

[56] *See* Mo Zhang, *Party Autonomy and Beyond: An International Perspective of Contractual Choice of Law*, 20 Emory Int'l L. Rev. 511 (2006).

[57] *See, e.g.*, the European Community Convention on the Law Applicable to Contract Obligations (Rome Convention), 19 I.L.M. 1492; Convention on the Law Applicable to Contracts for the International Sale of Goods (Hague Convention), 24 I.L.M. 1573; and the Inter-American Convention on the Law Applicable to International Contracts (Mexico City Convention), 33 I.L.M. 732.

[58] *See* Restatement (Second) of Conflicts of Laws §§ 6, 187.

[59] *See id.* § 187(2):

> "The law of the state chosen by the parties to govern their contractual rights and duties will be applied, even if the particular issue is one which the parties could not have resolved by an explicit provision in their agreement directed to that issue, unless either
> (a) the chosen state has no substantial relationship to the parties or the transaction and there is no other reasonable basis for the parties' choice, or
> (b) application of the law of the chosen state would be contrary to a fundamental policy of a state which has a materially greater interest than the chosen state in the determination of the particular issue and which, under the rule of § 188, would be the state of the applicable law in the absence of an effective choice of law by the parties."

[60] N.Y. Gen. Oblig. Law § 5–1401 (McKinney 2001).

amount in question is at least U.S. $1 million.[61] Thus, New York has chosen
to accept party autonomy in commercial cases if the amount in dispute is
sufficiently large. New York is apparently trying to secure and increase its
reputation as an international business center, with ease of access to its legal
system for parties with relatively significant transactions.

d. Dépeçage

In some instances, different laws may govern different issues in a transaction.
This is known as *dépeçage*, from the French verb *dépecer*, which means to
slice thinly or to cut in morsels. In the arbitration context, it is generally
translated in English as "splitting." Sometimes *dépeçage* occurs when the
parties choose one law but acknowledge that the mandatory law of a country
will also apply. At other times, a law may not cover all the issues, such as
the CISG, which does not cover validity of the contract, or issues outside of
sales law such as fraud or unfair business practices. In those cases, parties
should choose not only the CISG to govern issues arising out of the contract,
but also a national law that will govern issues not covered by the CISG.

e. Renvoi

When parties choose a national law to govern the contract, have they also
chosen the conflicts of laws rules of that national law? Conflicts of laws rules
(also referred to sometimes as the rules of private international law) are the
rules in a particular jurisdiction that are applied to determine which law is
the most appropriate when two or more substantive laws could govern the
transaction. For example, in a contract between a Dutch company and a
U.S. company, if the parties choose New York law to govern their contract,
should a tribunal or court consider New York conflicts of laws rules, which
may point to the Netherlands as the place with the most significant relationship to the transaction? If this should happen, the parties could end up with
Dutch law rather than New York law governing their contract.

    This problem is generally referred to as *renvoi*. It occurs when the forum
applies the conflicts of laws rules of the law chosen by the parties to select
a law different from that designated by the parties. Many jurisdictions
reject *renvoi* in an international setting, where parties have chosen a specific
national law.[62] Nonetheless, there are jurisdictions that still apply *renvoi*.

---

[61] *See id.*, § 5–1402.

[62] *See, e.g.*, UNCITRAL Model Law on Arbitration, art. 28(1) ("Any designation of the
law or legal system of a given State shall be construed, unless otherwise expressed, as
directly referring to the substantive law of that State and not to its conflict of laws
rules."); WIPO Arbitration Rules, art. 59(a) (virtually same as Model Law); Stockholm
Chamber of Commerce Arbitration Rules, art. 22(2) (2010) (virtually same as Model
Law); Rome Convention on the Law Applicable to Contractual Obligations (19 I.L.M.
1492, 1496 (1980)), art. 15, which is entitled "Exclusion of renvoi" ("The application

To avoid the problem, counsel should draft a clause that ensures that the "internal" laws of the State are chosen, rather than the "whole law," and that the State's rules of conflicts of laws are excluded. An example of a choice of law clause that would accomplish this is the following:

> This Agreement, and any disputes arising out of or relating to this Agreement or its validity, interpretation or construction, shall be governed exclusively by the internal laws of the state of California, without regard to its laws and rules governing conflicts of laws.

In the United States, if the agreement is an international agreement for the sale of goods, it is useful to add a clause excluding the CISG if the parties actually intend for California law to apply (*e.g.*, the Uniform Commercial Code ("UCC") Article 2, as enacted in California). Commentators have opined that if the CISG would otherwise apply (that is, if the two parties have their places of business in different contracting states, and the contract is for a business-to-business sale of goods), then the applicable law of California would be the CISG.[63] This is because in the United States, the body of law applying to domestic sales of goods is the UCC, and the body of law applying to international sales (where the CISG requirements are met) is the CISG. Thus, the following sentence could be added to the choice of law clause, if parties wanted the UCC, as enacted in California, to govern their sales contract, rather than the CISG:

> The United Nations Convention on Contracts for the International Sale of Goods shall not apply to the construction or interpretation of this Agreement or affect any of its provisions.

f. *Ex Aequo et Bono* and *Amiable Compositeur*

Another choice the parties have is that they may instruct the tribunal to decide the matter *ex aequo et bono*, or as *amiable compositeur*. Both phrases have been construed to mean that the tribunal does not have to strictly

of the law of any country specified by this Convention means the application of the rules of law in force in that country other than its rules of private international law.").

[63] *See* Joseph Lookofsky, *Understanding the CISG in the USA*, at 8 (2004) ("In a sales case where both parties have their places of business in different CISG Contracting States, American courts are "automatically" bound by the default rule in Article 1(1)(a) to apply the CISG as the applicable substantive law.").

apply the law, but can render a decision based on reasonableness and fairness. Although most modern arbitration rules and laws permit arbitrators to decide matters in this way, the power to do so must be expressly granted to the arbitrators by the parties. For example, the Model Law provides: "The arbitral tribunal shall decide *ex aequo et bono* or as *amiable compositeur* only if the parties have expressly authorized it to do so."[64] Most parties do not grant this authority to the tribunal, perhaps concluding that arbitrators have enough discretion without the parties adding this additional power.[65]

Parties generally have many choices in determining the law that will govern their contract and the seat of their arbitration. They are always better off if, first, they make the choice, and second, they keep the choice simple and clear. Unnecessary complications in the choice of law and the seat of arbitration can greatly increase the time and cost of the arbitration process. The next section will consider some of the situations that arise when the parties have either not made a choice or not made a choice that is clear, causing the task of determining the law and/or the seat of arbitration to fall on the arbitrators, the arbitral institution, or the courts.

E. WHEN PARTIES FAIL TO CHOOSE THE SEAT OR THE GOVERNING LAW

In a study of ICC arbitration agreements, Stephen Bond found that parties specified the city or country where the arbitration would take place 57 percent of the time in 1987 and 68 percent of the time in 1989.[66] They identified a particular law 75 percent of the time in 1987 and 66 percent of the time in 1989. If these studies are more or less representative of arbitration clauses generally, then at least 32 percent of the time the parties have not chosen the seat of the arbitration, and at least 25 percent of the time they have not chosen a national law. What happens next for these parties depends on the rules they have adopted. If parties have not adopted a law, a seat, an institution, or arbitration rules, then whether they can arbitrate, assuming one party resists, will depend on whether a court will accept jurisdiction to

---

[64] UNCITRAL Model Law on Arbitration, art. 28(3). *Accord*, UNCITRAL Arbitration Rules, art. 33(2); LCIA Rules, art. 22.4; ICDR Rules, art. 28(3); ICC rules, art. 21(3); WIPO Arbitration Rules, art. 59(a); Stockholm Chamber of Commerce (SCC) Rules, art. 22(3) (2010).

[65] A study by Stephen Bond of ICC arbitration clauses found that parties authorized arbitrators to decide on the basis of *amiable composition, ex aequo et bono* or in equity only 3% of the time in 1987, and only 4% of the time in 1989. *See* Bond, *How to Draft an Arbitration Clause (Revisited)*, 74, in TOWARDS A SCIENCE OF INTERNATIONAL ARBITRATION (Drahozal and Naimark, eds., 2005).

[66] *See id.*

decide these questions, or will simply find the arbitration clause too vague to be enforced.

1. Failure to Choose a Seat

If the parties have not chosen a seat, that choice will generally be made by the institution in an institutional arbitration. The London Court of International Arbitration (LCIA) rules provide that absent party agreement, the seat will be London, unless the Court decides otherwise after hearing from the parties.[67] The International Centre for Dispute Resolution (ICDR) rules state that the administrator decides, but can be overruled by the arbitral tribunal within sixty days after it is constituted.[68] The World Intellectual Property Organization (WIPO), International Chamber of Commerce (ICC), and the Arbitration Institute of the Stockholm Chamber of Commerce (SCC) rules all provide for institutional determination.[69] If the parties have agreed on an ad hoc arbitration, and have chosen the UNCITRAL rules, but not a seat, then the seat of arbitration will be decided by the tribunal.[70] The Model Law also provides for the tribunal to decide, absent party agreement.[71] In light of the importance of the seat of arbitration with respect to the law governing the arbitration, the law governing arbitrability, and possibly the law governing the arbitration agreement, the choice of the seat is not one that any prudent party would leave to be made by the institution or the tribunal. Moreover, having the choice made by someone other than the parties undermines any theory that the parties implicitly or tacitly chose the law of the seat of arbitration for any purpose.

2. Failure to Choose a Governing Law

When the parties have failed to choose a law governing the contract, who chooses the law and how is it chosen? Arbitration rules and laws uniformly provide that arbitrators will make this determination, and generally give them broad discretion to do so. The method of determining the law differs, however, by whether the arbitrators are specifically required to apply conflicts of laws rules to make the determination. The Model Law provides that the tribunal "shall apply the law determined by the conflict of laws rules which it considers applicable."[72] Most of the more modern institutional rules, however, do not mention conflicts of laws and expand the arbitrators' discretion by providing that when parties have not designated a governing

---

[67] LCIA Rules of Arbitration, art. 16.1.
[68] ICDR Rules, art. 13(1).
[69] WIPO Rules, art. 39(a); ICC Rules, 18(1); Stockholm Chamber of Commerce Rules (SCC) art. 20(1).
[70] UNCITRAL Rules, art. 18(1) (2010).
[71] UNCITRAL Model Law, art. 20(1).
[72] UNCITRAL Model Law, art. 28(2).

law, the tribunal "shall apply the law or rules of law which it considers to be most appropriate."[73] The 2010 UNCITRAL Rules simply provide that "the arbitral tribunal shall apply the law which it determines to be appropriate."[74] The difference between permitting the arbitrators to consider not just "law" but also "rules of law" is that the term "rules of law" is considered an authorization for arbitrators to apply the *lex mercatoria*, or general principles of law.[75] For example, tribunals are increasingly referring to the UNIDROIT Principles (which are not law, but can be considered "rules of law") when the parties have failed to choose a governing law, or when the arbitrators perceive a need to interpret or supplement the national law.[76]

3. Conflicts of Laws

Traditionally, when arbitrators have had to determine the law of the contract, they have applied conflicts of laws rules to determine which substantive law is most appropriate. Normally, they do this by considering various factors that connect a particular State law to the transaction. Different jurisdictions may consider different factors important. For example, in some jurisdictions, the place where the contract was negotiated or concluded is important. In others, the place where the "characteristic performance" occurs is more significant, or the place with the most significant relationship or the closest connection. When arbitrators have to use conflicts of laws rules to determine the proper choice of law, they use a two-step process. First, they have to decide which country's conflicts of laws rules they should use. Second, they have to determine, according to those rules, which law will govern the contract. Determining the law by means of a conflicts of laws analysis is considered an indirect approach (*voie indirecte*), whereas determining the law directly without applying conflicts of law rules is considered a direct approach (*voie directe*).

---

[73] SCC Rules, art. 22(1). *See also*, ICDR Rules, art. 28(1); WIPO Rules, art. 59(a); ICC Rules, art. 21(1); LCIA Rules, art. 22.3.

[74] UNCITRAL Rules, art 35(1).

[75] *See* Emmanuel Gaillard, *Transnational Law: A Legal System of a Method of Decision Making?*" 17 Arb. Int. 59, 65 (2001) ("[Some] arbitration rules chosen by the parties have enlarged the scope of the arbitrators' options by granting them the freedom to apply 'rules of law',... [for example] the 1998 ICC Rules, the 1998 LCIA Rules or the 1997 International Arbitration Rules of the AAA. This language ('rules of law'), which was first used in the French law on arbitration in 1981, was in fact specifically intended to bypass the issue of whether *lex mercatoria* or general principles qualify as a genuine legal order.") *See also* Blessing, *Regulations in Arbitration Rules on Choice of Law*, ICCA Congress series No. 7 at 391 (1996) (Rules of law include "legal rules pertaining to notions of a transnational law, *lex mercatoria* or general principles of law... or the... UNIDROIT Principles.").

[76] *See, e.g.*, Derains & Schwartz, *supra* note 54, at 238. *Citations omitted.*

4. *Voie Indirecte*

In the past, arbitrators would typically choose the conflicts of laws rules of the seat of arbitration. That practice is much less common today, because increasingly arbitrators are coming to understand that unlike judges, they have no particular obligation to a State to use its rules for determining the law. The seat of arbitration, as noted previously, may be chosen for many reasons, unconnected to the particular conflicts of laws rules in the jurisdiction. When the parties have not chosen a seat of arbitration and the seat has been selected by an institution or by the tribunal, there is even less reason for the State's conflicts of laws rules to be considered. Thus, arbitrators are more likely today to use other conflicts of laws rules, if they use conflicts of laws rules at all. They may determine that the appropriate conflicts of laws rules are those that they find most closely connected with the proceedings (*voie indirecte*). In modern times, however, arbitrators are more likely either not to use conflicts of laws rules or to use a cumulative approach. In the cumulative approach, they look at various conflicts of laws rules and find, in some instances, that all the relevant conflicts rules point to the same law; thus, that law becomes the applicable law. If the various conflicts rules point to different substantive laws, however, then the arbitrators must make a choice.

5. *Voie Directe*

Because modern arbitration rules permit arbitrators to determine the law or rules of law based on the law or rule of law they think is most appropriate, they are not tied to any particular legal system. They can consider the implicit or tacit intent of the parties. However, for the most part, unless the parties' intent is relatively clear, the arbitrators are not likely to use this as the basis for their determination.[77] They could determine that a law of one of the parties was the most appropriate, but they might also determine that an unrelated law was most appropriate because it was "highly developed and sophisticated and suitable for the contract or dispute,"[78] even if not closely connected to the dispute. Moreover, as noted earlier, the use of the expression "rules of law," referred to in a number of arbitration laws and rules, permits arbitrators to choose nonlegal standards, such as *lex mercatoria* or general principles of law, to the extent they believe this to be appropriate.[79] The modern trend, influenced by the movement toward

---

[77] *See, e.g.,* Convention on the Law Applicable to Contractual Obligations (Rome Convention), art. 3(1), Official Journal L 266, 09/10/1980 (Choice of law must be "expressed or demonstrated with reasonable certainty by the terms of the contract or the circumstances of the case.").

[78] *See* Lew et al., COMPARATIVE INTERNATIONAL COMMERCIAL ARBITRATION, 435, § 17–73 (2003).

[79] *See supra* note 75.

delocalization and independence from national law systems, is to provide arbitrators with substantial discretion to choose whatever law or rules of law they determine are appropriate, without having to engage in a conflict of laws analysis (*voie directe*).

F. AN ARBITRATOR'S DUTY TO APPLY THE LAW

1. Law or Equity

There is an enduring belief that an arbitrator does not necessarily have to apply the law; the obligation is simply to do justice. This may well have been true in former times, but today, an arbitrator is generally expected to apply the law. Nonetheless, there remains a widely held belief that arbitrators have more flexibility than a judge to soften the impact of a law that appears to work too harshly against one of the parties. There is some truth to this because arbitrators know that in most jurisdictions, an award cannot be vacated or refused enforcement on the grounds of a mistake of law. Therefore, they may be tempted to render an award that meets their personal standard of justice rather than the letter of the law, particularly if they view a strict application of law as being unfair. This raises the question of what the arbitrator's obligation is with respect to applying the law. Can or should the tribunal render awards giving each party one-half of what it asked for? Should it consider equitable solutions rather than a strict application of law?

There is also a persistent belief that arbitrators render compromise awards, giving something to each party. However, recent studies indicate that this is not the case.[80] Based on empirical research, scholars conclude that "arbitrators do not engage in the practice of 'splitting the baby.'"[81] Moreover, anecdotal evidence also indicates that arbitrators do not usually divide an award between the parties, except perhaps with respect to costs when the decision on the merits has a heavy impact on one of the parties.[82]

Today, parties expect that the arbitrator will enforce the law, especially if that law has been chosen by the parties.[83] Studies have shown that only a handful of counsel, in drafting an arbitration clause, will grant an arbitrator

---

[80] An American Arbitration Association study of commercial cases administered by the ICDR in 2005 showed that only 7% of the cases had awards in the midrange of the amount claimed. Approximately 93% had awards that were outside of the midrange. *International News*, American Arbitration Association. Available at http://www.adr.org/sp.asp?id=32004.

[81] *See* Stephanie Keer & Richard Naimark, *Arbitrators Do Not "Split the Baby," in* Towards a Science of International Arbitration, 311 (Drahozal & Naimark, eds., 2005) (Studies show "majority of awards resulted in outright 'wins' or 'losses'").

[82] *See* Pierre Mayer, *Reflections on the International Arbitrator's Duty to Apply the Law*, 17 Arb. Int. 235, at 242 (2001).

[83] *See id.*

the right to decide a matter *ex aequo et bono,* or as *amiable compositeur.*[84] According to Professor Pierre Mayer, companies that use arbitration are seeking certainty, which they believe will result only from the application of law.[85]

Although an arbitrator's award usually cannot be reversed for a mistake of law, it can be challenged if it is against the public policy of a jurisdiction, or if the arbitrator has acted in a way that exceeds his or her powers. The obligation to avoid these problems is tied to the arbitrator's duty to make best efforts to render an enforceable award, which will be discussed next.

2. Duty to Render an Enforceable Award

It is generally agreed in the arbitration world that an arbitrator has a duty to make best efforts to render an award that is enforceable.[86] After all, the point of the arbitration process is to end the dispute, which is expected to be accomplished by the issuance of a final and enforceable award. Some institutional rules make the obligation explicit. For example, the LCIA Rules state, "[T]he LCIA Court, the Arbitral Tribunal and the parties . . . shall make every reasonable effort to ensure that an award is legally enforceable."[87] The ICC Rules state that "the Court and the arbitral tribunal . . . shall make every effort to make sure that the award is enforceable at law."[88]

An arbitrator cannot guarantee an enforceable award and will not have liability if the award is not enforced. Nonetheless, the parties expect that the arbitrator they choose will be competent to render an award they can enforce. If an arbitrator's award is vacated because the arbitrator did not understand what he or she was supposed to be doing, or not supposed to be doing, this individual likely will not be chosen as an arbitrator again. To render an enforceable award, an arbitrator must understand that for an award to survive either a motion to vacate or an opposition to enforcement, it must generally meet formal requirements and not be against public policy. The award and the underlying agreement must therefore comply with the *lex arbitri* and with other relevant mandatory laws.

3. Applying the Law

a. The *Lex Arbitri*

Normally, to prevent an award from being vacated at the seat of arbitration, the arbitration agreement should be valid, and the subject matter should be

---

[84] *See* Bond, *supra* note 65, at 74 (Drahozal & Naimark, eds., 2005).

[85] *See* Mayer, *supra* note 82, at 243.

[86] *See, e.g.,* Derains & Schwartz, *supra* note 54, at 385 ("Enforceability of the award . . . is . . . the raison d'être of the arbitration process.").

[87] LCIA Rules, art. 32.2.

[88] ICC Rules, art. 41.

arbitrable. As discussed earlier, compliance with the law of the seat of arbitration may be critical to withstanding a motion to vacate. If the agreement is not valid under the law of the seat, the award may also be refused enforcement in the enforcing jurisdiction. Thus, an arbitrator should be very careful both in determining the applicable law governing the arbitration agreement, and in applying that law.

b. Mandatory Law

Although the arbitral tribunal may be obligated to apply the mandatory law of the seat of the arbitration in order not to have the award vacated, does it also have to apply the mandatory law of any state where the award might be enforced? The answer has generally been no. As commentators Derains and Schwartz have noted with regard to the ICC Rule cited earlier, the duty to render an enforceable award does not require the tribunal

> to ensure that the Award would be subject to execution in any particular country, provided normally that it has been rendered in accordance with the formal requirements of the place where made. Indeed, an international arbitrator will not necessarily be in a position to know, in any event, where execution of an award is likely to be sought."[89]

Even though an arbitral tribunal might not be expected to take into account the local peculiarities of every possible enforcing jurisdiction, nonetheless, it should consider the more significant international conventions that bear on enforcement. It should particularly be aware of the requirements of the New York Convention because so many countries are parties.[90] A tribunal should be careful to conduct its arbitral proceedings and craft its award in a manner that does not provide grounds for nonenforcement under the New York Convention.[91]

c. Mandatory Law and Public Policy

Although traditionally an arbitrator might not have been expected to take into account the law of the enforcing jurisdiction when rendering an award, increasingly, this is changing with regard to regulatory areas that fall under the heading of public policy, or *ordre public*. In the antitrust or competition law area, for example, the courts in both the United States and Europe expect arbitrators to take into account not just the law chosen by the parties, but also the law governing competition. In Mitsubishi Motors Corp. v. Soler

[89] *See* Derains & Schwartz, *supra* note 54, at 385–86 (2005).
[90] *See* Martin Platte, *An Arbitrator's Duty to Render Enforceable Awards*, 20 J. Int. Arb. 307 (2003).
[91] *See* Chapter 10 *infra* for further discussion of enforcement of awards under the New York Convention.

Chrysler-Plymouth, Inc.,[92] the U.S. Supreme Court held that even though the law chosen by the parties to govern the contract was Swiss law, the arbitrators were required to determine antitrust claims arising in connection with the contract under U.S. antitrust law, or assume the risk that the award would be condemned as against public policy if any enforcement attempt was made in the United States.[93] Similarly, the European Court of Justice (ECJ), in the *Eco Swiss* case,[94] held that issues of competition law were arbitrable. Moreover, even if competition law issues were not raised by the parties or by the arbitrable tribunal, if the contract at issue was in violation of competition law, the award would be subject to annulment under domestic law.[95] Presumably, the award would also be subject to nonenforcement under the New York Convention.[96]

These decisions indicate that courts, at least in Europe and the United States, expect an arbitrator to have obligations to do more than just resolve a private dispute between parties. Because statutory and regulatory claims are increasingly declared to be arbitrable, matters involving more than simply the parties' private contract claims are coming before tribunals in commercial cases. Although tribunals have usually seen their responsibility as primarily to the parties appearing before them, and have not generally assumed a duty to enforce the public interest, the duty to render an enforceable award in a case involving statutory and regulatory claims appears to impose new responsibilities. A tribunal that does not consider the public interest in ways expected under the enacted statutes at issue in the arbitration risks offending the public policy in the seat or in the jurisdiction of enforcement and thereby rendering an unenforceable award.

Similar issues concerning the obligation to apply mandatory law arise out of the decision of the ECJ in Ingmar GB Ltd. v. Eaton Leonard Technologies, Inc.[97] Although the decision did not arise in an arbitration context, it is likely to affect an arbitrator's obligation to apply a law not chosen by the parties. The *Ingmar* case involved a commercial agent agreement between an English agent and a U.S. principal. The agreement provided that California law applied. The question was whether the indemnity (a payment to the agent upon termination) required under the provisions of the European Community Directive Relating to Self-Employed Commercial Agents[98] was

---

[92] 473 U.S. 614 (1985).

[93] *See id.* at 637–38, n. 19.

[94] Case C-126/97, Eco Swiss China Time Ltd. v. Benetton International NV, [1999] ECR I-3055.

[95] *See* Robert B. von Mehren, *The Eco-Swiss Case and International Arbitration*, 19 Arb. Int. 465, 468 (2003).

[96] *See id.*

[97] Case C-381/98, [2000] ECR I-9305.

[98] Council Directive 86/653/EEC, 18 December 1986, OJ L 382, at 17.

mandatory, or whether it was not required because the parties had chosen California law to govern the contract. Under California law, no indemnity was required. The ECJ held that a foreign principal "whose commercial agent carries on his activity within the Community, cannot evade [the] provisions [of the Directive Relating to Self-Employed Commercial Agents] by the simple expedient of a choice-of-law clause."[99] Thus, if the agent is in a Member State, the parties cannot contract out of the European Community's commercial agent directive by choosing the substantive law of a nonmember state to govern the contract.

If an arbitration on similar facts were held in California, with California the enforcing jurisdiction as well as the seat of the arbitration, the question would be whether the European agent could persuade the tribunal in California that European Community (EC) mandatory law should apply despite the parties' choice of California law. In light of the ECJ decision, it would seem clear that the arbitrators should apply the EC mandatory law. However, if the tribunal applied California law to deny the indemnity, a U.S. court might not vacate or refuse to enforce the award. Even if the court believed the tribunal was mistaken in its application of law, mistake of law is not a ground for either annulment or refusal to enforce. As long as the court found that application of California law did not offend U.S. public policy, the award would probably be enforced.

On the other hand, if the arbitration were held in a Member State of the EC, an award that relieved the U.S. company of liability for the indemnity would most likely be annulled under the ECJ decision. Thus, in certain circumstances, when the mandatory law constituting public policy is clear, arbitrators should take this law into account in their deliberations and in crafting an award that will meet the parties' expectations by being enforceable.

---

[99] Case C-381/98, [2000] ECR I-9305, para. 25.

CHAPTER FIVE

Judicial Assistance for Arbitration

In international commercial arbitration, most of the time parties and arbitrators do not want interference from a court. There are, however, times when the support of a court can prove essential. The primary reason is that courts have resources that are lacking to a tribunal – in particular, coercive powers – that is, the ability to make someone do something. Courts can require performance because they have the ability to impose negative consequences if a person does not perform – in the form of fines, incarceration, or other penalties. Although tribunals have some ability to impose negative consequences on parties, such as drawing an adverse inference if a party does not produce documents, they have no ability to make a party carry out an order, and no coercive powers that can be applied to persons who are not party to the arbitration.

Courts also have an oversight role. Although arbitration is a private system of justice, organized and regulated by the parties in light of the rules and procedures they have chosen, it is still governed by law, and almost always by the arbitration law (*lex arbitri*) of the seat of the arbitration. Courts expect to retain a level of control to ensure that the private system of justice meets at least minimum standards of fairness – so that arbitration is not a system that is fraudulent, corrupt, or lacking in essential due process.

Parties also generally want some recourse to the court, if, for example, the arbitral procedure seems biased or unfair. As noted in Chapter 4, when Belgium law provided that there would be no court review of arbitral awards for parties arbitrating in Belgium who had no links to Belgium, parties began to avoid Belgium as the seat of arbitration. Businesses did not like being denied the opportunity for recourse to the courts if the award was in some way improper. As a consequence, the law was revised in 1998 to permit parties to have recourse to the court, unless they opted out of such recourse.[1] William W. Park refers to the legislation as "Belgium's failed

---

[1] *See* William W. Park, *The Specificity of International Arbitration: The Case for FAA Reform*, 36 Vand. J. Transnat'l L. 1241, 1267 (2003).

experiment in mandatory 'non-review' of awards."[2] Most parties want the safety net of judicial review, narrow though that review may be.

Parties tend to call on courts for assistance in very specific ways. For example, they may ask a court to enforce an agreement to arbitrate, sometimes by staying court proceedings while the arbitration goes forward, or in some jurisdictions by issuing an order compelling arbitration. Other times, courts may be asked to rule on the tribunal's decision that it has jurisdiction, or on a challenge to one of the arbitrators for conflict of interest. In an ad hoc arbitration, if parties cannot agree on an arbitrator, and have not named an appointing authority, they may ask a court to appoint the arbitrator. A party may ask the court for emergency relief, sometimes before the tribunal has even been formed. The emergency relief may be in the form of an order to the other party to maintain the status quo during the arbitration – for example, by not selling disputed property, or by not using or licensing disputed intellectual property. The court can issue an order for attachment of assets that seem likely to disappear, or an order requiring a party to provide security for costs, or providing for other measures that one party views as necessary to make sure the relief sought will still be possible at the time the arbitration concludes. Parties may also want judicial assistance with discovery, particularly from witnesses who are not under the control of one of the parties. In addition, courts also may be asked to rule on issues of consolidation and on motions to vacate, or to recognize and enforce the arbitration award.

Although courts generally respect the parties' autonomy in an arbitration, their assistance is sometimes more and sometimes less than what the parties want. There is a wavering line between helpful assistance and unhelpful interference. This chapter considers some of the ways in which courts have an impact on arbitration proceedings and results.

A. ENFORCEMENT OF ARBITRATION AGREEMENTS

1. Extent of Judicial Review

When one party to an arbitration agreement has begun litigation, the other party may ask the court to refer the matter to arbitration under the New York Convention. Article II(3) requires the court "at the request of one of the parties [to] refer the parties to arbitration, unless it finds that the said agreement is null and void, inoperative or incapable of being performed."[3] In determining whether the agreement is valid, a question arises whether the court should engage in a complete review of the facts and circumstances,

---

[2] *See id.* Switzerland, as well, permits noncitizens arbitrating in Switzerland to opt out of any court review. Swiss Private International Law Act of 1987, ch. 12, art. 192. Available at http://www.umbricht.ch/pdf/SwissPIL.pdf.

[3] New York Convention, art. II(3).

or merely a *prima facie* review. Under the lower *prima facie* standard, the court would only have to find there was a *reasonable likelihood* that the party bringing the suit had in fact previously agreed to arbitrate.[4]

Professor Frédéric Bachand argues that because Article II(3) of the Convention is silent on the question of *prima facie* or full review, only a *prima facie* review is required when the Convention is applicable.[5] He further argues that under the Model Law, which was always intended to comply with the Convention's provisions, a *prima facie* approach should be preferred over a full review.[6]

The argument in favor of a complete review is that it is more likely to prevent a defective arbitration agreement from ultimately causing an award to be vacated, thereby wasting the time, effort, and resources expended during the arbitration process. The argument in favor of the *prima facie* review is that it is more likely to prevent a party from being able to engage in dilatory and obstructionist tactics. When the parties are promptly referred to the tribunal, which will make a ruling on the validity of the arbitration agreement, and therefore on its own jurisdiction, a party whose arbitration agreement is *prima facie* valid will not be able to delay the arbitration and cause substantial increases in costs by pursuing a full litigation process.

Courts in different countries interpret differently the amount of review required.[7] In the United States, both approaches exist. Some U.S. courts have tended to provide a comprehensive review,[8] whereas others take a more restrained approach.[9] The U.S. Fifth Circuit has described its approach as follows:

> In applying the Convention, we have held that it contemplates a very limited inquiry by courts when considering a motion to compel arbitration, and that the court should compel arbitration if (1) there is an

---

[4] *See* Frédéric Bachand, *Does Article 8 of the Model Law Call for Full or Prima Facie Review of the Arbitral Tribunal's Jurisdiction?* 22 Arb. Int. 463 (2006).

[5] *See* Frédéric Bachand, *supra* note 4, at 470–71 (2006). Professor Bachand acknowledges, however, that there are cases that hold otherwise, but he finds them not persuasive. *See id.* at 470.

[6] *See id.*

[7] In France, a court will only review an arbitration agreement if the dispute is not yet before an arbitral tribunal, and then will refer it to arbitration unless it is *manifestly* void. French Code of Civil Procedure, art. 1448. Germany and England, on the other hand, permit more extensive review. *See* Lew, Mistelis, & Kroll, Comparative International Commercial Arbitration at 349–50 (2003).

[8] *See, e.g.,* Sandvik AB v. Advent International Corp., 220 F.3d 99 (3d Cir. 2000) *citing* Par-Knit Mills, Inc., v. Stockbridge Fabrics Co., 636 F.2d 51 (3d Cir. 1980) (The court ordered a jury trial on the existence of the arbitration agreement, specifically whether the person who signed the agreement had authority to bind the company.).

[9] Bautista v. Star Cruises, 396 F.3d 1289 (11th Cir. 2005) ("In deciding a motion to compel arbitration under the Convention Act, a court conducts 'a very limited inquiry.'"). *Citations omitted.*

agreement in writing to arbitrate the dispute, (2) the agreement provides for arbitration in the territory of a Convention signatory, (3) the agreement arises out of a commercial legal relationship, and (4) a party to the agreement is not an American citizen. If these requirements are met, the Convention requires district courts to order arbitration.[10]

A great variation also exists among other jurisdictions concerning the extent to which a court should review of the validity of an arbitration agreement. The UNCITRAL Model Law echoes the requirements of Article II(3) of the New York Convention. Like the Convention, the Model Law, in Article 8(1), provides for courts to refer a matter to arbitration, unless the arbitration agreement is null and void, inoperative, or incapable of being performed.

Professor Bachand's position is that there is substantial evidence in the *travaux préparatoires*[11] of the Model Law and in its basic structure and principles that the drafters valued most highly the prevention of dilatory and obstructionist conduct. That was more important than the possibility that mere *prima facie* review could result in a fatally flawed arbitral award.[12] Thus, a *prima facie* review would move the arbitration forward more quickly, consistent with the goals and expectations of the parties.

Although courts continue to differ on the amount of review required, a *prima facie* review of whether the agreement is "null and void, inoperable, or incapable of being performed" seems reasonable in light of the subsequent review available, at least in Model Law countries, under Article 16. Section 3 of Article 16 provides that if the tribunal rules that it has jurisdiction as a preliminary question, a party can appeal that ruling to the court. At that point, the court has the benefit of the tribunal's reasons for determining that it has jurisdiction.

Of course, if the tribunal does not rule on its jurisdiction until a final award on the merits, rather than as a preliminary question, substantial additional costs will be involved if it turns out at the award enforcement stage that the arbitration agreement was fatally defective. On balance, however, in light of the increasingly litigious means of conducting international arbitration, it makes sense to try to limit the ability of a party to obstruct and delay the arbitration process by permitting only a *prima facie* review of an

[10] Ernesto Francisco v. Stolt Achievement Mt, 293 F.3d 270, 273 (5th Cir. 2002). *Citations omitted.*
[11] The literal translation of *travaux préparatoires* is "preparatory works." In English, the words essentially mean "negotiating history" or "drafting history." *Travaux préparatoires* are the recorded history of the negotiation and drafting of a treaty (or a Model Law, as the case may be), and are frequently referred to as an aid to interpretation.
[12] *See* Bachand, *supra* note 4, at 470.

arbitration agreement under Model Law 8(1) or the New York Convention, Article II(3).

2. Competence-Competence

The doctrine of competence-competence,[13] which is followed in most jurisdictions, provides that arbitrators are competent to determine their own competence – that is, they are empowered to decide their own jurisdiction to hear and determine the dispute before them.[14] Sometimes the doctrine is criticized by those who assume that arbitrators will most likely find that they have jurisdiction in order to avoid losing a good job opportunity. However, the view in many countries is that by choosing arbitration, parties intend for an arbitrator to decide all disputes arising out of the contract, even those concerning the jurisdiction of the arbitrator. Not all countries endorse the competence-competence doctrine, however. Moreover, the varied application of the doctrine in different countries may necessitate consultation with local counsel to understand how competence-competence is applied in a particular country.[15]

The preceding discussion focused on the extent to which a court should review the question of validity of an arbitration agreement when, in the case before it, one party asks the court to refer the matter to arbitration. The doctrine of competence-competence may well be related to a court's approach as to whether it will give a full or a *prima facie* review of the validity of the arbitration agreement, because a strong competence-competence doctrine, as in France, will tend to result in very slight review by a court. But some jurisdictions, such as China, have no competence-competence doctrine, so the tribunal will never determine its own competence.[16] France and China, in effect, are countries that appear to be at opposite ends of the scale in terms of who decides the jurisdiction of the tribunal. In France, court intervention is generally not allowed until after a final arbitral award has been rendered.[17] This appears to be true for the most part even in cases in which the arbitral proceedings have not yet begun.[18] Article 1448 of the French

---

[13] The doctrine is frequently referred to by the German term *kompetenz-kompetenz*.

[14] *See, e.g.*, UNCITRAL Model Law, art. 16(1); French Code of Civil Procedure, art. 1465; Netherlands Arbitration Act, art. 1052(1); ICDR Rules, art. 15(1); LCIA Rules, art. 23.1; ICC Rules, art. 6(3).

[15] *See* John J. Barcelo III, *Who Decides the Arbitrators' Jurisdiction? Separability and Competence-Competence in Transnational Perspective*, 36 Vand. J. Transnat'l L. 1115 (2003), for a discussion of competence-competence in a number of different countries.

[16] *See, e.g.*, Jingzhou Tao & Clarisse Von Wunschheim, *Articles 16 and 18 of the PRC Arbitration Law: The Great Wall of China for Foreign Arbitration Institutions*, 23 Arb. Int'l 309, 312 (2007).

[17] French Code of Civil Procedure, art. 1448. Article 1485 provides for a very limited review of an arbitral award.

[18] *See* Christian Herrer Petrus, *Spanish Perspectives on the Doctrines of Kompetenz-Kompetenz and Separability*, 11 Am. Rev. Int'l Arb. 397, 407 (2000).

Code of Civil Procedure does provide a slight possibility that before the arbitral tribunal has begun to function, the court might decide the validity issue if "the arbitral agreement is manifestly void."[19] It has been suggested, however, that an agreement is very unlikely to be found "manifestly void" unless, for example, the agreement pertains to patents or other subject matter that is not arbitrable under French law.[20] Thus, under French law, a question of the arbitration agreement's validity (and, therefore, whether the arbitrators have jurisdiction to determine the dispute) will virtually always be decided by the arbitrators, subject to court review only after the final award.

Because the Arbitration Law of the People's Republic of China does not recognize the doctrine of competence-competence,[21] either an arbitration commission (generally, CIETAC, China's main international arbitration institution) or the People's Court will rule on the validity of the arbitration agreement, thereby determining the jurisdiction of the tribunal.[22] The tribunal itself has no voice in the decision. If one party raised the issue of the tribunal's jurisdiction with CIETAC, and the other with the People's Court, then conflicting decisions could result. In such a situation, the People's Court would prevail.[23]

Under the 2005 CIETAC rules, the People's Court has the power to intervene in disputes on the validity of arbitration agreements.[24] However, if the court does not intervene, CIETAC will make the decision as to validity.[25] Thus, the arbitral institution, rather than the tribunal, has the primary responsibility for determining validity, with the court also having the ability to intervene. The rules make it possible, however, for CIETAC to delegate its decision-making authority to the tribunal.[26] It is not yet clear in

---

[19] French Code of Civil Procedure, art. 1448.

[20] Bernard G. Poznanski, *The Nature and Extent of an Arbitrator's Powers in International Commercial Arbitration*, 4 J. Int. Arb. 71, 100 (1987).

[21] *See, e.g.*, Jingzhou Tao & Clarisse Von Wunschheim, *Articles 16 and 18 of the PRC Arbitration Law: The Great Wall of China for Foreign Arbitration Institutions*, 23 Arb. Int'l 309, 312 (2007).

[22] Arbitration Law of the People's Republic of China (CAL), art. 20. CAL was adopted on October 31, 1994 at the Ninth Session of the Standing Committee of the Eighth National People Legislation's Congress and implemented on September 1, 1995. English translation available at http://www.cietac.org/.

[23] Arbitration Law of the People's Republic of China, art. 20.

[24] *See* Michael J. Moser & Peter Yuen, *The New CIETAC Arbitration Rules*, 21 Arb. Int. 3, at 395, n. 13 (2005).

[25] *See id.*

[26] "The CIETAC shall have the power to determine the existence and validity of an arbitration agreement and its jurisdiction over an arbitration case. The CIETAC may, if necessary, delegate such power to the arbitral tribunal." 2005 CIETAC Arbitration Rules, art. 6(1). CIETAC is expected to have new rules sometime in 2012. However, Rule 6(1) does not appear to have changed in any significant way in the new rules. The 2012 rules were made available to students participating in the 19th Annual Vis

practice how often this may occur. Thus, in China, it appears that tribunals will rarely be able to determine the validity of an arbitration agreement, and therefore their own jurisdiction, although this may change over time.

Other countries, particularly countries that have adopted the UNCITRAL Model Law, permit arbitrators in most instances to decide the issue of an arbitration agreement's validity, viewing them as competent to determine their own competence to hear the arbitration. As noted earlier, under the Model Law, a tribunal can rule on a question of its own jurisdiction either as a preliminary question or in a final award.[27] If, however, the tribunal rules as a preliminary matter that it has jurisdiction, a party can request within thirty days that a court review the decision and determine whether jurisdiction is proper.[28]

The English Court of Appeal has found that even in cases in which bribery was alleged, arbitrators were competent to rule on their own jurisdiction. In Fiona Trust & Holding Corporation (and 20 Others) v. Yuri Privalov (and 17 Others) (Fiona Trust),[29] the Court held that an allegation of bribery would not cause the arbitration clause to be ineffective, so arbitrators would still have jurisdiction to determine their jurisdiction. In an earlier case, Harbour Assurance Co. (UK) Ltd v. Kansa General International Insurance (Kansa),[30] an English court had held that an arbitration clause could be invalidated in two instances: (1) where a party denied that an agreement had been concluded, or (2) where there was a mistake as to who the other contracting party was. In such cases, the arbitration clause could be invalidated and an arbitral tribunal would have no jurisdiction. But an allegation of illegality was not enough to invalidate the entire agreement, including the arbitration clause, according to the *Kansa* court. The *Fiona Trust* court held that as with allegations of fraud or illegality, the allegation of bribery alone was not enough to invalidate the arbitration clause. Something more was needed. Unfortunately, the court did not provide any guidelines as to what the "something more" should be. Nonetheless, it is clear that in England, when claims of bribery are alleged in the formation of a contract, arbitrators will still have jurisdiction to consider the claims arising out of the contract, including the bribery claim.

In the United States, the presumption that a tribunal will determine the validity of an arbitration agreement is reversed. In First Options v. Kaplan,[31] the Supreme Court held that there must be clear and unmistakable evidence

---

Moot Arbitration Competition, at http://www.cisg.law.pace.edu/cisg/moot/CIETAC_Rules_2011.pdf.

[27] UNCITRAL Model Law, art.16(3).

[28] *See id.*

[29] [2007] EWCA Civ. 20.

[30] [1993] QB 701.

[31] 514 U.S. 938 (1995).

that the parties agreed to submit to the arbitrator the question of the arbitrator's jurisdiction ("the arbitrability question").[32] Otherwise, the court will decide whether the arbitrator had a mandate to arbitrate. The presumption, therefore, is that the court should decide the question of the arbitrator's jurisdiction.

Nonetheless, the U.S. Supreme Court, in a number of decisions, has made it clear that many "arbitrability questions" are for the arbitrator. First, if the parties have adopted particular institutional rules that give the arbitrator the right to determine her competence, that is clear and unmistakable evidence that at least certain arbitrability questions go to the arbitrator. Moreover, the Supreme Court has adopted the separability doctrine, holding that an arbitrator has jurisdiction even if there was fraud in the inducement of a contract, as long as fraud was not alleged specifically with respect to the arbitration clause within the contract.[33] This is true even if the contract itself is alleged to be void under state law, not just voidable.[34] Scope issues, at least in cases in which parties agreed to institutional arbitration rules permitting the arbitrator to determine competence, will probably be decided by the arbitrator.[35] In addition, the court has found that certain procedural questions, such as allegations of waiver or delay, should be decided by the arbitrator, as well as issues such as time limits, notice, *laches* (neglecting to assert a claim for an unreasonable amount of time), estoppel, and other conditions precedent to an obligation to arbitrate.[36]

Thus, what remains for a U.S. court to determine is rather circumscribed. It appears that the court will still hear questions of whether the parties actually have a valid arbitration agreement – that is, issues of existence and validity of the arbitration agreement, as opposed to the container agreement.[37] Even if parties have chosen institutional rules that provide for arbitrators to determine their own jurisdiction, it is doubtful that U.S. law would permit an arbitrator to decide whether a valid arbitration agreement was ever concluded.[38] The relevant dispute is whether the parties agreed to give the

---

[32] *See id.* at 945.

[33] Prima Paint Corp. v. Flood & Conklin Mfg. Co., 388 U.S. 395 (1967).

[34] Buckeye Check Cashing v. Cardegna, 546 U.S. 440 (2006).

[35] However, the U.S. Supreme Court has essentially denied arbitrators the discretion to determine whether there should be a class action arbitration when the contract is silent on this question. Stolt-Nielsen v. Animal Feeds, 130 S.Ct. 1758 (2010).

[36] Howsam v. Dean Witter Reynolds, 537 U.S. 79, 84–85 (2002).

[37] As examples of issues a court should decide, the Supreme Court has referred to "whether the arbitration contract bound parties who did not sign the agreement" and "whether an arbitration clause . . . applies to a particular type of controversy." *See id.* at 84.

[38] *See* Three Valleys Municipal Water District v. E.F. Hutton & Co., 925 F.2d 1136, 1141 (9th Cir. 1991) ("If there was never an agreement to arbitrate, there is no authority to require a party to submit to arbitration."), *citation omitted.* Although in Buckeye Check Cashing v. Cardegna, 546 U.S. 440 (2006), the U.S. Supreme Court

arbitrator that power. Even if rules adopted in the arbitration agreement provided the arbitrator the power to decide the existence of the arbitration agreement, the question remains whether the resisting party ever agreed to those rules.[39]

When a party asks a court to dismiss a court case because the parties agreed to arbitrate, the court clearly has the power to do so if the case is in its own court. A question arises, however, whether a court that has jurisdiction over a party can order that party not to proceed with a claim in a foreign court. The answer, as will be discussed in the next section, may depend on where the two courts are located.

B. ANTI-SUIT INJUNCTIONS

An anti-suit injunction is an order by a court that has personal jurisdiction over a party to require the party either not to file a claim in a foreign jurisdiction or not to proceed with a claim that has already been filed. The reason for the anti-suit injunction is usually that the same issues between the same parties are currently being litigated or arbitrated within the jurisdiction of the court issuing the order. Concerns underlying the injunction are that the foreign action would frustrate efficient results in the forum court, imperil its jurisdiction, threaten some strong national policy, or that the party carrying on litigation in the foreign jurisdiction is doing so in bad faith and in order to harass the other party.[40]

When any court enjoins a party from bringing a suit in a foreign jurisdiction, questions of international comity come into play. International comity involves respect for and deference toward another country's laws and court decisions. "'Comity'...is neither a matter of absolute obligation...nor of mere courtesy and good will.... But it is the recognition which one nation allows within its territory to the legislative, executive or judicial acts of

---

eliminated the distinction between void and voidable contracts for purposes of determining whether an arbitration clause contained in such a contract was valid, thus perhaps putting in doubt one of the underpinnings of *Three Valleys*; nonetheless, the Court made clear that it was not deciding the issue of whether the court or the arbitrator should decide the issue of whether the arbitration agreement was ever concluded. ("Our opinion...does not speak to the issue...[of] whether the alleged obligor ever signed the contract, whether the signor lacked authority to commit the alleged principal, and whether the signor lacked the mental capacity to assent.") *Id.* at n.1. *Citations omitted.*

[39] *See* Three Valleys, *supra* note 38.

[40] *See, e.g.,* Quaak v. Klynveld Peat Marwick Goerdeler Bedrijfsrevisoren (KPMG-B), 361 F.3d 11 (1st Cir. 2004) (KPMG-B was enjoined by a U.S. court from maintaining an action in Belgium in which it requested that penalties be imposed on anyone seeking discovery of its records in Belgium. A U.S. magistrate judge had ordered KPMG-B to produce these records.).

another nation."[41] When a court enjoins a party from proceeding in a foreign court, even though the basis for the injunction is the first court's jurisdiction over the party, there is nonetheless an impact on the jurisdiction of the foreign court.[42] As the European Court of Justice noted with respect to anti-suit injunctions in litigation:

> [A] prohibition imposed by a court, backed by a penalty, restraining a party from commencing or continuing proceedings before a foreign court undermines the latter court's jurisdiction to determine the dispute. Any injunction prohibiting a claimant from bringing such an action must be seen as constituting interference with the jurisdiction of the foreign court.[43]

1. Anti-Suit Injunctions in the United States

Because of the inevitable impact on a foreign court's jurisdiction, most court systems are reluctant to grant anti-suit injunctions. Common law jurisdictions, however, are much more likely than civil law jurisdictions to issue anti-suit injunctions. In the United States, different courts have adopted different standards for whether to grant an anti-suit injunction.[44] In the more conservative or restrictive jurisdictions, the court must find that the foreign action undermines its own jurisdiction or threatens a strong national policy.[45] In the more liberal jurisdictions, courts generally will grant an anti-suit injunction if the parties and issues are the same, and if proceeding with

---

[41] Hilton v. Guyot, 159 U.S. 113, 163–64 (1895).

[42] This point has been noted in many cases. *See, e.g.*, Turner v. Grovit and Harada Ltd. and Changepoint S.A., ECR 2004, 1–3565, para. 27; Quaak, *supra* note 40, at 17, Paramedics Electromedicina Comercial, Ltda. v. GE Medical Systems Information Technologies, Inc., 369 F.3d 645, 654–55 (2d Cir. 2004).

[43] Turner v. Grovit, *supra* note 42, at para. 27.

[44] The anti-suit injunction is a particular subspecies of the preliminary injunction. Generally, the requirements in the United States for a preliminary injunction are some variation of the following: (1) likelihood of success on the merits, (2) irreparable injury if relief not granted, (3) a balancing of the equities (threatened injury greater than threatened harm from injunction), (4) granting the injunction will not disserve the public interest. *See* Karaha Bodas v. Negara, 335 F.3d 357, 363 (5th Cir. 2003). However, according to the Fifth Circuit, "the suitability of such relief [*i.e.*, a foreign antisuit injunction] ultimately depends on considerations unique to antisuit injunctions." *Id.* at 364.

[45] *See* Quaak, *supra* note 40. Decisions from the Second, Third, Sixth, and District of Columbia Circuits are described as taking the conservative approach. *See* China Trade & Dev. Corp. v. M.V. Choong Yong, 837 F.2d 33, 35 (2d Cir. 1987): Stonington Partners, Inc., v. Lernout–Hauspie Speech Prods., 310 F.3d 118, 126 (3d Cir. 2002); Gau Shan Co. v. Bankers Trust Co., 956 F.2d 1349, 1355 (6th Cir. 1992); Laker Airways Ltd. v. Sabena, Belgian World Airlines, 235 U.S. App. D.C. 207, 731 F.2d 909, 916 (D.C. Cir. 1984).

the foreign litigation would impede the prompt and efficient resolution of the case in the forum.[46]

Although the framework of legal analysis tends to be the same for anti-suit injunctions whether they are intended to protect rights in litigation or in arbitration, courts in common law countries seem to be somewhat more likely to issue an anti-suit injunction to protect an arbitration agreement, because of the strong public policy favoring arbitration.[47]

Several kinds of anti-suit injunctions may arise in connection with arbitration. One is when a party brings a lawsuit in a foreign jurisdiction, even though it had agreed to arbitrate the dispute that forms the basis of the lawsuit. A second is when a party tries to enjoin another party from either vacating an award, or enforcing an award that has been vacated. In another, a party, asserting that it has not agreed to arbitrate, seeks to enjoin the other party from proceeding with arbitration. This is sometimes called an *anti-arbitration injunction*. Courts are generally willing to grant anti-arbitration injunctions when there is no agreement to arbitrate, or when a party seeks to arbitrate in a venue not agreed upon by the parties.[48]

In some cases, each side will try to enjoin the other. For example, in Paramedics Electromedicina Comercial Ltda. v. GE Medical Systems Information Technologies, Inc., one party, GE, commenced an arbitration.[49] The other party, Paramedics, known as Tecnimed, began a lawsuit in Brazil, and petitioned in New York state court for a stay of the arbitration.[50] GE removed Tecnimed's New York state case to federal court, and then counterclaimed, seeking to compel arbitration and asking for an anti-suit injunction to stop the action in Brazil.[51] There were thus three proceedings: (1) the arbitration proceeding in the United States, (2) the Brazilian lawsuit that Tecnimed commenced to have substantive claims resolved by a court

---

[46] *See id*. The Quaak court, *supra* note 40, describes decisions from the Fifth and Ninth Circuits as taking the liberal approach. *See* Kaepa, Inc., v. Achilles Corp., 76 F.3d 624, 626 (5th Cir. 1996); Seattle Totems Hockey Club, Inc., v. Nat'l Hockey League, 652 F.2d 852, 855–56 (9th Cir. 1981) (Courts taking the liberal approach tend to assign little weight to international comity.). See Quaak, *supra* note 40, at 17. The Quaak court itself endorses the conservative approach, although finding it a little too rigid in application, and preferring a totality of the circumstances approach. *See id.* at 17–18.

[47] *See* Daniel Tan, *Anti-Suit Injunctions and the Vexing Problem of Comity*, 45 Va. J. Int'l L. 283, 327, 331–34 (2005). *See also* Paramedics Electromedicina Comercial, Ltda. v. GE Medical Systems Information Technologies, Inc., 369 F. 3d 645, 654 (2d Cir. 2004).

[48] *See, e.g.*, Société Générale de Surveillance, S.A., v. Raytheon European Management and Systems Co., 643 F.2d 863, 868 (1st Cir.1981) ("[T]o enjoin a party from arbitrating where an agreement to arbitrate is absent is the concomitant of the power to compel arbitration where it is present.").

[49] *See Paramedics*, *supra* note 47, at 648.

[50] *See id.* at 649.

[51] *See id.*

rather than by arbitration, and (3) the U.S. federal court lawsuit in which (a) Tecnimed wanted to enjoin the arbitration proceeding in the United States, and (b) GE wanted to enjoin the Brazilian lawsuit and force Tecnimed to arbitrate. Tecnimed was ultimately ordered by the U.S. federal district court to arbitrate and to take steps to cause dismissal of the Brazilian lawsuit.[52] Tecnimed refused initially to comply, and was held in contempt. The court ordered Tecnimed, so long as it was not in compliance, to pay U.S. $1000 per day for the first three months, and U.S. $5000 per day subsequently.[53] Eventually, it complied. Thus, the *Tecnimed* case is an example of one party trying to enjoin the other party's arbitration, and the second party responding by enjoining the first party's lawsuit.

Although normally a party seeking an anti-suit injunction will go directly to a court, there may be another way of obtaining the same relief. In at least one case, an arbitral tribunal has issued a partial award that (1) required a recalcitrant party to arbitrate and (2) forbade it from litigating in another forum. The award then became enforceable under the New York Convention.[54] When enforced, it had the same effect as an anti-suit injunction. This occurred in the case of Four Seasons Hotels and Resorts v. Consorcio Barr S.A. (Four Seasons).[55] Consorcio Barr had built a hotel in Venezuela and hired Four Seasons to run it. When disputes arose, the parties, the arbitral tribunal, and the pertinent national courts responded as follows:

1. Four Seasons brought an action in federal court in Miami, Florida, concerning certain claims that the parties agreed were nonarbitrable.
2. Four Seasons also commenced an arbitration in Miami.
3. Consorcio began litigation in Venezuela to stop the arbitration.
4. Four Seasons asked the federal court in Miami to issue an injunction compelling Consorcio to arbitrate and requiring it to withdraw the Venezuela litigation.
5. The U.S. federal district court in Miami denied Four Seasons' request for an injunction.
6. The arbitral tribunal in Miami then issued a partial arbitral award, which essentially granted the relief Four Seasons had failed to obtain from the district court. The award required Consorcio to participate in the arbitration and to withdraw any Venezuelan actions.

---

[52] *See id.* at 650, 659.

[53] *See id.* at 649. The Second Circuit affirmed the district court decision, except that it held that because the fine was compensatory (it was to be paid to GE, not to the court), the amount of the fine must be adjusted to reflect the actual expenses justifiably incurred by GE as a result of Tecnimed's noncompliance. *See id.* at 658.

[54] *See* Four Seasons Hotels and Resorts v. Consorcio Barr S.A., 377 F.3d 1164 (11th Cir. 2004).

[55] *See id.* Two cases were consolidated on this appeal.

7. The Venezuelan court held that arbitration of the disputes was improper.
8. Four Seasons brought a new case in the federal district of Florida for the purpose of confirming the arbitral award.
9. The U.S. federal district court confirmed the award under the New York Convention.

On appeal, the Eleventh Circuit disagreed with one aspect of the district court's reasoning and remanded to the district court for reconsideration of that part of its decision.[56] Subsequently, the district court, in an unpublished order, again confirmed the partial award.[57] What is noteworthy here is that if an arbitral tribunal can be persuaded to issue – as a partial award – relief that is essentially an anti-suit injunction, then there may be a treaty obligation that favors its enforcement. The treaty obligation may make a court more likely to grant the relief requested than if it is asked to issue an anti-suit injunction in the first instance. The *Four Seasons* case is a stark illustration of this: Four Seasons' motion for a preliminary injunction was denied by a court, but it obtained the same relief previously denied when that relief was packaged as a partial award by the arbitral tribunal.[58]

C. Ryan Reetz, an attorney in Miami, has noted that anti-suit injunctions are generally most effective if they can be issued at an early point in the arbitration.[59] To that end, under institutional rules that provide for appointment of an emergency arbitrator empowered to grant interim relief, a partial award could potentially be rendered that would function as an anti-suit injunction, even before the tribunal was constituted.[60] In this way, a party might succeed in stopping vexatious litigation at a very early point in the arbitration process.

For the most part, courts are more likely to grant an anti-suit injunction to enforce a party's agreement to arbitrate than to enjoin efforts either to vacate or enforce an award. Once an award has been rendered, the New York Convention provides for enforcement, but it does not include any

---

[56] *See id.* at 1171–72. The district court had rejected Consorcio's argument that the award should not be confirmed because the Venezuelan courts found the issue not arbitral, giving as the reason for its rejection that Consorcio had participated in the arbitration. The Eleventh Circuit found that reason invalid, and remanded for the issue to be considered under the New York Convention Article V(1)(a), that an award can be vacated if not valid under the law the parties have chosen.

[57] Case 1:02-cv-23249-KMM, Document 157, entered on FLSD docket 09/23/2005, K. Michael Moore, U.S. District Judge.

[58] A potential drawback, however, is that the two-step procedure, going first to the arbitrators and then to the court, may make the process quite time consuming.

[59] *See* C. Ryan Reetz, *United States Anti-Suit Injunctions in the Arbitration Context*, INTERNATIONAL ARBITRATION AND MEDIATION – FROM THE PROFESSIONAL'S PERSPECTIVE (Robert Carrow & Anita Alibekova, eds., 2007), 135–43, n. 20.

[60] *See supra* Chapter 3, Section B(2).

provision for issuing an injunction against foreign challenges to an award.[61]
Rather, the New York Convention allows for simultaneous proceedings in
different jurisdictions.[62]

Nonetheless, when a party pushes the envelope a little too far, a court
may grant an injunction against undermining an arbitration award. In the
ten-year *Karaha Bodas* case,[63] a U.S. federal district court enjoined the losing
party, Pertamina, from taking actions seeking to prevent enforcement of an
arbitral award. The arbitration, which had begun in 1998, had taken place
in Switzerland. By 2006, the matter seemed to be finally resolved, despite
numerous efforts by Pertamina to vacate the award or block its enforcement,
including more than one petition for certiorari in the U.S. Supreme Court.
One of the steps Pertamina had taken along the way, after the Swiss court
had refused to vacate the award, was to seek an annulment of the award
by an Indonesian court. Karaha Bodas Co. (KBC) asked a U.S. court to
enjoin this action. The U.S. court had denied the injunction request, and
had essentially ignored the resulting annulment in Indonesia.[64]

At the point when KBC was on the verge of finally collecting U.S. $260
million in the United States (it had previously collected some of the award in
Hong Kong), Pertamina brought an action in the Cayman Islands. It alleged
fraud and sought both damages and an injunction restraining KBC from
disposing of any sums received as a consequence of the fraud, including
any benefit from the arbitral award. Pertamina claimed that its action in
the Cayman Islands was not an action to set aside the arbitral award, but
rather a totally new fraud claim. Nonetheless, the U.S. court found that the
objective of the lawsuit was to nullify judgments in Texas and New York
allowing KBC to recover the award: "The main objective of Pertamina is to
have the Cayman Islands court reach out to the United States and frustrate
the consummation of the long and difficult litigation in the United States."[65]
The court not only enjoined Pertamina from seeking an order restricting
KBC's disposition of the funds received pursuant to the arbitral award, but
took the rather unusual step of also issuing a declaratory judgment. It ruled
that KBC had full rights to the funds, and that if Pertamina should obtain
an order from the Cayman Islands court or any other court, purporting
to interfere with KBC's right to dispose of the funds, KBC would have
no obligation to comply with any such order.[66] The court did not view

---

[61] *See* Karaha Bodas Co. v. Negara, 335 F. 3d 357 (5th Cir. 2003).
[62] Karaha Bodas Co. v. Negara, 465 F. Supp. 2d 283, 296 (2006), *aff'd in part, modified in part*, 500 F.3d 111 (2d Cir. 2007), *cert. denied*, 554 U.S. 929 (2008).
[63] *See id.*
[64] *See* Karaha Bodas Co. v. Negara, 335 F. 3d 357 (5th Cir. 2003).
[65] Karaha Bodas, 465 F. Supp. at 298–99, *aff'd in part, modified in part*, 500 F.3d 111 (2d Cir. 2007), *cert. denied*, 554 U.S. 929 (2008).
[66] *See id.* at 300–01.

Pertamina's action as protected under the New York Convention because it was not seeking to annul the award under the Convention's proceedings.[67] Rather, it was seeking to undermine a legitimate result in order to postpone its payment obligation.[68]

Thus, we see that although courts do not always grant anti-suit injunctions readily, and sometimes refuse even when a party believes there are good reasons to enjoin, the more egregious the behavior of the other party, the more likely that the court will issue an anti-suit injunction. Nonetheless, because a court's actions may simply be ignored by a foreign court, the success of the anti-suit injunction depends on the amount of coercive power a court can bring to bear over the party subject to its jurisdiction.

2. Anti-Suit Injunctions in Europe

In England, courts have had a robust record of granting anti-suit injunctions in cases of breach of an arbitration agreement.[69] However, their ability to continue to do so has been limited by the European Court of Justice (ECJ),[70] leaving uncertain the future of anti-suit injunctions in Europe in connection with arbitration. The question is whether the Brussels Regulation,[71] which does not permit anti-suit injunctions in litigated matters, should also prohibit such injunctions with respect to arbitration, even though the Brussels Regulation specifically excludes arbitration.[72] Currently, with respect to a litigated matter, a court of one Member State cannot enjoin or restrain parties over whom it has jurisdiction from bringing or continuing a second action arising out of the same facts in another Member State.[73] As to

---

[67] *See id.* at 296.

[68] The court noted that Pertamina's Finance Director told an Indonesian newspaper in December 2003 that the arbitration decision could no longer be disputed, but that "what Pertamina is doing now is actually only buying time." *Id.* at 298.

[69] *See, e.g.*, Welex AG v. Rosa Maritime Limited, [2003] 2 Lloyd's Rep. 509 (Eng.C.A.); Through Transport Mutual Insurance Association (Eurasia) Ltd. v. New India Assurance Co. Ltd. [2004]1 Lloyd's Rep. 206; *see also* Daniel Tan, *Anti-Suit Injunctions and the Vexing Problem of Comity*, 45 Va. J. Int'l L. 283, 331–32 (2005).

[70] *See* Allianz SpA v. West Tankers, Inc., Case C-185/07 [February 10, 2009].

[71] Council Regulation (EC) No. 44/2001 of December 22, 2000, on jurisdiction and the recognition and enforcement of judgments in civil and commercial matters, 2001 O.J. (L 12) 1 (January 1, 2001) (Brussels Regulation). The Brussels Regulation provides rules that govern courts and the recognition and enforcement of judgments in civil and commercial matters in European Union countries.

[72] Council Regulation (EC) No. 44/2001 of December 22, 2000, Article 1(2)(d). Article 1 provides in pertinent part: "2. This Regulation shall not apply to:

...

(d) arbitration"

[73] *See, e.g.*, Turner v. Grovit and Harada Ltd. and Changepoint S.A. (Turner), Case C-159/02 (E.C.R.) [2004], in which the European Court of Justice held that defendants could not be restrained even when they were acting in bad faith for the purpose of obstructing proceedings properly before the English Courts.

arbitration, despite the exclusion of arbitration from the Brussels Regulation, the ECJ in 2009 found in Allianz SpA v. West Tankers, Inc., that anti-suit injunctions intended to protect an arbitration agreement were incompatible with the Brussels Regulation.[74]

In *West Tankers*, The ECJ ruled that a Member State court could not restrain parties from commencing or maintaining a suit before a court of another Member State on the grounds that such action was contrary to an arbitration agreement.[75] *West Tankers* appeared to portend the end of anti-suit injunctions to ensure enforcement of arbitration agreements in situations involving two Member States. However, as will be discussed later, the ECJ decision may be limited by proposed amendments to the Brussels Regulation.

In *West Tankers*, a ship called the *Front Comor*, which was owned by West Tankers and chartered by Erg Petroli SpA (Erg), collided with a jetty in Syracuse, Italy, that was owned by Erg. In accordance with the charter party (the contract), Erg brought an arbitration in London against West Tankers for damages it incurred in excess of its insurance policy. Its insurers, Allianz SpA and Generali Assicurazioni Generali SpA, which had paid Erg under Erg's policy, then brought their subrogated claim against West Tankers in the Italian court, the Tribunale di Siracusa, to recover the amount they had paid to Erg.[76] In response, West Tankers went to court in England seeking a declaration that any dispute between itself and the insurers had to be settled in arbitration. West Tankers also asked the English court for an injunction restraining the insurers from bringing an action outside of arbitration and requiring them to terminate the court proceedings they had started before the Italian court.[77]

After the court granted the anti-suit injunction and the insurers appealed, the court certified the question to the House of Lords. The House of Lords referred to the ECJ the question of whether an anti-suit injunction restraining parties from beginning or continuing proceedings in another Member State would violate the Brussels Regulation when such proceedings were in breach of an arbitration agreement.[78] The ECJ answered that such an injunction was incompatible with the Brussels Regulation. The anti-suit injunction, even though directed at parties and not the Italian court, would strip the foreign court of the power to rule on its own jurisdiction under the Brussels Regulation.[79] The ECJ noted further that "such an anti-suit injunction also runs counter to the trust which the Member States accord to one another's

---

[74] Case C-185/07 2009 E.C.R., 2009 WL 303723.

[75] *See id.*, para. 34.

[76] *See id.*, paras. 9–12.

[77] West Tankers, [2005] EWHC (Comm.) 454, [2005] All E.R. (Comm.) 240, [1].

[78] West Tankers, Inc., v. Ras Riunione Adriatica di Sicurta SpA (the "Front Comor"), [2007] UKHL 4, [2007]1 Lloyd's Rep. 391, [8].

[79] *See id.*, para. 28.

legal systems and judicial institutions and on which the system of jurisdiction under Regulation No. 44/2001 [the Brussels Regulation] is based."[80]

The *West Tankers* decision was made during a period when various studies and proposals regarding the Brussels Regulation were being undertaken, with respect not only to arbitration but also to other issues.[81] The European Commission was subject to an obligation under Article 73 of the Regulation to present within five years after the 2001 entry into force of the Regulation, a report on its application and possible proposals for adaptations.[82] Rather belatedly, in 2009, the Commission presented a report[83] and a Green Paper[84] that took into account a number of studies and other reports, including a 2007 study known as the Heidelberg Report.[85] Although a discussion of these reports is beyond the scope of this chapter, it is worth noting that one proposal included by the Commission was a partial deletion of the arbitration exclusion of the Regulation, in order to bring all arbitration-related court proceedings and judgments within the scope of the Regulation. The arbitration community was not pleased with the proposals dealing with arbitration, and a number of groups submitted responsive

---

[80] *Id.*, para. 30. Thus, the Italian court proceedings continued. In November 2008, prior to the ECJ decision, the arbitral tribunal in London had issued an award declaring, *inter alia*, that West Tankers had no liability to the insurers. (*See* West Tankers, Inc., v. Allianz SpA & Generali Assicuarzzione Generali [2011] EWHC 829, para. 6.) Because West Tankers was concerned that the Italian court might grant a decision in favor of the insurers, who might then seek to have it enforced in England under the Brussels Regulation, it sought to have the English court enforce the arbitral award as a judgment. *See id.*, para. 10. An order to that effect was issued in November 2010, by Simon, J., and in April 2011, the High Court of England concluded that there was a proper jurisdictional basis for the order, and dismissed the insurer's application to set the order aside. *See id.*, paras. 1, 30–32.

[81] There were concerns about whether *exequatur* (the intermediate procedure for recognition and enforcement of a judgment in another Member State) should be abolished, whether the jurisdiction rules of the Regulation should be extended to disputes involving third-country defendants, how the effectiveness of choice of court agreements could be enhanced, how proceedings before the courts of Member States could be better coordinated, how access to justice for certain specific disputes could be improved, and how conditions under which provisional and protective measures circulate in the EU could be clarified. *See, e.g.*, Summary of the Proposed Action, in Proposal for a Regulation of the European Parliament and of the Council on jurisdiction and the recognition and enforcement of judgments in civil and commercial matters (Recast) [SEC(2010) 1547 final] [SEC(2010) 1548 final], page 5, available at http://ec.europa.eu/justice/policies/civil/docs/com_2010_748_en.pdf.

[82] Council Regulation (EC) No. 44/2001 of 22 Dec. 2000, Article 73.

[83] Report from the Commission to the European Parliament, the Council and the European Economic and Social Committee (COM (2099) 174 final).

[84] The Green Paper on the Review of Council Regulation (EC) no. 44/2001 (COM (2099) 175 final).

[85] Conducted by Professors Burkhard Hess, Thomas Pfeiffer, & Peter Schlosser and available at http://ec.europa.eu/justice_home/doc_centre/civil/studies/doc_civil_studies_en.htm.

comments.[86] For example, a Working Group of the International Bar Association commented, *inter alia*, that the arbitration exclusion should not be deleted.[87] In addition, the European Parliament passed a resolution opposing the deletion of the arbitration exclusion.[88]

After considering numerous comments and reports, as well as the Parliamentary Resolution, the European Commission changed course with regard to the arbitration exclusion. In its proposal for the reform of the Brussels Regulation issued in December 2010,[89] the Commission kept the exclusion of arbitration in the Regulation.[90] However, it included a rule that once proceedings had begun in the arbitral tribunal or in a court in the Member State that was the seat of the arbitration, then a court in another Member State would be required to stay proceedings if a challenge based on an existing arbitration agreement was brought.[91] This lis pendens rule appears to create a kind of anti-suit injunction, without calling it an anti-suit injunction. The Commission further stated, "This modification will enhance the effectiveness of arbitration agreements in Europe, prevent parallel court and arbitration proceedings, and eliminate the incentive for abusive litigation tactics."[92]

---

[86] Some of the concerns included a belief that the proposals would cause a substantial interference with obligations arising under the New York Convention of 1958 and the European Convention of 1961, that they would interfere with the doctrine of competence-competence, and that they would produce a regionalization of the law of arbitration in the European Union that would not serve well either the Member States or the broader international community. *See, e.g., AIA's Response to the Commission's Green Paper on the Brussels I Regulation Reform*, in AIA newsletter, In Touch (August 2009), pp. 1–3.

[87] *See* Report of International Bar Association Arbitration Committee Working Group, available at http://www.ibanet.org/LPD/Dispute_Resolution_Section/Arbitration/Default.aspx.

[88] September 7, 2010, available at http://www.europarl.europa.eu/sides/getDoc.do?pubRef=-//EP//TEXT+TA+P7-TA-2010-0304+0+DOC+XML+V0//EN&language=EN.

[89] Proposal for a Regulation of the European Parliament and of the Council on jurisdiction and the recognition and enforcement of judgments in civil and commercial matters. COM (2010) 748 final – 2010/0383 (COD). Available at http://ec.europa.eu/justice/policies/civil/docs/com_2010_748_en.pdf.

[90] *See id.*, Initial Provisions ("*Whereas*"), para. 11.

[91] *See id.*, Article 29(4), which provides as follows: "Where the agreed or designated seat of an arbitration is in a Member State, the courts of another Member State whose jurisdiction is contested on the basis of an arbitration agreement shall stay proceedings once the courts of the Member State where the seat of the arbitration is located or the arbitral tribunal have been seized of proceedings to determine, as their main object or as an incidental question, the existence, validity or effects of that arbitration agreement." The Proposal also defines "seat" as follows: "The seat of the arbitration should refer to the seat selected by the parties or the seat designated by an arbitral tribunal, by an arbitral institution or by any other authority directly or indirectly chosen by the parties." *See id.*, Initial Provisions, paragraph 20.

[92] *Id.*, Explanatory Memorandum, at 9.

It appears that the Commission proposal would substantially limit the effect of the *West Tankers* decision. If the proposal had been the law at the time of the *West Tankers* decision, the Italian court would have been required to stay the proceedings brought by the insurers, and the English decision on the validity of the arbitration agreement would have been binding as to the Italian proceedings.[93] It may be two or three years before the amendments to the Brussels Regulation are finalized. If the provisions concerning arbitration are adopted in the form proposed, however, it would be a favorable development for arbitration.

C. INTERIM MEASURES

Not so very long ago, interim relief – that is, relief granted before the final award, generally to ensure that once the award is rendered, relief would still be possible – was available only through the courts. Moreover, in some jurisdictions, once a party sought such relief from the courts, particularly if the relief was sought on an urgent basis before the tribunal was constituted, the party would be held to have waived its right to arbitrate. In other jurisdictions, it was believed that once a party agreed to arbitrate, it had no right to seek court-ordered provisional relief in support of arbitration.[94] Today, however, it is generally accepted that parties can obtain relief from a court when needed, without losing the right to arbitrate.[95]

1. Kinds of Interim Measures

The kinds of interim measures that a party to an arbitration agreement generally would seek are measures that would prevent the other side, for example, from hiding or removing assets, from using licensed intellectual property in a way that would devalue the licensor's interest, or from dispersing or destroying evidence that the party needed to prove its case. The term "interim measure" has traditionally been used without a very precise definition, but UNCITRAL has provided one in its amended Model Law on International Commercial Arbitration. Chapter IV A, Article 17, deals

---

[93] *See* Martin Illmer, *Brussels I and Arbitration Revisited*, RabelsZ Bd. 75 (2011), p. 664. *See also* Luca G. Radicati di Brozolo, *Arbitration and the Draft Revised Brussels I Regulation: Seeds of Home Country Control and of Harmonization?*, J. Private Int'l. Law, Issue 4 (2011).

[94] McCreary Tire & Rubber Co. v. CEAT, SpA, 501 F.2d. 1032 (3d Cir. 1974), is often cited for that proposition.

[95] A number of arbitration laws and rules specifically provide for parties to be able to obtain court relief when needed without waiving the agreement to arbitrate. *See, e.g.*, Japan Arbitration Law of 2003, art. 15; German Arbitration Act of 1998, § 1033; UNCITRAL Rules art. 26(9); ICDR Rules, art. 21(3), ICC Rules, art. 28(2).

with interim measures and preliminary orders. The UNCITRAL definition of interim measures is as follows:

> An interim measure is any temporary measure, whether in the form of an award or in another form, by which, at any time prior to the issuance of the award by which the dispute is finally decided, the arbitral tribunal orders a party to:
>
> (a) Maintain or restore the status quo pending determination of the dispute;
> (b) Take action that would prevent, or refrain from taking action that is likely to cause current or imminent harm or prejudice to the arbitral process itself;
> (c) Provide a means of preserving assets out of which a subsequent award may be satisfied; or
> (d) Preserve evidence that may be relevant and material to the resolution of the dispute.[96]

By this definition, interim measures, also sometimes referred to as conservatory measures, are basically those measures intended to protect the ability of a party to obtain a final award. Note that paragraph (b) in this definition appears to include anti-suit injunctions. The UNCITRAL Working Group stated in its Report that there were reservations expressed about including this paragraph "given that such injunctions were unknown or unfamiliar in many legal systems and that there was no uniformity in practice relating thereto. As well, it was said that anti-suit injunctions did not always have the provisional nature of interim measures."[97] Nonetheless, the Working Group decided to include the paragraph, and UNCITRAL adopted it. This provision would permit a party to bypass domestic anti-suit injunction law and simply get an anti-suit injunction from the arbitral tribunal. It could then be enforceable in another country under sections 17 H and I of the Model Law, which will be discussed below in Section C(4). It remains to be seen whether Model Law countries that decide to amend their law to adopt Article 17 will include this particular paragraph.

In trying to add clarity to the rather murky area of interim and conservatory measures, UNCITRAL also defines "preliminary order." A preliminary order is essentially the same as an interim measure with one major exception: it is obtained *ex parte* – that is, the tribunal has heard from only one of the

---

[96] UNCITRAL Model Law, art. 17(2) (2006), available at UNCITRAL.org/uncitral/en/uncitral_texts/arbitration.html. The 2006 amendments to the UNCITRAL Model Law are included in this book in Appendix C.

[97] Report of the Working Group on Arbitration and Conciliation on the Work of Its Forty-fourth session (New York, January 23–26, 2006), at 6, para. 18. A/CN.9/592.

parties. This would be done only when the party seeking the relief believes that if the other party knows in advance that the measure will be sought, it will do something to thwart the protection to be granted (for example, hide assets, distribute source code, or destroy evidence). A preliminary order expires after twenty days; within that time, at the earliest possible moment, the tribunal must hear from the other party.[98] After that party has been given notice and an opportunity to present its case, the tribunal may issue an interim measure that either adopts or modifies the preliminary order, or it can simply let the order expire.[99] Unlike a regular interim measure, which can be in the form of an award, and therefore may be enforceable by a court, a preliminary order is binding on the parties, but is not an award and cannot be enforced by a court.[100]

The Model Law has taken a big step toward harmonizing an approach to interim measures. However, even if its proposed amendments regarding interim measures are adopted by countries that currently have in place some version of the Model Law,[101] these amendments may not be adopted uniformly. Additionally, the many countries whose arbitration laws are not based on the Model Law will continue to take diverse approaches to interim measures. Nonetheless, Article 17 of the Model Law can serve as a useful guideline that may encourage courts and tribunals to take a more consistent approach to interim measures.

2. Tribunal or Court – Where to Go for Interim Relief?

Today, most arbitration laws and rules assume that the courts and the arbitral tribunal have concurrent jurisdiction to grant interim relief. There are, however, variations among jurisdictions as to how and when each decision maker should be involved. In a few jurisdictions, such as Argentina and Italy, arbitrators do not have the power to issue interim decisions.[102] In others, such as England, the arbitrator, for the most part, is expected to be much more active than the courts with respect to interim measures. Under the English Arbitration Act of 1996, certain powers are granted to the arbitrator, as long as the parties have not agreed otherwise.[103] Other powers, including the power to order provisional relief with respect to money or

---

[98] See UNCITRAL Model Law, art. 17C.

[99] See id. para. 4.

[100] See id. para. 5.

[101] At least 70 countries, states, administrative regions, and territories, including seven states within the United States – California, Connecticut, Florida, Illinois, Louisiana, Oregon, and Texas – have adopted a version of the Model Law. See supra Chapter 1, note 11. See also www.UNCITRAL.org.

[102] Argentine Code of Civil Procedure, art. 753; Italian Code of Civil Procedure, art. 818.

[103] See English Arbitration Act of 1996, § 38. These powers include the power to order security for costs, to inspect and preserve property, and to preserve other evidence.

property, are permitted only if the parties are in agreement.[104] Agreement occurs, however, when parties have chosen arbitration rules that grant the arbitrators such power. In that instance, most interim decisions will be made by the arbitrator. Parties are not expected to turn to the courts for assistance unless they have the permission of the tribunal or the permission of all other parties, or the matter is one of urgency.[105]

In most jurisdictions, if the tribunal has not yet been constituted, parties may choose to seek provisional measures from a court to protect against some immediate harm. In such a case, if urgent relief is needed, it may be attainable only through the local court. Once the tribunal has been constituted, however, then the rules may differ somewhat. For example, under some rules, once the tribunal is in place, the parties are supposed to apply to a court only "in appropriate circumstances,"[106] or, according to other rules, "in exceptional cases."[107]

Taking account of the sometimes urgent need to grant relief, a number of arbitral institutions have provided for the appointment of emergency arbitrators.[108] This permits prompt appointment of an arbitrator who has the power to order or award any interim or conservancy measure deemed necessary.[109] The procedure is applicable unless parties have opted out of it. As more arbitral institutions follow suit in providing this level of emergency relief, there will be less need for parties to seek court assistance at a point in time before the tribunal has been constituted.[110]

Although at present, some rules make a distinction between seeking court relief before or after the tribunal has been appointed, under other laws and rules there is full concurrent jurisdiction, even after the constitution of the tribunal. In those jurisdictions, parties may seek interim relief from either the tribunal or the court at any point during the proceedings, unless the parties themselves have provided otherwise. The Rules of Arbitration of the German Institution of Arbitration (DIS), for example, provide: "It is not incompatible with an arbitration agreement for a party to request an interim measure of protection in respect of the subject-matter of the dispute from a court before or during arbitral proceedings."[111]

---

[104] *See id.* § 39.

[105] *See id.* §§ 42–44.

[106] ICC Rules, art. 28(2).

[107] LCIA Rules, art. 25.3.

[108] *See* discussion *supra* Chapter 3, Section B(2).

[109] *See id.*

[110] The LCIA provides an expedited procedure for constituting the tribunal, in cases of "exceptional urgency." LCIA Arbitration Rules, art. 9.

[111] German Institution of Arbitration, Arbitration Rules, § 20.2. This is consistent with German law, which provides as follows: "It is not incompatible with an arbitration agreement for a court to grant, before or during arbitral proceedings, an interim

In the United States, because the Federal Arbitration Act (FAA) does not deal with interim measures, other than the court's ability to stay an action or to compel arbitration,[112] it is less clear when courts will grant interim measures. The ICDR Rules of the American Arbitration Association state that if a party seeks interim relief from a court, that request is not incompatible with arbitration, and does not constitute a waiver of the right to arbitrate.[113] Some cases in the United States suggest, however, that a court will not grant interim relief if the relief sought is also available through a tribunal. In Simula, Inc., v. Autoliv, Inc.,[114] for example, the Ninth Circuit held that a district court had properly denied Simula's request for a preliminary injunction because provisional relief was available from the Swiss Arbitral Tribunal where the arbitration would take place under the ICC Rules of Arbitration.[115] In an earlier case in the Third Circuit, McCreary Tire & Rubber v. CEAT, SpA,[116] the court discharged a foreign attachment because it had been obtained in a court proceeding, which the court viewed as an impermissible bypass of the agreement to settle the dispute by arbitration.[117]

McCreary has been much criticized, however; more recent decisions suggest that in other circuits in the United States, particularly in the Second Circuit, courts have the authority to grant injunctions and provisional remedies in the context of pending arbitrations.[118] Further, the Second Circuit has made clear that such authority exists even if the parties could also seek relief directly from the tribunal.[119] Thus, in the United States, parties need to

---

measure of protection relating to the subject matter of the arbitration upon request of a party." German Code of Civil Procedure, art. 1033. *See also* ICC Rules, art. 28(2), which provides that "the application of a party to a judicial authority for [interim] measures or for the implementation of any such measure ordered by an arbitral tribunal shall not be deemed to be an infringement or waiver of the arbitration agreement and shall not affect the relevant powers reserved to the arbitral tribunal."

[112] 9 U.S.C. §§ 3, 4. The FAA also provides subpoena power for a tribunal, but this does not fit under some definitions of interim measures.

[113] ICDR Rules, art. 21(3).

[114] 175 F.3d 716 (1999).

[115] *See id.* at 725.

[116] 501 F.2d 1032 (1974).

[117] *See id.* at 1038.

[118] Bahrain Telecommunications Co. v. Discoverytel, Inc., 476 F. Supp. 2d 176, 180, 182 (D. Ct. 2007) ("A prejudgment remedy does not interfere with the arbitral process but merely ensures that there will be assets available to satisfy any judgment the arbitrators themselves may render.").

[119] *See id.* at 180 ("[T]he Second Circuit has made it clear in a series of decisions that the Court has both the power and duty to entertain a motion for preliminary injunction pending the results in [an] arbitration. And this is true even though, as is the case here, the parties are entitled under the rules of the arbitral tribunal they have chosen to seek *pendente lite* relief directly from the arbitrator."). *Citations omitted.*

know how a particular circuit of the federal court will respond to a request for interim relief.

There are practical reasons why a party might prefer to go to the court in the first instance, even if the tribunal has already been constituted. If the interim relief sought would ultimately require court assistance to be effectuated, such as attachment of a bank account, then going to court immediately could save time. Thus, particularly if the relief is needed urgently, requesting the interim measure from the court may be the most efficient and effective way to proceed.

Moreover, arbitral tribunals tend to be somewhat reluctant to grant interim measures. They must apply appropriate standards before granting relief, and one of the standards usually applied is a determination whether the requesting party has a reasonable possibility of prevailing on the merits. Tribunals hesitate to make this preliminary decision, because they fear this may cause some prejudice on their part with respect to the final determination of the merits. Courts, on the other hand, are less concerned about making a preliminary decision about the merits of the case because the merits will ultimately be determined by the arbitral tribunal. Therefore, courts may be less reluctant to grant the requested relief.

A downside to seeking relief from the court is that valued confidentiality may be lost. Frequently, detailed factual information will be needed in support of a request, which may include information that one or both parties would prefer to remain confidential. It may be feasible in some courts to seal the records and close the hearings. However, even if this is possible, a court might require a very strong showing of need before it would agree to take steps to keep the information confidential.

Although there are valid reasons for seeking relief through a court rather than a tribunal, the increasing attention focused on providing arbitrators with the power to grant interim measures suggests a trend in international arbitration to keep as much decision making as possible under the aegis of the arbitral tribunal.

3. Basis for Interim Measures

In addition to defining interim measures and preliminary orders, Article 17 of the amended UNCITRAL Model Law also sets forth a series of conditions that must be satisfied before the measure will be granted. The party requesting the interim measure must demonstrate to the tribunal that (1) if the relief is not granted, harm will result that is not adequately remedied by money damages, and such harm is greater than any harm that might occur to the other party if the measure is granted, and (2) the requesting party has a reasonable possibility of succeeding on the merits of the claim. In addition, the tribunal may require a requesting party to provide appropriate security when it is seeking an interim measure, and *must* require security when the party seeks a preliminary order, unless the tribunal determines that it would be inappropriate.[120] Moreover, the party requesting a preliminary order must disclose all pertinent circumstances.[121] Not only is this a requirement, but it also makes good practical sense. If a party presents a very one-sided picture of the facts at an *ex parte* hearing, the untold facts will come out at the later hearing with the other party. If the whole story is, in fact, quite different from the one initially presented, the tribunal most likely will not allow the relief granted in the preliminary order to continue, will award costs against the requesting party, and will view the requesting party as lacking credibility.

4. Enforcement of Interim Measures

If an arbitral tribunal grants an interim measure, and court enforcement is needed, normally the local court at the seat of the arbitration will provide for enforcement. But what if the interim measure needs to be enforced in a different jurisdiction? It is quite likely that the jurisdiction where enforcement will be sought will not be the seat of the arbitration, because parties generally choose as the seat a place that is not the home country of either party. Thus, if the purpose of the interim measure is to attach a bank account, or prohibit sale of property, the bank account and the property are likely not to be in the same country as the arbitration, and therefore will need to be enforced in the country where they are located. Few laws deal with this, so the Model Law, by including this matter in its amended Article 17, provides a helpful step toward improving the possibility that interim measures will be enforced by foreign courts. The Model Law provides that "[a]n interim measure issued by an arbitral tribunal shall be recognized as binding and . . . enforced upon application to the competent court, irrespective of the country in which it was issued, subject to the provisions of Article 17 I."[122] Being made subject to Article 17 I means that the measure must be enforced, unless there are reasonable grounds for its nonenforcement, as set forth in Article 36. Those grounds for nonenforcement are essentially the same grounds that are set forth in the New York Convention. Thus, as discussed previously, any interim measure issued by an arbitral tribunal would be enforceable in a Model Law country, that had adopted Article 17 I, without the need to consider the applicability of the New York Convention.

The Model Law is creating a framework for Model Law countries to be able to enforce interim measures granted by arbitral tribunals in other

---

[120] UNCITRAL Model Law, art. 17 E (2006).
[121] UNCITRAL Model Law, art. 17 F (2006).
[122] UNCITRAL Model Law, art. 17 H.

countries, independently of the New York Convention. The Convention was not intended by its drafters to deal with interim measures, but rather with the enforcement of final awards. Occasionally, an interim measure has been enforced under the Convention when the relief granted by the tribunal was termed a partial award,[123] or the measure was determined by a court to be a final and enforceable award.[124] The Model Law, however, avoids any need to establish whether the interim measure is an order or a final award. If the measure fits the Model Law definition of "interim measure," then it is binding, and a court in a country that has adopted this provision of the Model Law should enforce it. If Article 17 is adopted in the countries where the Model Law is in effect, it should significantly facilitate the enforcement of interim measures issued by an arbitral tribunal. Moreover, wide adoption could encourage non–Model Law countries either to adopt similar legislation, or to refer to the Model Law provisions as guidelines.

D. COURT ASSISTANCE IN OBTAINING EVIDENCE

1. Procedural Orders

Although the rather vague definition of "interim measure" has sometimes been used to cover virtually any kind of order issued by a tribunal that does not resolve the entire case, in this chapter the orders of a tribunal that do not meet the definition of interim measure or preliminary order provided in Article 17 of the UNCITRAL Model Law will be referred to as procedural orders. Thus, a distinction is made here between an order for "preservation of evidence" and one for "taking of evidence." "Preservation of evidence" involves an interim measure under the UNCITRAL Model Law, which might consist, for example, of an order to preserve goods that were the subject matter of the dispute. On the other hand, "taking of evidence" involves a procedural order about evidence needed for the arbitration hearings.

Although the distinction may not always hold, generally, a procedural order is not a conservatory measure, or one that seeks to maintain the status quo. Rather, it is an order whose purpose is to move the arbitration forward. Procedural orders can be issued on many different topics, and basically constitute the various decisions of the tribunal concerning the management of the arbitration process. Such orders may concern scheduling or taking evidence or may delineate various obligations of the parties. Procedural orders are not generally considered to be final, are subject to change by

---

[123] *See, e.g.*, Four Seasons v. Consorcio Barr, *supra* notes 54–57 and accompanying text.
[124] *See* Yasuda Fire & Marine Ins. Co. v. Continental Cas., 37 F.3d 345 (7th Cir. 1994).

the tribunal, and may or may not be subject to enforcement by a court. Nonetheless, even when a tribunal has denominated its ruling as an "order," a court may enforce it under the New York Convention if the court is persuaded that the ruling is in fact a final award.[125]

Seeking a procedural order from a tribunal concerning the taking of evidence is, in some ways, a last resort. From a practical standpoint, the first step a party should take in trying to obtain documents would be to simply ask the other party for the information. If the other party does not cooperate, then a party could confer with both the other party and the tribunal, and the tribunal could suggest to the other party that it should produce the information. If this does not work, then a party may be able to persuade a tribunal to order the opposing party to produce documents or to produce witnesses under its control. If the tribunal agrees, the party subject to the order has a strong incentive to comply with the order, because arbitrators can draw adverse inferences from any noncompliance. Moreover, a party generally does not want a tribunal to think that it has reason to hide relevant information. Thus, compliance is usually forthcoming, and resort to the court to enforce such an order may not occur frequently. On the other hand, court assistance is more likely to be needed when documents and witnesses are under the control of a third party, that is, a party that is not subject to the arbitration agreement.

2. National Laws Concerning Court Assistance

Many national laws specifically provide for court assistance in obtaining evidence. The Model Law, for example, in Article 27, provides that "[t]he arbitral tribunal or a party with the approval of the arbitral tribunal may request from a competent court of this State assistance in taking evidence. The court may execute the request within its competence and according to its rules on taking evidence."[126] Although it is clear the court can provide assistance within its own jurisdiction ("within its competence"), it is less clear whether it can provide assistance for requests for obtaining evidence from a foreign jurisdiction. A narrow reading of the language could view court assistance as only available in the jurisdiction where the request is made.

German[127] and Swiss law,[128] on the other hand, though not specifically referring to obtaining evidence outside the jurisdiction, do not include

---

[125] See Publicis Communication v. True North Communications, Inc., 206 F. 3d 725, 728 (7th Cir. 2000) ("The content of a decision – not its nomenclature – determines finality.").
[126] UNCITRAL Model Law, art. 27.
[127] See German Code of Civil Procedure, § 1050.
[128] See Swiss Private International Law Act, art. 184(2).

language that would tend to limit the court's reach. Thus, it appears possible in those countries that a court may assist with requests from a tribunal or a party regarding evidence or witnesses outside the court's jurisdiction. This might be done, for example, through letters rogatory,[129] an international convention,[130] or, if exclusively within the EU, pursuant to an EU Regulation.[131]

English courts have the power under the English Arbitration Act to assist an arbitral tribunal or parties in securing attendance of a witness to give testimony or produce documents, by means of the same court procedures that could be used in litigation.[132] Thus, English courts would presumably be able to obtain evidence in support of arbitration from foreign third parties, through the EU Regulation on Cooperation Between the Courts of the Member States in the Taking of Evidence in Civil or Commercial Matters.[133] Moreover, the courts' powers apply not only to arbitrations held within England, Wales, and Northern Ireland, but also to arbitrations whose seat is in a foreign country.[134] The court is not required to provide such assistance to foreign tribunals, however, if the location of the arbitration tribunal makes it inappropriate to do so, presumably, if the assistance sought should more appropriately be provided in a different jurisdiction.[135]

3. Summons Issued by U.S. Arbitrators

In the United States, the Federal Arbitration Act gives arbitrators the ability to issue a summons requiring any person to appear as a witness and bring any documents deemed material as evidence in the case.[136] The summons is to be served in the same manner as a subpoena to appear and testify in court, and the witness can be compelled or punished for contempt in the same manner as provided in federal court.[137]

---

[129] A Letter Rogatory is a court's formal request to a foreign court for some kind of judicial assistance, such as taking of evidence or service of process.

[130] The 1970 Hague Convention on the Taking of Evidence Abroad in Civil or Commercial Matters formalized procedures for taking of evidence. There are at least 54 contracting States. *See* the website of the Hague Conference on Private International Law, http://www.hcch.net.

[131] Council Regulation (EC) No. 1206/2001 of 28 May 2001 on Cooperation Between the Courts of the Member States in the Taking of Evidence in Civil or Commercial Matters superseded the Hague Convention for matters exclusively among member states of the European Union. 2001 O.J. (L 174) 1 (June 27, 2001).

[132] *See* English Arbitration Act of 1996, §§ 43 and 44.

[133] *See supra* note 131.

[134] *See* English Arbitration Act § 2(3).

[135] *See id.*

[136] 9 U.S.C. § 7.

[137] *See id.*

U.S. FEDERAL ARBITRATION ACT – SECTION 7

The arbitrators selected either as prescribed in this title or otherwise, or a majority of them, may summon in writing any person to attend before them or any of them as a witness and in a proper case to bring with him or them any book, record, document or paper which may be deemed material as evidence in the case. . . . Said summons shall issue in the name of the arbitrator or arbitrators, or a majority of them, and shall be signed by the arbitrators, or a majority of them, and shall be directed to the said person and shall be served in the same manner as subpoenas to appear and testify before the court; if any person or persons so summoned to testify shall refuse or neglect to obey said summons, upon petition the United States district court for the district in which such arbitrators, or a majority of them, are sitting may compel the attendance of such person or persons before said arbitrator or arbitrators, or punish said person or persons for contempt in the same manner provided by law for securing the attendance of witnesses or their punishment for neglect or refusal to attend in the courts of the United States.[138]

There are two areas of controversy concerning this provision. First, does the language of the provision mean that a nonparty can be summoned and required to produce documents only *at* the final hearing, or can the documents be produced for inspection prior to the final hearing? There is a split in the circuits on this question. This means that the law will be different in different federal circuits until the U.S. Supreme Court resolves the issue.

Although the language of Section 7 indicates that the arbitrators may summon any person to appear before them, the Second Circuit has held that this does not mean only at the final hearing on the merits. Rather, arbitrators can hold a hearing prior to the main hearing in order to receive this evidence.[139] However, this ruling does not apply to a pretrial inspection of documents or deposition of a witness with no arbitrators present.[140] In 2008, the Second Circuit clarified its position by specifically holding that Section 7 of the FAA does not authorize arbitrators to compel non-parties to produce pre-hearing documents other than at a hearing before the arbitrators.[141] The Sixth and Eighth Circuits have ruled that the arbitrator's powers include the power to compel production of documents either before

---

[138] *See id.*
[139] Stolt-Nielsen, S.A., v. Celanese, 430 F.3d 567, 577–79 (2005).
[140] *See id.* at 579.
[141] Life Receivables Trust v. Syndicate 102 at Lloyd's of London, 549 F.3d 210 (2008).

or at the hearing.[142] The Third Circuit, on the other hand, has held that Article 7 of the FAA requires a nonparty to produce documents only at a hearing on the merits, and not before.[143] In addition, the Fourth Circuit held that an arbitrator can summon a third party for prehearing discovery only if there is a showing of "special hardship."[144] In the Third and Fourth Circuits, therefore, there would be little, if any, ability to obtain documents or witness testimony prior to the hearing on the merits.

The second controversy concerns the geographic limitation on enforcement of an arbitral summons. Although an arbitrator has the authority to issue a summons to "any person," the right to enforce that summons is limited to the way a subpoena can be enforced in federal court. Under the Federal Rules of Civil Procedure, a subpoena can be served only within the jurisdiction where the request is made, or, if outside the district, then within one hundred miles of the place of the hearing or place of production of documents or deposition.[145] The Federal Arbitration Act does not provide for nationwide service, according to the Second Circuit.[146] The Second Circuit has also held that the FAA Section 7 permits subpoenas to be issued and enforced only in the district where the arbitrators are sitting.[147] These kinds of restrictions suggest that courts may provide little support in obtaining evidence that is not within the district where the arbitration is being held.

The geographic restrictions on enforcement can present a significant problem if the documents or witnesses needed are not in the district where the arbitrators are sitting. In litigation, the problem is resolved because an attorney admitted to practice in District A, where the case is being tried, is empowered to issue a subpoena in District B, where the production of documents or testimony will take place.[148] The courts in District B will then enforce the subpoena. Under Section 7 of the FAA, however, the power to

---

[142] *See* American Fed'n of Television and Radio Artists, AFL-CIO v. WJBK-TV, 164 F.3d 1004, 1009 (6th Cir. 1999) (Arbitrators have implicit authority to compel production of documents for inspection prior to a hearing); Security Life Ins. Co. of America and Duncanson–Holt, Inc., 228 F. 3d 865 (8th Cir. 2000).

[143] *See* Hay Group, Inc., v. EBS Acquisition Corp., 360 F.3d 404 (3rd Cir. 2004).

[144] *See* Comsat Corp. v. National Science Foundation, 190 F.3d 269 (1999).

[145] Dynegy Midstream Servs., LP, v. Trammochem, 451 F.3d 89 (2006). Subpoenas by arbitrators, according to the FAA, must be served in the same manner as in federal court. This brings into play Federal Rule of Civil Procedure 45(b)(2), which permits a subpoena to be served "within the district of the court by which it is issued, or at any place without the district that is within 100 miles of the place . . . [of the hearing]."

[146] *See* Dynegy, 451 F.3d at 95–96. Nonetheless, Fed. R. Civ. Pro. 45 (b)(2) provides that "[w]hen a statute of the United States provides therefor," the court may authorize service at any other place. Some statutes that authorize broader service of process include the Commerce and Trade Act, 15 U.S.C. § 23, and the Veterans' Benefits Act, 38 U.S.C. § 1984(c).

[147] Dynegy, 451 F.3d at 95.

[148] Fed. R. Civ. Proc. 45 (a)(3)(B).

issue subpoenas is provided only to arbitrators. Thus, even though there are no territorial restrictions in the FAA on arbitral discretion to serve subpoenas – "any person" can be served – the courts have no authority, according to the Second Circuit, to enforce an arbitral subpoena for documents and witnesses located outside the district where the arbitrators are sitting.[149]

A few courts have taken a more creative and commonsense approach to resolving this problem than has the Second Circuit. In Amgen, Inc., v. Kidney Center of Delaware County Ltd. (Amgen)[150] a federal district court determined that subpoenas in support of arbitration should be treated in the same way as subpoenas in support of litigation. The normal way of collecting evidence in federal court litigation includes having an attorney issue a subpoena that could be enforced in the jurisdiction where the documents or witnesses were located.[151] Therefore, according to the court, the attorney for the party in an arbitration seeking this information could also issue a subpoena enforceable in the foreign jurisdiction. It seems logical that Congress, in making arbitral subpoenas enforceable in the same way as federal court subpoenas, did not intend to artificially limit the scope of the arbitral subpoena. Nonetheless, the Second Circuit specifically disagreed with the decision in *Amgen* on the grounds that the FAA did not give subpoena power to attorneys in arbitration, but only to arbitrators.[152]

A district court in Minnesota followed the decision in *Amgen*, and ordered the petitioner's attorney to issue a subpoena under the case name in Minnesota, to be enforced by the district court in California.[153] On appeal, the Eighth Circuit did not decide whether this procedure was proper because the party had voluntarily complied with the subpoena.[154] Therefore, the court dismissed as moot the portion of the appeal dealing with witness testimony.[155] As for the documents, the court held that an order for production of documents did not require compliance with the territorial limit under Rule 45, because increased distance did not cause the same burden for producing documents as for producing witnesses.[156] Therefore, the documents, even though outside the territorial limit, would have to be produced.[157]

---

[149] *See* Dynegy, 451 F.3d at 95.

[150] 879 F. Supp. 878 (N.D. Ill. 1995), remanded with instructions, 95 F.3d 562 (7th Cir. 1996), dismissed for lack of subject-matter jurisdiction, 1996 U.S. App. LEXIS 28250 (7th Cir. 1996).

[151] Fed. Rule Civ. Proc. 45 (a)(3)(B).

[152] Dynegy, 451 F.3d at 96.

[153] Security Life Ins. Co. of America v. Duncanson & Holt, Inc., 1999 U.S. Dist. LEXIS 23385 (1999).

[154] Security Life Ins. Co. of America v. Duncanson & Holt, Inc., 228 F.3d 865, 869 (2000).

[155] *See id.*

[156] *See id.* at 872 ("[T]he burden of producing documents need not increase appreciably with an increase in the distance those documents must travel.").

[157] *See id.*

Because these kinds of subpoenas are relatively rare in arbitration, it may be a while before a clear rule emerges about service outside the district where the arbitrators are seated. A logical result would be to permit service to the same extent that it is permitted in federal litigation, including subpoenas issued by attorneys. Although a tribunal does not often seek court enforcement of an order for taking evidence, once a tribunal has determined that the evidence is material, and a party or a nonparty has refused to produce it, it makes sense for the court to help the tribunal obtain it.

4. Tribunal in the United States Seeking Evidence Outside the United States

What about obtaining evidence from a jurisdiction outside of the United States? If a tribunal seated in the United States thought that evidence was needed from a third party in Spain, for example, could it obtain court assistance to compel production of this evidence? Under 28 U.S.C. § 1783, in a litigated matter, a subpoena may be served abroad on a U.S. national (citizen) or resident, but not on a nonresident alien.[158] It is not clear, however, whether this provision would apply to an arbitral subpoena. The same issues that arise with respect to the enforcement of an arbitral subpoena outside the federal district in which the arbitrators are seated would appear to be pertinent here.

Is there a way to obtain evidence abroad from a nonresident alien – that is, from someone who is not a citizen or a resident of the United States? Although it would seem logical that a court could make a request pursuant to the Hague Evidence Convention[159] in support of an arbitral tribunal's request, there is little evidence to suggest that this is done. Some courts might resist the use of this Convention because it refers to requests for evidence for use in "judicial proceedings."[160] Courts may not readily consider arbitrations to be "judicial proceedings." There may also be a reluctance on the part of some courts to help with broad discovery in arbitration, because they believe one of the reasons parties arbitrate is to limit the discovery process. Moreover, FAA § 7 restrictions on the geographic reach of an arbitral

---

[158] The court must also find that particular testimony or the production of the documents is necessary in the interest of justice, and that it is not possible to obtain this testimony in admissible form without the personal appearance of the witness or to obtain the production of the document or other thing in any other manner. This tends to restrict the use of 28 U.S.C. § 1783.

[159] 23 U.S.T. 2555, 847 U.N.T.S. 1971. *See* Jack J. Coe, INTERNATIONAL COMMERCIAL ARBITRATION: AMERICAN PRINCIPLES AND PRACTICE IN A GLOBAL CONTEXT, 194 (1997) ("[I]t does seem plausible that letters of request sent by courts of the situs of arbitration acting at the request of the tribunal should be honored.").

[160] *See* Hague Evidence Convention, *supra* note 159, art. 1.

subpoena may also be viewed as restricting the extraterritorial service of subpoenas on persons located outside the United States.[161]

5. Court Assistance in the United States to Foreign Tribunals

There is also a question about how much help a U.S. court will provide to a foreign arbitral tribunal or a foreign party that seeks pertinent discovery within the United States. The relevant statute, 28 U.S.C. § 1782, provides a federal district court with the discretion to order a person in its district to give testimony or produce documents, "for use in a proceeding in a foreign or international tribunal."[162] There is controversy, however, about whether "a foreign or international tribunal" includes an arbitral tribunal. Two circuit cases have said no.[163] However, a more recent Supreme Court decision, Intel Corp. v. Advanced Micro Devices, Inc.,[164] which did not decide this issue, nonetheless may be read as suggesting that 28 U.S.C. § 1782 could cover arbitral tribunals.

In the *Intel* case, a U.S. company, Advanced Micro Devices (AMD), filed an antitrust complaint against another U.S. company (Intel) before the Directorate-General for Competition of the Commission of the European Communities (EU Commission). AMD then applied to the federal district court in Northern California under 28 U.S.C. § 1782 for an order requiring Intel to produce certain documents. The U.S. Supreme Court ultimately held that the statute permitted, but did not require, a federal court to provide judicial assistance in this situation. One of the questions resolved was whether the EU Commission was a tribunal, because § 1782 permits the discovery only "for use in a proceeding in a foreign or international tribunal."[165] The Court found that because the EU Commission proceeding leads to a final action that is reviewable in court, it is a tribunal within the meaning of the statute. The Court further noted that when § 1782 was amended, the words "for use in any judicial proceeding," were replaced by the words "for use in a proceeding in a foreign or international tribunal." The Court explained that "Congress understood that change to 'provid[e] the possibility of U.S. judicial assistance in connection with [administrative and quasi-judicial proceedings abroad].'"[166] The court, in *dicta*, cited with approval the following quote from an article by Professor Hans Smit, who was considered a chief

---

[161] *See* Gary Born, INTERNATIONAL COMMERCIAL ARBITRATION, Vol. II, 1929 (2009) at 492–96.

[162] 28 U.S.C. § 1782(a).

[163] NBC v. Bear Stearns & Co., 165 F.3d 184 (2d Cir. 1999); Republic of Kazakhstan v. Biedermann Intern., 168 F.3d 880 (5th Cir. 1999).

[164] 542 U.S. 241 (2004).

[165] 28 U.S.C. § 1782(a).

[166] 524 U.S. 241 at 258, *citing* S. Rep. No. 1580.

architect of the statute:[167] "[t]he term 'tribunal'... includes investigating magistrates, administrative and *arbitral tribunals*, and quasi-judicial agencies, as well as conventional... courts."[168]

Commentators have viewed *Intel* as raising a question whether the two circuit decisions that found that arbitral tribunals were not covered by § 1782 have continued validity.[169] The Court in *Intel* recognized that Congress intended the language of § 1782 to be read broadly to provide district courts discretion to accommodate increasing international needs, in various kinds of tribunals, for appropriate judicial assistance in taking of evidence.[170] Since *Intel*, some district courts have found that arbitral tribunals are covered by § 1782.[171] Even assuming that § 1782 covers arbitral tribunals, however, a number of commentators take the position that § 1782 discovery should be granted only if it is requested by the arbitrator, not by the parties.[172] The reason would be to try to avoid potential abuses of discovery by parties seeking tactical advantages.

6. Conclusion

Thus, although court assistance to arbitral tribunals in taking evidence is possible today in many jurisdictions, courts tend to have a great deal of discretion, which contributes to a lack of clarity with respect to how much help a court will actually provide. There is clearly resistance on the part

---

[167] *See* Barry H. Garfinkel & Yuval M. Miller, *The Supreme Court's Reasoning in Intel Calls into Question Circuit Court Rulings on Inapplicability of 28 U.S.C § 1782 to International Commercial Arbitration*, 19–8 Mealey's Int'l. Arb. Rep. 17, n. 3 (2004), noting that Professor Smit was recognized by the Second and D.C. Circuits as a "chief architect" and the "dominant drafter" of § 1782.

[168] *See id. citing* Smit, *International Litigation under the United States Code*, 65 Colum. L. Rev. 1026–27, and nn.71, 73 (1965). *Emphasis added.*

[169] *See* Garfinkel and Miller, *supra* note 152.

[170] *See id.*

[171] *See, e.g.,* In re Application of Oxus Gold PLC, 2007 U.S. Dist. LEXIS 24061 (D.N.J. 2007) (Court extended reach of § 1782 to a tribunal involved in a treaty arbitration, distinguishing it from a tribunal in a commercial arbitration.); *In re* Application of Roz Trading Ltd. 469 F. Supp. 2d 1221 (N.D. Ga. 2006) (Court held that a tribunal in a commercial arbitration was an "international or foreign tribunal" within the meaning of § 1782.); In re Hallmark Capital Corp. 534 F. Supp. 2d 951, 957 (D. Minn. 2007) ("[T]he assistance permissible under Section 1782 may extend to private arbitration bodies.").

[172] *See, e.g.,* Gary Born, INTERNATIONAL COMMERCIAL ARBITRATION, Vol. II, 1935 ("§1782 should generally not be interpreted to grant discovery applications by a *party* to foreign arbitral proceedings, rather than by the *tribunal* itself."); Committee on International Commercial Disputes of the Association of the Bar of the City of New York, *28 U.S.C. §1782 as a Means of Obtaining Discovery in Aid of International Commercial Arbitration – Applicability and Best Practices*, 63 The Record 752 (2008). *See also* In re Technostroyexport, 853 F. Supp 695, 687 (S.D.N.Y. 1994), where the court did not permit discovery under § 1782 because the parties had "made no effort to obtain any ruling from the arbitrators."

of some courts to providing the same level of assistance in arbitration as they provide in litigation. No doubt this resistance stems in part from a sense that one advantage of arbitration is that the disclosure obligations are not as arduous as in litigation. Nonetheless, as arbitration proceedings have expanded to cover more complex issues, including, for example, statutory rights in areas such as antitrust and employment contracts, there may be a justifiable need for more extensive discovery. When a tribunal has determined that certain disclosure is needed, court assistance in obtaining it becomes increasingly important to a fair process and a reasonable result.

CHAPTER SIX

The Tribunal

Because arbitration is a private dispute resolution process lacking some of the safeguards of a national legal system, the quality of the tribunal has a significant impact on maintaining parties' confidence in arbitration as a system that works. This chapter focuses on issues of the tribunal's appointment, qualifications, and duties – all of which bear on the integrity of the process and on the efficiency and effectiveness of the dispute's resolution.

A. APPOINTMENT OF ARBITRATORS

Choosing arbitrators who will preside over the proceedings and issue an award is perhaps the most important thing a lawyer does with respect to resolving the client's dispute. The skill, experience, and knowledge of the arbitrators will have a significant impact on the quality of the process and of the award. In addition, arbitrators are fundamentally more powerful than judges, because unlike judges, their decision usually cannot be overturned on the basis of fact or law. An arbitrator can misinterpret the law or make an egregious mistake based on the facts of the case, and counsel will generally be unable to vacate the award resulting from the mistakes.[1] Thus, it behooves lawyers to plan carefully how they are going to select their decision makers.

1. How Many Arbitrators?

In a commercial arbitration, usually either one or three arbitrators are appointed.[2] A number of considerations should affect the decision whether to choose one arbitrator or three. With one arbitrator, the main advantages are that the costs will be less and it will be easier to schedule hearings.

---

[1] There are a few exceptions. For example, an award may be challenged under certain circumstances on a question of law under the English Arbitration Act of 1996, § 69.

[2] In a few situations, including in some trade associations, an even number of arbitrators may be chosen. *See* Alan Redfern & Martin Hunter et al., REDFERN AND HUNTER ON INTERNATIONAL ARBITRATION, § 4.24 at 249 (2009).

Moreover, the process should move more quickly, because a sole arbitrator can make decisions without the necessity of conferring with colleagues at any stage of the arbitration. In international arbitrations, however, there is frequently a preference for three arbitrators, particularly if the amount of money at stake justifies the cost. Although it is more expensive to have three arbitrators, they will bring more to the table in terms of their experience and knowledge than one arbitrator alone. In addition, it is generally believed that the award is more likely to be within the parties' expectations when considered by three arbitrators, and that unusual or inexplicable awards are less likely to occur. If the dispute is particularly large and complex, three arbitrators may be more likely to arrive at a better, more comprehensive understanding than one arbitrator. In addition, when parties are from different countries and cultures, a comfort level is provided when each party is able to select one arbitrator who comes from a similar cultural or legal background.

Although it is generally a good idea to specify in the arbitration clause whether the parties want one or three arbitrators, a party may not know at the beginning of the dispute whether the dispute will be complex and whether the amount in dispute will be large. One option is to state in the arbitration agreement that if the amount in dispute is over a certain amount, there will be three arbitrators; otherwise, there will only be one.

The various arbitral rules have different resolutions as to the number of arbitrators if the parties have not agreed as to the number. Some rules will default to a sole arbitrator unless the matter seems particularly complex.[3] Others default to three arbitrators, regardless of the circumstances.[4]

2. Qualifications

a. Knowledge and Experience
One of the advantages of arbitration is that parties can choose decision makers who have knowledge and experience in the area that is the subject of the dispute. This eliminates the time and effort that would be necessary, if parties were litigating before a randomly selected judge, to educate the judge about the particular industry or the matter at issue.

b. Lawyers or Nonlawyers
Although it is not necessary to have a law degree to be an arbitrator, parties generally choose an arbitrator who is also a lawyer. Arbitrators must make many decisions that require an understanding of the law, such as questions of contract interpretation or validity. If there are three arbitrators, however, parties might want to have one who is a lawyer – usually the chair – and one or two who are individuals with experience in the field. In a construction

---

[3] *See, e.g.*, LCIA Rules, art 5.4; ICC Rules, art. 12(2), ICDR Rules, art. 5.
[4] *See, e.g.*, UNCITRAL Rules, art. 7.

arbitration, for example, parties might want to select a chair who is a lawyer, one arbitrator who is a contractor, and one who is an architect.

Nonlawyers who serve as arbitrators are understandably enthusiastic about nonlawyer participation. They assert the importance of understanding the practical, and sometimes complicated, industry-based side of the dispute. Many arbitrators acknowledge that nonlawyers can contribute substantially by helping the tribunal to understand technical issues. In addition, the non-lawyer is sometimes called on to write the part of the award dealing with technical questions.

If specific industry knowledge is not crucial, however, parties tend to pre-fer arbitrators with a legal background. The parties' preference for lawyers is based in part on a number of concerns they may have about nonlawyer arbitrators. For example, there is a fear that the nonlawyer may use his or her specialized knowledge to unfairly sway the tribunal. For that reason, some arbitrators believe that technical issues are better dealt with by expert wit-nesses, as opposed to nonlawyer members of the tribunal. There is also a risk that nonlawyers will not understand the bases for procedural or substantive rulings, and that too much time may be lost educating them about the law. In addition, there have been occasional complaints about nonlawyers who lacked a judicial temperament, made editorial comments on the testimony, or openly ridiculed participants. Despite these concerns, many arbitrators and parties appreciate the significant contributions of experienced nonlawyer arbitrators who are also reasonably well-versed in the relevant law.

c. Professors as Arbitrators

Experienced counsel have differing views on whether professors make good arbitrators. Some counsel with a civil law background seem to think that the best arbitrators are professors. Lawyers with a common law background, and some civil law lawyers, tend to be more skeptical. The biggest concern is that professors are too focused on doctrine, and do not have sufficient practical experience to make wise decisions. Sylwester Pieckowski, a Polish arbitrator and counsel, told of a tribunal in which all three arbitrators were professors:

> The dispute concerned an agreement to distribute vodka in the U.S. None of the professors had experience either in arbitration or in the vodka business. They grossly misapplied the law, and rendered a very bad award, which was ultimately vacated.[5]
>
> Sylwester Pieckowski
> Poland

---

[5] Interview with Sylwester Pieckowski, April 2007. Notes of interview on file with author.

   Particularly in fact-intensive cases, such as construction arbitrations, there is concern that professors will be too theoretical, will not focus on the facts, and may not have the skill set to deal with complex factual issues. On the other hand, professors can be very effective if they are knowledgeable about arbitration, about the law in question, and about the pertinent industry. There seems to be a consensus that if professors are also involved in practice, that experience, along with an intellectual level that is generally quite high, can make them valuable members of a tribunal. Chris Seppälä, a frequent counsel in international arbitration and an arbitrator in Paris, observes, "Professors can be excellent if they have had a lot of practical experience, *e.g.*, as legal practitioners. Otherwise, they can be dangerous as they may lack the necessary familiarity with the business world as well as experience in dealing with fact intensive litigation (arbitration)."[6]

d. Language Fluency
The ability to be fluent in a particular language, or sometimes in two languages, may be important to the parties. An arbitrator lacking in fluency in the language of the arbitration may not understand some of the critical issues necessary to the resolution of the dispute.

e. Availability
Another important qualification to assess is availability. Parties often want to engage very well-known arbitrators, but these arbitrators may be so busy with other arbitrations that scheduling hearings becomes extremely difficult. It is important to have a clear idea of the arbitrator's availability, and a commitment of time from the arbitrator.

f. Reputation
The arbitrator's reputation is also important. A reputation for fairness, integrity, and wisdom is a great asset to an arbitrator[7] and also benefits the parties. For the arbitration process to work well, both parties need to have confidence in the integrity and the abilities of the arbitrator. Moreover, in the selection of a chair, or a sole arbitrator, parties are particularly interested in an individual's ability to manage the arbitration and to move it along so it does not drag on for years. This skill may be hard to determine from a resume but knowing what experience the individual has had, and if possible, speaking with others who have had arbitrations before this person can be helpful. In general, because parties know that they will not be able to appeal any decision on the merits, they want to choose the best arbitrator they can to make that decision.

---

[6] Interview with Chris Seppälä, April 2007. Notes of interview on file with author.
[7] *See* Yves Dezalay & Bryant G. Garth, DEALING IN VIRTUE, 18–29 (1996).

g. Specifications and Requirements

Qualifications agreed on by the parties can be spelled out in the arbitration clause. The parties could assert, for example, that all arbitrators must speak French, they all must have experience in the construction industry, and the language of the arbitration will be French. There is a risk in being too specific, however, because if the arbitration agreement contains a laundry list of qualifications, it may be too difficult to actually find arbitrators who have all of the desired qualifications.

Arbitrators are expected to be independent and impartial.[8] They are also expected to be neutral, which could include the requirements of independence and impartiality, but may also refer to nationality. There is generally an expectation that the presiding arbitrator, or a sole arbitrator, will not have the same nationality as either of the parties. Institutional rules may specifically provide for national neutrality.[9]

3. Method of Selection

The arbitrator selection procedure can vary, depending on the parties' agreement and on the institutional rules.[10] If parties do not state in their arbitration clause how they want to select arbitrators, but they choose rules to govern the process, the selection will take place according to the institutional rules. However, even if parties did not agree on a method of selection in their arbitration clause, if they can agree at the time of the arbitration, they can generally select the arbitrators, depending on institutional rules. If parties cannot reach agreement, however, the institution will choose the arbitrators. Some of the differences parties should be aware of, when they have not chosen a selection process, are whether (a) the institutional rules provide parties freedom to choose the arbitrators, (b) they will be limited to a list of names provided by the arbitral institution, (c) the institution will choose the arbitrators, or (d) some variation of the above.

a. Three Arbitrators

i. The Rules. When there are three arbitrators, the most frequent method of selection is for each party to select one arbitrator and for the two party-selected arbitrators to pick a third arbitrator, who will be the chair of the tribunal. If the parties want to ensure that this method will be used, they

---

[8] *See infra* Section B.

[9] *See, e.g.,* ICSID Arbitration Rules, Rule 3(1) (none of arbitrators may have same nationality as parties); LCIA Rules, art. 6.1 (sole arbitrator or presiding arbitrator may not have same nationality of parties unless parties agree in writing); *cf.* UNCITRAL Model Law, art. 11(1) ("No person shall be precluded by reason of his nationality from acting as an arbitrator, unless otherwise agreed by the parties.").

[10] Appointment of arbitrators in ad hoc arbitrations will be discussed later in this chapter in Section A(3)(c).

can state the method of selection in their arbitration clause. On the other hand, the rules of certain arbitral institutions may provide this method of selection, sometimes with variations. The ICC Rules provide that parties may each select one arbitrator, but unless the parties have agreed otherwise, the third arbitrator, who will be the presiding arbitrator, will be selected by the ICC Court of Arbitration.[11] In the Court of International Arbitration attached to the Chamber of Commerce and Industry of Romania, if the parties did not agree on a selection process, then each party will appoint its arbitrator, the Appointing Authority will select the presiding arbitrator, and all arbitrators must be chosen from a list provided by the Court of Arbitration.[12]

In its 2012 arbitration rules, effective March 1, 2012, CIETAC, the major arbitral institution in China, provides that parties can nominate arbitrators outside the list of arbitrators maintained by CIETAC, as long as the parties agree and the Chairman of CIETAC confirms the appointment.[13] If parties are unable to agree on a presiding arbitrator, they can each propose to CIETAC a list of one to three candidates.[14] If no name is common to both lists, CIETAC will appoint a person who was not nominated by either party.[15]

In general, if any party fails to appoint an arbitrator within the time frame agreed to by the parties or set forth in the arbitral rules, the institution selected by the parties in their arbitration clause has the authority to choose the arbitrators. If the two party-selected arbitrators cannot agree on the person to serve as chair, the institution will appoint the chair.

When an arbitrator is selected by only one party, he or she is nonetheless obliged to be independent and impartial.[16] All international rules require that once chosen, arbitrators cannot favor in any way the party that selected them.

ii. The Practice. Experienced practitioners agree that the appointment of arbitrators is a critical step in the arbitral process. As Sylwester Pieckowski has noted, "The quality of the tribunal is decisive, and the consequences are tragic if you choose wrong."[17] Jingzhou Tao, an arbitrator and counsel in Beijing, says, "The arbitrator is one-half of your case."[18] Inexperienced

---

[11] ICC Rules, art. 12(5).

[12] Court of International Commercial Arbitration attached to the Chamber of Commerce and Industry of Romania, Rules of Arbitration, art.17.

[13] CIETAC 2012 Arbitration Rules, art. 24(2)

[14] CIETAC 2012 Arbitration Rules, art. 25(3).

[15] *See id.*

[16] *See infra* Section B.

[17] Interview with Sylwester Pieckowski, April 2007. Notes of interview on file with author.

[18] Interview with Jingzhou Tao, April 2007. Notes of interview on file with author.

counsel may unfortunately learn this lesson a little too late. This section focuses on the strategies and methods used by experienced practitioners in choosing arbitrators.

(1) Choosing the Party-Appointed Arbitrators (Coarbitrators). There are, of course, many different theories of how to choose an arbitrator, but one common denominator that experienced counsel assert as crucial is that they always choose someone they know. Either they know the arbitrator personally, or they know of him or her because the particular arbitrator has a reputation of being among the best international arbitrators in the world. This desire to have a known quantity sometimes has a downside, however, because when many parties choose the same small number of arbitrators, these arbitrators become very busy and cannot always give sufficient attention to each arbitration. This can cause difficulties in moving an arbitration along quickly and efficiently and in obtaining an award in a timely manner. For this reason, some experienced counsel say they never choose an arbitrator who is "the flavor of the month."

When selecting the arbitrator they are entitled to appoint, parties and their representatives look for an arbitrator who will be the best for their particular case. This may mean not only that the arbitrator should have knowledge and experience in the subject matter of the dispute, and the applicable law, but also that he or she should be someone with sufficient stature, presence, and personality to be persuasive to the other arbitrators.

Some of the strategy involves weighing the merits of the prospective arbitrator against those of the other party's arbitrator. If respondent's counsel knows which arbitrator the claimant has chosen, then the strategy is generally to find someone who could not be considered subordinate to the claimant's appointed arbitrator. Rather, respondent's counsel wants someone who is equivalent to the claimant's arbitrator in experience, knowledge, age, and reputation.

Claudia Kälin-Nauer, a Swiss counsel and arbitrator, gives this example of some factors to be considered in choosing a party-appointed arbitrator and a chair.

> Assume the claimant is from Austria, and the law applicable to the merits is Swiss law. Should claimant now appoint a Swiss arbitrator or perhaps an Austrian arbitrator? If claimant decides to appoint an Austrian arbitrator, the other side may well appoint a Swiss arbitrator. At this point, claimant may be concerned about whether the chair should be Swiss, because it might not want the chair and the other arbitrator to be too close on the legal questions. However, if the chair is well-known, and highly respected for both his knowledge of Swiss law and the strength of his character and personality, then it would

not really matter if the chair is also Swiss. Depending on the case, knowledge of the applicable law may not be as important as other qualities, such as understanding pertinent industry practices, technical matters or other elements in dispute.[19]

Claudia Kälin-Nauer
Switzerland

Because the choice of arbitrator is so influenced by personal knowledge, an inexperienced lawyer would be well-advised to consult with more experienced counsel to understand how to choose the best arbitrator for the case. Additionally, clients may have their own views, which may or may not be well-founded, on who the arbitrator should be. The final choice of an arbitrator may involve some negotiation between client and counsel. Counsel should do extensive research, such as reading any articles written by the prospective arbitrator, reading any available decisions (for example, ICSID cases that are published),[20] and making numerous phone calls in search of people with first-hand knowledge of the arbitrator's abilities. Although such due diligence can be critical in the selection of an appropriate arbitrator, counsel do not always do a thorough job.

Parties can be incredibly casual in making appointments of arbitrators – they may do so without full study of their track record or published writings. Many times parties' lawyers just have not done their homework.[21]

Chris Seppälä
Paris

Although a coarbitrator is chosen by one party, she is not supposed to have any biases in favor of that party. The appointing party, of course, wants an arbitrator who it believes shares its cultural or legal background, or holds views that may be helpful to resolving the dispute in favor of the appointing party. Even though party-appointed arbitrators are expected to be independent and impartial, it is generally understood and accepted that they can consult with the appointing party concerning the choice of a chair.[22] It is also understood that a party-appointed arbitrator has a duty to make sure that the arguments presented by the appointing party are understood

---

[19] Interview with Claudia Kälin-Nauer, April 2007. Notes of interview on file with author.

[20] Available at http://icsid.worldbank.org/ICSID/Index.jsp.

[21] Interview with Chris Seppälä, April 2007. Notes of interview on file with author.

[22] See, e.g., IBA Rules of Ethics for International Arbitrators (1987), art. 5.2.

and fully considered by the tribunal.[23] This arbitrator cannot, however, act as an advocate for the party that appointed him. Arbitrators and counsel sometimes complain that certain party-appointed arbitrators do not act in an impartial manner. The problem seems particularly acute with some arbitrators who are appointed by governments or government-controlled entities. The problem for such arbitrators, and for any arbitrator who appears to be advocating for one party, is that he loses credibility with the two other members of the tribunal. He is therefore less able to help the party who appointed him, because he is no longer persuasive. In such a case, the other two arbitrators will essentially decide the case.

(2) Choosing the Presiding Arbitrator (Chair of the Tribunal). Once the party-appointed arbitrators have both been chosen, the next step is to choose the chair. Normally, the two coarbitrators make this choice in consultation with the parties who appointed them. Some experienced counsel, however, want to choose the chair themselves, without the participation of the party-appointed arbitrator. Generally, this can be done as long as the counsel for the other side also agrees that counsel for the parties, rather than the party-appointed arbitrators, will choose the chair.

> Choosing the chair of the tribunal is far too important to delegate to anyone. It is perhaps the most important decision in a case. Arbitration is for the parties, and the parties should always try to find a way to agree on the chair, if at all possible.[24]
>
> Chris Seppälä
> Paris

Other counsel believe that, in general, it is easier for coarbitrators to reach agreement on a chair than for the parties (or the parties' counsel) do so. Parties are always suspicious of the other side's choice. Thus, some counsel assert that having party-appointed arbitrators choose the chair will work more smoothly than having parties make the choice. As proof, they point out that parties' attempts to choose a sole arbitrator end in disagreement more often than coarbitrators' efforts to appoint a chair. The coarbitrators act as a filter for the parties' suspicions of each other's choices.

[23] *See* Doak Bishop & Lucy Reed, *Practical Guidelines for Interviewing, Selecting and Challenging Party-Appointed Arbitrators in International Commercial Arbitration,* 14 Arb. Int. 395, 404 (1998).

[24] Interview with Chris Seppälä, April 2007. Notes of interview on file with author. *See also* Seppälä, *Obtaining the Right International Arbitral Tribunal: A Practitioner's View* 22 Mealey's International Arbitration Report, Issue #10, October 2007 (Explains methodology for parties to follow to reach agreement and make a wise choice of the chair of the panel.).

Of course, as in any negotiation, success in reaching agreement on a chair or a sole arbitrator will depend in large part on the skill of the participants and on the incentives to reach agreement. In arbitration, the incentive to agree on a chair or on a sole arbitrator is strong because otherwise an unknown arbitrator will be parachuted in who may not be the best person for the case. Moreover, if this person is the chair, she may not work well with the other arbitrators. Some counsel refer to this situation – when, for example, the arbitrator is chosen by the ICC – as "ICC roulette."

Sometimes, however, agreement will not be possible. Occasionally, a party-appointed arbitrator, usually one appointed by a government or a government-controlled entity, will simply announce that he will not agree on anyone proposed by the other side. Generally, it appears that this individual does not want to accept responsibility if his government is ultimately unhappy with the presiding arbitrator. In such a case, the appointment will, of necessity, be made by the institution or other appointing authority.

Arbitrators who do a lot of international arbitrations tend to know each other. They sometimes have worked together as arbitrators, they are members of the same associations, they attend the same conferences, and they may serve together on boards of institutions or of publications. In some industries, they may all know each other reasonably well. Hew Dundas, an arbitrator in London, tells this story about trying to agree on a chair for a dispute in the oil and gas industry:

> I was a coarbitrator in a case where the other coarbitrator (who had never been involved in any arbitration before) asked me how we should proceed to select a chair. I suggested five names of prospective arbitrators. He asked me if I knew any of them. I replied that I knew them all, on a first name basis. He then said, "I don't want them, if you know them." I said, "Look. Why don't you consider it for a couple of days and consult your appointor, and then get back to me?" Two days later he agreed on one of the five I had suggested (a leading English QC with a long track record as an international arbitrator, particularly as Chairman), having found out in the interim (a) that my knowing the Chairman professionally in no way put him or his appointor at any disadvantage in the tribunal, and (b) my personal assurance of the proposed chairman's qualities was in itself of value and greatly preferable to picking unknowns off a list.[25]
>
> Hew Dundas
> London

---

[25] Interview with Hew Dundas, March 2007. Notes of interview on file with author.

Although the characteristics one seeks in a chair may vary, depending on the kind of case at issue, parties look for some general traits. Pierre Mayer, professor, arbitrator, and counsel in Paris, describes his perfect chair as follows:

- Bright and knowledgeable
- Impartial
- Has common sense
- Has a lot of authority, but not too much
- Listens carefully
- Thoughtful (hesitates), but is able to decide
- Available
- Not self-conscious, not arrogant
- Will draft a beautiful award[26]

Most parties would probably be satisfied with an arbitrator who had these characteristics, and as a result would have confidence in the arbitration process. One arbitrator told the author that she considered it quite a compliment when a party that had lost before her when she was an arbitrator later hired her as counsel in a different matter.

Although parties that agree on a procedure can usually nominate or have their coarbitrators nominate the chair, some institutions take the position that they have the right to confirm that appointment.[27] The ICC will generally confirm an arbitrator only if she filed a statement of independence without qualification, or, if the statement is qualified, there were no objections to the circumstances causing the qualification.[28] The position of the LCIA is that the LCIA Court alone is empowered to appoint arbitrators, although it will do so with "due regard for any particular method or criteria of selection agreed in writing by the parties."[29]

b. A Sole Arbitrator

If only a sole arbitrator is to be appointed, the parties will need to reach agreement on who should be chosen. It is generally not a good idea to select an arbitrator in advance and put his name in the arbitration clause. By the time a dispute arises, that arbitrator may be unavailable for any number of reasons, or may not have the necessary expertise or qualifications for the particular dispute that has arisen. Thus, it is better for the parties to agree on an arbitrator once the dispute has arisen. Even if no method for selection is

---

[26] Interview with Pierre Mayer, April 2007. Notes of interview on file with author.

[27] *See, e.g.*, ICC Rules, art. 12(5), 13(1–2). Under its 2012 Arbitration Rules, the ICC refers to the chair of the tribunal as the "president" of the tribunal. *See id. See also* CIETAC Rules, art. 21(2).

[28] *See* ICC Rules, art. 13(2).

[29] LCIA Rules, art. 5.5.

already established in the arbitration clause, if the parties agree at the time the dispute arises, most arbitral institutions will follow the choice of the parties. The difficulty is that once a dispute has arisen, many parties cannot reach agreement on anything.

Nonetheless, if the parties are willing to try to agree on a sole arbitrator – which is probably in the best interest of both parties – one of the ways to do this is for the parties first to agree generally on the qualifications they are looking for. They should then exchange a list of three to five arbitrators who have those qualifications. If any arbitrator's name is on both lists, that should be the arbitrator chosen. If not, the parties should try to see whether any arbitrator on the other party's list would be acceptable. In the event the parties do not reach a decision, the arbitral institution will choose the sole arbitrator. As noted earlier, parties should make a strong effort to agree, because the arbitration will begin more smoothly, and the parties are likely to have greater confidence in the process if they have been able to agree on the arbitrator.

c. Ad Hoc Arbitration

In an ad hoc arbitration, parties need to be particularly careful to specify their method of arbitrator selection because there is no institution to intervene. The selection method should be clear. There should be a time frame for making the selection, and a statement of how the issue will be resolved if parties cannot agree on a sole arbitrator or if they do not make their choice of a party-selected arbitrator within the allotted time frame. Normally, this is done by choosing an appointing authority who will select the arbitrator if the parties have not been able to do so. If the parties choose the UNCITRAL Arbitration Rules, but do not choose an appointing authority, or if the appointing authority chosen by the parties does not fulfill its function, the UNCITRAL Rules provide that one of the parties may ask the Secretary-General of the Permanent Court of Arbitration at the Hague to designate an appointing authority.[30]

If the parties did not provide for an appointing authority, and did not choose rules that provide for an appointing authority, then in most jurisdictions, the court at the seat of the arbitration can be called on to appoint an arbitrator. However, if no seat was chosen by the parties, they will have to see if they can persuade a court somewhere to take jurisdiction – perhaps the court in the country whose substantive law applies to the arbitration (assuming they have chosen a substantive law). It becomes readily apparent that in an ad hoc arbitration, even more than in an institutional arbitration, the arbitration clause must be carefully and thoughtfully drafted. A carelessly drafted clause may result in the parties litigating rather than arbitrating their dispute.

---

[30] *See* UNCITRAL Rules, art. 6(2).

4. Interviewing Prospective Arbitrators

Because the choice of an arbitrator is so important, parties may want to interview prospective arbitrators before making a decision to choose them. These interviews are sometimes referred to colloquially as "beauty pageants." Parties may believe that although resumes, reputation, and even personal acquaintance provide much of the information needed, a face-to-face meeting, or even a telephone interview, can provide a different and valuable kind of information.

There is a tension, however, between counsel's desire for information and an arbitrator's obligation to remain impartial. In interviewing a potential arbitrator, a lawyer is not supposed to ask questions involving the merits of the case.[31] There should not be any discussion that might cause the potential arbitrator to view the case in a particular light, or that would indicate how he or she felt about any given issues in the case. The interview should be limited to information about the arbitrator's qualifications, experience, and availability.

If the parties are choosing a sole arbitrator, normally they would both meet with the arbitrator at the same time. This avoids any sense that one party was unduly influencing the prospective arbitrator about the case. When three arbitrators are to be chosen, however, parties meet individually with the one arbitrator they intend to select, if that arbitrator is willing to do so. Some experienced arbitrators are not willing to meet with lawyers, and expect the lawyers to make a decision based on their resumes and reputation.[32]

THE INTERVIEW DILEMMA

I generally don't submit to interviews where the party is a U.S. or multinational company. However, I do bend my prohibition in the situation of a foreign party that is relatively unfamiliar with the international arbitral process. In that event, I will meet with a party representative and counsel for a half-hour meeting... with only counsel asking questions. However, my ground rules prohibit discussion of detail or merits of the case.[33]

Gerald Aksen
United States

---

[31] *See, e.g.,* IBA Rules of Ethics (1987), art. 5(1); ICDR Rules, art. 7(2). *See also* Doak Bishop & Lucy Reed, *Practical Guidelines for Interviewing, Selecting and Challenging Prospective Arbitrators*, 14 Arb. Int. 395, 424 (1998).

[32] *See* Gerald Aksen, *The Tribunal's Appointment*, 35, *in* Lawrence W. Newman, THE LEADING ARBITRATORS GUIDE TO INTERNATIONAL ARBITRATION (2004).

[33] *Id.*

The Chartered Institute of Arbitrators has developed guidelines for inter-viewing arbitrators (CIArb Guidelines).[34] According to Hew Dundas, a for-mer President of the Chartered Institute, this means an arbitrator willing to permit an interview can simply say to parties seeking the interview, "I will agree to be interviewed in accordance with the Guidelines of the Chartered Institute of Arbitrators."[35] This should make clear to the arbitrator and to the party the permissible scope and content of the interview.

CIArb Practice Guideline 16 sets forth in paragraph 9 what can and cannot be discussed. Obviously, the merits of the case cannot be discussed, and this Guideline delineates other areas that either are not appropriate for discussion, or that may be discussed. Guideline 16 provides further guidance on questions such as the location of the interview (business setting, not over a meal or drinks), the time period (should be limited), reimbursement of travel expenses (no reimbursement for time), tape recording or file note (should be made and disclosed to the other side and the appointing party), as well as other issues.[36]

The difficulty for counsel is to try to find some level of comfort with the prospective arbitrator without engaging in any discussions of the merits of the particular case. Counsel should also be aware that their meeting may not be considered confidential by the potential arbitrator. Some arbitrators will disclose any discussions they hold with one party to the opposing party or to the other party-selected arbitrator if they deem disclosure to be appropriate. These particular practices go beyond the standard set forth in the Interna-tional Bar Association Rules of Ethics for International Arbitrators.[37] Article 5 of those Rules requires disclosure only when a prospective sole arbitrator is approached by one party alone, or a prospective presiding arbitrator is approached by one party-appointed arbitrator alone.

B. OBLIGATIONS OF ARBITRATORS

1. Independence and Impartiality

Arbitrators have the obligation to be impartial and independent. This obli-gation is stated in numerous laws and rules.[38] *Impartiality* generally means

---

[34] *See* Chartered Institute of Arbitrators Practice Guideline 16. The Interviewing of Prospective Arbitrators, available at http://www.ciarb.org/information-and-resources/ Practice%20Guideline%2016%20April2011.pdf.

[35] Interview with Hew Dundas, March 2007. Notes of interview on file with author.

[36] *See generally, e.g.,* CIArb Practice Guideline 16. paras. 7, 15, 16, 18, 19.

[37] *See* IBA Rules of Ethics for International Arbitrators (1987). *See infra* sections B(1))(b) and B(2).

[38] *See, e.g.,* UNCITRAL Model Law, art. 12(1–2); UNCITRAL Rules, art. 12(1); LCIA Rules, arts. 5.2, 10.3; ICDR Rules, art. 7(1); ICC Rules, art. 11(1). *See also* IBA Rules of Ethics, art. 3.1.

that the arbitrator is not biased because of any preconceived notions about the issues and has no reason to favor one party over another. *Independence* generally means that the arbitrator has no financial interest in the case or its outcome. It can also mean that the arbitrator is not dependent on one of the parties for any benefit, such as employment or client referral, and that the arbitrator does not have a close business or professional relationship with one of the parties.

As international law firms and multinational corporations have grown exponentially, the question of what conflicts prevent an arbitrator from being impartial and independent has become more complex. If an arbitrator has a serious conflict, she should not accept an appointment as arbitrator. If there is some possible conflict, which may not be serious, the arbitrator is supposed to disclose this to the parties, so they can decide whether they wish to challenge the arbitrator's appointment. The UNCITRAL Model Law and a number of arbitration rules require that an arbitrator disclose without delay any circumstances likely to give rise to justifiable doubts as to her impartiality or independence.[39] This obligation occurs not only at the time of appointment, but continues throughout the entire arbitral proceedings.

Many arbitrators have found it difficult to know what should be disclosed, and have concerns about "overdisclosing," because some parties may be interested in challenging an arbitrator for the wrong reasons – perhaps simply to delay the process. Moreover, some arbitral institutions will pass over arbitrators and not actually appoint them if any doubt is raised.[40]

a. The IBA Guidelines on Conflicts of Interest

To attempt to deal with some of these issues, the International Bar Association (IBA) appointed a Working Group that has created the *IBA Guidelines on Conflicts of Interest in International Arbitration*.[41] The IBA had already promulgated Rules of Ethics for International Arbitrators in 1987, which dealt with these same issues in Rules 3 and 4. The Working Group viewed these earlier rules as more stringent than most national rules on the subject.[42] In developing the Guidelines, the Working Group asserted that it was "setting forth the best international practice with regard to impartiality

---

[39] *See* UNCITRAL Model Law, art. 12(1). *See also* CIETAC rules, art. 25; LCIA Rules, art 5.3; ICDR Rules, art. 7(1).

[40] *See* For the Working Group, Otto L.O. de Witt Wijnen, Nathalie Voser & Neomi Rao, *Background Information on the IBA Guidelines on Conflicts of Interest in International Arbitration*, 5 Business Law International 433, 444 (2004) (hereinafter, "Background Information"). *See also* Stephen R. Bond, *The Selection of ICC Arbitrators and the Requirement of Independence*, 4 Arb. Int. 306 (1988).

[41] *See infra* Appendix G.

[42] *See Background Information, supra* note 40, at 458.

and independence."[43] Its goal was to develop useful standards and concrete examples of their application.[44]

i. Part I: The General Standards. The Guidelines contain two parts. Part I is entitled "General Standards Regarding Impartiality, Independence and Disclosure." Part II is called "Practical Application of the General Standards." Part I provides seven General Standards for dealing with conflicts of interests and obligations to disclose, as well as issues of waiver, scope, and relationships. General Standard 1 is that every arbitrator must be and remain impartial and independent. General Standard 2, "Conflicts of Interests," sets forth the standards for determining whether a particular conflict would require the arbitrator to decline appointment. The first standard listed under General Standard 2 is subjective: an arbitrator must decline appointment if he has doubts as to his impartiality or independence. The second listed standard is objective: an arbitrator must decline appointment if a reasonable person would have justifiable doubts about the arbitrator's impartiality and independence. The objective standard for disqualification requires more than the mere possibility that the circumstances in questions could create doubts about impartiality and independence. Rather, the circumstances must raise doubts that are *justifiable* about the arbitrator's neutrality. Justifiable doubts are those that would persuade a reasonable third party that the arbitrator might make a decision based on factors other than the merits of the case.[45]

Although the tests for disqualification of an arbitrator in General Standard 2 are both subjective and objective, the test in General Standard 3 for what an arbitrator should disclose is purely subjective: arbitrators must disclose facts that may, *in the eyes of the parties*, create doubts as to the arbitrator's impartiality and independence.[46] Thus, the arbitrator has to try to put himself in the shoes of the parties, and determine what circumstances might cause the parties to have doubts about his independence and impartiality. This standard provides for broad disclosure not only because it is subjective, but also because there is no requirement that the doubts be "justifiable."[47] Nonetheless, as will be discussed later, limitations are placed on the breadth of the subjective standard.

An arbitrator's nondisclosure should not in itself, according to the Guidelines, result automatically in any kind of penalty, such as removal of the

---

[43] *See id.* at 434.
[44] *See id.*
[45] *See* General Standard 2(c).
[46] *See* General Standard 3, "Disclosure by the Arbitrator."
[47] General Standard 3(a) of the Guidelines provides in pertinent part, "If facts or circumstances exist that may, in the eyes of the parties, give rise to doubts as to the arbitrator's impartiality or independence, the arbitrator shall disclose such facts or circumstances to the parties."

arbitrator or a setting aside of an award. In the view of the Working Group, "nondisclosure cannot make an arbitrator partial or lacking independence; only the facts or circumstances that he or she did not disclose can do so."[48] This position conflicts with some national laws, which provide that an arbitrator's failure to disclose a nontrivial circumstance can be grounds for an award to be set aside.[49]

Finally, the Guidelines apply equally to all arbitrators, whether chair, party-appointed, or sole arbitrator.[50] In addition, they place a duty on both arbitrators and parties to investigate the direct and indirect relationships between them.[51]

ii. Part II: Practical Application of the General Standards. In Part II of the Guidelines, the Working Group provides examples of how the General Standards of Part I should be applied. Lists of specific situations are divided into three different groups. The groups are named after the colors of the traffic light: red, orange, and green. All of the lists in Part II are referred to as "nonexhaustive," meaning that additional situations could fit within any list, based on an application of the General Standards of Part I.

The Red List contains examples of serious conflicts of interests. The Red List is divided into two subgroups, nonwaivable and waivable situations. When a situation is nonwaivable, it means the conflict is so serious that it is not permissible for the parties to waive it and go forward with the arbitration. The arbitrator simply must not accept appointment. If the situation is waivable, it means the conflict is still serious, but if the parties are informed, and if they agree, then the arbitrator can accept the appointment. Some arbitrators refer to the waivable Red List as the "Pink List." The arbitrator must, of course, make full disclosure in situations described in this list.

EXAMPLES

Red List – Nonwaivable
1.3 The arbitrator is a manager, director or member of the supervisory board, or has a similar controlling influence in one of the parties.

Red List – Waivable
2.1.2 The arbitrator has previous involvement in the case.

---

[48] *See* Guidelines, Part II, Introduction, ¶ 5.
[49] *See, e.g.*, Commonwealth Coatings Corp. v. Continental Casualty Co., 393 U.S. 145 (1968).
[50] *See id.* General Standard 5.
[51] *See id.* General Standard 7.

The situations on the waivable Red List (or Pink List) appear for the most part unlikely to be waived. It was apparently believed by the Working Group, however, that if parties are fully informed, and nonetheless want the candidate to be the arbitrator, the parties should be permitted to waive the conflict.

The Orange List also contains situations that the arbitrator must disclose. If, after disclosure, the parties do not make a timely objection, then they are deemed to have accepted the arbitrator and to have waived any potential conflict of interest based on the facts and circumstances disclosed.[52]

EXAMPLES

Orange List

3.1.2 The arbitrator has within the past three years served as counsel for one of the parties or an affiliate of one of the parties . . . in an unrelated matter, but the arbitrator and the party or the affiliate of the party have no ongoing relationship.

In the Orange List, three years is considered a cutoff point, so if the circumstances occurred more than three years earlier, they do not have to be disclosed, and they would therefore fall within the Green List. There is an acknowledgment, however, in the introduction to the lists, that in any particular case, the three-year period could be either too long or too short.[53]

The Green List contains examples of situations that the Working Group believes would not raise questions of impartiality or independence, and would therefore require no disclosure. The Green List provides a safe harbor. It also serves to limit the subjective standard of disclosure set forth in General Standard 3, so that even if, *in the parties' eyes*, disclosure should be made, the arbitrator would not be expected to disclose if the kind of circumstances at issue were included in the Green List.[54]

EXAMPLES

Green List

4.4.2 The arbitrator and counsel for one of the parties or another arbitrator have previously served together as arbitrators or as co-counsel.

---

[52] *See id.* General Standard 4(a).
[53] *See id.* Part II: Practical Application of the General Standards, ¶ 7.
[54] *See Background Information, supra* note 40, at 450.

In the above example, parties might well think the arbitrator should disclose if he had been co-counsel in a matter with the attorney for the other side. A party might also be interested in knowing whether two arbitrators had previously served together, particularly if the two included the chair and the arbitrator selected by the other party. One might wonder whether these two arbitrators would tend to be of one mind because of previous shared experiences, rather than approaching the matter at hand completely independently. Here, however, the position of the Guidelines is that this circumstance of shared prior experience does not need to be disclosed. Of course, General Standard 3(c) provides that "[a]ny doubt as to whether an arbitrator should disclose certain facts or circumstances should be resolved in favour of disclosure."[55] Because under national laws courts may not reach the same conclusions about the necessity of disclosure as the Working Group, an arbitrator is probably better off disclosing, if he has any doubts, rather than relying on the Green List.

Although the Working Group certainly deserves praise for tackling a difficult issue, it remains to be seen whether the Guidelines will be persuasive to courts and to arbitral institutions. Some arbitral institutions have not expressed great enthusiasm about the new Guidelines, perhaps in some cases because their own rules are more strict.[56] Nonetheless, even though somewhat agnostic with respect to the Guidelines, some arbitral institutions have acknowledged that they may take the Guidelines into account in reviewing arbitrator challenges.[57] Courts may or may not refer to the Guidelines in reviewing a challenge to an arbitrator.[58] The parties could, of course, incorporate the Guidelines into their arbitration clause, which might make their application more likely. The Working Group, however, chose not to propose a model clause that parties could use to incorporate the Guidelines, because it believed that this might cause a negative inference that the Guidelines should not be applied unless incorporated.[59] The expressed goal of the Working Group is that the Guidelines

> will find general acceptance within the international arbitration community . . . and that they thus will help parties, practitioners, arbitrators, institutions and the courts in their decision-making process on

---

[55] Guidelines, General Standard 3(c).

[56] *See, e.g.*, discussion of AAA-ABA Code of Ethics for Arbitrators in Commercial Disputes *infra* Section B(1)(c).

[57] *See* Geoff Nicholas & Constantine Partasides, *LCIA Court Decision on Challenges to Arbitrators: A Proposal to Publish*, 23 Arb. Int. 1, 3 (2007).

[58] In a case in the Netherlands, for example, the court ignored the Guidelines, even though they were cited by one of the parties, and applied instead the Dutch Code of Civil Procedure. The Republic of Ghana v. Telekom Malaysia Berhad, Docket Nos. HA/RK 2004.667 and HA/RK 2004.788, cited in Vera Van Houtte, Stephan Wilske, & Michael Young, *What's New in European Arbitration?* 60-APR Disp. Resol. J. 6 (2005).

[59] *See Background Information, supra* note 40, at 440.

these very important questions of impartiality, independence, disclosure, objections and challenges in that connection.[60]

Although the Working Group asserted that prior IBA rules on disclosure were more strict than many national rules and laws, there has been criticism of the approach of the IBA. Basically, that criticism suggests that the rules are being relaxed so that conflicts arising from the complex and intertwined operations of multinational corporations and large international law firms will not prevent partners of globally based firms from serving as arbitrators. If some partners of such firms disclose every possible connection between their huge international firm with thousands of lawyers, and a multinational corporation that has worldwide operations and is looking for an arbitrator, there will likely be numerous connections which may or may not be considered conflicts. However, there is concern that disclosure of distant relationships may lead to bad-faith challenges. The Guidelines try to strike a balance between disclosing everything and disclosing actual or potentially actual conflicts. This is, of course, a very difficult line to draw, but many arbitrators are referring to the Guidelines and finding them useful. Sarah François-Poncet, an arbitrator and counsel in Paris, observed as follows:

> The Guidelines are imperfect, because they cannot address every possible fact situation. But they are better than nothing. In the arbitration community, they pass muster, but for people not in the community, they may not. If, as an arbitrator, you have any possible concern about a conflict, you sleep better at night if you disclose. But of course there is the problem of the abusive party who seizes on a precautionary disclosure to sabotage an arbitration. Thus, over-disclosure may open the door to abusive challenges. Unfortunately, you can't guideline away bad faith.[61]
>
> Sarah François-Poncet
> Paris

It is important for arbitrators to remember, however, that the Guidelines do not create a safe harbor; some courts may consider them relevant, but others may give them little, if any, deference.

b. The 1987 IBA Rules of Ethics for Arbitrators

One of the problems not dealt with very well by the Working Group is the interaction of the Guidelines, which were adopted in 2004, with the IBA Rules of Ethics, adopted in 1987. Rather than combining the two into

---

[60] Introduction to Guidelines, ¶ 6.

[61] Interview with Sarah François-Poncet, April 2007. Notes of interview on file with author.

one document, the IBA now has two different, overlapping documents in circulation. At the end of the Introduction, the Guidelines state that the 1987 Rules are still in effect, and cover more topics than the Guidelines, but they are superseded "as to matters treated here."[62] In other words, Rule 3 (impartiality and independence) and Rule 4 (duty of disclosure) of the 1987 Rules are now replaced by the Guidelines.[63] It might have been simpler if the IBA had deleted Rules of Ethics 3 and 4, and substituted the Guidelines, or in some fashion had combined the two documents, but it has not done so. Adding to the confusion is that the 1987 Rules of Ethics, which are widely available in appendices to arbitration treatises and in documentary supplements to casebooks on arbitration, include a proposed model clause for incorporating the Rules into a party's arbitration agreement.[64] This could create a trap for the unwary if a party used the Rules' model clause to incorporate the 1987 Rules, believing that Rules 3 and 4 applied, only to discover later that the Rules had been replaced by the Guidelines. To be clear, a prudent party that wished to adopt the Rules but not the Guidelines should not use the Rules' model clause. Rather, it should, in adopting the Rules of Ethics, expressly exclude the Guidelines, and specifically adopt Rules 3 and 4 of the Rules of Ethics in lieu of the Guidelines. The remaining rules – 1, 2, and 5 through 9 – include, *inter alia*, issues governing diligence, acceptance of appointment, communication with parties, and confidentiality.[65]

c. American Arbitration Association–American Bar Association Code of Ethics for Arbitrators in Commercial Disputes

The IBA's Rules and Guidelines are not the only ones that can be used to measure arbitrator conduct. The Code of Ethics for Arbitrators in Commercial Disputes, originally prepared in 1977 by representatives of the American Arbitration Association (AAA) and the American Bar Association (ABA), was revised, effective in 2004, by members of both groups. The revised Code differs in significant respects from the IBA Rules and Guidelines. First, with respect to party-appointed arbitrators, the AAA has a tradition in domestic arbitrations in the United States of having party-appointed arbitrators who are not neutral and are not expected to be impartial or independent. Rather,

---

[62] Introduction to Guidelines, ¶ 8.

[63] *See also Background Information, supra* note 40, at 456.

[64] The model clause does state that the rules being adopted are those "in force at the date of any arbitration under this clause." This would make the Guidelines applicable, but would not deal with the problem that parties might have no clue that the rules they thought they were adopting had changed. The IBA bears some responsibility for this, because it did not issue new Rules of Ethics, and the Rules of Ethics and the Guidelines are found in two separate documents. Normally, when institutions issue new rules, they issue one whole set of new rules. One must really go to the fine print of the Guidelines to understand how they affect the Rules of Ethics.

[65] See *infra* section B(2).

they are expected to advocate for the parties that chose them. Currently, however, in international arbitrations, the AAA does not permit non-neutral arbitrators. The international division of the AAA, the International Dispute Resolution Centre (ICDR), makes clear that under its international arbitration rules, all arbitrators, including party-appointed arbitrators, must be impartial and independent.[66] Nonetheless, in domestic arbitrations, parties may still decide to have non-neutral, party-appointed arbitrators. The AAA deals with this in its Code of Ethics by establishing a presumption that all arbitrators are neutral, but then providing special rules in Canon X for arbitrators in domestic arbitrations to be non-neutral, if that is what both parties choose. Canon X arbitrators, as the non-neutral arbitrators are called, still have a number of obligations. For example, a Canon X arbitrator cannot at any time during the arbitration disclose any deliberations of the arbitrators, or disclose any final decision or interim decision before it is disclosed to all parties.[67]

The second major difference between the IBA Guidelines and the AAA-ABA Code of Ethics is the AAA-ABA's very broad requirement of disclosure. A number of items under the Green List of the IBA Guidelines would be required to be disclosed under the AAA-ABA Code of Ethics. For example, Canon II (A)(2) of the AAA-ABA Code is similar to the IBA Guidelines in that it provides that prospective arbitrators should disclose any "financial, business, professional or personal relations which might reasonably affect impartiality or lack of independence in the eyes of any of the parties." But it also provides, as an example, that "prospective arbitrators should disclose "any such relationships which they personally have with any party or its lawyer [or] with any co-arbitrator."[68] As you will recall from the Green List example given earlier,[69] a prospective arbitrator would not be expected under the IBA Guidelines to disclose that she had served as co-counsel or coarbitrator with another arbitrator or as counsel for one of the parties. Although in particular cases, one might be able to argue that the relationship was not one that should be disclosed, the thrust under the AAA-ABA Code suggests that an arbitrator would most likely be expected to disclose such a relationship.[70] In addition, the AAA advises its arbitrators that "[a]rbitrators must disclose any relationship between themselves and a party, a party's representative or a witness," and that "[e]very disclosure, no matter how insignificant, should be communicated to the parties."[71]

---

[66] ICDR Rules, art. 7.

[67] The Code of Ethics for Arbitrators in Commercial Disputes, Canon X(c)(4)(a)&(c). Available at http://www.adr.org/si.asp?id=4582.

[68] The Code of Ethics for Arbitrators in Commercial Disputes, Canon II (A)(2).

[69] *See supra* Section B(1)(a)(ii).

[70] *See* discussion *infra*, text accompanying notes 90–91, of Positive Software Solutions, Inc., v. New Century Financial Corporation, 476 F.3d 278 (5th Cir. 2007, *en banc*).

[71] See AAA, Neutrals eCenter, at http://www.adr.org/si.asp?id=4217.

Thus, an arbitrators' duty to disclose is subject to different standards, with a higher standard under the AAA-ABA Code than under the IBA Guidelines. A general rule that prudent arbitrators should follow, however, is that when in doubt, disclose. This rule is contained in the IBA Guidelines, the AAA-ABA Code of Ethics, and a number of institutional rules.

d. Duty to Investigate

To what extent does a duty to disclose possible conflicts also mandate a duty to investigate? Although some courts have been known to vacate awards when an arbitrator has not investigated a potential conflict of interest,[72] laws and rules are not clear on the extent of the obligation of an arbitrator to actively investigate potential conflicts. The U.S. Second Circuit Court of Appeals has indicated that although there is no free-standing duty for an arbitrator to investigate potential conflicts, if the arbitrator has reason to believe a potential conflict exists, then he must investigate.[73] The U.S. Ninth Circuit has gone a step further. In New Regency Productions, Inc., v. Nippon Herald Films, Inc., it appeared to impose a duty on the arbitrator to investigate even if he was not aware of an actual or potential conflict.[74] In reaching its conclusion, the Ninth Circuit referred to both the AAA-ABA Code of Ethics and the IBA Guidelines.[75] The AAA-ABA Code requires arbitrators "to make reasonable efforts to inform themselves" of potential or actual conflicts,[76] and the IBA Guidelines, as noted earlier, place a duty on the arbitrator "to make reasonable enquiries to investigate any potential conflicts of interests."[77] It seems quite reasonable for a duty to be placed on parties as well as arbitrators to investigate possible conflicts, which is what the IBA Guidelines require.[78] Although Codes and Guidelines are soft law and not binding unless specifically agreed to by the parties, the *New Regency Productions* case indicates that courts may use these standards in determining whether an arbitrator has a conflict of interest serious enough to undermine her impartiality or independence. It therefore behooves arbitrators to investigate any potential conflict, and, in accordance with the IBA Guidelines, "disclose any facts or circumstances that may cause his or her

---

[72] *See, e.g.*, Applied Industrial Materials Corp. v. Ovalar Makine Ticaret Ve Sanayi, A.S., 492 F.3d 132 (2d Cir. 2007); Schmitz v. Zilveti, 20 F.3d 1043 (9th Cir. 1994); New Regency Productions, Inc., v. Nippon Herald Films, Inc., 501 F. 3d 1101 (9th Cir. 2007).

[73] *See* Applied Indus. Materials, 492 F.3d at 139.

[74] *See* New Regency Productions, 501 F.3d at 1109. *See also* Kathryn A. Windsor, *Defining Arbitrator Evident Partiality: The Catch-22 of Commercial Litigation Disputes*, 6 Seton Hall Cir. Rev. 191, 206 (2009).

[75] *See New Regency Productions*, at 1109–10.

[76] Code of Ethics for Arbitrators in Commercial Disputes, Canon II(B).

[77] IBA Guidelines, General Standard 7(c).The Guideline further notes that "[f]ailure to disclose a potential conflict is not excused by lack of knowledge if the arbitrator makes no reasonable attempt to investigate."

[78] IBA Guidelines, General Standard 7(a).

impartiality of independence to be questioned."[79] In practice, it is helpful if parties provide to arbitrators a list of companies and individuals that should be reviewed by the arbitrator for possible conflicts of interest.

2. Other Obligations

Arbitrators have a number of obligations. Some are embodied in rules and laws, whereas others are based on ethical concepts and on the parties' expectations, or are based on the usual practices in international arbitration.[80] Perhaps the most fundamental obligation is to render an enforceable award, or at least to make best efforts to render an enforceable award.[81] Although this could be considered an ethical or a moral obligation, some arbitral institutions impose the obligation in their rules.[82]

Arbitrators should read carefully the arbitration agreement to see whether the parties have imposed specific obligations. For example, the parties may have agreed that the arbitrator should decide the arbitration *ex aequo et bono*, that is, that the arbitrator is free to reach an equitable result as opposed to strictly applying the law. The arbitrator may also have specific duties imposed by an arbitral institution or by the arbitration rules, such as the obligation to be impartial and independent, and not to have *ex parte* communications with parties, except when a party is choosing its arbitrator pursuant to agreement.[83] Moreover, the arbitrator may be required under local law to be fair and impartial, to act with due care, to treat parties equally, and to give each party a full opportunity to present its case.[84]

Various codes of ethics also set forth duties for arbitrators. The 1987 IBA Rules of Ethics for International Arbitrators, for example, imposes the following duties:

Article 1

- To proceed diligently and efficiently to provide parties with a just and effective resolution
- To be free from bias

Article 2

- Not to contact parties to solicit an appointment
- Not to accept an appointment unless:

---

[79] IBA Guidelines, General Standard 7(c).

[80] *See*, generally, Catherine A. Rogers, *The Ethics of International Arbitrators*, in LEADING ARBITRATORS' GUIDE TO INTERNATIONAL ARBITRATION (Juris Publishing, 2008).

[81] *See, e.g.*, Martin Platte, *An Arbitrator's Duty to Render Enforceable Awards*, 20 J. Int'l Arb. 307 (2003).

[82] LCIA Rules, art. 32.2; ICC Rules, art. 41.

[83] *See, e.g.*, ICDR Rules, art. 7.

[84] *See, e.g.*, UNCITRAL Model Law, arts. 12, 14, 18.

- Free from bias
- Competent to determine the issue
- Knowledgeable of the language of the arbitration
- Available to give the matter reasonable time and attention

Article 3

- To be impartial and independent

Article 4

- To disclose facts and circumstances giving rise to justifiable doubts as to impartiality or independence

Article 5

- To respond to enquiries from parties about suitability to be an arbitrator, so long as the merits of the case are not discussed
- If a sole arbitrator is approached by one party or a presiding arbitrator is approached by one party-nominated arbitrator, to ensure that the other party has consented, and to inform the other party of the substance of the conversations
- To avoid unilateral conversations with any party or its representatives
- To alert the other arbitrator if one arbitrator has engaged in improper conduct, such as *ex parte* communications, and to jointly request the offending arbitrator to refrain from improper conduct; if the conduct continues, to alert the innocent party
- Not to accept from any party any gift or substantial hospitality
- To avoid substantial professional or social contacts with any party to the arbitration, unless all parties are present

Article 6

- Not to make unilateral arrangements for fees or expenses, unless a party defaults or parties agree otherwise

Article 7

- To devote time and attention needed
- To conduct proceedings with regard to efficiency and parties' costs

Article 8

- To make proposals for settlement if parties request or consent, but to refrain from doing so *ex parte*, unless first explaining to parties that *ex parte* participation will normally disqualify arbitrators from continuing to arbitrate

Article 9

- To keep the deliberations of the tribunal and the contents of awards confidential in perpetuity, unless released by the parties, or required to disclose the misconduct of fellow arbitrators

The IBA Rules of Ethics include many provisions that are generally accepted in international practice. The AAA-ABA Code of Ethics deals with many of the same issues, but is more detailed in many areas, and, as noted earlier, requires broader disclosure by a prospective arbitrator of his present or past relationships with any party, lawyer, arbitrator, or witness.

C. CHALLENGES TO THE ARBITRATOR

A party can challenge the appointment of an arbitrator and seek his removal at the time the tribunal is constituted – or later, if new facts come to light. The primary ground for challenging an arbitrator is a conflict of interest, but arbitrators can also be challenged for improper conduct – for example, repeatedly falling asleep at the hearings, having inappropriate *ex parte* conversations with one of the parties, or simply not moving the arbitration forward in a timely manner.

In an institutional arbitration, the rules of the institution will provide the bases for bringing the challenge and the procedure to do so. For example, the LCIA Rules provide that an arbitrator may be challenged on the basis of "justifiable doubts as to his impartiality or independence," or if she "becomes unable or unfit to act."[85] The Rules explain further that the arbitrator may be considered unfit if she does not act fairly or impartially or does not conduct the proceedings with diligence.[86]

If a party intends to challenge an arbitrator, it must do so promptly or risk being deemed to have waived any objection. Under the LCIA Rules, a written statement must be sent to the LCIA Court, the arbitral tribunal, and all other parties within fifteen days of becoming aware of any circumstances that would support a challenge.[87] Under the ICC Rules, the period is thirty days.[88] In both cases, unless the arbitrator has decided to withdraw, it is the administrative body of the institution that decides whether to remove the arbitrator.

---

[85] LCIA Rules, arts. 10.1, 10.3.

[86] *See id.* art. 10.2.

[87] *See id.* art. 11.2.

[88] ICC Rules, art. 14(2). More specifically, the challenge must be made within thirty days from notification of appointment or confirmation, or thirty days from being informed of circumstances on which the challenge is based. *See id.*

If the challenge is not successful, in many jurisdictions the party that brought the challenge may take the issue to a court. The UNCITRAL Model Law permits such a challenge within thirty days of receipt of notice that the challenge was rejected.[89] No appeal is permitted from the court's decision.[90] If the particular jurisdiction does not provide for review of a rejected challenge to an arbitrator, a party may have to wait until the final award to obtain court review of the decision.

If the arbitration is ad hoc, unless the parties have adopted the UNCITRAL rules,[91] or unless the parties have a carefully structured agreement dealing with this issue, local law will determine whether a party has the right to challenge an arbitrator prior to the rendering of a final award.

As international arbitration becomes increasingly adversarial, possibilities increase that a challenge to an arbitrator is simply a tactic to delay the proceedings. It is important, however, that parties have confidence in the arbitrators and the proceedings, which means they must have the right to challenge an arbitrator who does not inspire confidence. Challenges may be very well grounded. Moreover, many arbitrators will simply withdraw if they believe the parties do not have confidence in them.

If a party does bring a challenge, it will be difficult to win.[92] In addition, the loss of a challenge may leave the particular arbitrator, as well as the tribunal, with some resentment against the challenging party, particularly if they believe the challenge was merely a strategy to delay. Parties whose intention is to delay can expect that the challenge will probably slow down the proceedings, but should understand that the process could be damaging to their case if it causes them to lose credibility before the tribunal. Moreover, even challenges that may seem reasonable frequently do not succeed.

EXAMPLE OF A CHALLENGE THAT FAILED

In an arbitration in Australia arising out of a contract for sale of offshore natural gas, the plaintiff buyer sought to remove an arbitrator at the beginning of the arbitration. The grounds were as follows:

---

[89] UNCITRAL Model Law, art. 13(3).

[90] *See id.* This rule preempts the normal rules for appeal that would generally apply in cases brought in the particular national court.

[91] *See* UNCITRAL Rules, arts. 12–13, which deal with challenges to arbitrators.

[92] The LCIA recently published abstracts of arbitrator challenges between 1996 and 2010, 27 Arb. Int'l, issue 3, 2011. Among the 28 challenges, the challengers prevailed in only six cases. *See* Jean Kalicki, *Reflections on the LCIA Arbitrator Challenges*, Kluwer Arbitration Blog (Dec. 12, 2011). *See also* Thomas W. Walsh & Ruth Teitelbaum, *The LCIA Decisions on Challenges to Arbitrators: An Introduction*, 27 Arb. Int'l at 283–313.

1. The arbitrator had decided technical issues in favor of the sellers in another arbitration, and the buyer asserted those issues were similar to the issues in the instant case.
2. The arbitrator had been lead counsel for some producers in a prior arbitration concerning onshore natural gas, and had made submissions criticizing expert witnesses who were expected to be called in the instant case.
3. The arbitrator had failed to disclose pertinent information concerning his participation in the earlier arbitrations.

The Court of Appeal, Supreme Court of Victoria, refused to order the removal of the arbitrator, finding that the first two grounds did not suggest bias, and that failure to disclose circumstances that did not themselves lead to a reasonable apprehension of bias did not constitute grounds for removal.[93] There was no suggestion in the case of actual bias, according to the Court. The standard for apprehended bias in Australia was whether "a fair-minded lay observer with knowledge of the material objective facts might entertain a reasonable apprehension that the [arbitrator] might not bring an impartial and unprejudiced mind to the resolution of the matters before him."[94] The Court found that plaintiff buyer's evidence did not meet this standard.

There is clearly tension between the position that arbitrators should disclose any possible conflict and let parties decide what might indicate bias, and the position that arbitrators should not have to disclose broadly because parties may take advantage of any minor or insignificant relationship to try to delay the proceedings or to deny the other party its choice of arbitrator. Related to this tension is the question of what the standard for requiring disclosure is or should be.[95] Courts have taken different positions on when an arbitrator's nondisclosure is sufficient to result in removal of an arbitrator, or to set aside an award.[96]

A leading U.S. case on the proper standard for disclosure is Commonwealth Coatings Corp. v. Continental Cas. Co. (Commonwealth

---

[93] Gascor v. Ellicott (1996), 1 VR 332, 1996 VIC Lexis 1373.

[94] *Id.* at *19.

[95] *See, e.g.,* Catherine A. Rogers, *Regulating International Arbitrators: A Functional Approach to Developing Standards of Conduct,* 41 Stan. J. Int'l L. 53, 117–20 (2005) ("[D]isclosure obligations [should] be defined by categorical rules that limit arbitrator discretion."). *Id.* at 118–19.

[96] *Compare* Betz v. Pankow, 31 Cal. App. 4th 1503, 1511–12 (1995) (Arbitrator's lack knowledge of former firm's conflict did not create sufficient impression of bias to warrant overturning award.) *with* Schmitz v. Zilveti, 20 F.3d 1043, 1048–49 (9th Cir. 1994) (Arbitrator without actual knowledge can still have constructive knowledge of actual conflict, and failure to investigate is breach of duty to reasonably inform self of conflict.).

Coatings).[97] In that case, the U.S. Supreme Court vacated an award where the presiding arbitrator had not disclosed that one of the parties was a regular customer. The Court was interpreting the Federal Arbitration Act's provision that an award may be vacated for "evident partiality."[98] Even though the district court had found that the arbitrator was "entirely fair and impartial,"[99] the Supreme Court stated that arbitrators must disclose "any dealings that might create an impression of possible bias."[100] Because the opinion was a plurality opinion (only four of nine justices), for it to become an opinion of the court, it needed the concurrence of at least one more justice. In a separate concurring opinion, Justice White made clear that nondisclosure of trivial relationships does not result in disqualification. He stated that although arbitrators do not have to give the parties their "complete and unexpurgated business biography,"[101] they should nonetheless "err on the side of disclosure."[102]

Lower courts have tended to follow Justice White's concurring opinion. Recently, the Fifth Circuit, in an *en banc* decision, reconsidered a three-judge panel decision and reversed a lower court's decision that an award should be vacated because of the arbitrator's nondisclosure.[103] In that case, an arbitrator had not disclosed that he had previously been co-counsel with the counsel for one of the parties in a complex case in which, even though both the arbitrator and the counsel had signed many of the same papers, they had never met nor spoken to each other. The Fifth Circuit, relying heavily on Justice White's concurrence in *Commonwealth Coatings*, stated that *vacatur* was not appropriate unless the nondisclosure created "a concrete, not speculative impression of bias,"[104] which it did not find in the instant case.

There was, however, a very strong dissent by five Fifth Circuit judges. The dissenters believed that because decisions of arbitrators are not subject to judicial review, parties should be entitled to broad information in order to make a reasonable choice of their decision maker. Judge Wiener stated:

> The system fails when the nominee for the post of arbitrator takes it upon himself to make the value judgment whether a relationship is so inconsequential that it need not be disclosed at all. Arbitration's scant protection against bias and favoritism obviously breaks down completely when the question whether a relationship should be disclosed is assumed *sub silentio* by the potential arbitrator rather than

---

[97] Commonwealth Coatings Corp. v. Continental Cas. Co., 393 U.S. 145 (1968).
[98] *Id.* at 147.
[99] *Id.* at 151 (Justice White, concurring).
[100] *Id.* at 149.
[101] *Id.* at 151.
[102] *Id.* at 152.
[103] Positive Software Solutions, Inc., v. New Century Fin. Corp., 476 F. 3d 278 (5th Cir. 2007) (*en banc*).
[104] *Id.* at 286.

by disclosing all and allowing the parties to make that call following their receipt of all facts through an unabridged disclosure. . . . It cannot therefore be left to the fox, who is the potential arbitrator, to guard the arbitration henhouse, secretly identifying to himself alone all "prior or present relationships," then just as secretly deciding which are worthy of disclosure and which or not.[105]

Different courts and different judges obviously see the issues differently. From a practical perspective, a party is more likely to be successful if it challenges the arbitrator's nondisclosure at the beginning of the arbitration, rather than after an award has been issued.[106] In the Fifth Circuit case discussed earlier, it was only after the award had been rendered, and had been overwhelmingly in favor of the other party, that the challenging party did its investigation of the arbitrator and came up with information it believed the arbitrator should have disclosed. At that point, however, a court will be reluctant to set aside an award, given all the time, effort, and resources that have been expended. There may be a greater possibility of getting an arbitral institution to remove an arbitrator at the beginning of the arbitration if a party can show that the arbitrator failed to disclose information that was required to be disclosed by institutional or agreed-upon rules. Thus, parties should consider undertaking due diligence as soon as they know about an arbitrator's appointment, because their chances of reversing an award later for nondisclosure are slim.

When challenges are decided by an institution, the normal practice has been that, like awards, the information is considered confidential. The LCIA Court, however, has published its decisions on challenges to arbitrators in the form of digests, removing identifying information to preserve confidentiality.[107] Providing reasoned decisions to the parties and publishing digests of decisions should provide greater transparency as well as appropriate guidance to parties and arbitrators about the bases for the various decisions.[108]

D. FLAWED CONDUCT OF ARBITRATORS

Sometimes arbitrators do not conduct themselves as they should, even though such conduct may not arise to the level of warranting a challenge. The most common complaints are that arbitrators do not move the proceedings along efficiently and do not provide an award in a timely manner.

---

[105] *Id.* at 293 (5th Cir. 2007) (Judge Wiener, dissenting).
[106] *See* Stephen R. Bond, *The Selection of ICC Arbitrators and the Requirement of Independence*, 4 Arb. Int. 300, at 306 (1988).
[107] The digests have been published in 27 Arb. Int'l, issue 3 (2011). *See supra* note 92.
[108] *See* Geoff Nicholas & Constantine Partasides, *LCIA Court Decision on Challenges to Arbitrators: A Proposal to Publish*, 23 Arb. Int. 1 (2007).

Anecdotal tales abound of an arbitrator waiting over a year to schedule the preliminary conference, or waiting more than three years after the conclusion of the arbitration to render an award. This kind of conduct undermines confidence in arbitration as an effective dispute resolution system.

> The number one issue for users and counsel with respect to arbitrators is the length of time it takes them to issue an award.[109]
>
> Claudia Salomon
> New York

Counsel sometimes complain that once an arbitrator is chosen, he is a law unto himself, and there are little or no controls on his conduct. Increasingly, there are proposals for fines and reductions in fees for arbitrators who do not perform as they should. Some institutions hold back at least some fees until the award is rendered, and some have been known to cut fees for poor performance and enhance them for excellent performance. In addition, when arbitrators tend to be chosen from a list that is put together by an institution, removal from the list, or even threat of removal, can be an effective mechanism to encourage proper conduct. Diana Droulers, Executive Director of the Arbitration Center of the Caracas Chamber (Centro de Arbitraje de la Camara de Caracas), observes:

> In Caracas, the Chamber of Commerce has a list of arbitrators. Parties are free to choose someone not on the list, but generally they tend to choose from the list. The list is revised every two years, and individuals can be removed from the list for various reasons, including improper conduct.[110]
>
> Diana Droulers
> Venezuela

Institutions should exercise their right to refuse to appoint or to confirm arbitrators when they know that, in previous cases, the arbitrators have not met their responsibilities in a timely manner. Imposing sanctions on arbitrators who perform improperly sends a message to all arbitrators of the importance of conducting themselves in a way that encourages confidence in the arbitral process.

[109] Interview with Claudia Salomon, July 2011. Notes of interview are on file with author.
[110] Interview with Diana Droulers, April 2007. Notes of interview on file with author.

E. REPLACEMENT OF ARBITRATORS

If an arbitrator is successfully challenged, or if one resigns or withdraws for any reason, it will be necessary to choose a replacement. Generally, institutional rules will provide the method for replacement. With an ad hoc arbitration, if pertinent rules have not been adopted by the parties and the parties cannot agree on the method for replacing an arbitrator, usually the court at the situs of the arbitration can be called on to make an appointment.

If the vacancy occurs and is filled before the arbitration begins, there should be little disruption. However, if the replacement arbitrator is chosen after the arbitration has been in process for some time, the question arises as to how much, if any, of the testimony must be repeated. Most of the time, parties and tribunals take a commonsense approach. If there is a transcript, the replacement arbitrator can generally get up to speed by reading the transcript.[111] If not, then institutional rules tend to give arbitrators, upon consideration of the views of the party, the authority to determine how much of the testimony needs to be repeated.[112]

It may be the case, however, that an arbitrator resigns at or near the end of the arbitration proceedings, sometimes without sufficient reason.[113] In a number of cases, the proceedings have nonetheless continued and the award has been rendered by two arbitrators. Some arbitration rules specifically provide that the other two arbitrators may determine, in their sole discretion, whether to continue the arbitration with a truncated tribunal.[114]

F. ARBITRATOR IMMUNITY

If an arbitrator fails in one or more duties, is he liable to the parties for any damages they may suffer? The arguments in favor of granting immunity to arbitrators are that they perform a quasi-judicial function, and they should

---

[111] One counsel the author spoke with, Sarah François-Poncet, said that in one of her cases, an arbitrator died before the award was rendered. There had been a week-long hearing with extensive factual and expert testimony. The parties had also made oral closing arguments in lieu of post-hearing briefs, it having been agreed that there would be no post-hearing briefs. There was no transcript. Since that time, she has always requested that the hearings where she acts as counsel be transcribed.

[112] Many arbitral rules deal specifically with this issue. The WIPO Rules provide that when a substitute arbitrator has been appointed, "the Tribunal shall, having regard to any observations of the parties, determine in its sole discretion whether all or part of any prior hearings are to be repeated." WIPO Rules, art. 34. The ICC Rules state that once the replacement arbitrator has been appointed, "the arbitral tribunal shall determine if and to what extent prior proceedings shall be repeated before the reconstituted arbitral tribunal." ICC Rules, art. 15(4).

[113] *See, e.g.*, Redfern & Hunter et al., *supra* note 2, § 4.141 at 288.

[114] *See, e.g.*, WIPO Rules, art. 34; ICDR Rules, art. 11.

not be subject to suit by disgruntled parties. It is also argued that immunity helps ensure the finality of arbitral awards. Moreover, the suggestion is made that if arbitrators are subject to damage awards, this may encourage a party to try to intimidate an arbitrator during the arbitration by hinting that if things turn out "wrong" from the party's point of view, it will sue the arbitrator. Finally, it is argued that without immunity, many well-qualified individuals will not be willing to arbitrate.

Arguments against granting immunity to arbitrators include the concern that relieving arbitrators of liability will tend to encourage carelessness, fraud, and abuse of power, and that finality of awards should not be more important than individual justice. In addition, there are no readily available disciplinary measures that can be taken against arbitrators. These concerns are magnified by the fact that, generally, arbitral awards cannot be reversed for errors of law or fact.

How does a legal system balance the various concerns? Not surprisingly, different legal systems take different approaches to arbitral immunity. In all systems, however, arbitrators are not immune from criminal liability. If they are found to have accepted bribes or embezzled funds, they will be subject to criminal laws. There are wide variations, however, particularly between common-law and civil-law jurisdictions, in the way that various courts deal with immunity of arbitrators for noncriminal acts.

In common law countries, courts tend to provide immunity to arbitrators when they are acting in a quasi-judicial function. The United States probably takes the most protective stance toward arbitrators, providing almost absolute immunity to an arbitrator acting in a decision-making capacity. Some states within the United States even provide for immunity by statute.[115] The Australian International Arbitration Act of 1974, as amended, provides that "[a]n arbitrator is not liable for anything done or omitted to be done by the arbitrator in good faith in his or her capacity as arbitrator."[116] In England, an arbitrator may be liable for acting in bad faith and also if a court determines that she withdrew from the arbitration without good reason.[117]

Many civil law countries, although never granting absolute immunity, nonetheless recognize rather broad immunity for arbitrators.[118] For the most part, arbitrators are not going to be found liable for negligence, but only

---

[115] *See, e.g.*, California, Florida, and Alaska statutes, Cal. Civ. Code, § 1297.119 (1994); Fla. Stat. § 684.35 (1998); AS 09.43.410 (providing immunity when arbitrators are performing in their decision-making capacity).

[116] Australian International Arbitration Act (CTH.), Act No. 136 of 1974 as amended, § 28.

[117] English Arbitration Act of 1996, §§ 25, 29.

[118] *See* Gary Born, INTERNATIONAL COMMERCIAL ARBITRATION (2009) at 1657.

for gross negligence or intentional wrongdoing.[119] Liability is usually determined on the basis of contract or tort. With respect to contract liability, the arbitrator has sometimes been viewed as having a contract for services with the parties.[120] As with other professionals, if the arbitrator does not perform as agreed, he will have liability. The most likely breach for which an arbitrator may be found liable is if he simply does not render an award. In that case, the parties' entire effort is fruitless, and there may well be damages. When the violation is based on tort, the arbitrators' conduct may be viewed as violating a duty of due care.[121]

Disgruntled parties may want to sue not just the arbitrator, but also the institution that handled the arbitration. In most jurisdictions, arbitral institutions have immunity because they function as a quasi-judicial organization. Again, the rules may differ depending on the jurisdiction. In France, for example, arbitration centers are potentially liable if they fail to provide the means for an efficient and effective arbitration.[122]

Various arbitration rules have included provisions proclaiming immunity for arbitrators. Many provide that the arbitrator will be immune except in cases of deliberate wrongdoing.[123] Others provide for immunity except to the extent prohibited by applicable law.[124] Regardless of the level of immunity provided in the rules, most legal systems will not permit parties to waive intentional acts of wrongdoing, or gross negligence. Although arbitrators may in theory be liable for such acts, showing that an arbitrator engaged in such conduct can present difficult problems of proof.

---

[119] *See id.*

[120] In the case of Jivraj v. Hashwani, [2010] EWCA Civ 712, the UK Court of Appeal found that there was an employment contract between the parties and the arbitrators. However, the UK Supreme Court unanimously overturned the decision [2011] UKSC 40. Rather than finding the arbitrator to be an employee of the parties, the Supreme Court held that the arbitrator was independent of the parties, and was a quasi-judicial adjudicator. A concern in the arbitration community had been that because the Court of Appeals decision had found arbitrators were employees subject to nondiscrimination rules, the ruling would prevent parties from specifying requirements as to an arbitrator's nationality. The Supreme Court decision is seen as preserving this significant element of neutrality.

[121] *See* Susan D. Franck, *The Liability of International Arbitrators: A Comparative Analysis and Proposal for Qualified Immunity*, 20 N.Y.L. Sch. J. Int'l & Comp. L. 1, 11 (2000), for a discussion of tort or tort-like issues in Germany, Iraq, and Saudi-Arabia.

[122] *See* Matthew Rasmussen, *Overextending Immunity: Arbitral Institutional Liability in The United States, England, And France*, 26 Fordham Int'l L.J. 1824, 1864 (2003) ("Cour de Cassation held that . . . the ICC is contractually obligated to fulfill its essential function as an arbitral institution"), *citing* Société Cubic Defense System v. Chambre de Commerce Internationale, 1e Civ., 20 Feb. 2001.

[123] *See, e.g.*, LCIA Rules, art. 31; ICDR Rules, art. 35; WIPO Rules, art. 77.

[124] *See, e.g.*, ICC Rules, art. 40, NAI Rules, art. 66.

G. COSTS AND FEES

An arbitration is not necessarily less expensive for the parties than a lawsuit. However, cost savings may come from the fact that there is generally no appeal on issues of fact or law. In addition, arbitral tribunals generally do not permit the same level of discovery as courts, which can reduce costs substantially. On the other hand, the parties have to pay for the arbitrators and the costs of any institution that administers the arbitration, as well as legal fees, and those costs can be extensive.

In an institutional arbitration, the arbitrators' fees generally must be approved by the institution and are sometimes determined by it. Parties may discuss fees with their party-appointed arbitrator, but not with the other two arbitrators. In ad hoc arbitrations, on the other hand, in which fees may be discussed, all parties should participate in discussions with all arbitrators about their fees. Sometimes the presiding arbitrator is paid more than the party-selected arbitrators because he or she has additional obligations and duties.

An arbitrator is also entitled to reimbursement for expenses. In institutional arbitrations, these are dealt with by the institution. In ad hoc arbitrations, the parties may want to put some limitations on expenses, such as providing a per diem allowance and agreeing to reimburse flights at a particular level, such as "one above coach," coach being the lowest economy class.

Normally, parties are expected to pay some initial fees and costs in advance. If the respondent refuses to pay its share, the arbitration will not go forward unless the claimant pays the respondent's share. Although this initially burdens the claimant, the payments may be allocated against the respondent in the final award.

CHAPTER SEVEN

The Arbitral Proceedings

In a major international commercial arbitration, specific steps in the dispute-resolving process are reasonably well defined. First, the claimant must submit a notice of arbitration, to which the respondent answers. Depending on the relevant rules, the notice and response may include detailed pleadings. Other times the notice may be quite succinct, and written submissions constituting the pleadings will be provided at a later point. Next, the arbitrators are appointed, generally according to party agreement or pursuant to the rules the parties have chosen. Normally, some kind of organizational meeting will follow, to discuss how the arbitration will proceed. Subsequently, there may be further written submissions and pre-hearing disclosure will begin, including exchanges of documentary evidence and witness statements, all in preparation for the oral hearings.

The oral hearings may take place in one meeting that lasts several days, or in a number of multiday hearings that may occur over weeks or months. At the hearing, there may be short opening statements, followed by oral testimony, submission of documentary evidence, and perhaps legal argument on certain points, if requested by the tribunal. At the end of the hearing, there may be short closing statements, and the arbitrators may request post-hearing submissions. After the arbitrators review the post-hearing submissions, they deliberate and render a decision in the form of a final award. This is the basic process, of which there are many variations. This chapter focuses on the various elements of the arbitral proceedings, and some of the ways a tribunal may conduct the proceedings.[1]

Because international arbitration often involves parties and arbitrators from different legal systems, the procedures used in the arbitration may

---

[1] Some specific issues, such as the appointment of arbitrators, determination of the arbitrators' jurisdiction, interim relief, and court intervention, are dealt with in other chapters.

tend to reflect one system somewhat more than another, usually influenced by the background of the presiding arbitrator. Increasingly, however, the international arbitration process is becoming more of a standardized, hybrid process, taking elements from both civil and common law traditions. Lawyers from both systems are becoming more accustomed to this hybrid procedure and are adapting their methods of practice accordingly. This chapter considers how elements from common law and civil law combine to provide procedures that are generally accepted in international commercial arbitration.

A. BEGINNING THE ARBITRATION

When parties have not been able to resolve a dispute and one party decides to begin an arbitration, the first step for counsel is to read the arbitration agreement, then read and follow the rules chosen by the parties in that agreement.[2] The procedures for beginning an arbitration vary in accordance with the chosen rules. One difference that may prove important in some cases is how the time of commencement of an arbitration is determined. Does the arbitration begin when the claimant files a notice with the institution, when the respondent receives a notice, or some other time? This can make a difference for the purposes of time limits that may have been imposed by a statute of limitations or by the parties' own contract.

Under the ICDR Rules, the arbitration is deemed to begin on the date the administrator receives written notice of arbitration from the claimant.[3] The same is true for the ICC and LCIA Rules.[4] Under the UNCITRAL Rules, however, the arbitration is deemed to commence on the date the request for arbitration is received by the respondent.[5] The prudent claimant, of course, should ensure that it obtains proof of delivery of the notice to all the appropriate addressees, so the date of commencement will be clearly established.

Moreover, some arbitration laws provide that if the parties have not agreed otherwise, the arbitration is not commenced until appointment is accepted by the arbitrator[6] or the request to appoint an arbitrator has been served.[7] Thus, if there is an approaching deadline by which arbitration must

---

[2] If no rules have been chosen, counsel would look to the law governing the arbitration. The first step would likely be to send a demand for arbitration.
[3] ICDR Rules, art. 2(2).
[4] ICC Rule, art. 4(2); LCIA Rule, art. 1.2.
[5] UNCITRAL Rules, art. 3(2).
[6] Brazil Arbitration Law, art. 19.
[7] English Arbitration Act, § 14(4).

be commenced according to the parties' contract, or by virtue of a statute of limitations, the parties should make sure they understand what event triggers the beginning of the arbitration so the deadline can be met.

Another difference in how an arbitration is begun is whether the claimant must file with the arbitral tribunal (and/or with respondent) a simple notice, with a statement of claim to follow in a later document, or whether at the outset, it must submit a rather complete statement of claim. The UNCITRAL Rules, for example, require only a notice that sets forth "a brief description of the claim."[8] The claimant can then later, within a time period provided by the arbitrators, submit its more detailed statement of claim to the respondent and to each of the arbitrators.[9]

The ICDR, on the other hand, requires a written notice both to the institution and to the opposing party, and requires the notice to contain a statement of claim.[10] The rules state that the statement of claim should include the following:

- A demand for arbitration
- Contact information for the parties
- Reference to the arbitration agreement
- Reference to the contract which gave rise to the dispute
- A description of the claim, as well as the facts which support it
- The relief sought[11]

Optionally, the statement may also include a proposal about the method of choosing arbitrators, the number of arbitrators, the place of arbitration, and the language of arbitration.[12] This specification is not necessary if these issues have been dealt with in the arbitration clause or if the parties want to use the method provided in the arbitration rules.

Under the ICC rules, the claimant sends the Request for Arbitration only to the ICC Secretariat, not to the other party.[13] The Secretariat then sends a copy to the respondent.[14] Along with the Request, the claimant must also make advance payment on administrative expenses.[15]

---

[8] UNCITRAL Rules, art. 3 (3)(e). The notice must also include a demand for arbitration, contact information, identification of the contract and the arbitration clause, the amount at stake, the relief requested, and the number of arbitrators, if not previously agreed. *See id.* art 3(3).

[9] *See id.* art. 20(1).

[10] ICDR Rules, art. 2(1) & (3).

[11] ICDR Rules, art. 2(3).

[12] *See id.*

[13] ICC Rules, art. 4(1).

[14] *See id.* art. 4(5).

[15] *See id.* art. 4(4).

Once the respondent has received notice of the claimant's request for arbitration, normally it has either a time period to respond that is set by the pertinent rules, such as thirty days, or whatever time period may be determined by the arbitral tribunal. Generally, the respondent must assert any counterclaim at this time, as well as any objection to the tribunal's jurisdiction, or any assertion that the tribunal is exceeding the scope of its authority. Otherwise, the respondent may be deemed to have waived the right to assert a counterclaim or to object to jurisdiction or scope.[16]

B. PRELIMINARY MATTERS

Once the arbitrators have been appointed,[17] it is likely that the tribunal will schedule an initial meeting to discuss any preliminary matters and to organize the arbitral proceedings. If the issues are not complex, it may be sufficient to have the meeting by conference call or by video conferencing. For an arbitration that is likely to take significant time and deal with many issues, however, many arbitrators and parties consider it worthwhile to have a face-to-face meeting. At this meeting, it may be prudent to have not only the party's lawyers, but also an executive-level representative of the party, who has authority to make decisions for the party. Pierre Karrer, an arbitrator in Switzerland, explains factors to be considered in deciding whether to have a face-to-face meeting:

> Whether to have a face-to-face preliminary meeting depends upon 1. the size and complexity of the dispute, 2. the distance parties and counsel have to travel, and 3. whether the arbitrators and counsel know one another. Another factor is that sometimes clients want to come to a face-to-face conference to meet the arbitrators. Although telephone conferences are less expensive, if you are too cheap on the preliminary conference, you usually pay a price.[18]
>
> Pierre Karrer
> Switzerland

Although a telephone or video conference can provide cost savings, an old-fashioned, face-to-face meeting can provide good information to

---

[16] *See, e.g.*, LCIA Rules, art 23.2 (Objection to scope of tribunal's power is waived if not made in a timely manner.).

[17] *See* Chapter 6, *supra*, for a discussion of the appointment of arbitrators.

[18] Interview with Pierre Karrer, March 2007. Notes of interview on file with author.

everyone involved about the personalities of the various players, whose interactions can create an ambiance that will affect the arbitral process. Another advantage of the face-to-face meeting is that it provides the possibility that the parties can meet with each other before or after the principal meeting, and deal with certain issues in a more informal and comfortable setting than is possible through the medium of technology. Gillian Lemaire, counsel in Paris, explains why she prefers a face-to-face meeting:

> When acting as counsel, I almost always like to have a face-to-face meeting with the arbitrator(s) and opposing counsel at the beginning. As well as it being important to meet the arbitrator(s), the benefits of talking to counsel for the other side should not be underestimated. You get a better sense of who you are dealing with and a sharper focus on the real issues. You may find that A leads to B, and ultimately to an outcome that would be less likely to happen through telephone contact only.[19]
>
> Gillian Lemaire
> Paris

The preliminary meeting can deal with myriad issues. A good checklist of these kinds of issues can be found in a document produced by UNCITRAL in 1996, entitled "UNCITRAL Notes on Organizing Arbitral Proceedings."[20] If parties have not already agreed on rules, law, language, or place of arbitration, these will have to be discussed. In addition, issues such as the administration of the arbitration; use of technology (i.e., electronic submissions, technology at the hearings); confidentiality; a schedule for exchanging written submissions; documentary evidence; witness names and statements, as well as how many witnesses each side will call; whether expert witnesses will be needed; dates and length of future hearings; whether there will be a record of the hearings – these and other matters all should be considered and determined. Moreover, in an ad hoc arbitration, there should be a discussion of the deposit to be made by the parties for expenses and fees to be incurred in the arbitration. In institutional arbitrations, the institution will have already required this of the parties.

Frequently, the presiding arbitrator will send a letter to counsel to help them prepare for the preliminary conference. An example of the kind of letter that may be provided is set forth below, courtesy of David E. Wagoner, of Seattle, Washington.

[19] Interview with Gillian Lemaire, April 2007. Notes of interview on file with author.
[20] Available at www.UNICTRAL.org.

SAMPLE AGENDA LETTER FOR FIRST PRE-HEARING CONFERENCE

Dear Gentlemen:

May I express the appreciation of the Panel for being selected to serve as Arbitrators in this case.

I am writing to you to elaborate further on the matters to be discussed at the pre-hearing conference on Thursday, December 7, 2011, at 11:00 am.

The primary matter to be resolved is the setting of the dates for hearing. We estimate that the hearing will take five days. The Arbitrators have examined their calendars and are available for hearing on the following dates:

Week of February 20
Week of March 5
Week of March 26

Please confer with your client and witnesses and be prepared at the preliminary hearing to indicate your availability during one or more of these periods. May I ask you to confer with opposing counsel in an effort to reach an agreement.

Please be advised that the Arbitrators will expect the parties to adhere to the hearing dates that have been set. It is apparent from the arbitration provisions of the contract that the parties intended that the arbitration be handled in an expeditious and cost-effective manner.

The Arbitrators request that by noon on December 2, 2011 each party submit a brief letter of no more than 10 pages outlining with particularity the background of the dispute, its contentions and issues and the relief sought and listing the names and addresses of witnesses it intends to call at the hearing. The purpose of this is to help the Arbitrators understand the case.

Additional items to be discussed at the preliminary hearing are the following:

1. *Exchange of Reliance Documents* – The Arbitrators propose that within 20 days after the pre-hearing conference, there will be production to the other party of reliance documents, *i.e.*, all documents upon which either party relies in support of its claims and its defenses to the opponent's claims, both as to liability and to damages (and any other documents which the parties mutually agree to produce). Supplemental document production may be made within 20 days thereafter.

2. *Other Discovery* – Requires a showing of need for particular documents or classes of documents. With the early exchange of reliance documents and witness statements of direct testimony, there should be no need for depositions. Depositions will only be allowed on a clear showing that such discovery is necessary to ensure a fair hearing.

3. *Witnesses Statements of Fact* – The Arbitrators propose that 10 days before the hearing date the parties simultaneously exchange the direct testimony of fact witnesses in support of its case, by affidavit or declaration.

   For clarification, the fact witness statements will be expected to set forth the facts known to the witness and not argument or "testimony" by counsel. Each witness for whom a statement is offered will be expected to be available at the hearing for cross-examination, unless excused by opposing counsel. On a case-by-case basis, arrangements may be made to allow cross-examination by video conferencing, phone or otherwise. At the hearing, live direct testimony of each witness for approximately 15 minutes may be allowed to introduce the witness and outline the witness' position, allowing some time flexibility on a case-by-case basis.

4. *Experts* – Expert reports shall be exchanged 20 days before the hearing and rebuttal expert reports 10 days thereafter. Immediately after this exchange, the experts shall meet, confer, and file a joint report to the Arbitrators of the matters upon which they are in agreement and define the issues to be resolved at the hearing. It would be desirable to hear the totality of the expert testimony as a block of evidence at the hearing.

5. *Tutorials* – Would it be helpful for the parties to submit tutorial material to help the Arbitrators' general understanding of highly technical issues in the case? If so, what should the protocol be?

6. *Protective Order* – Is there a need? If so, please submit a draft by noon on December 6, 2011 agreed, if possible.

7. *Time Limitations* – Section 12.4 of the Agreement provides that the hearing shall be held within 90 days of the initial demand for arbitration, that the hearing shall be concluded within two days, and the arbitrator(s) written decision shall be made within 14 calendar days after the hearing. Obviously these time limitations cannot be met. It is suggested that the parties enter into a written stipulation waving these requirements or amending them to conform to reality.

8. *Governing Law* – Section 11 of the Agreement seems clear – laws of the State of Washington excluding conflicts of law rules.

9. *Briefs and Form of Award*– The Arbitrators propose that 10 days before the hearing date the parties submit briefs of no more than 15 pages outlining the facts and laws applicable to the case with copies of court opinions cited and relevant statutory provisions. At the same time, each party will submit a proposed form of award.

10. *Exhibits* – The Arbitrator proposes that 10 days before the hearing date, the parties will exchange proposed exhibits. The parties are requested to pare down the number of exhibits, emphasizing key documents and excluding irrelevant or cumulative documents. Any objections to the admissibility of exhibits must be filed 5 days before the hearing. The Arbitrator will admit any proposed exhibits as to which no objection has been made. The parties are requested to identify exhibits for Claimant as C-1, C-2, etc., and Respondent as R-1, R-2, etc., and to highlight in different colors the key portions of the exhibits. A joint set of exhibits would be helpful.

11. *Witness Scheduling* – Witnesses shall be scheduled to avoid delays. At least 24 hours notice shall be given to the other party of witnesses to be called the next day.

12. *The Hearing* – Each party will be allocated approximately one half of the hearing time. The primary purpose of the hearing will be to allow cross-examination of fact and expert witnesses and presentation of rebuttal testimony. There should be no need for opening arguments. A short closing argument can be helpful at the end of the hearing or the next day, by phone if necessary. A post-hearing brief may be preferable. The Arbitrators will focus the argument on important matters.

13. *Form of Award* – The arbitration agreement provides that the Arbitrators' decision "shall set forth the essential findings and conclusions upon which the decision is based." This needs further clarification. Absent agreement, the Arbitrators will issue a reasoned award.

14. *Communications* – Written communications shall be submitted directly to the opposing party with a copy to the Arbitrators and the Administrator and shall be by email. Lengthy documents such as briefs shall be by hardcopy.

15. *Other Matters* – To be identified by the parties 2 days before the pre-hearing conference.

16. *Procedural and Discovery Decisions* – With the concurrence of the other Arbitrators and the agreement of the parties, the presiding Arbitrator alone shall decide procedural and discovery matters without necessarily conferring with the other Arbitrators.

17. *Scheduling* – Another preliminary hearing in 30 days.

> 18. *Cooperation of Counsel* – Counsel are expected to cooperate fully
> to expedite the process and reduce costs.
>
> The Panel looks forward to working with the parties to obtain a
> fair and expeditious resolution of this case.
>
>
>
> Sincerely,
> David E. Wagoner, Presiding Arbitrator
>
>

Note that the letter is sent by the presiding arbitrator on behalf of all
three arbitrators. Before sending the letter to the parties, the presiding arbitrator usually sends a draft to the coarbitrators, and then incorporates their
comments into the final version. The letter tells the parties what they should
be prepared to discuss and decide at the preliminary hearing. It also lets
them know the arbitrators' preferences on a number of matters and suggests
that the parties try to agree on various issues in advance of the hearing.
By letting counsel know what to expect, and encouraging them to agree in
advance, the agenda letter contributes to the efficiency and effectiveness of
the preliminary conference.

Note also that paragraph 17 refers to scheduling another preliminary
conference. This serves to deal with any new issues that may arise, and
helps to keep the parties on track in their preparation for the hearing. The
second, and even third, preliminary conferences are likely to be telephone
conferences. Many of the issues raised in the agenda letter are discussed in
more detail later in this chapter.

Although all institutional rules vary somewhat, the ICC differs from
many, but not all, arbitration proceedings in its requirement that the arbitrators and the parties sign a document called the Terms of Reference.[21]
The Terms of Reference are based on the prior written submissions of the
parties,[22] for example, the request for arbitration, the answer, and possibly
the counterclaim and answer to counterclaim. Drafted by the arbitral tribunal, the Terms of Reference set forth the nature of all of the claims and
defenses of the respective parties, as well as "particulars of the applicable
procedural rules."[23] The ICC Rules also provide for a case management
conference when drawing up the Terms of Reference, or as soon as possible thereafter.[24] One purpose of the conference is to establish a procedural timetable for the conduct of the arbitration.[25] The case management

---

[21] ICC Rules, art. 23.
[22] *See id.* art. 23(1).
[23] *Id.*, art. 23(1)(g).
[24] *See id.* art. 24(1)
[25] *See id.* art. 24(2).

conference may be conducted through a meeting in person or by telephone, video conference, or other electronic means.[26]

Experienced arbitrators may make good use of the Terms of Reference in other ways. For example, they sometimes restate the original arbitration clause in the Terms of Reference, along with a statement that this arbitration clause (newly signed) is the original arbitration clause for purposes of the New York Convention. Because the New York Convention requires production of an original or certified arbitration clause, this eliminates the problem of trying to find the original version at the time of enforcement.

Essentially, the Terms of Reference provide the scope of the matters to be dealt with in the arbitration. Parties should prepare their submissions carefully prior to signing the Terms of Reference because, as a general rule, they are not permitted to submit new claims or counterclaims after the Terms of Reference are signed, unless the arbitral tribunal decides to admit them.[27] In practice, however, if new issues evolve during the course of the arbitration, the tribunal will generally consider them.[28] New issues that could easily have been included in the Terms of Reference and were simply overlooked by counsel, or which appear to be asserted in order to delay the process, are less likely to be permitted by the tribunal.

C. WRITTEN SUBMISSIONS

As noted earlier, depending on the rules, the initial pleadings of the parties may be succinct or detailed. If the pleadings are succinct, the tribunal will probably ask for additional written submissions later that will set forth the issues, define the scope of the arbitrator's mandate, and identify the facts and the law underlying the parties' claims and defenses.[29] On the other hand, if the parties have submitted extensive information in their pleadings, the arbitral tribunal may or may not wish to receive additional written submissions.[30]

The tribunal should provide specific information to the parties as to its expectations with respect to any written submissions, possibly including the issues it wishes to be discussed, whether it wants to know about facts

---

[26] *See id.* art. 24(4).

[27] *See id.* art. 19.

[28] *See* W. Laurence Craig, William W. Park, & Jan Paulsson, INTERNATIONAL CHAMBER OF COMMERCE ARBITRATION, § 15.01.

[29] *See, e.g.,* UNCITRAL Rules, arts. 20 and 21 (providing information about contents to be provided in statement of claim and statement of defence submitted after notice of arbitration).

[30] *See, e.g.,* ICDR Rules, art 17(1) ("The tribunal may decide whether the parties shall present any written statements in addition to statements of claims and counterclaims and statements of defense . . . ").

supporting only specific issues or all issues, whether it wants any discussion of law, and a page limit or range.

If the submissions essentially constitute the statement of claim and the response, they will probably be submitted sequentially. On the other hand, if both parties are knowledgeable about their respective positions on the issues as a result of prolific pleadings, but there is a question about which the arbitrators want to know more – for example, about a particular issue of law – the parties could be required to submit memoranda simultaneously.

Sometimes the parties may ask to submit post-hearing memoranda, or the arbitrators may require that post-hearing memoranda be submitted. Again, the arbitrators should make very clear to the parties exactly what they expect – for example, whether the memoranda should deal with all the issues of the arbitration, or simply certain points that the arbitrators would like to have clarified.

D. THE HEARING

Most institutional rules either require the tribunal to hold a hearing[31] or require a hearing if either one of the parties requests it.[32] Parties can agree, of course, to have the tribunal decide the dispute on documents only. Arbitrators may encourage parties, in the interest of efficiency, to agree to have the decision made on the documents. However, most counsel prefer to be heard orally in order to be available to respond to the arbitrators' questions and to satisfy their concerns or provide clarification or explanation.

1. Chair Can Decide Procedural Issues
In a three-arbitrator proceeding, parties will often agree that the chair alone can make decisions about procedural issues.[33] The chair, for example, might decide a question involving disclosure of documents or a time limitation for witness testimony. This permits matters to move along much more swiftly than if all three arbitrators were required to confer before rendering a decision. Under the UNCITRAL Model Law and under the LCIA Rules, however, the parties do not need to consent to the chair's authority to act independently; if the coarbitrators consent, the chair may make procedural rulings alone.[34]

---

[31] *See, e.g.,* ICDR Rules, art. 20(1).
[32] *See, e.g.,* ICC Rules, art. 25(6); LCIA Rules, art. 19.1; UNCITRAL Rules, art. 17(3); WIPO Rules, art. 53(a).
[33] *See* UNCITRAL Model Law, art. 29.
[34] *See* UNCITRAL Model Law, art. 29 ("[Q]uestions of procedure may be decided by a presiding arbitrator, if so authorized by the parties or all members of the arbitral tribunal."); LCIA Rules, art. 14.3 ("In the case of a three-member Arbitral Tribunal the

2. Scheduling the Hearings

Scheduling the hearing, or hearings, should be done early in the process, and may occur at the preliminary meeting. It is important to set hearing dates early, because finding a convenient time can be difficult, particularly when there are three arbitrators, as well as a number of lawyers, parties, and witnesses whose schedules must be coordinated. Parties will estimate the amount of time needed for the hearing; depending on the estimates, the decision must be made whether to have one hearing that may last a week or more, or whether to schedule several shorter hearings. Sometimes the problem will be that busy arbitrators do not have more than three or four days in a row when they can meet. When hearings are held in a number of shorter segments, however, it can greatly increase the cost, because usually everyone is required to travel internationally to get to the hearing. David Wagoner stresses the importance of making a schedule, and keeping to it.

> It is important to set hearing dates early, typically at the first pre-hearing conference, and not change them without a strong showing of need. If the hearing is expected to take two weeks, add a day or two for contingencies and for deliberations of the tribunal. Schedule the hearing on consecutive weeks at the earliest time available to counsel and the tribunal. During the hearing the tribunal should take steps to insure that the hearing will be completed on schedule. If rescheduling becomes necessary, it could be six months or a year before it is possible to reschedule and complete the hearing.[35]
>
> David E. Wagoner
> United States

3. Seat of the Arbitration

The seat of the arbitration is normally determined in the arbitration clause, but if not, the arbitrators will choose a seat, usually one that is neutral in the sense of not being in the country of either party. Once the seat is chosen, the tribunal will usually hold hearings there, but it can, on occasion, decide to hold meetings elsewhere, without changing the legal situs of the arbitration.[36] For example, if a site visit is necessary, one set of hearings could be held near the site, because all parties would generally want to be present for the site visit.

---

chairman may, with the prior consent of the other two arbitrators, make procedural rulings alone.").

[35] Interview with David E. Wagoner, March 2007. Notes of interview on file with author.

[36] *See, e.g.,* UNCITRAL Model Law, art. 20; LCIA Rules, art. 16.2; SCC Rules, art. 20 (2); ICC Rules, art. 18(2); ICDR Rules, art. 13(2).

4. Language of the Arbitration

The language of the arbitration generally and of any specific hearing is also normally determined by the arbitration clause. If not, and if the parties cannot agree on the language, the arbitrators will determine the language. If all the contract documents have been in one language, such as French, then French is likely to be chosen as the language of the arbitration, although this will not necessarily be the choice. It is important, of course, that the arbitrators all be able to understand the language of the arbitration. Although everything – documents, witness testimony, and legal argument – could be translated for an arbitrator who did not speak the language of the arbitration, this would be very costly and would slow down the process enormously. The IBA Rules of Ethics actually require an arbitrator not to accept an appointment unless she has an adequate command of the language of the arbitration.[37] This works well when the language of the arbitration is known in advance, but that may not be the case in some arbitrations.

Parties and witnesses who are not native speakers of the language of the arbitration have the right to testify in their own language but, generally, must pay for a translator. Documents not in the language of the arbitration must also be translated.

5. Local Bar Requirements

In most jurisdictions, the lawyers who are representing the parties in an arbitration do not have to be admitted to the local bar. Also, in most jurisdictions, the representative of a party does not even have to be a lawyer. Nonetheless, if the seat of the arbitration is in an area where arbitrations are less common, it would be prudent to confer with local counsel to see whether there are any special requirements as to who can represent a party in an international arbitration.[38]

6. Closed Hearings

Because arbitrations are private matters, a hearing is not open like a courtroom. Although parties have a right to be present at a hearing, any witness can be excluded whenever he or she is not testifying.[39]

---

[37] IBA Rules of Ethics, art. 2(2).

[38] In Portugal, for example, it appears that to represent a party in an international arbitration, one must be admitted as a lawyer in Portugal, although there is apparently no court decision on the subject. *See* ARBITRATION WORLD, European Lawyer Reference Series (2006) 284, § 10. It is also unclear under South Korean law whether a foreign lawyer is permitted to handle an international arbitration in South Korea. *See id.* 360, § 10. In China, however, "[a] party may be represented by its authorized Chinese and/or foreign representative(s)...," but a Power of Attorney must be forwarded to CIETAC. CIETAC 2012 Rules, art. 20.

[39] *See, e.g.,* ICDR Rules, art. 20(4) ("The tribunal may require any witness or witnesses to retire during the testimony of other witnesses.").

7. Record of Proceedings

The parties may determine that they want a verbatim record of the proceedings. This can be expensive, particularly if provided on a daily basis. Parties will generally share the cost of the transcript. If only one party wants a transcript, however, that party must pay for the transcript. Sometimes that party may be required to share the transcript, not only with the arbitrators but also with the other side.

8. Technology

Increasingly, in larger arbitrations, technology is being used by arbitrators and by parties. From PowerPoint and video to sophisticated database management systems, twenty-first-century arbitrations take advantage of technology developed for litigation purposes. In some arbitrations, everyone must have a laptop to keep up with what is going on in the hearing. On the other hand, some arbitrators may not even know how to use email. In arbitrations in which there are large numbers of documents, however, it behooves counsel to use technology to manage the process and try to present evidence in the clearest and most efficient way possible.[40]

A number of arbitral institutions and other organizations have introduced guidelines and protocols with suggestions of how to deal with E-Discovery. For example, the Chartered Institute of Arbitrators in 2008 issued its Protocol for E-Disclosure in Arbitration.[41] The ICC completed a Report on E-Discovery in August 2011.[42] The various guidelines, reports, and protocols seek to control costs by narrowing the focus of the requests, requiring a balancing of the benefits and hardships, and putting the burden on the requesting party to establish that the benefits outweigh the hardships.[43]

9. Time Limits per Side

Arbitrators may limit the time that each side can have to present testimony. The tribunal must strive for a balance, of course, between managing the hearing efficiently and ensuring two important results: that the parties are

---

[40] *See* Thomas Schultz, Information Technology and Arbitration: A Practitioner's Guide (2006).

[41] Available at http://www.ciarb.org/information-and-resources.

[42] *See*   http://www.stblaw.com/siteContent.cfm?contentID=4&itemID=81&focusID= 1247.

[43] *See, e.g.,* the 2010 IBA Rules on Taking of Evidence, arts. 3 (3)(a)(ii), 3 (12) (b), and 9 (2)(g), available at http://www.ibanet.org/Document/Default.aspx? DocumentUid=68336C49-4106-46BF-A1C6-A8F0880444DC; the ICDR Guidelines for Arbitrators Concerning the Exchange of Information, art. 4, available at http:// www.adr.org/si.asp?id=5288; the CPR Protocol on Discovery of Documents and Presentation of Witnesses, Section 1(d), available at http://cpradr.org/Resources/ ALLCPRArticles/tabid/265/ID/614/CPR-Protocol-on-Disclosure-of-Documents-and-Presentation-of-Witnesses-in-Commercial-Arbitration.aspx.

treated equally and that they have a fair opportunity to present their case.[44] Some arbitrators impose very strict time limits, giving each side exactly the same number of minutes, and reserving specific time for the arbitrators.[45] This can be important in managing large, complex cases and in ensuring that the arbitration is completed in the time allotted. Parties know exactly how much time they have, and know they will be held to the limits given. This is intended to prevent the situation in which, on the last day of the hearing, everyone realizes that, in fact, the hearing cannot be completed by the end of the day.

In setting time limits, however, arbitrators must always use their common sense to ensure fairness and equal treatment. It may not always be fair to provide exactly equal time to the parties because one side may have more witnesses or may have a much heavier burden of proof. Giving each side an equal opportunity to present its case fairly may, in fact, result in one side having more time than the other side. Arbitrators should be alert to this possibility in making reasonable allocations of time, and should consider allocating a comparable rather than an identical amount of time per side.

Even arbitrators who support strict time management in large, complex cases generally believe more flexibility is possible and makes more sense in smaller cases. Parties sometimes need somewhat more time than originally estimated; a tribunal should be willing to allow it if the time requested is reasonable and does not unduly extend the hearings.

10. Default of Appearance

If the claimant initiates proceedings but then fails to communicate the statement of claim, in many cases the tribunal can terminate the proceedings.[46] If the respondent does not appear at the hearing, despite proper notice, its default of appearance does not give the claimant an automatic win. Rather, the claimant still has the burden of proving its case. Therefore, the tribunal must hear testimony, examine documents, and weigh evidence to see whether the claimant has met that burden. The tribunal should also, at every stage of the process, make efforts to contact the respondent and give it the opportunity to participate in the hearing, and to make written submissions. Because a nonparticipating party is likely to challenge any award rendered against it, a prudent tribunal, in any award granted after an *ex parte* procedure, should

---

[44] *See, e.g.,* UNCITRAL Model Law, art. 18 ("The parties shall be treated with equality and each party shall be given a full opportunity of presenting his case.").

[45] When parties are given and held to a certain number of minutes on each side, this is sometimes referred to as a "chess clock," after the clocks used in chess tournaments. For a discussion of time management, *see* Jan Paulsson, *The Timely Arbitrator: Reflections on the Bockstiegel Method,* Arb. Int., 19–26 (2006).

[46] *See, e.g.,* UNCITRAL Model Law, art. 25(a); SCC Rules, art. 30(1).

set forth all of the efforts it made to permit respondent a fair opportunity to participate in the proceedings.

11. Expedited Proceedings

Finally, sometimes parties want to have an expedited arbitration proceeding. Some arbitration institutions provide that parties can simply agree to shorten time limits.[47] When parties agree to an accelerated schedule, this is generally referred to as *fast-track arbitration*. Some arbitration institutions provide special fast-track arbitration rules.[48] One of the traps that parties and arbitrators do not want to fall into, however, is a fast-track arbitration that does not give arbitrators any right to extend the time limits. Many things could happen that would make it necessary to extend the limits: an interim award might be necessary, one party could be uncooperative, or a coarbitrator could be uncooperative. If the arbitrators did not have the power to extend the time limits, and the time period were to elapse before the arbitrators were able to render an award, that would be the end of the arbitration. The arbitrators would have no further mandate to act, and the parties would receive nothing after all the effort that had gone into the proceeding. Depending on statutes of limitations, there might be a possibility of starting over with a different tribunal. However, this would completely defeat the purpose of having an expedited arbitration in the first place. It would be far better to provide the arbitrators from the beginning with the discretion to extend time limits, when necessary.[49]

E. PRESENTING EVIDENCE

In international arbitration, rules or procedures regarding the taking of evidence tend to be within the discretion of the tribunal. The tribunal generally has the power to determine the admissibility and the weight of the evidence.[50] Most arbitrators are not going to apply the rules of evidence that may be part of the procedural law of the seat of arbitration. Rather, they will use a flexible approach to establish the facts of the case.

---

[47] *See, e.g.*, ICC Rules, art. 38(1) ("The parties may agree to shorten the various time limits set out in these Rules.").

[48] *See, e.g.*, WIPO Expedited Arbitration Rules, available at http://www.wipo.int/freepublications/en/arbitration/446/wipo_pub_446.pdf.

[49] The ICC Rules deal with this issue by providing that, despite any mandatory time limits agreed to by the parties, the Court of Arbitration (not the tribunal) can extend the time to permit the tribunal and the Court to fulfill their responsibilities under the Rules. *See* art. 38(2).

[50] *See, e.g.*, ICDR Rules, art. 20(6) ("The tribunal shall determine the admissibility, relevance, materiality and weight of the evidence offered by any party.").

1. IBA Rules of Evidence

Because of the different approaches to evidence in the common law and civil law systems, the IBA adopted in 1999, and then amended in 2010, its Rules on the Taking of Evidence in International Arbitration (IBA Rules of Evidence).[51] The IBA Rules of Evidence themselves promote flexibility, stating in the Preamble that parties and tribunals may adopt them in whole or in part, or may vary them or simply use the Rules as guidelines. The IBA Rules of Evidence have contributed to harmonizing the approach used in many international arbitrations for the taking of evidence.

Most parties and arbitrators prefer that the IBA Rules of Evidence remain in the category of guidelines, rather than being imposed on the arbitrators by party agreement. This permits flexibility as needed to make the arbitral process responsive to the needs of the particular case. Pierre Karrer, for example, likes to put in the Terms of Reference that the arbitrators will be "inspired though not bound" by the IBA Rules of Evidence.[52] Some arbitrators, on the other hand, prefer that the IBA Rules of Evidence be adopted as binding, because they believe there is less discussion about evidentiary issues if the Rules are considered binding.

The following are some of the more significant changes in the 2010 rules:

1. The elimination of the word "Commercial" from the title, to indicate a broader application of the rules to disputes such as investment treaty-based arbitrations
2. A stronger emphasis on fairness (para 2 of Foreword; para. 1 of Preamble), and good faith (para. 3 of Preamble and art. 9(7))
3. A request for document production to be addressed to both the tribunal and the other parties, so that voluntary compliance can occur without intervention of the tribunal
4. Addition of specific language covering E-disclosure (art. 3(3)(ii)), submission of electronic documents (art. 3(12)), and using videoconferencing for witness testimony (art. 8(1))
5. More extensive requirements for expert reports of tribunal-appointed experts (art. 6(4))
6. A requirement that a party inform the tribunal and the other parties which witnesses it intends to request to appear at the hearing (many more witness statements may be submitted than witnesses who will be requested to testify) (art. 8(1))
7. More extended treatment of privilege, including factors that the tribunal may take into account, such as the expectations of the parties and "the

---

[51] Available at www.ibanet.org under "Publications," and "IBA guides and free materials."
[52] Interview with Pierre Karrer, March 2007. Notes of interview on file with author.

need to maintain fairness and equality as between the Parties, particularly if they are subject to different legal or ethical rules" (art. 9(3))

The issue of privilege has been a complicated one in light of the fact that differenct legal systems tend to recognize different privileges. For example, the attorney–client privilege in the United States tends to protect all communications between attorneys and their clients, including attorneys who serve as in-house counsel. In Europe, however, the European Court of Justice has made clear that under EU law there is no attorney–client privilege for an in-house counsel and his client, the corporation for whom he works.[53] The need for fair treatment under the IBA Rules would suggest that the tribunal should extend to the party with the lower level of privilege the same level of privilege that the opposing party enjoys.[54]

2. Burden of Proof

It is generally understood, and sometimes specifically expressed in various rules, that each party will have the burden of proof to establish its claim or defense.[55] But there is no specific rule establishing the standard of proof, for example, whether the standard to be met is (a) "preponderance of the evidence" or "balance of the probability" – two standards that both mean "more likely than not"; (b) "beyond a reasonable doubt," which means proved to a virtual certainty; or (c) a civil law standard known as *l'intime conviction du juge*, which means that the judge has to be convinced at an inner, deep-seated, personal level.[56] This civil law standard is higher than preponderance of the evidence, and appears closer to, though not the equivalent of, the common law standard of beyond a reasonable doubt. In some civil law countries, this standard – *l'intime conviction du juge* – appears to apply in both criminal and civil cases.[57]

At common law, the standard of beyond a reasonable doubt is normally applied only in criminal law cases. In international commercial arbitration, it would probably be applied only in cases involving bribery, fraud, or

---

[53] *See* Case C-550/07P, Akzo Nobel Chemicals Ltd. and Akcros Chemicals Ltd v. European Commisstion, Sept. 14, 2010.

[54] *See also* ICDR Guidelines for Arbitrators Concerning Exchanges of Information, art. 7, *Privileges and Professional Ethics* ("When the parties, their counsel or their documents would be subject under applicable law to different rules, the tribunal should to the extent possible apply the same rule to both sides, giving preference to the rule that provides the highest level of protection."), available at http://www.adr.org/si.asp?id=5288.

[55] *See, e.g.,* ICDR Rules, art. 19(1); UNCITRAL Rules, art. 27(1).

[56] *See* Michele Taruffo, *Rethinking the Standards of Proof*, 51 Am. J. Comp. L. 659, 667 (2003).

[57] *See* Kevin M. Clermont & Emily Sherwin, *A Comparative View of Standards of Proof*, 50 Am. J. Comp. L. 243, 245–46 (2002). *Cf.* Michele Taruffo, *Rethinking the Standards of Proof*, 51 Am. J. Comp. L. 659 (2003).

corruption.[58] In most international commercial arbitration cases, the common law approach of balance of the probabilities or preponderance of the evidence appears to be generally accepted,[59] although arbitrators may not necessarily state what standard they are using to make their decision. In any event, the arbitral tribunal is generally considered to have full discretion to determine what standard to apply when establishing the facts of the case, as part of its inherent power to determine the probative value of all of the evidence.[60]

Some arbitrators express concern that lawyers in arbitrations are not sufficiently skilled in meeting their burden of proof. Mauro Rubino-Sammartano, an arbitrator and counsel in Italy, believes that law schools, particularly in civil law jurisdictions, should place more focus on teaching students how to prove facts.

> Parties do not devote enough time to what they have to prove and how to prove it. In continental Europe, legal arguments have top priority. Students are not taught to give enough attention to evidence. They like beautiful legal doctrine, but don't understand that they have to prove facts. Common law students tend to have more practical preparation.[61]
>
> Mauro Rubino-Sammartano
> Italy

3. Documentary Evidence

The common law and civil law approaches to production of documentary evidence are quite different. In common law litigation, parties expect to (1) serve interrogatories to find out about documents in the possession of the other party, then (2) serve requests to produce those documents, as well

---

[58] The Iran-U.S. Claims Tribunal has applied the "beyond a reasonable doubt" standard to a case involving a bribery claim, stating: "The burden is on NIOC [National Iranian Oil Company] to establish its defence of alleged bribery in connection with the Lease Agreement. If reasonable doubts remain, such an allegation cannot be deemed to be established." Oil Field of Texas, Inc., v. Gov't. of the Islamic Republic of Iran (1986), 12 Iran-U.S. Cl. Trib. Rep. 315, Award in Case No. 43 (258-43-1).

[59] See Redfern & Hunter et al., *Redfern and Hunter on International Arbitration*, § 6.93 at 388(2009) ("The degree of proof... before an international tribunal is not capable of precise definition, but it may be safely assumed that it is close to the "balance of probability.").

[60] See Robert Pietrowski, *Evidence in International Arbitration*, 22 Arb. Int. 373, 379 (2006).

[61] Interview with Mauro Rubino-Sammartano, April 2007. Notes of interview on file with author.

as (3) take depositions of witnesses to learn how they will testify, and to have them identify, produce, and authenticate documents. The goal is to obtain all relevant documents, including documents adverse to the opposing party's position. In civil law litigation, on the other hand, the documents that must be produced are those on which each party intends to rely. For other documents to be obtained, generally the requesting party must specifically identify the documents, or category of documents, and have reason to know they are in the other party's possession.

In international arbitration, production of documentary evidence tends to follow the civil law model. The goal is to keep down the costs of massive discovery before the hearing, to prevent long delays in the pre-hearing stage, and to encourage a speedy and efficient resolution of the dispute. As in civil law cases, in many arbitrations, primary importance is placed on documentary evidence.[62] Oral testimony is generally considered less important, although this may well be different, depending on the facts of the particular case and the background of the arbitrators.

a. Hearsay Evidence

Tribunals will generally admit all documents, even those that may contain what common law lawyers consider to be hearsay evidence. With respect to documents, hearsay evidence is a statement by one person contained in a document, reporting that a second person has made a particular statement, and the statement of the second person is being offered to establish the truth of the matter in question. Hearsay evidence is considered not reliable because the second person is not available to be cross-examined about her statement or its context. Arbitrators will generally admit such evidence, but will assert that it will be given appropriate weight, which may mean it will be disregarded.

b. Authentication

Documents are generally assumed to be authentic unless objected to. If a document's authenticity is challenged, the party submitting the document will probably be asked to establish its authenticity, usually by producing the original. If the party is unable to do so, the document may be rejected. On the other hand, if some justification is given for the missing original, the document could be admitted (unless patently fraudulent), with a caveat by the tribunal that it will give the document appropriate weight, presumably less than if its authenticity were not at issue.

c. Document Requests

Parties are charged with providing to the tribunal and the other party all documents on which they intend to rely to support their claims or defenses.

---

[62] *See* Pietrowski, *supra* note 60, at 374, 391.

In addition, once parties have produced to each other the documents on which they intend to rely, they may determine that they need additional documents under the control of the other party. Under the IBA Rules of Evidence, in order to obtain documents from an opposing party, the requesting party has a relatively heavy burden of establishing the existence of the documents as well as their importance to the outcome of the case. Arbitrators generally have broad discretion to order a party to produce relevant documents that are identified by the opposing party.[63] However, most arbitrators are not receptive to document requests that they believe amount to "fishing expeditions." In practice, requests for documents must be quite specific. The specificity required by the IBA Rules is set forth below:

REQUEST TO PRODUCE

A Request to Produce shall contain:

a. (i) a description of each requested Document sufficient to identify it, or
   (ii) a description in sufficient detail (including subject matter) of a narrow and specific requested category of Documents that are reasonably believed to exist; in the case of Documents maintained in electronic form, the requesting Party may, or the Arbitral Tribunal may order that it shall be required to, identify specific files, search terms, individuals or other means of searching for such Documents in an efficient and economical manner;
b. a statement as to how the Documents requested are relevant to the case and material to its outcome; and
c. (i) a statement that the Documents requested are not in the possession, custody, or control of the requesting Party, or a statement of the reason why it would be unreasonably burdensome for the requesting Party to produce such Documents, and
   (ii) a statement of the reasons why the requesting Party assumes the documents requested are in the possession, custody or control of another Party.

IBA RULES OF EVIDENCE
Article 3(3)

Managing the parties' disputes over documents is an important aspect of controlling time and costs. Some arbitrators will require the parties to

---

[63] *See, e.g.*, ICDR Rules, arts. 19 (2–3); LCIA Rules, art. 22.1(e); UNCITRAL Rules, art. 27(3).

submit their requests for rulings on disputed documents in the form of a "Redfern Schedule," named after noted English scholar and arbitrator Alan Redfern. In a Redfern Schedule, parties submit a joint schedule with four columns. The first column identifies the documents or categories of documents requested, the second column provides the reason for the party's request, the third column gives a summary of the other party's objection to the request, and the fourth column is left blank for the tribunal's decision on each request. This method of promoting efficiency, along with many others, is proposed in the ICC publication, Techniques for Controlling Time and Costs in Arbitration.[64]

Although arbitrators can order parties to produce documents, what happens if some of the desired documents are in the hands of nonparties? The power of the arbitrator is a product of the parties' consent, and nonparties have not consented to be subject to that power. Nonetheless, U.S. law gives the arbitrators subpoena power, enabling them to subpoena nonparties to appear as witnesses and to produce documents.[65] Most laws, however, do not give this power to arbitrators, so if a party believes the appearance of a nonparty is critical to its case, it will probably need to seek assistance of the court, which it can do only if the local laws and pertinent rules permit such assistance. Under the UNCITRAL Model Law, the tribunal, or a party with the approval of the tribunal, may request assistance from the court in taking evidence.[66] In England, if a party can persuade the tribunal or the other party to agree, it can use court procedures "to secure the attendance before the tribunal of a witness in order to give oral testimony or to produce documents or other material evidence."[67]

Thus, depending on the jurisdiction, court assistance may or may not be available to obtain evidence from third parties. But what about a recalcitrant party? What happens when a party has been ordered by the tribunal to produce documents and has simply refused? As with third parties, court assistance may be available in some jurisdictions to enforce an arbitrator's order. However, commentators opine that "obtaining documents from courts is rarely an effective remedy in international arbitration."[68] Instead,

---

[64] ICC Publication 843, available at http://www.iccwbo.org/uploadedFiles/TimeCost_E. pdf. *See also* 2010 ICC Arbitration and ADR Rules, Appendix IV, Case Management Techniques. Another effort to encourage efficiency in international arbitration is found in the ICDR Guidelines for Arbitrators Concerning Exchanges of Information, available at http://www.adr.org/si.asp?id=5288.

[65] *See, e.g.*, the U.S. Federal Arbitration Act, § 7, which provides arbitrators with power to subpoena "any person" and require him to bring with him "any book, record, document or paper which may be deemed material as evidence in the case." *See supra* Chapter 5(D)(3).

[66] *See* UNCITRAL Model Law, art. 27.

[67] English Arbitration Act of 1996, § 43.

[68] Jerome K. Sharpe, *Drawing Adverse Inferences from the Non-Production of Evidence*, 22 Arb. Int. 549 (2006), *citing* M. Hunter, *Modern Trends in the Presentation of Evidence in International Commercial Arbitration*, 3 Am. Rev. Int'l Arb. 204 (1992).

arbitrators may draw an adverse inference from the failure of the party to comply.[69] The possibility that arbitrators will draw such an inference can be an effective means of compelling production, at least when the other party actually possesses the documents requested. Because arbitrators have so much power (i.e., their decision is unlikely to be overturned), most practitioners and parties do not wish to offend the arbitrators by refusing to comply with their order.

d. Arbitrator Discretion

As a general rule, arbitrators are going to admit any evidence they believe will help establish the facts of the case. They have the power, however, to refuse to admit evidence that is irrelevant, duplicative, defamatory, unduly burdensome, or otherwise inappropriate. The challenge for arbitrators in managing the arbitration is to find a balance so that they neither accept massive amounts of marginally relevant documents, nor restrict document production to such an extent that a party can assert subsequently it was not allowed to present its case.[70]

4. Fact Witnesses

a. Testimony Prior to the Hearing

The treatment of witnesses also differs markedly between common law and civil law. In litigation, common law lawyers tend to take lengthy depositions in order to learn what information witnesses for the opposing side possess. Another purpose of depositions is to lock in the testimony of the witness, so she cannot change it later. Because depositions are taken under oath, if the witness changes her story, counsel will bring this out on cross-examination at the trial, using the prior deposition testimony. The purpose of doing so is to undermine the credibility of the witness.

For civil law lawyers, on the other hand, fact witnesses in litigated matters are generally not considered very important.[71] Witnesses generally cannot be questioned in advance by opposing counsel, and at the hearing, they will be questioned only by the judge, not the counsel.[72]

---

[69] *See* Redfern & Hunter et al., *supra* note 59, § 6.129 at 399.

[70] Not having been allowed to present one's case is one of the grounds for resisting enforcement under the New York Convention, art. V(1)(b).

[71] *See, e.g.,* James Beardsley, *Proof of Fact in French Civil Procedure*, 34 Am. J. Comp. L. 459 (1986) (In France, there is "a distrust of oral evidence," and "a settled habit of fact avoidance." *Id. at* 459, 469. Moreover, "parties to civil proceedings [in France] don't take an oath before testifying, although non-party witnesses do." Apparently, "the expectation is that parties won't tell the truth anyway." *Id.* at 464.). *See also* Hans Van Houtte, *Counsel-Witness Relations and Professional Misconduct in Civil Law Systems*, 19 Arb. Int'l 457, 457–458 (2003) ("In civil and commercial court proceedings, witnesses are not much used.").

[72] *See, e.g.,* Van Houtte, *supra* note 71, *id.* at 457–58.

In an international arbitration, the treatment of witness testimony prior to the hearing tends to follow a hybrid law model. Depositions are almost never allowed unless both parties agree to them. Even then, they are likely to be few in number and limited in time. The parties are usually asked at a fairly early point in the proceedings to provide the names of witnesses and the subject matter about which they will testify. They are then asked at some point to submit statements by each witness that include all the relevant evidence the particular witness is going to provide. It is important that the witness statement be complete because sometimes the witness will not actually be allowed to testify – for example, if the arbitrators decide not to hold a hearing, but rather to resolve the matter based on the documents alone. The witness statement may also be used in lieu of direct testimony, and the witness may be subject only to cross-examination.

b. Witness Statements

In many jurisdictions, it is generally recognized that the witness statements are prepared by counsel.[73] Nevertheless, the statement should be written so it resembles the witness's own words and manner of speaking. It should deal with facts known to the witness, and should not contain legal conclusions. The witness should probably not, for example, use legal terms of art in the statement, such as "irreparable harm." Nonetheless, the lawyer generally works closely with the witness in the preparation of the statement, because the witness probably will be subject to cross-examination by the other party on the contents of the statement. Thus, the witness should feel confident about whatever facts are contained in the statement. Moreover, the statement should be complete, because the witness may not be permitted to add to the statement at the oral hearings. The point of providing pre-hearing disclosure is so that there will be no surprises at the hearing. On the other hand, under the IBA Rules of Evidence, witnesses may, within a time period determined by the tribunal, submit revised witness statements, generally limited, however, to responding to matters that were stated in a witness statement filed by the opposing party.[74]

c. Who Can Testify

Generally, any person may testify at the hearing, including a party. This is despite rules in certain civil law jurisdictions, such as Germany, which provide that a party cannot testify as a witness for its own cause, although it can be "called by the opponent to give a party's statement."[75]

---

[73] *See* David P. Roney, *Effective Witness Preparation for International Commercial Arbitration*, 20 J. Int'l Arb. 429, 430, n. 6 (2003).
[74] IBA Rules of Evidence, art. 4 (6).
[75] ARBITRATION WORLD, *Germany* (2006), 102, § 12.1.

In international arbitrations, however, the restriction usually does not apply, and parties regularly testify.[76]

d. Meeting with Witnesses

In some countries, Rules of Professional Conduct or case law prohibit prior meetings with witnesses. However, it is generally expected in international arbitrations that witnesses will be interviewed.[77] The IBA Rules of Evidence specifically provide that "[i]t shall not be improper for a Party, its officers, employees, legal advisors or other representatives to interview its witnesses or potential witnesses and discuss their prospective testimony with them."[78]

Lawyers from different jurisdictions may have a different understanding of what "interview" means. To a lawyer from a common law system, it means to "prepare" the witness. This involves helping the witness to be able to present his or her testimony clearly and consistently. It does not mean coaching a witness to give evidence in a manner that is false or misleading. Preparation of a major witness can involve a great deal of time and effort by the lawyer, including making sure the witness understands the issues and understands how his or her testimony fits into the overall legal strategy. The preparation may also include having mock direct and cross-examinations, to help the witness feel more confident when testifying.[79] This is important because a confident witness tends to have more credibility than a nervous one.

Civil law lawyers must be careful to ensure that whatever contact they have with the witness does not cause them to violate local Rules of Professional Conduct.[80] As a general rule, they are not supposed to write the witness statement for the witness, nor influence the witness's testimony. There have been instances of complaints being filed by opposing counsel regarding the level of interaction between civil law lawyers and their witnesses.

e. Examining Witnesses

The method counsel is permitted to use for examining the witnesses at the hearing may reflect the legal background of the arbitrators. In civil law, the system for examining witnesses is called "inquisitorial," which means that most of the questioning is done by the judge or arbitrator. In common law, on the other hand, in which the lawyers do most of the questioning by direct examination and cross-examination, followed by redirect examination, the system is referred to as "adversarial." In international arbitration, the common law system of examination and cross-examination is frequently

---

[76] *See id.*
[77] *See* Roney, *supra* note 73, at 429–30.
[78] IBA Rules of Evidence, art. 4(3).
[79] *See* Roney, *supra* note 73, at 433–35.
[80] *See* Van Houtte, *supra* note 71, at 457–58.

used, although arbitrators may intervene from time to time to question a witness, and, as will be discussed below, direct examination is frequently eliminated.

Although cross-examination is usually permitted in international arbitration, the tone of the examination should be professional and polite. Arbitrators, particularly those from a civil law background, can become quite annoyed if they think that counsel is badgering a witness. A cross-examination that appears abusive will probably be cut short, and the arbitrators may suspend the hearing long enough to talk privately with counsel (both counsel being present) about the proper approach to cross-examination. Nicolas Simon, an arbitrator and counsel in Vienna, notes that arbitrators are concerned about the purpose of the cross-examination.

> Arbitrators do not like cross-examination where witnesses are badgered. In the continental tradition, arbitrators see cross-examination as a method for eliciting information, not for destruction of a witness.[81]
>
> Nicholas Simon
> Vienna

A tribunal will frequently dispense with direct examination because the witness statements basically set forth the same facts that would be elicited on direct examination. Thus, the witness's testimony may begin with cross-examination. Although this is a time-saver, which may be important in a long arbitration, there are some disadvantages. First of all, any witness, no matter how well prepared, is likely to be nervous about having to testify. If the witness is taken through her direct testimony by her own lawyer, she starts to feel more confident and comfortable in her role, and will tend to be perceived by the arbitrators as credible. Because of this, some arbitrators may allow a ten- or fifteen-minute "warm-up," in which the witness gives a very brief summary of her testimony. If there is no warm-up, however, and as soon as the witness takes the stand, she is attacked by a rather aggressive cross-examiner, the arbitrators are more likely to perceive her as nervous, confused, and lacking credibility. Even if the cross-examination is restrained, and the witness holds up well, the arbitrators will still be more likely to remember what was said in front of them, rather than what was written in the witness statement, which they may have read rather perfunctorily. Moreover, on cross-examination, counsel may deliberately avoid asking questions about certain issues in the witness statement. The effect could be

[81] Interview with Nicholas Simon, April 2007. Notes of interview on file with author.

that these issues in the witness statement, because they were not subjected to cross-examination, may not be raised at all in oral testimony, and may be forgotten by the arbitrators.

Arbitrators deal with this problem differently. Some, for example, do not allow scope objections. Scope objections are objections made by the opposing counsel if, for example, an attorney during redirect examination asks questions that go beyond the scope of the cross-examination. If scope objections are not allowed, the attorney who wanted to bring out points from the witness statement that were not raised during cross-examination could do so, even though the questions went beyond the scope of the cross-examination.

Other arbitrators permit scope objections, thereby limiting redirect examination. Their view is that the attorney who believes points in the witness statement have not been sufficiently addressed during cross-examination can nonetheless refer to these points in closing arguments, and possibly again in any post-hearing submissions.

In some instances, an arbitrator may want to hear direct testimony, instead of relying on the witness statement.

I would not discourage direct examination. The witness statement is drafted by counsel. I prefer to hear directly from the witness.[82]

Mauro Rubino-Sammartano
Italy

Some arbitrators believe that although there has been a commendable effort to make arbitrations shorter and more efficient, it has come at a cost to oral presentations and to interaction between counsel and the tribunal. Increasingly, arbitrators do not permit opening arguments, closing arguments, or direct testimony. This means that what mostly takes place at the hearings is cross-examination of the witnesses. Currently, this tends to disadvantage civil law lawyers, who do not receive training in cross-examination as part of their law school education. But it also means – for all counsel – that they have less opportunity to engage the arbitrators, to understand their questions and concerns, and to help the tribunal understand their client's position. Eric Schwartz, an arbitrator and counsel in Paris, notes the importance of closing oral arguments.

---

[82] Interview with Mauro Rubino-Sammartano, April 2007. Notes of interview on file with author.

When arbitrators dispense with closing arguments in favor of written submissions, it is not clear that this saves time or money. The cost of preparing post-hearing briefs may far exceed the cost of preparing a closing argument. Moreover, after arbitrators read the post-hearing submissions, they may well have questions, but they do not want to re-open the hearings to hear from counsel. On the other hand, when closing arguments are permitted in lieu of briefs, arbitrators can raise questions about the points that are troubling them and counsel has the opportunity to explain and clarify.[83]

Eric Schwartz
Paris

f. Arbitrator Intervention

In general, most arbitrators prefer flexibility in the hearing as opposed to strict enforcement of rules. They feel comfortable asking the witnesses questions themselves and, for the most part, will allow counsel a certain amount of leeway. Most arbitrators, however, do not believe they have an obligation to step in and come to the aid of a party who is represented by inexperienced or incompetent counsel. If a party is represented by inexperienced in-house counsel, however, arbitrators have been known to ask in-house counsel gently whether they have considered involving a lawyer experienced in arbitration.

On the other hand, arbitrators generally feel differently about intervening when there appears to be a gap in the evidence. If arbitrators have questions that have not been answered by the evidence presented, most would not hesitate to inquire of the parties about their concerns. Louise Barrington, an arbitrator and counsel in Hong Kong, supports some kinds of intervention.

Arbitrators need to be discreet and even-handed when they intervene. But they should be willing to tell parties if there are certain matters that they think are important for them to know. For example, the tribunal might say to the parties, "We need to know about X. What can you tell us about X?"[84]

Louise Barrington
Hong Kong

---

[83] Interview with Eric Schwartz, April 2007. Notes of interview on file with author.
[84] Interview with Louise Barrington, April 2007. Notes of interview on file with author.

g. Availability of Witnesses

According to the IBA Rules of Evidence, a fact witness or expert, if requested by any party or by the tribunal, must appear in person for testimony at the hearing, unless the tribunal has agreed to permit the use of videoconference or other technology for that particular witness.[85] If the witness does not show up for the hearings, and there is no valid reason, then the tribunal will disregard the witness statement unless there are exceptional circumstances.[86]

h. Compelling Witness Testimony

The IBA Rules of Evidence also state that if a party wants to call a witness who will not appear voluntarily, the party may ask the tribunal to take whatever steps are legally available.[87] Taking any such steps, however, remains entirely within the discretion of the tribunal, and will depend on how relevant or material the tribunal thinks the particular testimony would be.[88] The party may also seek leave from the tribunal to take legal steps itself to compel witness testimony, though court assistance.[89] In some jurisdictions, arbitrators may have subpoena power. As noted earlier, the U.S. Federal Arbitration Act provides arbitrators with power to subpoena "any person" and require him to bring "any book, record, document or paper."[90] In other cases, if the reluctant witness appears to be under the control of one of the parties, the IBA Rules of Evidence state that the tribunal may order any party to provide, or make best efforts to provide, the appearance of any person for testimony at the hearing.[91]

5. Expert Witnesses

When international arbitrations involve highly technical issues, such as what caused cracks in the concrete of a new bridge and whether the cracks make the bridge unsafe, or who bore the responsibility for an explosion at a recently completed oil refinery, the testimony of an expert may be required. Unlike fact witnesses, experts provide opinions based on their expertise, which are applied to the facts at hand. When an expert is needed, the parties generally decide whether each side will call an expert, or whether they prefer that the tribunal choose an expert. The tribunal generally has the discretion to choose an expert even if the parties have not asked it to do so.

Selecting an expert witness is probably the most important decision made by counsel in the arbitration after the selection of the arbitrators. Counsel need to exercise great care and diligence in finding the best international

---

[85] IBA Rules of Evidence, art. 8(1).
[86] *See id.* art. 4(7).
[87] *See id.* art. 4(9).
[88] *See id.*
[89] *See id.*
[90] 9 U.S.C. § 7. *See supra* Chapter 5(D)(3).
[91] *See* IBA Rules of Evidence, art. 4(10).

expert in the particular field. If counsel is able, for example, to retain the leading expert in the field, and the expert agrees with counsel's view of the issues, the case will be very likely to settle. Counsel may want to interview the expert witness before engaging him. Sarah François-Poncet explains why it is helpful to meet the expert.

> I always try to meet potential expert witnesses. I want to know how they will hold up before a tribunal. How will Texas play in Stockholm?[92]
>
> Sarah François-Poncet
> Paris

If the tribunal is appointing an expert, it is likely to first consult with the parties, and invite them to agree on the choice of expert. One of the concerns when a tribunal appoints an expert is whether it is simply delegating its decision-making authority to the expert. The tribunal does not have the authority to delegate its powers to decide.[93] It should therefore make clear in its award that it has not just adopted an expert report as its final decision, but has scrutinized all the evidence, including the parties' various comments and objections to the expert's report.

The expert is normally empowered to obtain from the parties information he or she needs to render an opinion. This could take the form of documents, goods, samples, or even access to property for a site inspection. The expert normally prepares a report, which is provided to each of the parties. The report contains opinions and conclusions, and usually describes how the expert reached those conclusions – the method, information, and evidence that were relied on.

Under the IBA Rules of Evidence, if an on-site inspection is needed, the tribunal may, on its own motion, or at the request of a party, require inspection of "any site, property, machinery, or any other goods, samples, systems, processes, or Documents, as it deems appropriate."[94] The parties or their representatives have the right to be present at the inspection.[95]

Parties generally have the right not only to examine an expert's report and submit a response in writing prepared by the party or by a party-appointed expert, but also to examine any of the documents, goods, or other information on which the expert based the report. Generally, if one of the parties so requests, or the tribunal thinks it necessary, the expert

---

[92] Interview with Sarah Francois-Poncet, April 2007. Notes of interview on file with author.
[93] *See* Redfern & Hunter et al., *supra* note 59, § 6.157, at 407.
[94] IBA Rules of Evidence, art. 7.
[95] *See id.*

will be available at the hearing to testify and respond to questions. When the matter is complex, each party may want its own expert to be able to analyze, understand, and agree or disagree with a tribunal-appointed expert. In complex matters, each party's expert may prepare a report, and will be present at the hearing either to aid the questioning, or to testify.

It is helpful in the management of the arbitration if the parties, before the hearing where the tribunal-appointed expert will testify, have their experts meet and set forth in writing all the areas where they agree and where they disagree with the tribunal-appointed expert. This will narrow the issues for the hearing. Another possible scenario would be that the tribunal does not appoint an expert, and the parties simply have dueling experts who exchange reports and who testify at the hearing. Again, it is helpful if the experts can discuss and narrow their areas of disagreement prior to the hearing. The IBA Rules of Evidence state that the tribunal, in its discretion, may order party-appointed experts to meet, confer, and record in writing any issues on which they reach agreement, as well as any remaining issues of disagreement and the reasons therefor.[96]

Some arbitral tribunals have at times asked the experts, after examination and cross-examination, to respond essentially at the same time, issue by issue, to questions raised by the tribunal.[97] The technique, sometimes referred to as "confrontation" or "conferencing," or more informally, "hot-tubbing," can be very effective, according to arbitrators. Counsel, on the other hand, may oppose this means of examining expert witnesses, perhaps because they feel they have less control of their expert. Jose Rosell, an arbitrator and counsel in Paris, values the confrontation technique.

Having confrontation with expert witnesses can be very effective, particularly with experts on damages or legal experts. The tribunal asks each expert his or her view on the same issue, and asks each one to respond to the other's answers. It is particularly helpful when you can get them in a dialogue with each other. They tend to cross-examine themselves.[98]

Jose Rosell
Paris

---

[96] See id. art. 5(4).

[97] See, e.g., Redfern & Hunter et al., supra note 59, §§ 6.223–227 at 424–25, describing expert conferencing techniques.

[98] Interview with Jose Rosell, April 2007. Notes of interview on file with author. Some arbitrators may ask the experts to confer with one another without counsel present. One concern by counsel is that if the arbitrators plan to use conferencing, either with or without counsel present, they should notify counsel at the beginning of the arbitration, because such a procedure could affect counsel's choice of an expert. Some experts may be better at holding their ground than others.

F. CLOSING THE HEARING

At the end of a hearing, the tribunal will generally declare the hearing closed. This means that the record is closed with respect to presenting oral or written evidence, although the parties can still submit post-hearing memoranda if requested to do so by the tribunal.

G. POST-HEARING PROCEEDINGS

Normally, the only post-hearing proceedings involve the submission of briefs that may summarize the evidence and arguments. Sometimes the arbitrators may ask for briefs only on one or two points of law. If one party has turned up new evidence at the end of the trial, sometimes the other party will have the opportunity to respond to that evidence in a post-hearing brief, rather than having to return for another hearing.

   If new evidence is somehow discovered by one of the parties after the close of the hearing, but before the award is made, the party can seek to reopen the hearing. The tribunal generally has discretion to reopen the hearings, but is probably more likely, if persuaded that the new evidence is relevant and material, to ask the parties to respond by written submissions to the issues raised. Finally, the award may on occasion be sent back to the tribunal by a court for clarification or interpretation.[99]

---

[99] *See* Chapter 8, *infra*, Section G, *Post-Award Proceedings*.

CHAPTER EIGHT

The Award

Parties generally expect an arbitration to result in an award that will be final and binding. The widely accepted meaning of "award" is that it is the final decision by the arbitrators, dispositive of the issues in the case. Tribunals may issue "partial awards" or "interim awards," however, which also may be final and binding on the parties. In addition, arbitrators may issue certain directions and orders during the course of the proceedings, which may be reviewable by the tribunal, and which do not constitute awards.

A. DIFFERENCE BETWEEN "ORDERS" AND "AWARDS"

Various laws, rules, and tribunals may use the terms "orders" and "awards" differently, but there are some generally accepted distinctions. The main difference between orders and awards is that orders are not usually reviewable by a court prior to the rendering of the final award, although they may be subject to review by the tribunal.[1] Orders that are considered sufficiently final to permit judicial review, however, can in some instances be challenged in courts.[2] In particular, orders for prehearing security have been found to be reviewable by some courts because of sufficient finality.[3]

---

[1] There are, however, many gray areas. When a tribunal makes a ruling that it has jurisdiction under the UNCITRAL Model Law, that ruling is appealable to a court within thirty days, whether the ruling is designated as an award or an order. Art. 16(3).

[2] *See, e.g.,* France, Braspetro Oil Servs. Co. v. Mgmt and Implementation Auth. of the Greater Man-Made River Project (Brasoil), XXIVa YBCA 296 (1999) (Although the tribunal's ruling was characterized as an order, the court determined it was in fact an award, which it then set aside.).

[3] *See* Banco de Seguros del Estado v. Mut. Marine Office, Inc., 344 F.3d 255 (2d Cir. 2003) (Interim order requiring posting of pre-hearing security was properly confirmed by court); Pac. Reinsurance Mgmt. Corp. v. Ohio Reinsurance Corp., 935 F.2d 1019 (9th Cir. 1991) (Order granting temporary equitable relief is enforceable by court at time it is granted, not after a final award on the merits.).

Even when a party cannot appeal an order to a court, if it believes the order is improper, it should express forthwith its objection to the tribunal. It must do this to preserve the right to challenge the final award if it believes that the order caused an unfair, inappropriate, or biased procedure that prevented it from fairly presenting its case.[4] If a party does not object to an order when issued, it may later be held to have waived any right to challenge the final award based on that ground.[5]

Orders usually pertain to procedural issues that must be resolved so the arbitral process can move forward. Orders may, for example, deal with discovery issues, evidence issues, or places and times of hearings. They essentially deal with the conduct of the proceedings. Awards, on the other hand, generally resolve substantive rights of the parties. Awards are normally enforceable under the New York Convention, and can be challenged on limited legal grounds in the courts at the seat of the arbitration. Several different kinds of awards will be discussed in the following section.

B. TYPES OF AWARDS

1. Final Award

The term "final award" is generally used to refer to the award by the tribunal that resolves all the remaining disputes between the parties. Significant consequences flow from a final award. First, a final award is challengeable by the losing party, which may attempt to have it annulled or vacated under the laws of the seat of the arbitration. In addition, assuming the award is made in a Convention State, it may be enforced under the New York Convention. Finally, issuance of the award terminates the duties of the tribunal, which becomes *functus officio* – without further jurisdiction – subject in some instances to review and to any necessary corrections or interpretation.[6]

---

[4] *See, e.g.*, English Arbitration Act, § 73. Most arbitral rules require that a party raise an objection at the time of an order or ruling, or be deemed to have waived any right to object. *See, e.g.*, ICC Rules, art. 39; UNCITRAL Rules, art. 32; ICDR Rules, art. 25; LCIA Rules, art. 32.1; ICSID Rules, art. 27; WIPO Rules, art. 58.

[5] *See, e.g.*, Cour d'appel de Paris, SA Caisse Federale de Credit Mutuel du Nord de la France v. Banque Delubac et Compagnie, 2001 Revue d'Arbitrage 918 (Party that did not raise allegation of arbitrator lack of impartiality during the arbitral proceedings implicitly waived right to raise it later); The Republic of Kazakhstan v. Istil Group, Inc., [2006] 2 Lloyd's Rep. 370 (By not objecting to a perceived irregularity at the proper time, party lost right to object at a later time). *See also* UNCITRAL Model Law, art. 4 (Party that does not timely object waives right to do so) and English Arbitration Act of 1996, § 73 (Party who participates in an arbitration and does not make timely objections may not raise the objections later before a tribunal or a court, unless it can show that it did not know of the basis for the objection at the time.).

[6] BLACK'S LAW DICTIONARY explains that *functus officio* means "without further authority or legal competence because the duties and functions of the original

2. Partial and Interim Awards

The term "interim award" is sometimes used synonymously with partial award. However, some commentators distinguish between the two by saying that partial awards refer to substantive claims, whereas interim awards refer to issues such as jurisdiction or applicable law.[7] Such awards do not resolve all the issues in dispute between the parties. Depending on the jurisdiction, however, in some cases parties may either challenge or seek to confirm the partial or interim award in court, without waiting for the final award, which resolves the entire dispute.[8]

Various arbitral rules tend to refer to awards without defining them as partial, interim, or final, thereby perhaps contributing to the confusion about any distinction between them, as well as to their sometimes interchangeable use. The UNCITRAL Arbitration Rules, for example, simply provide that "[t]he arbitral tribunal may make separate awards on different issues at different times."[9]

The UNCITRAL Rules also provide that the tribunal may take "interim measures" prior to the issuance of a final award – for example, by ordering a party to maintain the status quo or preserve assets out of which a subsequent award could be satisfied.[10] This suggests that the tribunal's decision would constitute an order as to the interim measure. The UNCITRAL Rules do not discuss whether the interim measure could be in the form of an award. Under other rules, however, such as the Stockholm Chamber of Commerce Rules and the ICC Rules, the tribunal has the discretion to provide for interim measures in the form of either an order or an award.[11] In some instances, courts have determined that what a tribunal designated as an

---

commission have been fully accomplished." BLACK'S LAW DICTIONARY (8th ed., 2004). *See also* Green v. Ameritech Corp., 200 F.3d 967, 977 (6th Cir. 2000) ("A remand is proper ... to clarify an ambiguous award or to require the arbitrator to address an issue submitted to him but not resolved by the award.").

[7] *See Final Report on Interim and Partial Awards*, 2 ICC International Court of Arbitration Bulletin 26 (1990).

[8] A partial award may be confirmed in the United States if it determines with finality a discrete issue among those within the tribunal's mandate. *See* Metalgesellschaft v. M/V Capitan Constante, 790 F.2d 280, 283 (2d Cir. 1986) (partial award for freight charges properly confirmed because it was a separate, independent claim); Hart Surgical v. Ultracision, Inc., 244 F.3d 231, 234 (1st Cir. 2001) ("[T]he FAA permits a district court to confirm or vacate a partial award."). *See also* Robert Von Mehren, *The Enforcement of Arbitral Awards under Conventions and United States Law*, 9 Yale J. World Public Order 343, 362–64 (1983).

[9] Art. 34(1). *See also* ICDR Rules, art. 27(7). The Stockholm Chamber of Commerce Rules avoid the nomenclature problem by simply providing that "[t]he Arbitral Tribunal may decide a separate issue or part of the dispute in a separate award." SCC Rules, art. 38.

[10] UNCITRAL Rules, art. 26(1–2).

[11] *See* the SCC Rules, art. 32(3) and the ICC Rules, art. 28(1).

order was in fact an award.[12] In Publicis Communication v. True North Communications,[13] for example, the U.S. Seventh Circuit Court of Appeals affirmed a lower court's ruling that a tribunal's order to turn over tax records, although designated as an "order," was a final award, ripe for confirmation. The appellate court held that the "award" had been properly confirmed by the lower court under the New York Convention. It found that the tribunal's decision was more than "just some procedural matter" because "it was the very issue True North wanted arbitrated."[14] Thus, even though other issues were yet to be decided, and even though the decision was denominated an "order," the substance and impact of the tribunal's decision demonstrated finality and made it a final award. The substantive content and effect of the decision were the determining factors.[15]

A decision designated as an "interim award," dealing with interim relief, is generally not considered a final award enforceable under the New York Convention.[16] As noted earlier in Chapter 5, the drafters of the New York Convention intended the Convention to apply to final awards, and not to interim awards.[17] In some jurisdictions, however, an interim award can be confirmed under local arbitration laws, if the award dealt with a "separate, discrete, independent, severable issue."[18] Enforcement of such awards is viewed as "essential to the integrity of [the arbitral] process."[19]

3. Consent Award
The parties may, at any time during the proceedings, decide to resolve their dispute by consent, without the benefit of an arbitral decision. Most rules

---

[12] See Brasoil, *supra* note 2; Publicis Communication & Publicis SA v. True North Communications, Inc., 206 F.3d 725 (7th Cir. 2000).

[13] 206 F.3d 725 (2000).

[14] *Id.* at 729.

[15] See Brasoil, *supra* note 2. *See also* Yasuda Fire & Marine Ins. Co. of Europe v. Continental Cas. Co., 37 F.3d 345 (7th Cir. 1994) ("interim order of security" found to be a final award under the U.S. Federal Arbitration Act).

[16] *See, e.g.*, Resort Condominiums Int'l, Inc., v. Ray Bolwell et al. (S. Ct. Queensland), XX YEARBOOK COMMERCIAL ARBITRATION 628, 642 (1995) ("It does not appear that the . . . Convention contemplates any type of 'award' or 'order' of an arbitrator, other than an award which determines at least all or some of the matters referred to the arbitrator for decision.").

[17] *See* Chapter 5 *supra* Section C(4).

[18] Island Creek Coal Sales v. City of Gainesville, Florida, 729 F.2d 1046, 1049 (6th Cir. 1984). (Court upheld an interim arbitration award that required the defendant to continue performance of a contract until the arbitration panel issued its final award.) *See also* Yasuda, *supra* note 15.

[19] Pacific Reinsurance v. Ohio Reinsurance, 935 F.2d 1019, 1023 (9th Cir. 1991). (Court upheld tribunal decision establishing an escrow account with the money a plaintiff claimed to be due under its contract with the defendant.)

refer specifically to this possibility, and permit the parties, if they so request, to enter an award upon agreed terms.[20] Parties may have no need to have their settlement agreement recorded as a consent award if, at the time they sign the agreement, all monies are paid and any other disputes completely resolved. If, however, any obligation remains to be performed after the signing of the agreement, parties are well advised to convert their settlement agreement into an award. If they do not, and one party does not perform its obligations under the agreement, it would constitute a breach of contract. The other party would then have to go to court and prove the breach before it could begin enforcement proceedings. Enforcement would probably be more difficult because the judgment obtained for breach of contract would not be enforceable under the New York Convention. If the agreement has been converted into an award, however, enforcement would be more readily available by means of the New York Convention.

Another reason for converting the agreement into a consent award would be if the other party is a sovereign state or state agency. From a political perspective, the imprimatur of the arbitral institution and the signatures of the arbitrators could make a particular state system more willing to pay the amount of the award than if there was only a settlement agreement.[21]

4. Default Award

A default award is one made despite the failure of one party to participate in the proceedings. If a respondent does not participate, or withdraws, the tribunal cannot automatically make an award in favor of the claimant. Rather, it must still carefully review the evidence before it and make a determination on the merits. In some ways, this puts a heavier burden on the tribunal, which must ensure at each point in the process that the missing party has been notified and has had every opportunity to participate, both orally and in writing, in the arbitral process. To render an enforceable award, the tribunal must show that it has made reasonable, continuing, and even substantial efforts to permit the other party to present its case. It would be wise for the tribunal to note these efforts in its final award and to provide thoughtful and clear reasons in the award for how it reached its decisions on the merits of the case.

---

[20] *See* UNCITRAL Rules, art. 36(1), ICC Rules, art. 32. *See also* UNCITRAL Model Law, art. 30.
[21] *See* Redfern & Hunter et al., Redfern and Hunter on International Arbitration, § 9.34 at 525.

C. VALIDITY OF THE AWARD

A tribunal has an obligation to make best efforts to produce an enforceable award.[22] This obligation may be expressly stated in institutional rules.[23] Additionally, an arbitrator who renders an award unenforceable through carelessness or negligence will not likely be chosen to arbitrate in the future. Arbitrators work hard to develop a reputation for competence, and do not want to be perceived as having wasted both parties' time by issuing an award that cannot be enforced.

1. Formalities

To be valid, an award must conform with the parties' agreement, the chosen rules, and the applicable law. Certain formalities must be met, which are generally set forth in the rules. Under the UNCITRAL Rules, for example, an award must be:

- in writing
- final and binding
- supported by reasons
- signed by the arbitrators (if one arbitrator's signature is missing, reason for absence must be stated)
- dated, and place of arbitration named
- made public only if both parties consent, or if required by a legal duty or to protect a legal right
- communicated to both parties[24]

Arbitrators need to verify the rules under which the arbitration is conducted, to make sure that their award conforms in all respects. Although failing to meet some of the requirements as to form, such as not stating the date and place of arbitration, would not necessarily invalidate the award, there is no reason to give a disgruntled party any basis to begin an attack on the award.[25]

2. Communication

The award must be communicated promptly to both parties, so that if there are any corrections to be made, they can be done forthwith. In some

---

[22] *See, e.g.*, Martin Platte, *An Arbitrator's Duty to Render Enforceable Awards*, 20 J. Int'l Arb. 307 (2003).

[23] *See, e.g.*, LCIA Rules, art. 32.2.

[24] UNCITRAL Rules, art. 34.

[25] In Publicis, *supra* note 12, 206 F.3d at 729–30, the court, applying the UNCITRAL Rules, did not find an award invalid when it was signed only by the chair of tribunal, who stated he signed "for and on behalf" of the other arbitrators.

jurisdictions, the parties, rather than the tribunal, must register or file the award with the appropriate national authority.

3. Time Limits

There may also be time limits that have to be met in order for the award to be valid. The ICC, for example, imposes a six-month time frame from the beginning of the arbitration to the rendering of the final award.[26] The time frame may be extended, however, and frequently is.[27]

Parties should be wary of placing strict time limits on the tribunal by express agreement, without any possibility of extension. The risk of having an inflexible time frame is twofold. First, the time period may run out before the tribunal has been able to issue an award, leaving the arbitrators with no jurisdiction to proceed.[28] Second, the tribunal might be so rushed into meeting the deadline that the losing party could try to vacate the award on the grounds that it was not fully able to present its case.[29] Thus, anytime limits should be imposed only as guidelines, with the flexibility to extend them as needed.

4. Concurring and Dissenting Views

When a tribunal is composed of three members, a majority of two can decide the case. Usually, an arbitrator's dissent is expressed simply by his or her refusal to sign the award. On rare occasions, however, an arbitrator may wish to write a concurring or dissenting opinion. A concurrence generally expresses agreement with the result, but argues that the result should be based on different grounds. A dissent disagrees with the result. Few laws deal expressly with dissenting or concurring opinions, but it is generally understood that they do not form part of the award.[30] A concern about dissenting opinions is that they should not reveal the deliberations of the tribunal, which are confidential, and that they should not provide to the losing party a basis for challenging the award.

5. Scrutiny of the Draft Award

To ensure conformity of the award to the rules, some arbitral institutions, such as the ICC and the CIETAC, scrutinize every award before it is communicated to the parties.[31] The ICC rules provide that the ICC Court can make

---

[26] See ICC Rules, art. 30(1).

[27] See id. art 30(2).

[28] See Redfern & Hunter et al., *supra* note 22, § 9.127 at 557.

[29] See id. § 9.131 at 558.

[30] See Lew, Mistelis & Kroll, COMPARATIVE INTERNATIONAL COMMERCIAL ARBITRA-TION, at 641–42, §§ 24–46–24–49 (2003), *citing* Swiss Federal Tribunal, May 11, 1992, D.V.A., ASA Bulletin 381, 386 (1992).

[31] See ICC Rules, art. 33; CIETAC 2012 Rules, art. 49.

changes as to form, and can recommend changes as to substance, but the final decision as to substance remains with the arbitrators.[32] The CIETAC Rules similarly provide that CIETAC "may bring to the attention of the arbitral tribunal issues addressed in the award on the condition that the arbitral tribunal's independence in rendering the award is not affected."[33] The purpose of the scrutiny is to ensure that the form of the award is appropriate, and to be able to encourage arbitrators to revise the substantive core, if necessary. The process also provides an incentive to arbitrators, who know their work will be scrutinized, to draft the award properly in the first instance.

6. Finality, Clarity, and Scope

It is important that the arbitrators make clear whether an award is a final award, and if so, that they ensure that the award deals with all remaining issues in dispute between the parties. The award should also state clearly what the arbitrators have decided as to each issue. A lack of clarity could lead to requests for interpretation or even to attempts to vacate. Moreover, the tribunal should make sure that the award does not exceed the scope of powers granted to it by the parties' agreement. As will be discussed further in Chapter 10, an award may be refused enforcement if it exceeds the scope of the arbitration, as defined by the parties in the arbitration agreement.[34]

In sum, to ensure the validity of the award, arbitrators need to take the time to craft the award carefully, to meet the legal requirements as to form and content, to make a clear presentation of the substance of the award, and to ensure that the award does not exceed the scope of their authority.

D. REMEDIES AND COSTS

1. Monetary Damages

The most common remedy sought in international commercial arbitration is the payment of monetary damages. If the tribunal finds that one party has not performed its contractual obligations, it may award "make whole" relief – that is, relief that will put the nonbreaching party back in the position it would have been in if the breach had not occurred.

2. Interest

A tribunal is also likely to include an award of interest. This is fairly routine in an international arbitration, but the arbitrators must pay attention to

---

[32] *See* ICC Rules, art. 33.

[33] CIETAC 2012 Rules, art. 49.

[34] *See* discussion *infra* Chapter 10, Section D(3). *See also* New York Convention, art. V(1)(c).

the law of the place of arbitration, which may impose some limits or even prohibitions. The laws of the place of enforcement may also affect whether interest can be awarded.

Jurisdictions vary widely in their approach to interest awards. Some laws specifically grant arbitrators the power to award not just simple interest, but also compound interest.[35] Other jurisdictions, however, either limit or prohibit the award of compound interest. The rate of interest, and who determines the rate of interest, will also vary by jurisdiction: the rate may be within the discretion of the arbitrators, or it may be prescribed by statute.

In jurisdictions where an award of interest is prohibited by law, such as in certain Islamic states, international arbitrators have nonetheless found a way to award interest by referring to it as "compensatory indemnity in lieu of interest."[36]

3. Other Remedies

Arbitrators generally have discretion to award a variety of remedies. The tribunal can make a declaratory award, simply setting forth the rights of the parties. It may grant injunctive relief, either as preliminary or interim relief,[37] or in the final award. It may, in some instances, award specific performance, but the effectiveness of such an award may depend on the willingness of the enforcing court to enforce it. Punitive damages are rarely awarded in arbitrations, but may be awarded if permitted by law. They are not recoverable in most civil law countries, and may be recoverable only in tort law, not contract law, in many common law countries. Even if punitive damages were awarded, however, there could be problems of enforcement. If awarded by a tribunal in the United States, for example, punitive damages might be refused at the place of enforcement, if the enforcing court was in a jurisdiction that considered punitive damages to be contrary to public policy.[38]

4. Costs

Although the fees and costs of the arbitral tribunal and the arbitral institution are usually determined in advance, the arbitrators will have discretion as to the allocation of those costs between or among the parties, unless the parties predetermined the allocation in their arbitration agreement. "Costs" will usually refer to administrative costs of the institution (including fees and expenses of the tribunal) as well as costs and legal fees for the parties. If

---

[35] *See, e.g.*, English Arbitration Act of 1996, § 49.

[36] *See* Klaus Peter Berger, *International Arbitration Practice and the UNIDROIT Principles of International Commercial Contracts*, 46 Am. J. Comp. L. 129, 136 (1998), and cases cited therein.

[37] *See* discussion in Chapter 5 *supra* Sections B & C.

[38] *See* Redfern & Hunter et al., *supra* note 22, § 9.49 at 530.

parties are allocating these costs by agreement; however, they should make clear whether they are referring to administrative costs, legal fees, or both.

If the parties have not agreed otherwise, the arbitrators have the discretion to award all the reasonable costs, including the prevailing party's legal fees, against the losing party. In civil law jurisdictions, it is common for the losing party to pay the other side's attorney's fees. In many cases, however, the winning party may win some, but not all, of its claims. The arbitrators may, in those cases, award costs pro rata – that is, if the prevailing party won 65 percent of its claims, the losing party would pay 65 percent of the other party's costs and fees. The arbitrators may also decide to award all the administrative costs against the losing party, but provide that each party will bear its own legal costs. However, in a large case, the winning party might be awarded a six- or even seven-figure amount for its costs and legal fees.[39] Because the amount and allocation of costs and fees can vary enormously, parties may find it useful to limit the arbitrators' discretion in this regard by setting forth in the arbitration clause how the costs and fees will be allocated.[40]

E. *RES JUDICATA* EFFECT OF THE AWARD

A final and binding arbitral award has *res judicata* effect.[41] This means that the same issues cannot be arbitrated or litigated again between the same parties, as long as the award is not vacated. Once an award has been confirmed by a court, it normally has the same *res judicata* effect as a court judgment. Moreover, even unconfirmed awards may be treated as *res judicata*. In the United States, not only will courts preclude parties from litigating a claim that has already been decided in arbitration,[42] but they may also apply a *res judicata* bar to claims that could have been, but were not, arbitrated in a prior proceeding.[43]

---

[39] *See* Southern Pacific Properties Ltd. v. Egypt, May 20, 1992 (ICSID), where costs and attorneys fees of U.S. $5 million were awarded. (The prevailing party received in addition an award of damages in the amount of U.S. $27.7 million.) XIX YEARBOOK COMMERCIAL ARBITRATION 51, 82–83 (1994).

[40] *See* Y. Gotanda, *Awarding Costs and Attorneys Fees in International Commercial Arbitration*, 21 Mich. J. Int'l L 1, 2 (1999) ("[A]wards of costs and fees in international commercial arbitration are often arbitrary and inconsistent.").

[41] *See* Bernard Hanotiau, *The Res Judicata Effect of Arbitral Awards*, International Court of Arbitration Bulletin: Complex Arbitrations – Special Supplement 2003, at 47.

[42] *See, e.g.*, Schattner v. Girard, Inc., 668 F.2d 1366, 1369 (D.C. Cir. 1981) ("A party whose claims have been decided in arbitration may not then bring the same claims under new labels.").

[43] *See, e.g.*, Gary Born, INTERNATIONAL COMMERCIAL ARBITRATION 2883 (Vol. 2, 2009); Norris v. Grosvenor Marketing Ltd. 803 F.2d 1281, 1286 (2d Cir. 1986) ("Norris was

The point at which an award becomes *res judicata* may vary by jurisdiction.[44] It could occur when the award is made, when it is communicated to the parties, or when it can no longer be challenged.[45]

Res judicata is also referred to as "claim preclusion" because it precludes the same claims from being litigated again between the same parties. But *issues* that have been previously determined in an arbitration may also, under the doctrine of collateral estoppel, be precluded in a subsequent action that is not between the same parties, or does not involve the same cause of action. If a tribunal has determined an issue of fact or law necessary to the final award, the decision as to that issue may preclude relitigation or rearbitration of the issue as part of a different claim.[46] If, however, the arbitral award is one in which reasons are not given, some courts will not apply collateral estoppel, because it may be unclear what particular issues were dispositive of the claim.[47]

F. CONFIDENTIALITY OF THE AWARD

How important is it to parties to keep the arbitral award confidential? There have been cases in which the award appeared on the Internet within hours of being announced. When substantial amounts of money are at stake, this kind of disclosure could cause the stock prices of the parties involved to go up or down, depending on the result. If confidentiality is important to the parties concerned, there are various ways to help ensure the desired result.

As noted in Chapter 3, the parties can provide for confidentiality of the proceedings and the award in the arbitration agreement. This is particularly necessary if the arbitration is ad hoc, or if the parties have chosen

---

given his opportunity to argue his case to the arbitrator. He should not now be given another bite of the cherry."); Brotherhood of Railroad Trainmen v. Atlantic Coast Line R. Co., 383 F.2d 225, 227 (D.C. Cir. 1967), *cert. denied*, 389 U.S. 1047 (1968) ("[W]hether a party loses or wins relief in his initial action, the judgment embodies all his rights stemming from the transaction involved, and he is foreclosed from later seeking relief on the basis of issues he might have raised in the prior proceeding to support the original claim.").

[44] *See* Hanotiau, *supra* note 41 at 48 ("[T]he law of the seat of the arbitration must be taken into consideration . . . since the moment at which the award becomes *res judicata* may vary from one jurisdiction to another.").

[45] *See id.*

[46] *See, e.g.*, Allen v. McCurry, 449 U.S. 90, 94 (1980); Bryson v. Gere, 268 F. Supp. 2d 46 (D.D.C. 2003) ("[A]ll of plaintiff's claims against [defendants] center on allegations that are identical to issues already decided in arbitration [and are therefore] properly precluded.").

[47] *See* French v. Jinright & Ryan, 735 F.2d 433 (11th Cir. 1984); Murray v. Dominick Corp. of Canada, 631 F. Supp. 534, 537–38 (S.D.N.Y. 1986); Brownko Int'l, Inc., v. Ogden Steel Co., 585 F. Supp. 1432, 1435 (S.D.N.Y. 1983).

arbitration rules that do not offer much protection. Attorneys representing parties should be familiar with how confidentiality is treated in the chosen rules before they draft the arbitration agreement. If parties chose the LCIA Rules, for example, they would have broad protection of confidentiality of the proceedings and the award.[48] Their awards could not be published except with the consent of both parties.[49]

Parties would have less confidentiality protection if they chose the ICC Rules or the ICDR Rules. Although the ICC Rules provide that the tribunal can, "[u]pon the request of any party . . . take measures for protecting trade secrets and confidential information,"[50] the Rules themselves do not appear to impose on the parties any obligation to keep confidential the award or any evidence leading to the award. The ICDR Rules, on the other hand, provide that the award may not be published without the consent of both parties, but do not impose on the parties a confidentiality obligation as to information obtained during the arbitration. Rather, this obligation is imposed only on the administrators and the arbitrators.[51] If either of these sets of rules is chosen for the arbitration, it would be prudent to draft additional confidentiality protections in the arbitration agreement.

In the arbitral community, there are tensions between keeping awards private and confidential and making them generally available, to serve as guides, if not precedents. If parties have information about how similar cases have been decided, it may make their settlement discussions more fruitful. Thus, the ICDR will permit the publication of awards if identifying information has been removed, unless the parties have agreed otherwise.[52] The ICC has also made available abstracts of awards, without revealing names of the parties.[53] The WIPO Arbitration Rules will permit publication of the result of an arbitration in aggregate statistical data, as long as the parties or the particular circumstances of the arbitration are not identifiable.[54]

In addition to the choice of rules, the choice of place of arbitration will affect the extent of the confidentiality obligation. In England, the courts have found an implied obligation of confidentiality in connection with an arbitration clause, thereby creating a general rule of confidentiality even when the arbitration agreement does not expressly provide for it.[55] In the United

---

[48] *See* LCIA Rules, art. 30. Other rules pertaining to confidentiality of awards include, *e.g.*, ICDR Rules, art. 34, UNCITRAL Rules, art. 34(5), WIPO Rules, arts. 73–76.

[49] *See* LCIA Rules, art. 30.

[50] ICC Rules, art. 22(3).

[51] *See* ICDR Rules, arts. 27(4), 34.

[52] *See* ICDR Rules, art. 27(8).

[53] *See* Lew et al., *supra* note 30, at 661–662.

[54] *See* WIPO Rules, art. 76(b). The WIPO Rules provide perhaps the most comprehensive confidentiality protection. These rules were designed primarily, but not exclusively, for use by parties entering into commercial agreements pertaining to intellectual property.

[55] *See* Ali Shipping Corp. v. Shipyard Trogir (1997), E.W.J. No. 1781.

States and Australia, on the other hand, the courts have not placed any implied duty of confidentiality on parties to an arbitration, and, with a few exceptions, require that parties must specifically contract for confidentiality in order to protect confidential information.[56] In sum, the more important it is for parties to keep their award and the underlying evidence confidential, the more diligent their attorneys must be to ensure that if the laws and the rules do not adequately protect their client, the arbitration agreement will do so.

G. POST-AWARD PROCEEDINGS

Once the tribunal has rendered a final award resolving the issues in the case, its duties are generally deemed to be finished. There are occasions, however, when the award may turn out to have errors or be incomplete. Most institutional rules provide that a tribunal may take steps to correct typographical or clerical errors, or errors of computation.[57] Usually, the arbitral tribunal may make the correction on its own, or in response to a request from either party made within thirty days of the receipt of the award. Many rules also provide that in response to a timely request by one of the parties, the tribunal may make an additional award with respect to claims presented to the tribunal but not covered by the award.[58] The tribunal is generally not permitted, however, to correct any substantive error, such as a misinterpretation of a document or of witness testimony.[59]

Some rules may also permit arbitrators to "interpret" the award, in order to clarify ambiguities or inconsistencies.[60] This can be somewhat more complex than simply correcting a typographical or mathematical error. The dilemma for a tribunal is to distinguish between a legitimate need by a party to clarify the meaning of the award and a party's attempt to reargue or revise the decision that was made.[61]

---

[56] *See* Esso Australia Resources Ltd. v. Hon. Sydney James Ploughman (1995), 128 ALR 391; United States v. Panhandle Eastern Corp., 118 F.R.D. 346 (Del. 1988).

[57] *See, e.g.*, WIPO Rules, art. 66; LCIA Rules, art. 27; ICC Rules, art. 35(1); ICDR Rules, art. 30; UNCITRAL Rules, art. 38. *See also* UNCITRAL Model Law, art. 33(1)(b).

[58] *See, e.g.*, WIPO Rules, art. 66(c); LCIA Rules, art. 27.3; ICDR Rules, art. 30; UNCITRAL Rules, art. 39.

[59] *See, e.g.*, UNCITRAL Model Law, art. 33(1)(a) (Types of corrections are limited to "errors in computation, any clerical or typographical errors or any errors of similar nature.").

[60] *See, e.g.*, WIPO Rules, art. 66; ICC Rules, art. 35(2); ICDR Rules, art. 30; UNCITRAL Rules, art. 37.

[61] *See, e.g.*, Robert Knutson, *The Interpretation of Arbitral Awards – When Is a Final Award Not Final?* 11 J. Int'l Arb. 99, 106 (1994) ("A request for interpretation must, therefore, genuinely relate to the determination of the meaning and scope of the decision, and cannot be used as a means for its 'revision' or 'annulment,' processes of a

Almost all of the post-award proceedings permitted under the various rules have to be requested within thirty days and completed within sixty days of a party's receipt of the award. Any corrections or interpretations made by the tribunal are considered to be part of the final award. After the time period for correction and interpretation has passed, it appears under most rules that the award cannot be changed, and the tribunal has no further jurisdiction.

There is an exception, however, when the award is reviewed by a court. The Model Law, for example, provides that when a party moves to set aside an award, the court may, upon a party's request, remand to the arbitral tribunal to permit it to attempt to eliminate, if possible, the grounds for setting it aside.[62] On the other hand, when a party moves to confirm an award, if the other party can show that the award is ambiguous, a court may decide to remand the award to an arbitrator for a clarification. In M&C Corporation v. Erwin BehrGMBH Co., the U.S. Sixth Circuit Court of Appeals noted that even though the ICC Rules, which governed the arbitration, did not provide for remand, it was nonetheless appropriate under ICC policy for the court to remand to the arbitrator for a clarification.[63] The court found that the ICC policy – that every effort should be made to make sure that an award was enforceable at law – would permit a remand to ensure enforceability.[64] The court also noted that the place of arbitration was London, and that the English Arbitration Act provided that in instances of "uncertainty or ambiguity as to the effect of the award," it could be "remit[ted] to the tribunal, in whole or in part."[65] A number of other laws also provide for remission to the arbitrator in similar circumstances.[66]

The policy reasons for remand seem strong. Although remands should be used sparingly, they are appropriate when an award is ambiguous. Basically, a court does not want to guess how the award should be enforced or what the arbitrator actually meant. The authority to order a remand is an exception to the *functus officio* doctrine that an arbitrator's duties are discharged when the final award is rendered. Upon a remand by the court, the arbitrator is deemed to have jurisdiction to complete his duties by clarifying the award to make it properly enforceable.

---

different kind to which different considerations apply," *citing* U.K.-French Continental Shelf case, 54 ILR 139 (1978).).

[62] *See* UNCITRAL Model Law, art. 34(4).

[63] 326 F.3d 772, 783–84, *rev'd on other grounds*, 411 F.3d 749 (2005), *affirmed in part, rev'd on other grounds* (6th Cir. 2008).

[64] *See* 326 F.3d 772, 783–84.

[65] English Arbitration Act of 1996, §§ 68(2)(f) and (3)(a).

[66] *See, e.g.*, Swedish Arbitration Act of 1999, § 35; China Arbitration Law of 1994, art. 61.

CHAPTER NINE

Attempts to Set Aside an Award

A party that has lost before an arbitral tribunal faces an uphill battle if it wishes to set aside or vacate the award. Courts rarely overturn an arbitral award. Because arbitral awards are considered to be final and binding, for the most part they cannot be challenged on the merits, but only on procedural grounds or grounds of arbitrator misconduct or bias. One of the touted advantages of an arbitration is the finality of the award, and arbitration laws and rules support finality by making it difficult to set aside an award. Nonetheless, steps can be taken by a determined party that believes an award was improperly made.

A. METHODS OF CHALLENGE

The most common method of challenge is to bring an action to annul, set aside, or vacate the award (the terms differ in different jurisdictions) in the court at the situs of the arbitration.[1] This is the appropriate place to challenge the award, because the court at the situs is considered to have supervisory jurisdiction over the arbitral process to ensure that it was conducted in a fair and noncorrupt manner. The law that will govern the action will be the *lex arbitri*, or the curial law, which governs the arbitration proceedings at the situs.[2] In at least seventy jurisdictions, the procedural law for challenging an award will be based on the UNCITRAL Model Law on International Commercial Arbitration, which will provide the grounds on which an award can be challenged.

---

[1] The court at the seat of the arbitration is the proper court under the UNCITRAL Model Law, art. 34, and under most arbitration laws.

[2] Parties are unlikely to choose a law different from the curial law of the situs, and it is inadvisable for them to do so, because of the unnecessary complication of having a court apply (assuming it will do so) a procedural law different from its own.

As for methods of challenge, however, actions other than court challenges are available in particular kinds of arbitrations. In the maritime industry and in certain trade associations, for example, a challenge to an arbitration award may be brought to another arbitration panel or to a Board of Appeal.[3] Moreover, a party to an award under the ICSID Convention can appeal only to another ICSID arbitral tribunal.[4] If the second panel annuls the original award, either party can request yet another tribunal to render an award.[5]

An interesting formula adopted by the European Court of Arbitration is to have the initial arbitration heard by a sole arbitrator, with the possibility of an appeal to a panel of three arbitrators.[6] To have an appeal, the losing party must deposit the amount awarded against it with the registrar or the bank of the arbitral institution.[7] Thus, if the award is not vacated on appeal, the amount of the award can be paid immediately to the prevailing party.[8]

In most commercial arbitrations arising out of an international contract, however, any challenge to an award will be directed to a court. A losing party can bring an action to set aside an award on procedural or public policy grounds. If it loses in the local court, or if it does not bring an action to set aside, the losing party has still another opportunity to resist enforcement. It can oppose the prevailing party's efforts to enforce the award in a different jurisdiction, where the losing party's assets are located. Thus, the losing party has two opportunities to challenge an award: first, in the court of the situs and, second, in the court where the prevailing party is attempting to enforce the award against the assets of the losing party.

Courts have sometimes confused the two actions – an action to vacate and an action to enforce. It is possible, in some instances, to bring both actions in the same court. If, for example, the arbitration were held in the United States and the losing party's assets were also in the United States, the U.S. court could hear both a motion to vacate and a motion to enforce. Normally, however, the parties will have chosen a neutral situs for the arbitration, so the losing party's assets are likely to be in a jurisdiction other than the one where the arbitration is held. Thus, the motion to vacate will take place in the courts of the situs, but the motion to enforce will be in the jurisdiction where the relevant assets are located.

---

[3] The Grain and Feed Association (GAFTA), for example, provides for an appeal to a Board of Appeal, consisting of either three or five members of the Association.

[4] ICSID Arbitration Rules, art. 52.

[5] See id. art. 55.

[6] See Mauro Rubino-Sammartano, *Is Arbitration Losing Ground?*, 14 Am. Rev. Int'l Arb, 341, 344 (2003). See also Rules of European Court of Arbitration, 28(3), available at http://cour-europe-arbitrage.org/archivos/descargas/17.pdf.

[7] See Rubino-Sammartano, *supra* note 6; see also ECA Rules, art. 28(3).

[8] See Rubino-Sammartano, *supra* note 6; see also ECA Rules, art. 28(9)(10).

Although from time to time awards are vacated by the court of the arbitral situs, and enforcement is sometimes refused in the jurisdiction where it is sought, for the most part a challenging party is not likely to succeed because the grounds for challenging an award are quite narrow, as discussed next.

B. GROUNDS OF CHALLENGE

Because arbitrations are meant to be final and binding, in most jurisdictions there is no right to appeal if the arbitrators made a mistake of law or of fact.[9] Rather, there are only a few grounds on which a party can base a motion to set aside the award. The applicable law in the jurisdiction where the challenge is brought defines the grounds that can be used. In most jurisdictions, the grounds for a challenge tend to fall into two broad categories: (1) jurisdictional and (2) procedural.

1. Jurisdictional Challenges

Jurisdictional challenges may be made to an award, but they are more typically made at the beginning of the arbitration, rather than after the award is rendered. Under many laws, if a party does not challenge the jurisdiction at the beginning of the arbitration, it may lose the right to object.[10] It is obviously more efficient to determine whether jurisdiction is proper at the beginning of an arbitral procedure, rather than after parties have expended time, effort, and resources to reach the final award.

Thus, if a party waits until the award is handed down before it objects to the tribunal's jurisdiction, it may well have lost its opportunity to challenge. It is also not advisable for a party to boycott the proceedings, because even if permitted to challenge the award, the party is likely to have the award enforced against it despite its nonparticipation, and costs will probably be awarded against it as well.[11] For that reason, in most cases it would be better for a party to test the jurisdictional question at the beginning of the arbitration, and if that challenge fails, to participate in the arbitration.

A jurisdictional challenge to the award, however, may be based on a claim that the tribunal exceeded its powers. A tribunal may have had jurisdiction under the arbitration agreement, but nonetheless could have rendered an award that it was not entitled to make. For example, if a party claimed only

---

[9] *See infra* Section B(3) for exceptions.

[10] English Arbitration Act of 1996, §§ 31, 73; Cour d'Appel de Paris decision in SA Caisse Federale de Credit Mutuel du Nord de la France v. Banque Delubac et Compagnie, 2001 Revue d'Arbitrage 918 (R & H).

[11] *See* Redfern & Hunter et al., REDFERN AND HUNTER ON INTERNATIONAL ARBITRATION, § 5.121 at 355 (2009); Tweeddale & Tweeddale, ARBITRATION OF COMMERCIAL DISPUTES, 698–99, 789 (2005).

a certain quantum of damages, and the tribunal awarded more than that amount, the tribunal may have exceeded its jurisdiction.[12] The award may also be challenged if the tribunal either fails to consider all the issues before it, or if it decides certain issues that were not before it. In some instances, if a court finds that the tribunal has exceeded its powers, the issues that were improperly decided may be severed, leaving the award as to other issues intact.[13]

2. Procedural Challenges

Awards are most often challenged on procedural grounds. Most arbitration laws provide that certain standards of due process must be met.[14] Under the UNCITRAL Model Law, for example, a party can base a challenge on four grounds, all of which relate to some aspect of due process.[15] They include the following: (1) a party must not be under any incapacity, and the agreement must be valid; (2) a party must have been given proper notice of both the appointment of the arbitrator and the scheduling of the proceedings, and must have been able to present its case; (3) the subject matter has to be within the scope of the arbitration agreement; and (4) the arbitral tribunal must be constituted in accordance with the agreement of the parties.[16] On each of these grounds, the party making the challenge bears the burden of proof.

Two other grounds may be raised and determined by the national court *sua sponte*: (1) whether the subject matter is arbitrable and (2) whether the award conflicts with the public policy of the state.[17] The arbitrability ground will not cause many awards to be vacated, because few matters today are not considered arbitrable.[18] The second ground that a court could raise is a violation of public policy. Public policy is defined differently in different jurisdictions, but in most, an award could be vacated if it was not consistent with fundamental notions of justice, honesty, and fairness. Thus, corruption, fraud, or lack of integrity in the process could be considered a violation of public policy, requiring the award to be annulled.

In most Model Law jurisdictions, fraud or corruption would probably be considered a proper ground for challenging an award as a violation of

---

[12] *See* Paris Lapeyre v. Sauvate [2001] Rev. Arb. 806.

[13] *See, e.g.*, General Organisation of Commerce and Industrialisation of Cereals of the Arab Republic of Syria v. SpA Simer, Italy, Corte di Appello Trento (1981), VIII; YEARBOOK COMMERCIAL ARBITRATION 386–88 (1983).

[14] *See, e.g.*, Swiss PILA, Ch. 12, art. 190; U.S. FAA, § 10.

[15] UNCITRAL Model Law, art. 34.

[16] *See id.*

[17] *See id.*

[18] Some matters that are usually not considered arbitrable in most jurisdictions include family law matters, such as child custody, as well as criminal matters, tax issues, patent validity issues, and bankruptcy claims.

public policy. The U.S. Federal Arbitration Act (FAA) is more explicit. It provides specifically that grounds for vacating an award include the following: (1) "the award was procured by corruption, fraud or undue means," (2) "there was evident partiality or corruption in the arbitrators," (3) "the arbitrators were guilty of misconduct . . . or . . . other misbehavior by which the rights of any party have been prejudiced."[19] Similarly, the English Arbitration Act provides that a party may challenge an award based on "serious irregularity affecting the tribunal, the proceedings or the award."[20]

3. Challenges Based on the Merits

There are a few exceptions to the general rule in arbitration that the only grounds for challenging an award are based on jurisdiction, procedural irregularities, arbitrability, or public policy. These exceptions are found generally in common law legal systems. In England, for example, a party may appeal an arbitral award on a point of law, unless the parties have agreed otherwise.[21] This right of appeal, however, is subject to substantial limitations. The appeal cannot be brought unless all the parties agree, or unless the court grants leave to appeal.[22] The court should grant leave only if the tribunal was obviously wrong on the point of law, or the question is of general public importance and the decision of the tribunal is open to doubt.[23] Moreover, case law has established that only a point of English law can be appealed, so questions that arise under other countries' laws are not appealable.[24]

In the United States, courts have created some nonstatutory grounds for challenging an award. For example, an award can be vacated if it violates public policy, a nonstatutory ground under the FAA.[25] It is rare that a court

---

[19] U.S. Federal Arbitration Act, 9 U.S.C. § 10(a).

[20] English Arbitration Act of 1996, § 68(1). The Swedish Arbitration Act also permits a challenge based on "an irregularity . . . which probably influenced the outcome of the case." § 34(6).

[21] English Arbitration Act of 1996, § 69(1).

[22] *See id.* § 69(2).

[23] *See id.* § 69(3).

[24] *See* Reliance Industries Ltd. v. Enron Oil & Gas India Ltd. [2002], 1 All ER (Comm) (QBD) (Appeal not granted because issues related to Indian law, not English law.).

[25] Public policy is a nonstatutory ground for setting aside an award in the United States because it is not one of the grounds for nonenforcement provided under the Federal Arbitration Act, 9 U.S.C. § 10. The doctrine apparently originated in the context of labor arbitrations and collective bargaining. *See* United Paperworkers Int'l Union v. Misco, Inc., 484 U.S. 29, 49 (1987). Many courts recognize public policy as a potential ground for setting aside an award. Nonetheless, attempts to set aside an award on this ground usually do not succeed. *See, e.g.,* Seymour v. Blue Cross/Blue Shield, 988 F.2d 1020, 1023 (10th Cir. 1993); PaineWebber, Inc., v. Argon, 49 F.3d 347 (8th Cir. 1995); Brown v. Rauscher Pierce Refsnes, Inc., 994 F.2d 775 (11th Cir. 1994); Diapulse Corp. of America v. Carba Ltd., 626 F.2d 1108 (2nd Cir. 1980).

will set aside an award on this ground, however, courts generally find that *vacatur* on the grounds of "public policy" requires more than a mistake or misunderstanding of the law by the arbitrator. Courts differ as to whether the ground of public policy requires the court to inquire into the merits of the arbitration award.[26]

In some U.S. courts, "manifest disregard of the law" is a nonstatutory ground for setting aside the award.[27] This doctrine requires that a party show that the arbitrator knew and understood the law, but deliberately disregarded it.[28] The standard is rarely met, because it is quite difficult to show that an arbitrator deliberately disregarded law that he knew and understood. Moreover, the current status of the doctrine is quite uncertain.[29] In Hall Street Assoc. v. Mattel,[30] the U.S. Supreme Court appeared to eliminate manifest disregard as a ground for *vacatur*.[31] But in a subsequent case, Stolt Nielsen v. Animal Feeds,[32] the Court vacillated about the validity of the manifest disregard doctrine. The majority of justices asserted that the Court was not deciding whether the doctrine had survived its decision in *Hall Street*, either as an independent ground or as a judicial gloss on the enumerated statutory grounds.[33] Thus, lower courts have taken different positions on whether the ground still exists.[34] The American Law Institute, which is drafting a Restatement of the United States Law of International Commercial Arbitration, is expected to take a position on whether an award subject to enforcement in the United States under the New York Convention could ever be vacated based on an arbitrator's manifest disregard of the law. However, the Restatement will probably not be completed for several years.

---

[26] *See* Revised Uniform Arbitration Act, available at http://www.law.upenn.edu/bll/ulc/uarba/arbitrat1213.htm, Comment C to Section 23 on Vacating Awards, *Comment on Possible Codification of the "Manifest Disregard of the Law" and the "Public Policy" Grounds for Vacatur*.

[27] *See* Jock v. Sterling Jewelers, Docket No. 10-3247, c.v. note 1 (2d Cir. July 1, 2011) (stating that manifest disregard is a separate an independent ground for *vacatur*).

[28] *See* Prudential-Bache, 72 F.3d 234 at 240 (1st Cir. 1995).

[29] *See, e.g.*, Judge Posner's decision in Baravati v. Josephthal, Lyon & Ross, Inc., 28 F.3d 704, 706 (7th Cir. 1994).

[30] 552 U.S. 576 (2008).

[31] *See id.* at 586 (holding that the statutory grounds for vacatur under the FAA were exclusive).

[32] 130 S.Ct. 1758 (2010).

[33] *See id.* at 1768, note 3.

[34] *Compare* Jock v. Sterling, *supra* note 27 ("In addition to the section 10(a) grounds for vacatur, we have recognized a judicially-created ground, namely that "an arbitral decision may be vacated when an arbitrator has exhibited a manifest disregard of law."), with Louisiana Health Service Indemnity Co. v. Gambro, 756 F. Supp. 2d 760, 766 (W.D. La. 2010)("[T]o the extent that manifest disregard of the law constitutes a nonstatutory ground for vacatur, it is no longer a basis for vacating awards under the FAA.").

C. TIME LIMITATIONS

Challenges to an award must be brought promptly. Failure to act within the time limitations may preclude the challenge. Time periods range from twenty-eight days (England)[35] or a month from notification of the award (France)[36] to about six months (China).[37] In the Model Law jurisdictions and in the United States, the period is three months.[38] The Model Law, however, arguably permits the court some discretion, because it provides that "an application for setting aside *may* not be made after three months [from receipt of the award]."[39] The U.S. law, on the other hand, requires that notice *must* be served on the opposing party or counsel within three months from the date when the award was delivered or filed.[40] This does not appear to permit any flexibility.

D. EFFECTS OF A SUCCESSFUL CHALLENGE

Assume that a party persuades the local court to vacate the arbitration award. At that point, with some few exceptions, the award is null and void, having no further legal effect. What happens next? If the award was vacated because the court held that the arbitration agreement itself was invalid, then, assuming there is no time bar, the prevailing party should be able to initiate a court action on the same issues. Dutch law, for example, explicitly states that when a decision setting aside an award becomes final, the jurisdiction of the court shall revive.[41]

If the award is vacated because of some major procedural irregularity, however, the question is whether the case will be remitted to the arbitrators, and if so, whether it will be to the same tribunal or to a different one. Courts are likely to favor some kind of remission, so that the parties will not have wasted the entire arbitration effort. If the problem with the award can be resolved short of declaring it null and void, most courts will try to choose a solution that will not require the parties to start all over again. A substantial duplication of effort, time, and resources would not benefit either party. The English Arbitration Act, for example, specifically provides that a court shall not "set aside or . . . declare an award to be of no effect, in whole or in part,

---

[35] English Arbitration Act of 1996, § 70(3).
[36] French Code of Civil Procedure, art. 1519.
[37] China Arbitration Law, art. 59.
[38] UNCITRAL Model Law, art. 34(3); U.S. Federal Arbitration Act, 9 U.S.C. § 12.
[39] UNCITRAL Model Law, art. 34(3).
[40] U.S. Federal Arbitration Act, 9 U.S.C. § 12.
[41] Netherlands Arbitration Law, art. 1067. The provision appears to apply to all awards, not just those set aside on jurisdictional grounds.

unless it is satisfied that it would be inappropriate to remit the matters in question to the tribunal for reconsideration."[42]

As noted earlier, in Chapter 8, if an award needs to be corrected or interpreted, the court will generally remit the case to the same tribunal. German law provides that a court may "where appropriate, set aside the award and remit the case to the arbitral tribunal."[43] German law also provides that absent any indication to the contrary, the setting aside of the award will "result in the arbitration agreement becoming operative again in respect of the subject-matter of the dispute."[44] This suggests the possibility that if the court does not specifically remit to the prior tribunal, the parties could start over again with a new tribunal.

It would be logical, if the problem with the award were related to the integrity of the process, such as bias by the arbitrator, or some kind of misconduct, that the court would not remit the case to the same tribunal. The Uniform Arbitration Act in the United States, which has been adopted in forty-nine U.S. jurisdictions, was revised in 2000 to spell out more clearly what should happen after a court vacates an arbitral award.[45] Under the Revised Uniform Arbitration Act (RUAA), if the court vacates an award other than on the ground that the arbitration agreement was invalid, "it may order a rehearing."[46] However, if the award was vacated on grounds of corruption, fraud, or arbitrator misconduct or partiality, "the rehearing must be before a new arbitrator."[47] If the ground concerned a failure of procedure, or an arbitrator acting in excess of her powers, then the rehearing "may be before the arbitrator who made the award or the arbitrator's successor."[48] Presumably, in this latter case, the parties themselves, if they agreed, could have some ability to help determine whether the prior tribunal or a newly constituted one would conduct the rehearing.

Although this revised version of the Uniform Arbitration Act has not yet been adopted in many states, it provides reasonable guidelines for how remissions or remands should be handled. Ultimately, whether a case is remitted to a prior tribunal or the parties start over with a new tribunal will depend on the law of the jurisdiction and the reasons the award was vacated, and possibly on what the parties want to do and whether they can agree.

---

[42] English Arbitration Act of 1996, § 68(3)(c).

[43] German Arbitration Act, § 1059(4).

[44] German Arbitration Act, § 1059(5).

[45] At least 14 states plus the District of Columbia have amended their statutes to include the changes of the Revised Uniform Arbitration Act. *See* website of National Conference of Commissioners of Uniform State Laws, at http://www.nccusl.org/Act .aspx?title=Arbitration%20Act%20(2000).

[46] RUAA, § 23(c).

[47] *See id.*

[48] *See id.*

CHAPTER TEN

Enforcement of the Award

In many instances, a losing party will voluntarily comply with an arbitration award, so enforcement proceedings will not be necessary. If, on the other hand, the prevailing party is required to initiate judicial enforcement because of the recalcitrance of the losing party, the good news is that the award is likely to be enforced. One of the prime reasons parties include an arbitration clause in an international contract is the relatively certain enforceability of the award. The likelihood of enforcement is high because so many countries have adopted international conventions that are pro-enforcement – that is, they provide only narrow grounds for refusing to enforce. This chapter discusses some of the issues and procedures pertinent to recognition and enforcement of awards under international conventions and various national laws, as well as the limited grounds for refusing enforcement.

A. APPLICATION OF INTERNATIONAL CONVENTIONS

The Convention on Recognition and Enforcement of Foreign Arbitral Awards,[1] also known as the New York Convention, requires courts of Contracting States to enforce both arbitration agreements and arbitration awards. Currently, more than 145 countries are parties to the New York Convention.[2] The New York Convention has contributed to the growth of international arbitration because parties in Contracting States are confident that if they prevail in an arbitration, they will obtain a remedy. A 2005 study noted that for corporate counsel, the most important reason for choosing arbitration over litigation to settle disputes was the enforceability

---

[1] 21 U.S.T. 2517, 330 U.N.T.S 38 (1958).
[2] Available at http://www.uncitral.org/uncitral/en/uncitral_texts/arbitration/ NYConvention_status.html.

of awards.[3] Because the New York Convention is the predominant arbitration enforcement convention, this chapter focuses primarily on its function, requirements, and effect.

B. PRINCIPLES GOVERNING RECOGNITION AND ENFORCEMENT

Article III of the New York Convention (the Convention) requires countries to recognize arbitral awards as binding and to enforce them in accordance with national law, consistent with the provisions of the Convention. Although the terms "recognition" and "enforcement" tend to be used together, they mean different things. When a court "recognizes" an award, it acknowledges that the award is valid and binding, and thereby gives it a preclusive effect with respect to the matters determined in the award. Thus, a recognized award can be relied on as a set-off or defense in related litigation or arbitration. The award has an official legal status, so issues determined by the award usually cannot be relitigated or rearbitrated.[4]

Suppose, for example, the party that prevailed in the arbitration was the respondent, and the award simply said the respondent had no liability. The respondent might want to have the award recognized in order to defeat claims on the same facts that might be brought against it in other proceedings, before either a court or another arbitral tribunal.

Enforcement, on the other hand, may mean different things in different jurisdictions. In some jurisdictions, it may mean simply the process by which an international arbitration award is reduced to a judgment. In other jurisdictions, it may mean using whatever official means are available in the enforcing jurisdiction to collect the amount owed or to otherwise carry out any mandate provided in the award. However, another term frequently used for this purpose is "execution." Execution usually refers to the manner by which relief under an award is obtained pursuant to the legal process of the authorizing jurisdiction.

When an award has provided that the respondent is liable to the claimant for money damages and the respondent appears in no hurry to pay the amount awarded, then the claimant – the award creditor – may seek recognition and enforcement of the award in a jurisdiction where assets of the respondent – the award debtor – are located. In some jurisdictions, the award

---

[3] Loukas Mistelis, *International Arbitration-Corporate Attitudes and Practices* – 12 *Perceptions Tested: Myths, Data and Analysis Research Report*, 15 Am. Rev. Int'l Arb. 525, 545, describing results of a survey conducted in 2005.

[4] In the United States, an award can have *res judicata* effect even if it has not been confirmed or recognized. *See* Gary Born, INTERNATIONAL COMMERCIAL ARBITRATION 2883 (Vol. 2, 2009).

must first be recognized before the award creditor can use the enforcement mechanisms of the enforcing court.[5] Once the award is recognized, the award creditor may use whatever methods are normally used to collect the amount of the award – for example, by seizing assets in accordance with legal procedures in the enforcing jurisdiction. In other jurisdictions, there may be no practical difference between procedures for recognition and for enforcement.

C. REQUIREMENTS FOR ENFORCEMENT

1. Scope

The Convention was intended to apply to international awards, and expressly states that it covers awards made in a state other than the one where enforcement is sought.[6] It also, however, permits enforcement of awards considered "nondomestic" by the enforcing jurisdiction.[7] Because "domestic" is not defined in the Convention, that determination must be made by each of the Contracting States. In the United States, the implementing legislation found in the Federal Arbitration Act (FAA) provides that an award is nondomestic, even if between citizens of the United States, if the "relationship involves property located abroad, envisages performance of enforcement abroad, or has some other reasonable relation with one or more foreign states."[8] Thus, in the United States, for an award to be covered by the Convention, it can be either rendered in a foreign country, or it can be nondomestic in the sense that it has an international aspect involving in some way the legal system of another country.[9]

In China, on the other hand, the only nondomestic awards enforceable under the New York Convention are those rendered in another Contracting State with which China also has a treaty on Judicial Assistance.[10] Many other countries only enforce, under the Convention, awards that were rendered in a foreign state.[11]

---

[5] In Portugal, for example, the award must first be recognized before it can be enforced in accordance with the provisions of the Portugal Procedural Rules regarding enforcement of judicial decisions. ARBITRATION WORLD, EUROPEAN LAWYER REFERENCE SERIES, 290 (2006).

[6] See N.Y. Convention, art. I(1).

[7] See id. "[The Convention] shall also apply to arbitral awards not considered as domestic awards in the State where their recognition and enforcement are sought."

[8] 9 U.S.C. § 202.

[9] See Yusuf Ahmed Alghanim & Sons v. Toys "R" Us, Inc., 126 F.3d 15 (2nd Cir. 1997); Bergesen v. Joseph Muller Corp., 710 F.2d 928 (2nd Cir. 1983).

[10] ARBITRATION WORLD, EUROPEAN LAWYER REFERENCE SERIES, 273 (2006).

[11] For example, Japan, the Netherlands, and Portugal. See id. at 191, 231, 290.

Contracting States are permitted to make two reservations as to the scope of applicability of the Convention.[12] The first limitation is one of reciprocity: a Contracting State can provide that it will apply the Convention only to awards that are made in the territory of another Contracting State. This reservation has been adopted by approximately half the Contracting States.[13] Thus, if an enforcement action was brought in a Contracting State that had made a reservation as to reciprocity, and the award had been made in a non-Contracting State, the Convention would not apply. This would be true even if both parties had places of business located in a Contracting State. It is important to understand that neither citizenship nor location of the parties is a key determinant of the Convention's applicability. Rather, the significant consideration is the place where the arbitration occurred. Therefore, in drafting the arbitration clause, one is well advised to choose a location for the arbitration that is within a Contracting State. This will avoid the problem of lack of reciprocity, which can prevent enforcement under the Convention in many Contracting States.

The second permitted reservation is that a Contracting State may "declare that it will apply the Convention only to differences arising out of legal relationships, whether contractual or not, which are considered as commercial."[14] At least forty-four states have declared that they will apply the Convention only to commercial matters.[15] Because no definition of "commercial" is provided in the Convention, the law of the enforcing jurisdiction determines what is commercial. There does not appear to be a uniform understanding of the meaning of "commercial." In general, however, criminal matters and family matters, such as divorce, custody, and adoption, as well as wills and trusts, are not considered commercial.

2. Jurisdiction and *Forum Non Conveniens*

When an award creditor seeks enforcement in a Contracting State, the presence of the award debtor's assets in that state will usually suffice to provide a jurisdictional basis for the enforcement of the award under the Convention. In the United States, however, some courts have refused to enforce foreign arbitral awards either on the grounds that there was no personal jurisdiction over the award debtor, or that the forum was inappropriate under the doctrine of *forum non conveniens* (an inconvenient forum). For example, in Base Metal Trading Ltd. v. OJSC "Novokuznetsky Aluminum Factory"

---

[12] N.Y. Convention, art. I (3).

[13] *See* http://www.uncitral.org/uncitral/en/uncitral_texts/arbitration/NYConvention_status.html.

[14] N.Y. Convention, art. I(3).

[15] *See* http://www.uncitral.org/uncitral/en/uncitral_texts/arbitration/NYConvention_status.html.

(Base Metals),[16] the U.S. Fourth Circuit Court of Appeals found no personal jurisdiction because the property that was asserted as the basis for jurisdiction was unrelated to the claimant's cause of action. In contrast, the Ninth Circuit, in Glencore Grain Rotterdam B.V. v. Shivnath Rai Harnarain Co.,[17] held that any property, not just property related to the claimant's cause of action, would support jurisdiction.[18]

Most commentators have criticized the *Base Metal* decision as wrongly decided,[19] and some have also suggested that the Fourth Circuit's refusal to recognize a New York Convention award is a violation of U.S. treaty obligations under the Convention.[20] Professor William Park and Alexander Yanos argue convincingly that the standard under U.S. law for finding jurisdiction to enforce an award is more lenient than the standard to find jurisdiction to decide a case on the merits, and that the award in *Base Metals* should have been enforced.[21]

Another roadblock to enforcement of Convention awards that has been raised in the United States is the doctrine of *forum non conveniens*, which is derived from a court's inherent power to control its docket.[22] A court's determination that an adequate alternative forum exists, and that there are

---

[16] 283 F.3d 208 (2002), *cert. denied*, 537 U.S. 822 (2002).

[17] 284 F.3d 1114 (2002).

[18] *See id.* at 1127. The Ninth Circuit nonetheless refused to enforce the award on the grounds that there was no evidence that the respondent owned property, kept bank accounts, had employees, solicited business or had designated an agent for service of process in California. *See id.* at 1128.

[19] *See, e.g.*, William W. Park & Alexander A. Yanos, *Treaty Obligations and National Law: Emerging Conflicts in International Arbitration*, 58 Hastings L.J. 251, 279–81 (2006); Joseph E. Neuhaus, *Current Issues in the Enforcement of International Arbitration Awards*, 36 U. Miami Inter-Am L. Rev. 23, 27–30, 39 (2004); International Commercial Disputes Committee of the Association of the Bar of the City of New York, *Lack of Jurisdiction and Forum Non Conveniens as Defenses to the Enforcement of Foreign Arbitral Awards*, 15 Am. Rev. Int'l Arb. 407, 417–18 (2004). Park and Yanos also believe the Ninth Circuit wrongly decided *Glencore Grain*. *See* 58 Hastings L.J. 251, 297.

[20] *See* Park and Yanos, 58 Hastings L.J. at 281.

[21] Park and Yanos cite footnote 36 of Shaffer v. Heitner, 433 U.S. 186 (1977), which provides: "Once it has been determined by a court of competent jurisdiction that the defendant is a debtor of the plaintiff, there would seem to be no unfairness in allowing an action to realize on that debt in a State where the defendant has property, whether or not that State would have jurisdiction to determine the existence of the debt as an original matter." *Id.* at 210, n. 36. *See also* Aristides Diaz-Pedrosa, *Shaffer's Footnote 36*, 109 W. Va. L. Rev. 17, *20 (2006) ("[T]he presence of assets alone, however unrelated to the underlying cause of action they may be, should be enough to meet the minimum contacts test during a post-award proceeding.").

[22] *See* Monegasque de Reassurances v. Nak Naftogaz of Ukraine and State of Ukraine 311 F.3d 488, 498 (2002), *citing* In re Minister Papandreou, 329 U.S. App. D.C. 210, 139 F.3d 247, 255–56 (D.C. Cir. 1998) ("Forum non convenience does not raise a jurisdictional bar but instead involves a deliberate abstention from the exercise of jurisdiction.").

public or private interests that weigh more heavily in favor of a different forum, can cause it to dismiss a case. Although this doctrine should rarely justify a refusal to recognize or enforce a Convention award, in *Monegasque de Reassurances v. Nak Naftogaz of Ukraine and State of Ukraine*,[23] the Second Circuit Court of Appeals upheld a district court's dismissal on *forum non conveniens* grounds.[24] The circumstances in that case, however, make it one of those rare cases in which application of *forum non conveniens* may have been justified.[25] There was a serious issue of whether the proper party was before the court. Because the answer depended on Ukrainian law, the U.S. court held that the court in the Ukraine was better able to make that decision.[26]

Although the better view in the United States is that enforcement of Convention awards should not be thwarted by grounds such as *forum non conveniens* and lack of personal jurisdiction, the fact that some courts have refused enforcement on these grounds suggests that it may be prudent to address the issue in an arbitration clause, if enforcement is likely to be sought in the United States. The International Commercial Disputes Committee of the Association of the Bar of the City of New York recommends providing in the arbitration clause that "the parties consent to recognition and enforcement of any resulting award in any jurisdiction and waive any defense to recognition or enforcement based upon lack of jurisdiction over their person or property or based upon *forum non conveniens*."[27] They suggest further that this language could be limited to specific jurisdictions, or to any jurisdiction where property of the award debtor may be located.[28]

3. Procedures for Enforcement

Procedures for enforcing an award or executing on an award will vary by jurisdiction, because a Contracting State will provide for enforcement or execution in accordance with its own rules of practice.[29] It cannot, however, impose any higher fees or any more onerous conditions on the process than would be applicable with respect to a domestic award.[30] The only specific requirements imposed by the Convention are that the party applying for recognition and enforcement must provide the court with the authenticated original award or a certified copy, and the original arbitration agreement or a certified copy.[31] In addition, if the award or the agreement is not in the same language used in the enforcing jurisdiction, the party must provide

---

[23] 311 F.3d 488 (2002).
[24] *See id.*
[25] *See, e.g.*, Neuhaus, *supra* note 19, at 34–35 (2004).
[26] *See* Monegasque de Reassurances, 311 F.3d at 500–01.
[27] 15 Am. Rev. Int'l Arb. 407, 411 (2004).
[28] *See id.*
[29] *See* N.Y. Convention, art. III.
[30] *See id.*
[31] *See* N.Y. Convention, art. IV.

a certified translation of the documents.[32] Otherwise, the procedures are determined by each jurisdiction, but are frequently similar to the procedures used to enforce court judgments within that jurisdiction.

D. GROUNDS FOR NONENFORCEMENT UNDER THE CONVENTION

To support enforcement of arbitral awards, the Convention provides only a limited number of defenses to enforcement, and these are narrowly construed.[33] They are also considered exhaustive, meaning they are the only grounds on which nonenforcement can be based. Five kinds of defenses are found in Article V(1) and two additional defenses in Article V(2). In brief, the five Article V(1) defenses are (1) incapacity and invalidity, (2) lack of notice or fairness, (3) arbitrator acting in excess of authority, (4) the tribunal or the procedure not being in accord with the parties' agreement, and (5) the award not yet binding or having been set aside. The two Article V(2) defenses are (1) lack of arbitrability and (2) violation of public policy. The five Article V(1) defenses must be established by the party resisting enforcement, which has the burden of proof. The two additional defenses in Article V(2) can be raised by the court *sua sponte*, although it is likely that these defenses would, if pertinent, be raised by the resisting party.

The most important characteristic of the defenses is that they are not based on the merits. Under the Convention, a court cannot refuse enforcement of an award because the arbitrators got it wrong, either on the facts or the law. Rather, the permitted defenses focus on the integrity of the process, including fairness to the parties and a reasonable opportunity to be heard. An arbitration that has been conducted by competent, experienced arbitrators is unlikely to produce an award that is unenforceable. In fact, it has been estimated that voluntary compliance combined with court enforcement results in 98 percent of international arbitration awards being paid or otherwise carried out.[34]

1. Incapacity and Invalidity

Despite the odds against successfully resisting enforcement of an award, some parties will nonetheless undertake to do so. It is important therefore to understand the applicability of the defenses available under the Convention. The first defense found in Article V(1)(a) of the Convention has two parts: (1) there is some incapacity of the party, or (2) the agreement is

---

[32] *See id.*

[33] If an award were not covered by the Convention, in many countries it would be subject to the UNCITRAL Model Law. The defenses to recognition in the Model Law, found in Articles 35 and 36, are essentially the same as those in the Convention.

[34] Michael Kerr, *Concord and Conflict in International Arbitration*, Arb. Int. 121, 128, n. 24 (1997).

invalid, either under the law chosen by the parties, or, if the parties did not choose a governing law, then under the law of the country where the award was made.[35] The incapacity issue could involve issues such as sovereign immunity,[36] or perhaps a question of whether the arbitration agreement was signed by someone who did not have authority to act for the corporate party. The invalidity issue may simply be a question of meeting the form requirements of the law in question, which may be the law chosen by the parties or the law of the seat of arbitration. Questions of invalidity may also concern the proper formation of a contract to arbitrate. Generally, consent to arbitrate must be clear, and most laws require that it be demonstrated by a writing.

The Convention's writing requirement is contained in Article II, which requires Contracting States to recognize an arbitration agreement that is in writing, and further explains that this includes "an arbitral clause in a contract or an arbitration agreement, signed by the parties or contained in an exchange of letters or telegrams."[37] However, there is a question whether the writing requirement of Article II, which applies to agreements, also serves as a requirement for enforcement of awards under Articles IV through VII. Arguably, there is at least a minimal requirement of a writing in Article IV. That article establishes that to obtain recognition and enforcement of an award, a party must provide the original or a certified copy of both the original award and the original agreement.[38] The requirement of producing a certified copy of the original agreement suggests that the agreement must be in writing.

But the question remains whether the form requirements of Article II are actually incorporated into the requirements for determining validity of an award under the Convention, or whether compliance with a more lenient national law can meet the validity requirement. "Agreement" as used in Article V(1)(a) is specifically defined as the "agreement referred to in Article II."[39] Thus, for an award to be enforceable, must the underlying agreement

---

[35] *See* N.Y. Convention, art. V(1)(a).

[36] A State party might raise a defense of sovereign immunity. In general, however, if the State has participated in commercial activity, such as entering into a commercial contract containing an arbitration clause, a sovereign immunity defense will not be available. That defense applies only if the sovereign is acting in its governmental capacity. *See, e.g.,* Jasper Finke, *Sovereign Immunity: Rule, Comity or Something Else?*, 21 Eur. J. Int'l Law 853, 858 (2010) ("States therefore enjoy immunity as long as they act in their official capacity, but must submit to the jurisdiction of another state if they act as a private person.").

[37] N.Y. Convention, art. II(1–2).

[38] *See* N.Y. Convention, art. IV.

[39] The specific language is as follows: "The parties to the agreement referred to in Article II were, under the law applicable to them, under some incapacity, or the said agreement is not valid under the law to which the parties have subjected it or, failing

be "in a contract or an arbitration agreement, signed by the parties or contained in an exchange of letters or telegrams" as provided in Article II(2)? Or, if the agreement does not meet Article II standards, is it nonetheless valid for award enforcement purposes if under the pertinent national law it would be considered valid? For example, suppose one party sends another party a purchase order containing an arbitration clause. The second party accepts by shipping goods, but never signs a contract. In some jurisdictions, the arbitration agreement would be valid under national law, even though there was no contract signed by both parties, and no "exchange of documents." Because this agreement would not meet Article II standards, however, an award pursuant to such an agreement could be challenged.[40]

A modern way of making sense out of the interrelation of Articles II and V would be to interpret the Article II requirements as a ceiling, in the sense that if these requirements are met, then the agreement shall be valid. A Contracting State could not, for example, impose stricter requirements for validity by providing that an arbitration clause would not be valid if it was contained in an exchange of letters.[41] If Article II is a ceiling, and not a floor, then national law should be able to provide for a more lenient approach to validity of the arbitration agreement, without being preempted by the Convention. This interpretation would be consistent with the Convention's purpose of making agreements and awards readily enforceable, because a more lenient approach to validity of the underlying agreement would make enforcement of the award more likely.

Moreover, the words "shall include" in the statement in Article II(2) that "[t]he term 'agreement in writing' *shall include* an arbitral clause in a contract" suggest that the requirements stated therein do not create an exclusive definition of "agreement in writing," but rather indicate that if these particular requirements are met, the existence of a written agreement cannot be denied. The language does not appear to preclude other, more lenient definitions of an agreement in writing. Finally, it would seem to violate both the purpose and the language of the Convention to refuse to enforce an award rendered pursuant to an agreement valid under the law to which it was submitted, or under the law of the country where the award was made.

---

any indication thereon, under the law of the country where the award was made." New York Convention, art. V(1)(a).

[40] *See, e.g.*, Spain, Tribunal Supremo, 16 September, 1996, Actival International, S.A., v. Conservas El Pilas S.A., XXVII YEARBOOK COMMERCIAL ARBITRATION 528 (2002); Spain, Tribunal Supremo, July 7, 1998, Union de Cooperativas Agricolas Epis Centre (France) v. Agricersa SL (Spain), XXVII YEARBOOK COMMERCIAL ARBITRATION 546 (2002).

[41] *See* Lew, Mistelis & Kroll, COMPARATIVE INTERNATIONAL COMMERCIAL ARBITRATION, 113–14, § 6–39 (2003).

Thus, UNCITRAL's recommendation to interpret the definition of "in writing" in Article II(2) as not being exhaustive, discussed earlier in Chapter 2, appears to be reasonably supported by the text of Article II and by the purpose of the Convention.[42] UNCITRAL's second recommendation, that the "more favorable right" provision of Article VII should apply to agreements as well as awards, would support the enforcement of agreements that were valid under a more lenient national law. This appears consistent with the Convention's purpose of making arbitration awards readily enforceable.

If the agreement were valid under the laws of the enforcing country, a court, by regarding the Article II(2) definition of a writing as nonexhaustive and interpreting VII(1) to apply to agreements as well as to awards, should not refuse enforcement because the underlying arbitration agreement did not meet the narrow definition of writing in Article II(2). The UNCITRAL recommendations, if followed by courts, would make enforcement of an award more likely, and should discourage courts from refusing enforcement based on formalistic writing requirements.

2. Lack of Notice or Fairness

Article V(1)(b) provides the second ground for refusal to enforce, which is based on a lack of notice to the parties or a lack of fairness in the process. A party must be provided with notice of the appointment of the arbitrator and of the arbitral proceedings. Parties must also be given a full opportunity to present their cases. Thus, the award will not be enforced if the party did not receive proper notice or if the arbitrators prevented a party from being able to present its case – that is, if the party was denied a fair hearing. Generally, a court will not try to second-guess an arbitrator's handling of admission of specific evidence, or limitation on the number of witnesses or the extent of their testimony. However, arbitrator decisions as to the way parties can make their cases, if viewed as essentially denying justice, may cause a court to hold that there has been a denial of due process. One of the more famous examples of this is Iran Aircraft Industries v. Avco Corp.,[43] in which counsel were told to submit summaries of evidence but then had the case decided against them because they had not produced original documents. The award in that case was not enforced.[44]

3. Arbitrator Acting in Excess of Authority

The third ground for nonenforcement pertains to arbitrator conduct. An arbitrator's power comes from the consent of the parties, and if the arbitrator

---

[42] *See* Chapter 2 *supra* Section B(1)(a).
[43] 980 F.2d 141 (2d Cir. 1992).
[44] *See id.* at 144 ("Since Claimant did exactly what it previously was told to do by the Tribunal, the denial in the present Award . . . on the ground that more evidence should have been submitted constitutes a denial to Claimant of the ability to present its case to the Tribunal.").

exceeds the authority specifically given to her under the parties' arbitration agreement, then the resulting award is not enforceable under the Convention. Article V(1)(c) provides that an award will not be enforced if it deals with a difference not contemplated by the terms of the parties' agreement, or if the decision rendered applies to matters beyond the scope of the agreement. If, for example, the arbitration clause is narrowly drafted and applies only to issues arising out of the parties' contract, the tribunal may not properly be able to issue an award dealing with questions of unfair business practices that do not arise out of the contract. A savings clause in Article V(1)(c), however, provides that if some matters are beyond the scope, and some are within the scope, those matters within the scope may be recognized and enforced.[45]

Defenses based on a claim that the arbitrator acted in excess of authority have rarely succeeded.[46] Recently, however, the U.S. Supreme Court breathed new life into the "excess of authority" ground for *vacatur* under the Federal Arbitration Act, which is very similar to the defense under the Convention.[47] In Stolt-Nielsen v. Animal Feeds,[48] the parties asked the arbitral tribunal to decide whether a class action could be permitted when the agreement between the parties was silent on the issue. The tribunal said yes. The U.S. Supreme Court majority, which was hostile to class actions, held that the arbitrators had exceeded their authority because, according to the Court, "the task of the arbitrator is to interpret and enforce a contract, not to make public policy."[49] Essentially, the Court reversed a lower court decision upholding the award because, in the Court's view, the arbitrators got it wrong. The lower court had held unequivocally that the arbitrators did not exceed their authority because they decided exactly the question that both parties had asked them to decide.[50] Unfortunately, the Supreme Court decision raises the prospect that some courts may in the future use

---

[45] *See* New York Convention, art. V(1)(c). *See also* Redfern & Hunter et al., REDFERN AND HUNTER ON INTERNATIONAL COMMERCIAL ARBITRATION, § 11.79, at 647(2009), *citing* an Italian case where court found that arbitrator exceeded his jurisdiction, but granted enforcement of part of an award that was within arbitrator's jurisdiction. Vol. VIII YEARBOOK COMMERCIAL ARBITRATION 386 (1983).

[46] *See, e.g.,* Fertilizer Corp. of India v. IDI Management, Inc., 517 F. Supp. 948, 958–60 (S.D. Ohio 1981) (If award would not be set aside in India, the Court would enforce it under the Convention even though arbitrators had awarded consequential damages, which parties had prohibited in their contract.). *See also* Parsons & Whittemore Overseas Co., Inc., v. Societe Generale de L'Industrie du Papier, 508 F.2d 969, 976(1974) (Second Circuit affirmed a foreign arbitral award that granted damages for loss of production, although the contract excluded such liability.).

[47] 9 U.S.C. § 10(a)(4) provides that an award can be vacated when arbitrators act in excess of authority. It is very similar to the defense found in the New York Convention's art V(1)(c), which provides for nonrecognition of an award dealing with matters that are outside the scope of the parties' arbitration agreement.

[48] 130 S. Ct. 1758 (2010).

[49] 130 S. Ct. at 1767.

[50] 548 F. 3d 85 (2d Cir. 2009), *rev'd and rem'd,* 130 S. Ct. 1758 (2010).

the "excess of authority" ground under the FAA, and perhaps by analogy under the Convention, to overturn decisions they do not like.

4. The Tribunal or the Procedure Is Not in Accord with the Parties' Agreement

Article V(1)(d) provides for nonenforcement if either (1) the constitution of the tribunal or (2) the arbitral procedure was not consistent with the agreement of the parties. If the parties did not reach an agreement on either of these two matters, then the constitution of the tribunal and the arbitral procedure must be in compliance with the law of the country where the arbitration took place.[51] This defense is rarely asserted, and when it is asserted, is not usually successful.[52]

5. The Award Is Not Yet Binding, or Has Been Set Aside

a. A Binding Award

Under the fifth defense, found in Article V(1)(e), the award is not enforceable unless it has become binding on the parties. Although no definition of "binding" is provided in the Convention, most courts consider that an award is binding if there is no way of bringing an appeal on the merits. The choice of the word "binding" was made in the Convention to try to avoid issues raised under its predecessor, the 1927 Geneva Convention.[53] Under the Geneva Convention, in some countries, awards first had to be confirmed in the jurisdiction where they were made before they could be enforced in another jurisdiction. This requirement of two separate judicial processes was known as *double exequatur*.

One of the goals of the Convention drafters was to simplify enforcement by eliminating the first of the two judicial processes. Thus, an award that was binding could be enforced without first having to be confirmed in the rendering jurisdiction. Requiring the award to be "binding" rather than "final in the country in which it has been made," which was the Geneva Convention formulation, was expected to accomplish this. Because arbitration awards are generally not appealable on the merits, an arbitrator's award will most likely be considered binding. For the same reasons, a partial award rendered by the arbitrator is usually binding, and therefore enforceable.

b. Effect of a Vacated Award

Article V(1)(e) also provides that to be enforceable, the award should not have been previously set aside or vacated in the country where rendered

---

[51] *See* New York Convention, art. V(1)(d).
[52] *See, e.g.,* Lew et al., *supra* note 41, at 715, § 26–95.
[53] 92 LNTS 301.

or under the law to which it was subjected. Keep in mind that to vacate an award, a losing party must apply to the local court where the award was rendered. To enforce an award, the prevailing party must apply to a court where the losing party's assets are located. A number of courts and commentators take the position that under the Convention, a court is empowered only to recognize or enforce an award, not to vacate it.[54]

When a party succeeds in having an award vacated in the court of the jurisdiction where the arbitration took place, the traditional view is that such an award has no further legal force or effect, and cannot be enforced in any other jurisdiction.[55] Certainly, the award cannot be enforced in the jurisdiction where it was set aside. The effect is different, however, for an award for which enforcement has been refused. When an award is not enforced, unlike a vacated award, it is not annulled. Rather, if assets of the award debtor are available in more than one jurisdiction, then the award creditor that did not succeed in enforcing the award in the first jurisdiction can pursue the award in a second jurisdiction, perhaps with better results.[56]

c. The Article V(1)(e) Loophole

Under Article V(1)(e), the question of whether an award is binding will be determined by the law in the country where it was made. Thus, *vacatur* can be determined under local law according to local standards. This potentially creates a large loophole to the Convention's otherwise limited defenses to enforcement. Despite its strong purpose to enforce awards, the Convention provides for the possibility that a local court will vacate an award on a ground that is not among the narrow grounds listed in Article V of the Convention. If this happens, most Contracting States will refuse to enforce the award, because under V(1)(e) of the Convention, recognition and enforcement may be refused when the award is vacated under the law of the country where it was rendered.

---

[54] *See, e.g.,* Toys "R" Us, *supra* note 9 ("[M]any commentators and foreign courts have concluded that an action to set aside an award can be brought *only* under the domestic law of the arbitral forum, and can never be made under the Convention.").

[55] Albert Jan van den Berg, *Annulment of Awards in International Arbitration*, in INTERNATIONAL ARBITRATION IN THE 21ST CENTURY, TOWARDS JUDICIALIZATION AND UNIFORMITY 133, 137 (Richard B. Lillich & Charles N. Brower, eds, 1994).

[56] *See* Gary B. Born, INTERNATIONAL COMMERCIAL ARBITRATION 2673, Vol 2 (2009) ("[S]ignificantly different consequences may flow from (i) a national court's refusal to enforce an international arbitral award, as compared with (ii) a national court's decision annulling or setting aside or vacating the award. If an award is denied recognition..., the award nonetheless plainly remains in existence as a 'binding' award. It...can be taken to other jurisdictions, and efforts can be made to recognize and enforce it anew.").

d. The Court's Discretion to Ignore the Article V(1)(e) Loophole

However, the party that succeeds in vacating an award on the basis of a ground not listed in the Convention cannot be assured that another jurisdiction will refuse enforcement. Although in most cases, courts will follow Article V(1)(e)'s proscription, and not enforce a vacated award, Article V provides courts with some discretion. The first sentence of Article V(1) states that recognition and enforcement of the award *may* be refused (not "must" be refused) if the defenses listed in the Article are established. Thus, courts have discretion to determine whether they will or will not enforce an award vacated in another jurisdiction.

e. Deference to Local Law under Article VII

In addition, Article VII of the Convention provides a different loophole leading in another direction. It permits a party in an enforcing court to take advantage of any laws or treaties in the enforcing jurisdiction that are more favorable to enforcement of the award than the Convention. This "more favorable right" provision may not have been intended by the drafters to permit the enforcement of vacated awards, but there appears to be nothing in the language of the Convention that would preclude this interpretation.[57]

f. Enforcement of Vacated Awards

Various courts have taken the position that a vacated award can nonetheless be enforceable. In France, for example, the law governing international arbitrations provides that an award may be denied enforcement only on the basis of five specific grounds.[58] The setting aside of an award by the court in the country where the award was rendered is not one of those specific grounds.[59] Thus, a French court will enforce a vacated award unless the basis for vacating the award was one of the specific grounds listed in its law. Article VII permits a party whose award was vacated the ability to use more favorable French law to enforce the award in France. Like French law, German arbitration law also provides a list of exclusive grounds on which an award may be challenged.[60]

Moreover, the European Convention on International Commercial Arbitration also provides that an award will be set aside only on the basis of

---

[57] *See* Gary H. Sampliner, *Enforcement of Foreign Arbitral Awards after Annulment in Their Country of Origin*, 11–9 Mealey's Int'l Arb. Rep. 17 (1996).

[58] *See* French Code of Civil Procedure, arts., 1520, 1525. *See also* various rulings in the case of Hilmarton v. OTV, from 1994 to 1997, discussed in Hamid G. Gharavi, *Enforcing Set Aside Arbitral Awards: France's Controversial Steps beyond the New York Convention*, 6 J. Transnat'l L. & Pol'y 93 (1996).

[59] *See* French Code of Civil Procedure, art. 1520.

[60] *See* Hans Smit & Vratislav Pechota, NATIONAL ARBITRATION LAWS, GER B(2)-15 (2002).

one of the exclusive grounds set forth in the convention.[61] The European Convention applies only to parties that, when concluding the arbitration agreement, have their habitual place of residence or seat in different Contracting States.[62] Thus, under the New York Convention, a party from a European Convention country whose award had been set aside on a basis not permitted under the European Convention could nonetheless enforce the award in an enforcing jurisdiction that is a party to both the European Convention and the New York Convention. Under Article VII of the New York Convention, the party could use the more favorable provisions under the European Convention that would permit enforcement of the award, even though it had been annulled at the seat of the arbitration.[63] The European Convention thus makes the narrow grounds for refusing to enforce awards even narrower than the New York Convention, because European Convention grounds do not include the fifth defense under the New York Convention – that the award has not yet become binding, or that it has been set aside at the seat of arbitration – or the last two defenses – lack of arbitrability and violation of public policy.

In the United States, a vacated award was enforced in Chromalloy Aeroservices v. Arab Republic of Egypt (Chromalloy).[64] A U.S. company had obtained an award against the State of Egypt, which was then set aside by the Egyptian court. The U.S. court determined that under Article V it had discretion whether or not to enforce the vacated award. Applying Article VII of the Convention, the court found that the U.S. Federal Arbitration Act was a more favorable law that should permit the award to be enforced.[65] The court also held that in the arbitration clause, the parties had agreed not to challenge the award.[66] The *Chromalloy* decision not to enforce has not, however, been very influential in subsequent U.S. cases. Some cases have distinguished *Chromalloy*,[67] or have specifically rejected its reasoning.[68] It does not appear today that the reasoning of *Chromalloy*, particularly the view

---

[61] 484 U.N.T.S. 349 (1961), art. IX.

[62] *See id.* art. I(a). There are 31 members of the European Convention, including most but not all of the EU countries (the UK, for example, is not a member) and countries as diverse as Cuba, Kazakhstan, and Burkina Faso. Available at http://treaties.un.org/pages/ParticipationStatus.aspx.

[63] *See* Emmanuel Gaillard, *The Enforcement of Awards Set Aside in the Country of Origin*, 14 ICSID Rev. 16, 35–37 (1999).

[64] 939 F. Supp. 907 (D.D.C. 1996).

[65] *See id.* at 909–10.

[66] *See id.* at 912.

[67] *See* Baker Marine (Nig.) Ltd. v. Chevron (Nig.) Ltd. 191 F.3d 194 (2d Cir. 1999); Spier v. Calzaturificio Tecnica S.p.A., 71 F. Supp. 2d 279 (S.D.N.Y. 1999).

[68] Four Seasons Hotels and Resorts, B.V. v. Consorcio Barr, S.A., 267 F. Supp. 2d 1335 (S.D. Fla. 2003) (The question of enforcement of the award falls exclusively under the New York Convention, not the FAA.).

that the FAA provides grounds for the court to enforce annulled awards, has much, if any, precedential value.[69]

To the extent that local laws can undercut the ability to easily enforce an arbitration award, participants will tend to lose confidence in the process. That confidence is also undermined, however, if participants have no reasonable ability to challenge a tribunal or a procedure that is not fair or reasonable. Whether by vacating awards or by enforcing awards that were vacated, courts must try to ensure that the integrity of the arbitral process is maintained. It is no doubt for that reason that the drafters of the Convention included the additional two defenses, which are discussed below.

6. The Last Two Defenses under Article V

The second subsection of Article V deals with grounds for enforcement that can be raised by the court *sua sponte*. If a court finds that the subject matter of the dispute is not arbitrable under the law of its jurisdiction, or if it finds that enforcement would be contrary to the country's public policy, then recognition and enforcement may be refused.

a. Subject Matter Not Arbitrable

A country's laws may provide that certain types of disputes are not arbitrable. For example, child custody disputes, criminal matters, bankruptcy, the validity of trademarks or patents, and other kinds of disputes that will have an impact on third parties or have some kind of consequences in the public domain will usually have to be decided in a court of law. The most typical kinds of disputes that are arbitrated are those arising from contractual or commercial relationships, which parties are considered free to resolve without any supervision or interference by the court.

As noted earlier, in Chapter 4, one kind of dispute that was not considered arbitrable until relatively recently was in the area of antitrust, or competition law. The reason was that competition law is expected to protect not just the individual parties, but also the public at large. Arbitrators, on the other hand, are expected to be responsible only to resolve the dispute with respect to the parties before them, not to represent the public interest.[70] Thus, until fairly recently, competition law claims were not arbitrable in many jurisdictions.

---

[69] In Karaha Bodas Co., LLC v. Perusahaan Pertambangan Minyak Dan Gas Bumi Negara (Pertamina) 364 F. 3d 274 (2004); the Fifth Circuit, in affirming enforcement of an award that had been annulled in Indonesia, primarily relied on a doctrine of *judicial estoppel*. Because Pertamina had taken the position before the Arbitral Tribunal and the District Court that Swiss law was the procedural law (the arbitration was held in Geneva), it was estopped from asserting later that the procedural law was Indonesian. The Fifth Circuit therefore held the annulment by the Indonesian court should not bar enforcement.

[70] Some take the view, however, that an arbitral tribunal does owe a duty to the public as well as the parties. *See, e.g.,* Lew et al., *supra* note 41, at 220–21, § 9–97.

In 1985, however, the U.S. Supreme Court decided that the FAA applied not just to contract issues, but also to issues arising out of statutory claims involving U.S. antitrust law.[71] Although the decision has been criticized,[72] antitrust and other statutory claims, including securities and employment law claims, are routinely arbitrated in the United States today. In Europe, as well, competition law claims are considered arbitrable.[73]

In some nations, disputes between businesses and their consumers are not arbitrable if the arbitration agreement was entered into in advance of the dispute. Under the European Union Directive on Unfair Terms in Consumer Contracts,[74] most predispute arbitration agreements with consumers are invalid.[75] For a consumer arbitration to take place, the agreement to arbitrate must be entered into after the dispute has arisen. Apparently the Europeans, and most other nations, believe that consumers can reach an informed decision about the choice between arbitration and litigation only once the dispute has arisen. The United States appears to be fairly unique in enforcing predispute arbitration agreements with consumers.[76] The increasing use of mandatory arbitration clauses in adhesion contracts in the United States has closed access to the courts for a substantial segment of consumers, and has eliminated jury trials in most consumer cases.[77]

The arbitrability of various matters may vary widely from jurisdiction to jurisdiction. Therefore, before parties begin an arbitration in a particular jurisdiction, they should consult with local counsel to ensure that the matters

---

[71] Mitsubishi Motors Corp. v. Soler Chrysler-Plymouth, Inc., 473 U.S. 614 (1985).

[72] *See, e.g.,* Philip J. McConnaughay, *The Risks and Virtues of Lawlessness: A 'Second Look' at International Commercial Arbitration,* 93 Nw. L. Rev. 453, 481 (1999).

[73] *See* Eco Swiss China Time Ltd. v. Benetton International N.V., Case C-126/97 [1999] ECR I-3055, at 25, ¶ 41("[a] national court to which application is made for annulment of an arbitration award must grant that application if it considers that the award in question is in fact contrary to Article 85 of the Treaty, where its domestic rules of procedure require it to grant an application for annulment founded on failure to observe national rules of public policy."). *See also* Lew et al., *supra* note 41, at 201–03, §§ 9–42, 9–47, concerning acceptance of arbitrability of competition law issues in Europe. ("This European approach has been largely influenced by the prevailing opinion in the US case law for antitrust disputes.") *Id.* at 202, § 9–44.

[74] Council Directive 93/13/EEC, 1993 O.J. (L095).

[75] *See* Christopher R. Drahozal & Raymond J. Friel, *Consumer Arbitration in the European Union and the United States,* 28 N.C.J. Int'l L. & Com. Reg. 357 (2002) (discussing higher level of protection provided to European consumers over U.S. consumers); Jean R. Sternlight, *Is the U.S. Out on a Limb? Comparing the U.S. Approach to Mandatory Consumer and Employment Arbitration to that of the Rest of the World,* 56 U. Miami L. Rev. 831 (2002) (discussing uniqueness of practice of the United States in forcing consumers to arbitrate).

[76] *See* Sternlight, *supra* note 75.

[77] *See* Jean R. Sternlight, *Mandatory Binding Arbitration and the Demise of the Seventh Amendment Right to a Jury Trial,* 16 Ohio St. J. Disp. Res. 669 (2001).

they intend to arbitrate are arbitrable. In general, however, there are few cases in which awards have been denied on the ground of nonarbitrability.[78]

b. Public Policy

The Convention provides in Article V(2)(b) that recognition or enforcement of an arbitral award may be refused if a court finds that it would be contrary to the public policy of that country. Public policy is not defined in the Convention, and thus presents the possibility of another broad loophole for refusing enforcement. On the whole, however, most courts have viewed this defense narrowly, in keeping with the Convention's pro-enforcement purpose. One of the most-cited explanations of the concept comes from the case of Parsons & Whittemore Overseas Co., Inc., v. Société Générale de l'Industrie du Papier,[79] in which the U.S. Second Circuit Court of Appeals, in affirming the enforcement of an arbitral award against an American company, stated that "the Convention's public policy defense should be construed narrowly. Enforcement of foreign arbitral awards may be denied on this basis only where enforcement would violate the forum state's most basic notions of morality and justice."[80]

Although a number of countries construe the public policy defense narrowly, there is room for it to be used parochially to protect national political interests. To the extent that a country does this, it undermines the utility of the Convention. For example, the Turkish Supreme Court in 1995 refused to enforce an ICC award in which the tribunal in Zurich had applied Turkish substantive law, but the procedural law of the canton of Zurich.[81] The Turkish Court held that by not applying both Turkish substantive law and Turkish procedural law, the arbitrator had violated Turkish public policy.[82] Not only did this appear incorrect, but there also was no material difference in the procedural law of Turkey and the procedural law applied.[83] Here, the Turkish court used public policy as a basis for refusing enforcement on a point of law, and one that did not matter to the ultimate decision. This appears to be an unfortunate use of the public policy defense as a basis to reach a decision more favored by the Turkish court.

Although there are occasional examples of misuse of the public policy defense, in most countries courts have been reluctant to refuse enforcement

---

[78] See Lew et al., *supra* note 41, at 721, n. 171.
[79] 508 F.2d 969 (2d Cir. 1974). See also, Karaha Bodas Co., L.L.C. v. Perusahaan Pertambangan Minyak Dan Gas Bumi Negara, 364 F.3d 274, 306 (2004) ("The general pro-enforcement bias informing the convention . . . points to a narrow reading of the public policy defense.") *Citation omitted.*
[80] 508 F.2d at 974.
[81] See Kerr, *supra* note 34, at 140.
[82] See id.
[83] See id.

on public policy grounds. In fact, awards are so rarely refused enforcement on grounds of public policy that some commentators have urged courts to reconsider the application of the public policy defense of Article V(2)(b) to make it more than a theoretical defense, and to apply it somewhat more flexibly as a basis for refusing enforcement when enforcement would condone unjust or improper results.[84]

E. CONCLUSION

Overall, the New York Convention has been one of the most successful international treaties. Along with other conventions that support the enforcement of international awards, it has contributed to the growth of international arbitration as a preferred method of resolving disputes. Parties are willing to engage in international arbitration because they have confidence that if they obtain an award, it will be readily enforceable in almost any country in the world where the award debtor's assets can be found.

---

[84] *See, e.g.*, Eloise Henderson Bouzari, *The Public Policy Exception to Enforcement of International Arbitral Awards, Implications for Post-NAFTA Jurisprudence*, 30 Tex. Int'l L.J. 205, 217–18 (1995) ("[T]he equitable path for article V(2)(b) jurisprudence to take would be . . . [to preserve] a deferential stance toward arbitration while recognizing that the court system need not condone the unjust results that are sometimes reached in alternative dispute resolution.")

CHAPTER ELEVEN

Investment Arbitration

A. GROWTH OF FOREIGN INVESTMENT AND INVESTMENT ARBITRATION

Foreign investment is a critical component of the world's economy. Global flows of investment in 2010 amounted to U.S. $1.22 trillion.[1] The United Nations Conference on Trade and Development (UNCTAD) estimates for 2011 that foreign direct investment (FDI) flows will be between $1.3 and $1.5 trillion.[2] Although the highest capital inflows in 2010 in any single country went to the United States, significant increases were attained in Latin American and the Caribbean, as well as in South, East, and Southeast Asia.[3] Because many developing countries do not have the capital, technology, or other resources needed to modernize their infrastructure and develop their industries, foreign investment is seen as crucial to making them more competitive in a global economy. Developed countries, as well, know the importance of attracting foreign investment. Investment to developed countries in 2010 was approximately U.S. $ 526.6 billion.[4] It is thus not surprising that many countries have actively sought ways to encourage foreign investment.

Foreign investors considering major capital-intensive projects such as the financing and development of a power plant, the construction of a 5,000-unit housing project, the building of long-distance oil and gas pipelines, or the development of transportation or communications infrastructure want assurances that their investments will not be taken over (expropriated) by the host country or so undermined by changes in the host country's regulations or laws that the investment is constructively expropriated. They also want a way to resolve disputes that does not depend on the courts of the host

[1] See UNCTAD Global Investment Trends Monitor, No. 5, January 17, 2011, p. 3; available at www.unctad.org.
[2] See id., p. 7.
[3] See id., p. 3.
[4] See id.

country, for fear that they will not receive fair and equal treatment in those courts when the opposing party is the State or a State entity. The need for investors to feel secure in their investments has led national governments to take steps to make their laws and rules more investor friendly. Many have adopted investor protection legislation, and have entered into bilateral and multilateral investment treaties.

As investments have increased worldwide, so have arbitrations to resolve investor–State disputes. The obvious alternative to litigation in local courts is to provide for international arbitration. Provision for disputes to be arbitrated can generally be found in an investment agreement between the investor and the State or State entity, and in investment legislation and treaties. A highly contested issue is whether or when claims of a breach of an investment agreement also become a violation of an investment treaty. This and other issues are discussed in this chapter, which focuses on arbitration under the aegis of investment agreements and investment laws and treaties.

B. INVESTOR PROTECTION

1. The Washington (ICSID) Convention

a. Background

In 1965, the World Bank[5] sponsored a treaty to promote foreign investment by establishing a neutral forum for the resolution of investment disputes between States and nationals of other States. Known as the Washington Convention,[6] and also as the ICSID Convention, the treaty created an organization to deal with investment disputes: the International Centre for the Settlement of Investment Disputes (ICSID or "the Centre"). ICSID is an autonomous international organization with close links to the World Bank.

After a somewhat slow start, ICSID today is playing an important role in the investment community.[7] Traditionally, cases resolved by ICSID were

---

[5] The World Bank is made up of two international development institutions: the International Bank for Reconstruction and Development (IBRD) and the International Development Association (IDA). *See* http://www.worldbank.org. The work of these two institutions is complemented by that of the International Finance Corporation (IFC), the Multilateral Investment Guarantee Agency (MIGA), and the International Centre for the Settlement of Investment Disputes (ICSID).

[6] The formal name for the Washington Convention or the ICSID Convention is the Convention on the Settlement of Investment Disputes Between States and Nationals of Other States. Available at http://www.worldbank.org/icsid.

[7] As of December, 2011, the number of countries adhering to the ICSID Convention was 147 (http://www.worldbank.org/icsid/). Two countries, Bolivia in 2007 and Ecuador in 2010, withdrew from the Convention by depositing notices of denunciation.

based on arbitration provisions in parties' investment contracts. Subsequently, there was a period when ICSID cases were also based on the consents of governments as expressed in their national legislation on investor protection.[8] In the most recent decade, however, most cases have been based on the arbitration provisions of bilateral and multilateral investment treaties. In ICSID's fiscal year 2010, nineteen of twenty-seven new cases registered with the Centre were based on bilateral and/or multilateral investment treaties.[9] The twenty-seven new cases registered in 2010 are indicative of the expanding use of ICSID by investors and States. It took from 1966 until the end of the 1980s – almost twenty-five years – for ICSID to register its first twenty-six cases.[10] By the end of fiscal year 2010, however, ICSID had registered in total, since its inception, 319 cases.[11] Although the number of cases may appear small, the dollar amount of these cases is usually quite large, and the issues rather complex. The increase in cases, which began in the 1990s, is in large part attributable to the proliferation of bilateral investment treaties, which will be discussed in Section B(2) of this chapter.

b. ICSID Jurisdictional Requirements

ICSID, which is located at the World Bank headquarters in Washington, D.C., has an Administrative Council and a Secretariat. A staff member of the Secretariat serves as the secretary for each of the ICSID tribunals. ICSID has several sets of rules, including the Institution Rules, which set forth the procedure for beginning an arbitration or a conciliation. It has separate rules governing procedures for conciliation and for arbitration.

Parties must meet three jurisdictional requirements to have a dispute resolved by ICSID. First, both parties must have consented to arbitrate or conciliate pursuant to ICSID Rules. Second, one party must be a Contracting State, and the other party must be a national of a different Contracting State. Third, the dispute must be a legal dispute arising directly out of an investment.

i. Consent. The fact that a Contracting State is a party to the ICSID Convention does not automatically mean that it has agreed to submit disputes to ICSID's jurisdiction. That consent must be found elsewhere. It may be

---

[8] *See* ICSID, *News from ICSID*, Vol. 21, No. 1 (Summer 2004), at 12. Available at http://www.worldbank.org/icsid/news/news.htm.

[9] *See* ICSID, *ICSID Annual Report*, pp. 21–22 (2010). Available at http://www.worldbank.org/icsid/.

[10] *See* ICSID website, "List of Concluded Cases," available at http://www.worldbank.org/icsid/cases/conclude.htm. Use the following link for graph of ICSID cases over time, on page 7: http://icsid.worldbank.org/ICSID/FrontServlet?requestType=ICSIDDocRH&actionVal=ShowDocument&CaseLoadStatistics=True&language=English21.

[11] *See ICSID Annual Report*, p. 21 (2010).

found in a contract with the investor that contains an arbitration clause, or in national legislation. It may also be found in an investment treaty, such as a bilateral investment treaty between the host State and the home country of the investor. Complications can arise if the host State's consent to an ICSID arbitration is found in a bilateral investment treaty, but the investor and the State or a State agency have nonetheless entered into a contract that does not provide for arbitration. It could happen that the investor's treaty claims would still be arbitrated, whereas contract claims would be decided in accordance with the provisions of the investment contract. In practice, however, the investor will often try to arbitrate all its claims under the investment treaty.[12]

When the host country is party to an investment treaty, or when national legislation provides for arbitration of disputes, the provisions relating to arbitration are generally considered to be an offer to arbitrate, which can be accepted by an investor. There may, however, be certain preconditions that are part of the offer, such as a six-month notice period before the host country's offer can be accepted.

The investor's acceptance could be in a written letter of acceptance. However, the investor is also considered to have accepted the offer to arbitrate if it files a request for arbitration with ICSID. The host country's offer in a treaty or legislation is generally considered irrevocable, so it cannot change its position once it has entered into an agreement with an investor in which it consents to arbitrate.[13]

ii. Contracting State or National of Another Contracting State. It is not difficult to establish which states are Contracting States. That information is available on the ICSID website.[14] More complicated, however, is the situation in which the party to the investment agreement in the host country is not the Contracting State itself but an agency or a subdivision of the Contracting State, such as a geographic region or a municipality, or a public sector enterprise. Before such a region or entity can be subject to ICSID jurisdiction, two requirements must be met. First, the Contracting State must designate to the Centre that the constituent subdivision or agency is subject to its jurisdiction.[15] Second, the Contracting State must indicate its

---

[12] The difference in investment contract claims and treaty claims and the overlap between them will be discussed *infra* in section C.

[13] *See* Alcoa Mineral of Jamaica v. Gov't of Jamaica, IV YEARBOOK COMMERCIAL ARBITRATION at 206, 207 *et seq.* (1979) (Tribunal found that Jamaica could not unilaterally withdraw consent to arbitration contained in investment agreement. Jamaica had attempted to avoid an arbitration involving the mining of bauxite by notifying ICSID that ICSID would no longer have jurisdiction over disputes in Jamaica arising out of an investment relating to minerals or other natural resources.).

[14] *See* http://www.worldbank.org/icsid/ for current list.

[15] *See* ICSID Convention, *supra* note 6, art. 25(1).

approval to the consent of the subdivision or agency, or notify the Centre that State approval is not required.[16] An investor dealing with a subdivision or agency should therefore include in its arbitration clause a provision that would ensure that these requirements are met. An appropriate clause to accomplish this result is provided by ICSID on its website.[17]

Meeting the preceding requirements, however, does not necessarily mean that the host State itself has consented to arbitration. Independent consent by the host State must be provided before a claim can be raised directly against it in an ICSID tribunal.[18] This may be available, however, by means of a bilateral or multilateral investment treaty.

The jurisdictional requirement of being a "National of another Contracting State" also raises some issues. Generally, a national is an individual who is a citizen of, or an entity organized or incorporated in, a Contracting State. Nationality is determined as of the date on which the parties consent to arbitrate.

A more complicated question is whether an entity that is incorporated locally – that is, in the host State – but owned by foreign investors meets the ICSID jurisdictional requirement of being a national of *another* Contracting State. In many cases, sometimes because local laws or regulations require it, a foreign investor will incorporate a subsidiary in the host State, which will serve as the vehicle for its investment in that State. The question then is whether the nationality of the subsidiary-investor is local – that is, the same as the host State – which would not meet the ICSID jurisdictional requirement, or whether the subsidiary's nationality is determined by the foreign company that controls the subsidiary.

To deal with this issue, the ICSID Convention provides that a "'National of another Contracting State' means...any juridical person...which, because of foreign control, the parties have agreed should be treated as a national of another Contracting State for the purposes of this Convention."[19] Thus, even though the dispute may be between a host Contracting State and the subsidiary that is located in the host Contracting State, an ICSID arbitration will be available if the parties agree that the subsidiary is controlled by a national in a foreign State. In addition, however, tribunals have held that even if there was no express agreement about nationality based on foreign control, if the host State knew that the local entity was controlled by an investor in a foreign State,[20] or if the host State signed an

---

[16] *See id.* art. 25(3).
[17] *See* Model Clause 5, available at http://icsid.worldbank.org/ICSID/StaticFiles/model-clauses-en/9.htm#.
[18] *See* Lucy Reed, Jan Paulsson & Nigel Blackaby, GUIDE TO ICSID ARBITRATION, SECOND EDITION (2011), at 35–40, 53–56.
[19] ICSID Convention, *supra* note 6, art. 25(2)(b).
[20] *See, e.g.,* Amco Asia Corp. and Others v. Republic of Indonesia, Decision on Jurisdiction, 23 ILM 351, 359 *et seq.* (1984).

investment agreement with a local subsidiary in which it agreed to the ICSID arbitration clause,[21] the ICSID requirement can be met.

Instead of depending on a tribunal's interpretation about nationality, however, prudent counsel should include in any investment contract that contains an ICSID arbitration clause a stipulation as to the nationality of the investor. ICSID provides model clauses on its website that deal specifically with this issue.[22]

iii. Legal Disputes and Investments. With respect to the third jurisdictional requirement – that the dispute must be a legal dispute arising out of an investment – the ICSID Convention does not define either legal disputes or investments. However, for the most part, tribunals have interpreted both of these terms broadly. A legal dispute is generally considered to apply to a dispute over any legal right or obligation, or over any remedy for a breach of a legal obligation. An investment is basically a project or transaction having economic value. Tribunals have considered many different kinds of assets, projects, or transactions as investments, including not only capital contributions and other equity investments, but also nonequity investments such as construction and infrastructure projects, service contracts, transfers of technology, and even the issuing of promissory notes.[23]

There are limitations, however. A mere commercial sale may not qualify as an investment.[24] Moreover, expenses that a party incurred in pursuing a possible investment in a proposed power project that never materialized were found by a tribunal not to be an investment under the pertinent bilateral investment treaty.[25]

---

[21] Liberia Eastern Timber Corp. (LETCO) v. Republic of Liberia, ICSID Case No. ARB/83/2, Decision on Rectification (17 June 1986), 2 ICSID Reports 346 (1994), 26 ILM 647, *653 ("When a Contracting State signs an investment agreement, containing an ICSID arbitration clause, with a foreign controlled juridical person,... the Contracting State could be deemed to have agreed to [ICSID jurisdiction] by having agreed to the ICSID arbitration clause. This is especially the case when the Contracting State's laws require the foreign investor to establish itself locally as a juridical person in order to carry out an investment.").

[22] *See* Model Clauses 6 and 7. Available at http://icsid.worldbank.org/ICSID/StaticFiles/model-clauses-en/9.htm#.

[23] *See* Reed et al., *supra* note 18, at 65–71, *citing* Salini Costruttori S.p.A. and Italstrade S.p.A. v. Kingdom of Morocco, ICSID Case No. ARB/00/4, Decision on Jurisdiction (23 July 2001), 42 ILM 609 (2003) (construction contract found to have characteristics of an investment); Fedax N.V. v. Republic of Venezuela, ICSID Case No. ARB/96/3, Decision on Objections to Jurisdiction (July 11, 1997), 5 ICSID Reports 183 (2002) (promissory notes constituted an investment).

[24] *See* Redfern & Hunter et al., REDFERN AND HUNTER ON INTERNATIONAL ARBITRATION, § 8.29 at 477 (2009) ("ICSID Secretary-General refused to register a case that was merely a commercial sale because it did not qualify as an investment."). 1985 ICSID Annual Report 6.

[25] *See* Reed et al., *supra* note 18, at 70, *citing* Mihaly Int'l Corp. v. Democratic Socialist Republic of Sri Lanka, ICSID Case No. ARB/00/2 (March 15, 2002) 17 ICSID Review – Foreign Investment Law Journal 142 (2002).

c. Special Features of ICSID Arbitrations

i. Delocalization. An ICSID arbitration is entirely delocalized. The law of the place of arbitration generally has no impact at all on the ICSID arbitration process. It makes sense that court involvement would be excluded in arbitrations between a Contracting State and an investor, because the Contracting State would not expect to submit to the laws of another country, and the investor does not want to submit to the laws of the Contracting State.

The tribunal deals with interim measures, unless the parties agree otherwise.[26] In addition to interim measures being usually limited to the tribunal's discretion, there is also no review of a tribunal's award by a court. Instead, ICSID has a procedure for review of the award by another tribunal, called an "ad hoc committee." The three-member committee, which is appointed by the Chairman of the Administrative Council, can annul the award, or partially annul it, but it cannot modify it in any way. In reviewing the award, the committee cannot consider the merits of the award. There are only five grounds for annulment:

- The tribunal was not properly constituted.
- The tribunal manifestly exceeded its powers.
- There was corruption on the part of a member of the tribunal.
- There was a serious departure from a fundamental rule of procedure.
- The award did not state the reasons on which it is based.[27]

In practice, parties do not usually challenge the proper constitution of the tribunal, or corruption of a tribunal member. Rather, annulments are usually sought on the other three grounds: (1) the tribunal exceeded its powers, or (2) there was a serious departure from a fundamental rule of procedure, or (3) the tribunal did not provide reasons for the award. Frequently, all three of these reasons are raised. If the award is annulled by an ad hoc committee, the parties may submit the dispute to yet another tribunal, whose award may be reviewed by another ad hoc committee. Although, in the early years, there was criticism of the number of awards annulled, over time, the annulment procedure has been perceived as working as intended – to protect against any serious problems in the integrity of the arbitral process.

ii. Recognition, Enforcement, and Execution. When a party takes steps to recognize and enforce an ICSID award, if it is a monetary award, the enforcing court in a Contracting State is required to treat it as though it were a final judgment of a court in that state.[28] Thus, there is no court review of

---

[26] *See* ICSID Convention, *supra* note 6, art. 47.
[27] *See* ICSID Convention, *supra* note 6, art. 52(1).
[28] *See id.* art. 54(1).

a monetary award at the enforcement stage. Rather, enforcement is automatic. With respect to a nonmonetary award, however, there is automatic recognition of the award as binding, but enforcement is not automatic. Thus, enforcement would be subject to the New York Convention, if applicable, or subject to other applicable treaties or laws.[29]

The ICSID Convention differentiates between the enforcement of an award and the execution of an award. In many jurisdictions, enforcement (that is, actually collecting from the award-debtor the money owed, or otherwise ensuring compliance with the award) is synonymous with execution. For ICSID purposes, on the other hand, there is a difference. It is not entirely clear what "enforcement" means under ICSID, although it is evident that "recognition" is the official acknowledgment that an award is final and binding.[30] Taken together, recognition and enforcement under ICSID appear to refer to all the steps taken up to the execution of an award.[31] "Execution" means the actual collection of the money awarded. The reason the difference is important is that although recognition and enforcement of a monetary award are automatic, execution of the award is subject to the local rules of the enforcing jurisdiction.[32] Thus, at this point, delocalization ends, and the ability to execute against the award-debtor's assets will depend on the local rules on execution of a final judgment.[33]

The governing of execution procedures by local law is particularly significant with respect to the local jurisdiction's rules on sovereign immunity. The Convention devotes an entire article to making clear that the laws of the place of execution pertaining to sovereign immunity are not limited to any degree by the Convention's rules on recognition and enforcement. Article 55 provides, "Nothing in Article 54 shall be construed as derogating from the law in force in any Contracting State relating to immunity of that State or of any foreign State from execution."[34]

Article 55 should serve as a red flag to investors and their counsel to be very aware of the pertinent local laws on sovereign immunity. It is worth noting that in many countries, the laws provide that a waiver of sovereign immunity with respect to arbitration does not mean sovereign immunity has been waived with respect to execution of an award. The investor should try, if possible, to obtain in advance from the Contracting State a specific waiver of immunity from execution against assets.[35]

---

[29] See id. See also Reed et al., *supra* note 18, at 183.
[30] See id. at 179–180.
[31] See id. at 180.
[32] See ICSID Convention, *supra* note 6, art. 54(3).
[33] See id.
[34] See id. art. 55.
[35] See Reed et al., *supra* note 18, at 189–190.

Even if such a waiver is impossible to negotiate, investors can take some comfort in the fact that most parties have traditionally complied voluntarily with ICSID awards.[36] It is no doubt helpful that ICSID has close links to the World Bank. Contracting States probably do not want to be viewed as recalcitrant by World Bank authorities. Noncompliance with an ICSID award could conceivably cause a Contracting State to be regarded less favorably by the World Bank at a future point when the State might seek loans and credit.

Moreover, if a Contracting State does not comply with an ICSID award, then the investor's own country can, under Article 64 of the ICSID Convention, bring a claim before the International Court of Justice.[37]

iii. Publication of Awards.

Although information about most international arbitrations is confidential, records of the existence, status, and disposition of ICSID awards are made available on the ICSID website. If both parties consent, ICSID can publish the awards.[38] Whether or not the parties consent, however, ICSID must promptly publish "excerpts of the legal rules applied by the Tribunal."[39] In addition, the parties themselves may publish the awards. As a result, most ICSID awards are publicly available, which permits the development of a jurisprudence of investor–State arbitrations under the ICSID Convention.

d. Additional Facility Rules

In 1978, ICSID adopted Additional Facility Rules for administering arbitrations for certain kinds of proceedings that fall outside the scope of the ICSID Convention. For example, these proceedings may involve a situation in which either the State is not a party to the ICSID Convention, or the investor is not a national of a Contracting State.[40] The use of the Additional Facility is, however, subject to the specific consent of the Secretary-General

---

[36] *See id.* at 186.

[37] *See id.* at 190.

[38] *See* ICSID Arbitration Rules, Rule 48(4).

[39] *See id.* One of the changes in the arbitration rules that ICSID amended in 2006 was that ICSID is now required to publish promptly the legal reasoning underpinning an award. The change in the rule added the requirement of promptness, and made the obligation mandatory rather than precatory.

[40] On its website, ICSID describes the applicability of the Additional Facility Rules as follows: (i) fact-finding proceedings; (ii) conciliation or arbitration proceedings for the settlement of investment disputes between parties one of which is not a Contracting State or a national of a Contracting State; and (iii) conciliation and arbitration proceedings between parties, at least one of which is a Contracting State or a national of a Contracting State for the settlement of disputes that do not arise directly out of an investment, provided that the underlying transaction is not an ordinary commercial transaction. Available at http://icsid.worldbank.org/ICSID/StaticFiles/facility/AFR_English-final.pdf.

of ICSID.[41] Thus, parties that wish to avail themselves of ICSID's Additional Facility should plan ahead and seek approval of the Secretary General by submitting to ICSID a draft of their proposed agreement.[42]

Arbitration proceedings under the Additional Facility Rules are not subject to the ICSID Convention, although many principles from the Convention are incorporated into the Rules. However, the major significance of the inapplicability of the ICSID Convention is that the Convention's provisions on recognition and enforcement do not apply. Rather, an Additional Facility award, like an award under the auspices of the ICC or the LCIA, is subject to enforcement under the New York Convention. It is for this reason that the Additional Facility Rules on arbitration require that arbitration proceedings be held in States that are parties to the New York Convention.[43] In addition, because an award rendered under the Additional Facility Rules is not governed by the ICSID Convention, it can be attacked by an attempt to vacate under the laws of the seat of arbitration.[44] Thus, awards under the 1994 North American Free Trade Agreement (NAFTA),[45] for example, remain subject to attempts to vacate under local law, because Canada and Mexico have not yet ratified the ICSID Convention.[46]

2. Bilateral Investment Treaties

a. Background

As noted above, one of the reasons for the increase in ICSID arbitrations is the proliferation of bilateral investment treaties (BITs) containing arbitration provisions. BITs provide mutual protections for qualifying investors. For example, when Country A enters into a BIT with Country B, investors from Country A have certain protections for their investments in Country B, and investors from Country B have those same protections for their investments in Country A. As the name indicates, bilateral treaties are only between two countries, but Country A may be a party to thirty or forty BITs, each with a different country.[47] By the end of 2005, almost 2,500 BITs had been concluded.[48]

---

[41] Additional Facility Rules, art. 4(1).

[42] Article 4(1) of the Additional Facility Rules provides that "[t]he parties may apply for such approval . . . by submitting to the Secretariat a copy of the agreement concluded or proposed to be concluded between them."

[43] Arbitration (Additional Facility) Rules, art. 19.

[44] *See* Jack J. Coe, Jr., *Domestic Court Control of Investment Awards: Necessary Evil or Achilles Heel Within Nafta and the Proposed FTAA*, 19(3) J. Int'l Arb. 185, 185–86, 194–96 (2002).

[45] 32 I.L.M. 289 (pts. 1–3); 32 I.L.M. 605 (pts. 4–8) (entered into force Jan. 1, 1994).

[46] *See* list of Contracting States available at http://www.worldbank.org/icsid.

[47] *See* www.unctad.org. On its website, UNCTAD maintains lists by country of BITs that have been concluded.

[48] *See The Entry into Force of Bilateral Investment Treaties (BITs)*, UNCTAD/WEB/ITE/IIA/2006/9. Available at www.UNCTAD.org. Only about 1,900 (75.8%) of the

Because each BIT is negotiated between two different sovereign States, the contents of different BITs may vary substantially. Thus, any investor should carefully review the pertinent BIT when planning for an investment. BITs may define differently, for example, the investors who are covered and the investments that are protected, and may impose certain requirements on the investor's conduct as a precondition to the State's engaging in arbitration.

b. Substantive Rights

Despite many variations, most BITs tend to have some common features. Listed below are a number of substantive rights that may be included among the protections usually provided by BITs, along with a thumbnail sketch of how the rights are generally understood.

- *Fair and equitable treatment* – This essentially requires States to provide a reasonably stable investment environment, consistent with investor expectations.[49]
- *Full protection and security* – The investor should not suffer physical destruction of its property, or be subjected to serious threat of physical destruction. According to a number of tribunals, however, this right is not limited to protection from physical interference, but includes the right to be free from any act or measure that constitutes inequitable treatment.[50]
- *Protection against uncompensated expropriation or nationalization* – If a government expropriates or nationalizes an investment, it must be for a public purpose and not be done in a discriminatory manner, and the

treaties had entered into force at that time, however. As time passes, after a BIT has been concluded, a higher percentage will enter into force. For BITs concluded in 1996 and earlier, 90% were in force by the end of 2005. *See id.* at 2. The lag time is attributable to the often complicated or cumbersome process for approval or ratification in both countries.

[49] *See* Reed et al., *supra* note 18, at 74–78. There is, however, a controversy about whether fair and equitable treatment should be based on a minimum international standard, or simply plain meaning. NAFTA's Free Trade Commission has stated that fair and equitable treatment "do[es] not require treatment in addition to or beyond that which is required by the customary international law minimum standard of treatment of aliens." (www.naftaclaims.com/files/NAFTA_Comm_1105_Transparency.pdf). However, tribunals under certain BITs apply the plain meaning discerned by each tribunal based on the text of the BIT and the facts and circumstances of a particular case. *See* Richard H. Kreindler, *Perspectives on State Party Arbitration: The Future of BITs – The Practitioner's Perspective*, 23 Arb. Int. 43, 51–55 (2007). *See also* Compania de Aguas del Aconquija, S.A. & Vivendi Universal v. Argentine Republic, ICSID Award, 202, ¶ 7.4.7 (2007) ("The Tribunal sees no basis for equating principles of international law with minimum standards of treatment."). Available at http://ita.law.uvic.ca/chronological_list.htm.

[50] *See, e.g., Vivendi, supra* note 49, at 206–09 ¶¶ 7.4.15–7.4.17 (Obligation to provide full protection and security not limited to acts or measures "which threaten physical possession or the legally protected terms of operation of the investment."). *Id.* at ¶ 7.4.15.

investor must be promptly and adequately compensated. State actions that substantially diminish the value of an investment may also be treated as an expropriation.

- *National treatment* – The host country must treat the investor as well as it treats its own nationals. Exceptions may be provided for certain industries.
- *Most favored nation treatment* – The host country must treat the investor as well as it treats any other investor from another country. Exceptions may be provided for certain industries.
- *Free transfer of funds* – Funds related to the investment may be moved freely into and out of the host country.
- *Obligation to observe specific investment undertakings* – Sometimes called "umbrella clauses," these clauses require the State to observe all its obligations. There is a lack of agreement among tribunals as to whether application of an umbrella clause will cause a breach of an investment agreement to amount to a breach of a treaty obligation.[51]

A BIT may also deal with other issues, such as transparency, domestic labor laws, disclosure of information, and taxation.

c. Enforcing Rights under a BIT

Although many BITs provide for arbitration of disputes, there may be various requirements that an investor must meet before arbitration can be commenced. In some cases, there may be a period of about three to six months in which it is expected that parties will attempt to resolve the dispute through consultation and negotiation. These settlement attempts may include using nonbinding mediation or conciliation. Usually, the consultation period is triggered by a letter from the investor to the State. The letter should go to top officials of the State, and not just to the head of a State entity who perhaps signed the investment contract.

A few BITs contain a precondition that the investor is required to first try to resolve its dispute in the courts of the host country.[52] Generally, if the dispute has not been resolved by the local courts within a specified time period, then the State will be required to arbitrate.

Sometimes the BIT will provide a number of options to the parties about how they can proceed to resolve a dispute. The BIT may give the parties, or perhaps just the investor, the option to bring an ICSID arbitration, an arbitration with a different arbitral institution, an ad hoc arbitration, or

---

[51] *See infra* Section C.

[52] *See* Reed et al., *supra* note 18, at 99–100, describing the Argentina-Netherlands BIT, which entered into force in 1994. It requires a three-month negotiation period and then, if the dispute is not settled, submission to local courts. Arbitration is permitted only if no final decision is provided by the court after 18 months.

an action in the local courts of the Contracting State. A BIT that provides such options will also frequently provide that once a party has selected an option, the other options are no longer available. This is commonly known as a "fork in the road" provision. When this kind of provision exists in the applicable BIT, the investor should exercise care before raising claims in a domestic court, because this action could preclude the possibility of an ICSID arbitration or an arbitration with another institution or other rules.

3. Multilateral Investment Treaties

Multilateral investment treaties contain many protections similar to those found in BITs. They also tend to provide for international arbitration of disputes. A typical choice of forum includes ICSID or other arbitral institutions. The 1994 North American Free Trade Agreement (NAFTA),[53] which includes Canada, the United States, and Mexico, provides that a disputing investor may submit an arbitration claim under the ICSID Convention if both parties are Contracting States of the Convention, or under the Additional Facility Rules of ICSID, or under the UNCITRAL Arbitration Rules.[54] However, among the three countries, only the United States is currently a party to the ICSID Convention, so investor claims under NAFTA are brought under the Additional Facility Rules or the UNCITRAL Rules.[55] Because many provisions of NAFTA are similar to the substantive and procedural issues in a number of BITs, rulings under the more well-known NAFTA cases have tended to influence the jurisprudence of international investment arbitrations.

Another important multilateral treaty is the Energy Charter Treaty.[56] It was signed in December 1994 and entered into force in April 1998.[57] The Energy Charter website states that "[t]he fundamental aim of the Energy Charter Treaty is to strengthen the rule of law on energy issues by creating a level playing field of rules to be observed by all participating governments, thereby mitigating risks associated with energy-related investments and trade."[58] Investors covered by the Energy Charter Treaty have three

---

[53] 32 I.L.M. 289 (pts. 1–3); 32 I.L.M. 605 (pts. 4–8) (entered into force January 1, 1994).

[54] *See id.* art. 1120.

[55] Canada signed the ICSID Convention on December 15, 2006, but as of December 2011, the Convention was not in force for Canada. Enactment of implementation legislation must occur before Canada can deposit its instrument of ratification. *See* www.worldbank.org/icsid.

[56] 34 ILM 381 (1995).

[57] As of 2011, there were 46 members who had ratified, acceded to, or approved the treaty; 5 signatories whose ratifications were pending; 24 observers, some of whom were signatories; and 10 international organizations with observer status. *See* http://www.encharter.org/.

[58] *See* http://www.encharter.org/index.php?id=7.

choices as to arbitration procedures: (1) an ICSID arbitration, or, if they do not meet the jurisdictional requirements, the Additional Facility Rules; (2) an arbitration under the UNCITRAL Rules; or (3) an arbitration under the aegis of the Arbitration Institute of the Stockholm Chamber of Commerce.[59]

Similar to BITs, multilateral investment treaties contain provisions designed to protect cross-border investors and provide for settlement of investment disputes. By taking investment disputes out of the domestic courts, these treaties lessen the risk that harm to the investor resulting from arbitrary or unfair acts of the Contracting State will go unremedied. The treaties thereby encourage investment by providing recourse to neutral dispute resolution in the event an investor would be subject to unfair state action.

4. Investor Protection Legislation

Some States, in order to encourage investment, adopt investor protection laws. These laws generally provide some of the same protections found in BITs, such as national treatment, and protection against uncompensated expropriation or nationalization. In addition, the laws often contain an offer to submit to ICSID arbitration. Counsel for a potential investor should read such legislation very carefully to understand what the investor must do in order to accept the State's offer to arbitrate. Normally, the investor's consent must be in writing. It is best if the investor accepts the offer early, because otherwise the State may be able to withdraw its offer – for example, by amending or repealing the investor protection legislation.[60]

C. OVERLAP OF TREATY-BASED RIGHTS AND CONTRACT-BASED RIGHTS

1. The Source of the Right

There are fundamental differences between treaty arbitrations, which are based on a treaty between two sovereign States, and commercial arbitrations, which are based on a contract between two private entities. In treaty arbitrations, the role of the State and the application of a treaty necessarily implicate public international law. Although traditionally, international treaties do not provide rights to individuals, in most investment treaties, States have intended to permit individuals to assert claims under the treaty against the State party. The purpose of arbitration provided by the treaty is to avoid a perception of unfair advantage for the State, thereby giving a comfort level to investors that will encourage them to invest.

---

[59] Energy Charter Treaty, *supra* note 56, art. 26(4).
[60] *See* Reed et al., *supra* note 18, at 54.

In many investment situations, however, the State will have obligations both under a treaty and under a contract. The investor will typically enter into a contract with the State or a State agency, which will govern the parties' contract rights and obligations. If the parties are also subject to the provisions of an investment treaty, the investor's contract rights will be different from the treaty-based rights, with the contract rights generally being much more specific. In addition, the contract is likely to provide for resolving disputes by a method that may be different from the method provided in the treaty. For example, the contract may provide for disputes to be resolved in the courts of the Contracting State, rather than by arbitration, and may further assert that the courts of the Contracting State have exclusive jurisdiction over any dispute. The treaty, on the other hand, may provide for international arbitration under ICSID.

In this kind of situation, when a dispute arises, what is an investor to do? The focus in this section is on the difference between contract rights and treaty rights, and how disputes over those rights are resolved. The difference is particularly important in situations such as the one described previously, in which the only right to international arbitration is from the treaty, because the contract provides for resolution in the local courts. Investors may want to characterize any breach as a treaty breach, because they prefer to resolve the dispute by an international arbitration. The Contracting State may want to characterize a breach as breach of contract, but not a treaty breach, particularly if the investment contract provides for contract disputes to be resolved in its local courts. As will be discussed below, tribunals sometimes take the investor view and other times the Contracting State view, depending on the wording of the pertinent treaty and the pertinent contract, as well as other factors.

The main difference in contract and treaty rights is that the source of that right – the legal basis – is different. A contract claim will be based on the terms of a contract, whereas a treaty claim is based on the terms of a treaty. Contract rights tend to be very specific to the investment in question, whereas treaty rights are generally generic and tend to be defined by international law (such as most favored nation treatment, nondiscriminatory treatment, or compensation in the event of expropriation).

It is important to consider carefully who the parties are to the treaty and to the investment contract, and who the parties are to the treaty claim and the contract claim, because they are not the same. The parties to a bilateral treaty are two sovereign States. For a treaty claim, however, the parties will always be the investor, who is given the right under the treaty to claim against the State, and the State itself, not a State agency. If the treaty claim is based on acts of government conducted at a lower level by lower-level State officials, the investor must demonstrate that the State is responsible, in accordance with the doctrine of State responsibility under international law.[61] On the other hand, the parties to an investment contract may well be a subsidiary or affiliate of the investor and a Contracting State agency, rather than the Contracting State. Thus, a contract claim is likely to be brought by an investor's subsidiary against a State agency, whereas a treaty claim will be brought by an investor against a State.

In addition, different laws may apply to a contract claim or a treaty claim. Normally, under a BIT, in addition to applicability of the BIT provisions, the Contracting State law and international law may be applicable. Under the investment contract, Contracting State domestic law will probably be applicable.

2. Umbrella Clauses

An umbrella clause imposes an obligation on a Contracting State to observe all the obligations it has undertaken with respect to an investor from the other Contracting State. If there is an umbrella clause in the BIT, investors may argue that any breach of a contract-based obligation will trigger protection of the treaty. A typical umbrella clause provides, for example, that "[e]ach Contracting Party shall observe any obligation it has assumed with regard to investments in its territory by investors of the other Contracting Party."[62] The question is whether this clause means that if the State breaches some aspect of an investment contract, even if the breach is not a violation of international law, an investor can bring a treaty claim. In other words, does an umbrella clause make every contract breach amount to a breach of an investment treaty? Tribunals have given different answers to this question.

In one case, SGS v. Pakistan,[63] the tribunal determined that the umbrella clause does not permit an investor to seek redress of breach of an investment contract through international arbitration under a treaty. In another case, SGS v. Philippines,[64] the tribunal found that an umbrella clause did provide jurisdiction to consider breach of contract claims as a breach of the BIT, but then declined to exercise jurisdiction because there was a clause in the investment contract that designated a different, exclusive forum for

---

[61] Bernardo M. Cremades & David J. A. Cairns, Contract and Treaty Claims and Choice of Forum in Foreign Investment Disputes, 13–42, at 16, in Dossiers: PARALLEL STATE AND ARBITRAL PROCEDURES IN INTERNATIONAL ARBITRATION (2005).

[62] Umbrella clause from Swiss Model BIT. *See Interpretation of the Umbrella Clause in Investment Agreements*, OECD Working Papers on International Investment, October 2006 at 23. Available at http://www.oecd.org/dataoecd/3/20/37579220.pdf.

[63] *See* SGS Société Générale de Surveillance S.A. v. Islamic Republic of Pakistan, ICSID Case No. ARB/01/13. Decision on Jurisdiction (August 6, 2003). Available at www.worldbank.org/icsid.

[64] *See* SGS Société Générale de Surveillance S.A. v. Philippines, Decision of the Tribunal on Objections to Jurisdiction, ICSID Case No. ARB/02/6 (2004) reprinted in 19 Mealey's Int'l. Arb Rep. 6 (2004).

resolving contract disputes. Following these cases, a number of decisions have addressed the umbrella clause, with inconsistent results.[65]

Commentators and others have argued that the origins and history of the umbrella clause make very clear that the purpose of this clause is, in fact, to turn breaches of an investment contract into treaty breaches, so recourse can be obtained under the treaty.[66] For example, UNCTAD observed in the 1990s that "as a result of [an umbrella clause in a BIT], violations of commitments regarding investment by the host country would be redressible through a BIT."[67] After examining the history of the umbrella clause and a number of recent tribunal decisions interpreting the clause, Jarrod Wong, a former legal adviser at the Iran-United States Claims Tribunal, concluded:

> [T]he more reasonable and effective interpretation of the umbrella clause is that it applies to obligations arising under the relevant investor-State investment contract, and a BIT tribunal may thereby exercise jurisdiction over breach of contract claims, including when the contract contains an exclusive forum selection clause.[68]

Because the main value of a BIT for the investor is that it permits arbitration of investment disputes directly against the State, when a tribunal denies the effect of an umbrella clause the result can be a limitation on the protections accorded the investor under the BIT. Nonetheless, arbitral tribunals remain somewhat skeptical of a broad interpretation of an umbrella clause that would make any breach of a contract amount to a breach of the

---

[65] *See, e.g.,* Pan American Energy LLC and BP Argentina Republic v. Argentine Republic, ICSID Case No. ARB/03/14 (2006) (Tribunal follows SGS v. Pakistan in finding that umbrella clause does not elevate every contract claim to a treaty claim.). Available at http://italaw.com/chronological_list.htm. *Compare* Eureko BV v. Republic of Poland, Ad Hoc Proceedings, Partial award (2005) (Tribunal finds analysis in SGS v. Philippines convincing, and finds that umbrella clause makes breaches of contract amount to breaches of treaty.). Available at http://italaw.com/chronological_list.htm.

[66] *See, e.g.,* Jarrod Wong, *Umbrella Clauses in Bilateral Investment Treaties: Of Breaches of Contract, Treaty Violations and the Divide between Developing and Developed Countries in Foreign Investment Disputes,* 14 Geo. Mason L. Rev. 135, 166 (2006) ("As its history shows, the umbrella clause was specifically designed to ensure that disputes under investor-State contracts would be resolved in a neutral forum and enforced as a matter of international law."); Anthony C. Sinclair, *The Origins of the Umbrella Clause in the International Law of Investment Protection,* 20 Arb. Int. 411 (2004) (The author reviews the history and function of the umbrella clause to demonstrate that the clause was intended to make a breach of an agreement a breach of a BIT, and argues that this history should be relevant to tribunals interpreting and applying an umbrella clause in an investment treaty.).

[67] *See* Wong, *supra* note 66, at 150, *citing* UNCTAD, Bilateral Investment Treaties in the Mid-1990s, Geneva, Switz. Nov. 1998, U.N. Doc. UNCTAD/IIT/7.

[68] *See id.* at 174.

substantive standards of a BIT.[69] Tribunals have tended to take the position that a breach of a contract by a State will not be considered a breach of a treaty unless the conduct is "beyond that which an ordinary party could adopt and (would) involve State interference with the operation of the contract."[70]

3. Distinguishing Contract and Treaty Claims

Some tribunals, in trying to distinguish between contract and treaty claims, have mentioned with favor the *Vivendi* annulment decision in Compania de Aguas del Aconquija, S.A.(CAA) & Vivendi v. Argentine Republic (Vivendi).[71] This decision will be discussed in some detail, because it deals with a number of the issues mentioned previously. *Vivendi* involved a thirty-year concession contract[72] between an Argentine affiliate, CAA, of a French company, Compagnie Générale des Eaux (CGE)[73] and Tucumán, a province of Argentina.[74] The purpose of the concession contract was to privatize (transfer from public to private hands) the Tucumán water and sewage facility, which had been operated by a provincial authority. When

---

[69] *See, e.g.,* El Paso Energy Int'l Co. v. Argentine Republic, ICSID Case no. ARB/03/15. Decision Jurisdiction (2006). Available at http://icsid.worldbank.org/ICSID/FrontServlet?requestType=CasesRH&actionVal=showDoc&docId=DC511_En&caseId=C17 (Tribunal follows SGS v. Pakistan, interpreting umbrella clause restrictively.).

[70] Siemans A.G. v. Arg. Republic, ICSID Case No. ARB/02/8, Award, ¶ 248 (February 6, 2007), available at http://ita.law.uvic.ca/documents/Siemens-Argentina-Award.pdf. *See also* George K. Foster, *Striking a Balance between Investor Protections and National Sovereignty: The Relevance of Local Remedies in Investment Treaty Arbitration,* 49 Colum. J. Transnat'l. L. 201, 256 (2011) ("I concur in the view that an investor cannot establish a breach of fair and equitable treatment or an expropriation simply by identifying a contractual breach by the host State.").

[71] Compania de Aguas del Aconquija, S.A. & Vivendi Universal v. Argentine Republic, Decision on Annulment, ICSID Case no. ARB/97/3 (July 3, 2002), reprinted in 41 I.L.M. 1135 (2002). A second award was issued on August 20, 2007, and a decision denying the Argentine Republic's request for annulment of the award rendered on 20 August 2007 was rendered on August 20, 2010. *See infra* note 93.

[72] A concession contract generally provides a private firm (frequently a foreign party) with rights from a government to build, develop, or upgrade a project or facility, frequently something that is normally in the public domain – such as a water and sewage facility – and to operate it, collecting income for the period of the concession. Ownership rights generally remain with the government, and at the end of the concession period, the facility or project is usually turned over to the government.

[73] In 1998, Compagnie Général des Eaux changed its name to Vivendi.

[74] After the annulment, respondents moved for supplementation and rectification of the decision, which was denied in May 2003. 19 ICSID Rev. – FILJ 139 (2004); 8 ICSID Rep. 490 (2005). The case was resubmitted to a new tribunal in October 2003. That tribunal declared the proceedings closed in May 2007, and rendered its award in August 2007. Available at http://italaw.com/chronological_list.htm.

the concession contract ended prematurely, claimants CAA and CGE commenced an ICSID arbitration against Argentina under the Argentine-French BIT.[75] The Tribunal ruled that because of a clause in the concession contract providing for exclusive jurisdiction in the administrative courts of the Province, the claims against Tucumán would have to be adjudicated there. The Tribunal further declared that it could not determine "which actions of the Province were taken in exercise of its sovereign authority and which in the exercise of its rights as a party to the Concession Contract."[76] In other words, the Tribunal found it impossible to distinguish rights that should be determined under the BIT from rights that should be determined under the contract. The only way such a determination could be made, according to the Tribunal, would be "to undertake a detailed interpretation and application of the Concession Contract, a task left by the parties to that contract to the exclusive jurisdiction of the administrative courts of Tucumán."[77] Thus, in the Tribunal's view, it was impossible to separate potential breaches of contract from violations of the BIT unless the concession contract was first interpreted and applied. However, under the parties' agreement, the Tribunal viewed that task as exclusively for the local courts.

In the annulment decision, the ICSID ad hoc committee found that the Tribunal had jurisdiction over the claims against Tucumán, and that in failing to decide those claims, the Tribunal had exceeded its powers under ICSID Article 52(1)(b).[78] The committee made very clear that treaty rights were independent from contract rights: "A state may breach a treaty without breaching a contract, and vice versa."[79] It attempted, however, to provide guidance as to when contract or treaty claims would prevail, based on whether "'the essential basis of a claim'... is breach of contract,"[80] or whether "the fundamental basis of the claim... is a treaty."[81]

It is not so clear that in practice this guidance will prove helpful, because the parties in most cases could make arguments for either position. Nonetheless, in *Vivendi*, the committee appeared to be very supportive of treaty

---

[75] Agreement between the Government of the Argentine Republic and the Government of the Republic of France for Reciprocal Protection and Promotion of Investments of 3 July, 1991, http://icsid.worldbank.org/ICSID/FrontServlet.

[76] Award, Compania De Aguas Del Aconquija, S.A. v. Argentine Republic, 40 ILM 426, 443, ¶ 79 (2001).

[77] *Id.*

[78] The committee noted that "an ICSID tribunal commits an excess of powers not only if it exercises a jurisdiction which it does not have... but also if it fails to exercise a jurisdiction which it possesses." Annulment decision, 41 I.L.M. 1135 (2002), ¶ 86. The committee did not annul the Tribunal's finding with respect to claims "based directly on alleged actions or failures to act of the Argentine Republic." *Id.* at ¶ 16.

[79] *Id.* at ¶ 95.

[80] *Id.* at ¶ 98.

[81] *Id.* at ¶ 101.

rights. It specifically rejected the Tribunal's view that the exclusive jurisdiction clause in the party's contract could override a treaty right.

> [I]t is not open to an ICSID tribunal having jurisdiction under a BIT in respect of a claim based upon a substantive provision of that BIT, to dismiss the claim on the ground that it could or should have been dealt with by a national court. In such a case, the inquiry which the ICSID tribunal is required to undertake is one governed by the ICSID Convention, by the BIT and by applicable international law. Such an inquiry is neither in principle determined, nor precluded, by any issue of municipal law, including any municipal law agreement of the parties.[82]

Thus, according to the ad hoc committee, if a tribunal has jurisdiction to decide a BIT claim, a clause in a contract between the parties would not override that jurisdiction. The committee noted further that "[a] state cannot rely on an exclusive jurisdiction clause in a contract to avoid the characterization of its conduct as internationally unlawful under a treaty."[83]

Interestingly, the committee did not rely on an umbrella clause. It did, however, rely on specific language in the BIT, which gave the Tribunal jurisdiction over the contract claims. Article 8(4) of the Argentine-French BIT provides as follows:

> The ruling of the arbitral body shall be based on the provisions of this Agreement, the legislation of the Contracting Party which is a party to the dispute, including rules governing conflict of laws, *the terms of any private agreements concluded on the subject of the investment*, and the relevant principles of international law.[84]

Because the BIT specifically provided that the Tribunal could base its ruling on the terms of the parties' contract, the committee stated that under Article 8(4) of the BIT,

> the Tribunal had jurisdiction to base its decision upon the Concession Contract, at least so far as necessary in order to determine whether there had been a breach of the substantive standards of the BIT.[85]

Thus, from the committee's perspective, the allegations against Tucumán under the contract should have been examined in the arbitration to determine whether they amounted to a violation of Article 3 or 5 of the BIT, which provided for fair and equitable treatment, protection, and full security, and

---

[82] *Id.* at ¶ 102.
[83] *Id. at* ¶ 103.
[84] *Id. at* ¶ 53. Emphasis added.
[85] *Id.* at ¶ 110.

for no expropriation or nationalization except for a public purpose, without discrimination, and upon payment of prompt and adequate compensation.[86] The committee acknowledged that because claimants had taken the "fork in the road" under Article 8(2)[87] by choosing arbitration over the local courts, if the claimants could not establish that the acts complained of rose to the level of a breach of the BIT, they would lose both their treaty claim and their contract claim.[88] Although the committee asserted that it had not formed even a provisional view of whether the conduct alleged by claimants, if established, could have breached the BIT, it noted that the conduct complained of was not "peripheral to a continuing successful enterprise."[89] Rather, the conduct of the Tucumán government "had the effect of putting an end to the investment."[90]

After the partial annulment, the case was resubmitted by Vivendi to a second tribunal, which rendered an award against Argentina in August 2007.[91] The second tribunal followed the guidance of the committee, confirming that a tribunal can consider the background of parties' conduct under a contract in determining whether there has been a breach of a BIT.[92] A second ad hoc committee declined to annul the award of the second tribunal.[93]

4. Coordinating Contracts with Treaties

Given the potential pitfalls of having both a treaty and a contract applicable to the same fact situation, what steps can counsel take to minimize

---

[86] *Id. at* ¶ 11.
[87] *Id.* at ¶ 53. Article 8(2) provides that if the dispute is not settled within six months, upon the request of the investor it shall be submitted:

- Either to the domestic courts of the Contracting Party involved in the dispute;
- Or to international arbitration.

Once an investor has submitted the dispute to the courts of the Contracting Party concerned or to international arbitration, the choice of one or the other of these procedures is final.

[88] *Id.* at ¶ 113.
[89] *Id. at* ¶ 114.
[90] *Id.* The committee found the conduct of Tucumán attributable to Argentina." [I]n the case of a claim based on a treaty, international law rules of attribution apply, with the result that the state of Argentina is internationally responsible for the acts of its provincial authorities." *Id.* ¶ 96. *See also*, Cremades & Cairns, *supra* note 61, at 22 ("[I]n a Federal State all of the actions of a Federal unit are, as a matter of public international law, attributed to the State itself.").
[91] *See Vivendi, supra* note 74.
[92] *See id.* at 199, ¶ 7.3.10 ("It is permissible for the Tribunal to consider . . . alleged contractual breaches, not for the purpose of determining liability under domestic law, but to the extent necessary to analyse and determine whether there has been a breach of the Treaty.").
[93] *See* Compañiá de Aguas del Aconquija S.A. & Vivendi Universal v. Argentine Republic, ICSID Case No. ARB/97/3 (dispatched to the parties 10 August 2010). Available at http://italaw.com/documents/VivendiSecondAnnulmentDecision.pdf.

complications in future dispute resolution processes? Because more than 2,500 BITs have already been concluded, amending BITs to make the parties' intentions clearer is not a likely scenario in many cases. In new BITs, however, better drafting could alleviate some difficulties. Some BITs make the right to raise contract rights in a BIT arbitration relatively clear. The 2004 U.S. Model BIT, for example, provides that the claimant may, on its own behalf or on behalf of an enterprise it controls, submit to arbitration a claim that the respondent has breached obligations under the BIT, or an investment authorization, or an investment agreement. As to claims of a breach of an investment agreement, however, there is a proviso. That claim may be submitted to arbitration only "if the subject matter of the claim and the claimed damages directly relate to the covered investment that was established or acquired, or sought to be established or acquired, in reliance on the relevant investment agreement."[94] This language appears to accomplish two goals. First, in a complex investment project, there may be a number of collateral contracts that are indirectly rather than directly related to the covered investment. Breaches of the indirectly related contracts would not give rise to a claim under the BIT. Second, if the investor incurred substantial expenses trying to set up an investment that never became fully functional, those expenses should be recoverable if the inability to complete the investment resulted from a breach of terms of the treaty.

Although the investor will not be able to redraft an applicable BIT, it should be very careful in negotiating and drafting the dispute resolution provisions in its investment contract. If it has sufficient leverage, it should avoid agreeing to settle contract disputes in the local courts and try to provide for an international arbitration, preferably tracking the arbitration provisions found in the applicable BIT. In the case of a multinational enterprise, which could choose to have the investor located in any of a number of countries, it might be worthwhile to scrutinize each potentially applicable BIT and then use as the investor a company located in the country with the best protection under the applicable treaty.[95] Most important, in planning an investment, the investor and its counsel should always study carefully any applicable bilateral or multilateral treaty in order to understand how the scope and the content of that treaty will affect the investment.

---

[94] U.S. Model BIT, art. 24(1)(a–b) (2004). Available at http://ustraderep.gov/Trade_Sectors/Investments/Model_BIT/Section_Index.html.

[95] Dana H. Freyer, Barry H. Garfinkel, & Hamid G. Gharavi, *Bilateral Investment Treaties and Arbitration*, in HANDBOOK ON INTERNATIONAL ARBITRATION & ADR (Thomas Carbonneau & Jeanette A. Jaeggi, eds.) (2006), 289 ("The investor should identify the BIT that would provide it with the foremost protection ... and consider selecting the state of incorporation of the company which is to carry out the investment ... in order to fall within the scope of that BIT.").

The United Nations Convention on the Recognition and Enforcement of Foreign Arbitral Awards (The New York Convention) (1958)

Reprinted with permission of UNCITRAL

1. Completed in New York, on June 10, 1958, at the United Nations & the Convention entered into force on June 7, 1959. Treaty Series, vol. 330, p. 38, No. 4739 (1959)

Article I

1. This Convention shall apply to the recognition and enforcement of arbitral awards made in the territory of a State other than the State where the recognition and enforcement of such awards are sought, and arising out of differences between persons, whether physical or legal. It shall also apply to arbitral awards not considered as domestic awards in the State where their recognition and enforcement are sought.
2. The term "arbitral awards" shall include not only awards made by arbitrators appointed for each case but also those made by permanent arbitral bodies to which the parties have submitted.
3. When signing, ratifying or acceding to this Convention, or notifying extension under Article X hereof, any State may on the basis of reciprocity declare that it will apply the Convention to the recognition and enforcement of awards made only in the territory of another Contracting State. It may also declare that it will apply the Convention only to differences arising out of legal relationships, whether contractual or not, which are considered as commercial under the national law of the State making such declaration.

Article II

1. Each Contracting State shall recognize an agreement in writing under which the parties undertake to submit to arbitration all or any differences which have arisen or which may arise between them in respect of a defined

legal relationship, whether contractual or not, concerning a subject matter capable of settlement by arbitration.

2. The term "agreement in writing" shall include an arbitral clause in a contract or an arbitration agreement, signed by the parties or contained in an exchange of letters or telegrams.

3. The court of a Contracting State, when seized of an action in a matter in respect of which the parties have made an agreement within the meaning of this article, shall, at the request of one of the parties, refer the parties to arbitration, unless it finds that the said agreement is null and void, inoperative or incapable of being performed.

Article III

Each Contracting State shall recognize arbitral awards as binding and enforce them in accordance with the rules of procedure of the territory where the award is relied upon, under the conditions laid down in the following articles. There shall not be imposed substantially more onerous conditions or higher fees or charges on the recognition or enforcement of arbitral awards to which this Convention applies than are imposed on the recognition or enforcement of domestic arbitral awards.

Article IV

1. To obtain the recognition and enforcement mentioned in the preceding article, the party applying for recognition and enforcement shall, at the time of application, supply:
   (a) The duly authenticated original award or a duly certified copy thereof;
   (b) The original agreement referred to in Article II or a duly certified copy thereof.

2. If the said award or agreement is not made in an official language of the country in which the award is relied upon, the party applying for recognition and enforcement of the award shall produce a translation of these documents into such language. The translation shall be certified by an official or sworn translator or by a diplomatic or consular agent.

Article V

1. Recognition and enforcement of the award may be refused, at the request of the party against whom it is invoked, only if that party furnishes to the competent authority where the recognition and enforcement is sought, proof that:
   (a) The parties to the agreement referred to in Article II were, under the law applicable to them, under some incapacity, or the said agreement is not valid under the law to which the parties have subjected it or, failing any indication thereon, under the law of the country where the award was made; or

(b) The party against whom the award is invoked was not given proper notice of the appointment of the arbitrator or of the arbitration proceedings or was otherwise unable to present his case; or

(c) The award deals with a difference not contemplated by or not falling within the terms of the submission to arbitration, or it contains decisions on matters beyond the scope of the submission to arbitration, provided that, if the decisions on matters submitted to arbitration can be separated from those not so submitted, that part of the award which contains decisions on matters submitted to arbitration may be recognized and enforced; or

(d) The composition of the arbitral authority or the arbitral procedure was not in accordance with the agreement of the parties, or, failing such agreement, was not in accordance with the law of the country where the arbitration took place; or

(e) The award has not yet become binding on the parties or has been set aside or suspended by a competent authority of the country in which, or under the law of which, that award was made.

2. Recognition and enforcement of an arbitral award may also be refused if the competent authority in the country where recognition and enforcement is sought finds that:

(a) The subject matter of the difference is not capable of settlement by arbitration under the law of that country; or

(b) The recognition or enforcement of the award would be contrary to the public policy of that country.

Article VI

If an application for the setting aside or suspension of the award has been made to a competent authority referred to in Article V(1)(e), the authority before which the award is sought to be relied upon may, if it considers it proper, adjourn the decision on the enforcement of the award and may also, on the application of the party claiming enforcement of the award, order the other party to give suitable security.

Article VII

1. The provisions of the present Convention shall not affect the validity of multilateral or bilateral agreements concerning the recognition and enforcement of arbitral awards entered into by the Contracting States nor deprive any interested party of any right he may have to avail himself of an arbitral award in the manner and to the extent allowed by the law or the treaties of the country where such award is sought to be relied upon.

2. The Geneva Protocol on Arbitration Clauses of 1923 and the Geneva Convention on the Execution of Foreign Arbitral Awards of 1927 shall

cease to have effect between Contracting States on their becoming bound
and to the extent that they become bound, by this Convention.

Article VIII

1. This Convention shall be open until 31 December 1958 for signature on
   behalf of any Member of the United Nations and also on behalf of any
   other State which is or hereafter becomes a member of any specialized
   agency of the United Nations, or which is or hereafter becomes a party
   to the Statute of the International Court of Justice, or any other State to
   which an invitation has been addressed by the General Assembly of the
   United Nations.
2. This Convention shall be ratified and the instrument of ratification shall
   be deposited with the Secretary-General of the United Nations.

Article IX

1. This Convention shall be open for accession to all States referred to in
   Article VIII.
2. Accession shall be effected by the deposit of an instrument of accession
   with the Secretary-General of the United Nations.

Article X

1. Any State may, at the time of signature, ratification or accession, declare
   that this Convention shall extend to all or any of the territories for the
   international relations of which it is responsible. Such a declaration shall
   take effect when the Convention enters into force for the State concerned.
2. At any time thereafter any such extension shall be made by notification
   addressed to the Secretary-General of the United Nations and shall take
   effect as from the ninetieth day after the day of receipt by the Secretary-
   General of the United Nations of this notification, or as from the date of
   entry into force of the Convention for the State concerned, whichever is
   the later.
3. With respect to those territories to which this Convention is not extended
   at the time of signature, ratification or accession, each State concerned
   shall consider the possibility of taking the necessary steps in order to
   extend the application of this Convention to such territories, subject,
   where necessary for constitutional reasons, to the consent of the Governments of such territories.

Article XI

In the case of a federal or non-unitary State, the following provisions shall
apply:

(a) With respect to those articles of this Convention that come within the
    legislative jurisdiction of the federal authority, the obligations of the

federal Government shall to this extent be the same as those of Contracting States which are not federal States;

(b) With respect to those articles of this Convention that come within the legislative jurisdiction of constituent states or provinces which are not, under the constitutional system of the federation, bound to take legislative action, the federal Government shall bring such articles with a favourable recommendation to the notice of the appropriate authorities of constituent states or provinces at the earliest possible moment;

(c) A federal State Party to this Convention shall, at the request of any other Contracting State transmitted through the Secretary-General of the United Nations, supply a statement of the law and practice of the federation and its constituent units in regard to any particular provision of this Convention, showing the extent to which effect has been given to that provision by legislative or other action.

Article XII

1. This Convention shall come into force on the ninetieth day following the date of deposit of the third instrument of ratification or accession.

2. For each State ratifying or acceding to this Convention after the deposit of the third instrument of ratification or accession, this Convention shall enter into force on the ninetieth day after deposit by such State of its instrument of ratification or accession.

Article XIII

1. Any Contracting State may denounce this Convention by a written notification to the Secretary-General of the United Nations. Denunciation shall take effect one year after the date of receipt of the notification by the Secretary-General.

2. Any State which has made a declaration or notification under Article X may, at any time thereafter, by notification to the Secretary-General of the United Nations, declare that this Convention shall cease to extend to the territory concerned one year after the date of the receipt of the notification by the Secretary-General.

3. This Convention shall continue to be applicable to arbitral awards in respect of which recognition or enforcement proceedings have been instituted before the denunciation takes effect.

Article XIV

Contracting State shall not be entitled to avail itself of the present Convention against other Contracting States except to the extent that it is itself bound to apply the Convention.

Article XV

The Secretary-General of the United Nations shall notify the States contemplated in Article VIII of the following:

(a) Signatures and ratifications in accordance with Article VIII;
(b) Accessions in accordance with Article IX;
(c) Declarations and notifications under Articles I, X, and XI;
(d) The date upon which this Convention enters into force in accordance with Article XII; and
(e) Denunciations and notifications in accordance with Article XIII.

Article XVI

1. This Convention, of which the Chinese, English, French, Russian and Spanish texts shall be equally authentic, shall be deposited in the archives of the United Nations.
2. The Secretary-General of the United Nations shall transmit a certified copy of this Convention to the States contemplated in Article VIII.

UNCITRAL Model Law on International Commercial Arbitration (original 1985 version)

Reprinted with permission of UNCITRAL

CHAPTER I – GENERAL PROVISIONS

Article 1 – Scope of application

1. This Law applies to international commercial arbitration, subject to any agreement in force between this State and any other State or States.
2. The provisions of this Law, except articles 8, 9, 35 and 36, apply only if the place of arbitration is in the territory of this State.
3. An arbitration is international if:
    (a) the parties to an arbitration agreement have, at the time of the conclusion of that agreement, their places of business in different States; or
    (b) one of the following places is situated outside the State in which the parties have their places of business:
        (i) the place of arbitration if determined in, or pursuant to, the arbitration agreement;
        (ii) any place where a substantial part of the obligations of the commercial relationship is to be performed or the place with which the subject-matter of the dispute is most closely connected; or
    (c) the parties have expressly agreed that the subject-matter of the arbitration agreement relates to more than one country.
4. For the purposes of paragraph (3) of this article:
    (a) if a party has more than one place of business, the place of business is that which has the closest relationship to the arbitration agreement;
    (b) if a party does not have a place of business, reference is to be made to his habitual residence.

5. This Law shall not affect any other law of this State by virtue of which certain disputes may not be submitted to arbitration or may be submitted to arbitration only according to provisions other than those of this Law.

Article 2 – Definitions and rules of interpretation for the purposes of this Law:

(a) "arbitration" means any arbitration whether or not administered by a permanent arbitral institution;

(b) "arbitral tribunal" means a sole arbitrator or a panel of arbitrators;

(c) "court" means a body or organ of the judicial system of a State;

(d) where a provision of this Law, except article 28, leaves the parties free to determine a certain issue, such freedom includes the right of the parties to authorize a third party, including an institution, to make that determination;

(e) where a provision of this Law refers to the fact that the parties have agreed or that they may agree or in any other way refers to an agreement of the parties; such agreement includes any arbitration rules referred to in that agreement;

(f) where a provision of this Law, other than in articles 25 (a) and 32 (2) (a), refers to a claim, it also applies to a counter-claim, and where it refers to a defence, it also applies to a defence to such counter-claim.

Article 3 – Receipt of written communications

1. Unless otherwise agreed by the parties:

   (a) any written communication is deemed to have been received if it is delivered to the addressee personally or if it is delivered at his place of business, habitual residence or mailing address; if none of these can be found after making a reasonable inquiry, a written communication is deemed to have been received if it is sent to the addressee's last-known place of business, habitual residence or mailing address by registered letter or any other means which provides a record of the attempt to deliver it;

   (b) the communication is deemed to have been received on the day it is so delivered.

2. The provisions of this article do not apply to communications in court proceedings.

Article 4 – Waiver of right to object

A party who knows that any provision of this Law from which the parties may derogate or any requirement under the arbitration agreement has not been complied with and yet proceeds with the arbitration without stating his objection to such non-compliance without undue delay or, if a time-limit is provided therefor, within such period of time, shall be deemed to have waived his right to object.

Article 5 – Extent of court intervention

In matters governed by this Law, no court shall intervene except where so provided in this Law.

Article 6 – Court or other authority for certain functions of arbitration assistance and supervision

The functions referred to in articles 11 (3), 11 (4), 13 (3), 14, 16 (3) and 34 (2) shall be performed by . . . [Each State enacting this model law specifies the court, courts or, where referred to therein, other authority competent to perform these functions.]

CHAPTER II – ARBITRATION AGREEMENT

Article 7 – Definition and form of arbitration agreement

1. "Arbitration agreement" is an agreement by the parties to submit to arbitration all or certain disputes which have arisen or which may arise between them in respect of a defined legal relationship, whether contractual or not. An arbitration agreement may be in the form of an arbitration clause in a contract or in the form of a separate agreement.
2. The arbitration agreement shall be in writing. An agreement is in writing if it is contained in a document signed by the parties or in an exchange of letters, telex, telegrams or other means of telecommunication which provide a record of the agreement, or in an exchange of statements of claim and defence in which the existence of an agreement is alleged by one party and not denied by another. The reference in a contract to a document containing an arbitration clause constitutes an arbitration agreement provided that the contract is in writing and the reference is such as to make that clause part of the contract.

Article 8 – Arbitration agreement and substantive claim before court

1. A court before which an action is brought in a matter which is the subject of an arbitration agreement shall, if a party so requests not later than when submitting his first statement on the substance of the dispute, refer the parties to arbitration unless it finds that the agreement is null and void, inoperative or incapable of being performed.
2. Where an action referred to in paragraph (1) of this article has been brought, arbitral proceedings may nevertheless be commenced or continued, and an award may be made, while the issue is pending before the court.

Article 9 – Arbitration agreement and interim measures by court

It is not incompatible with an arbitration agreement for a party to request, before or during arbitral proceedings, from a court an interim measure of protection and for a court to grant such measure.

CHAPTER III – COMPOSITION OF ARBITRAL TRIBUNAL

Article 10 – Number of arbitrators

1. The parties are free to determine the number of arbitrators.
2. Failing such determination, the number of arbitrators shall be three.

Article 11 – Appointment of arbitrators

1. No person shall be precluded by reason of his nationality from acting as an arbitrator, unless otherwise agreed by the parties.
2. The parties are free to agree on a procedure of appointing the arbitrator or arbitrators, subject to the provisions of paragraphs (4) and (5) of this article.
3. Failing such agreement,
    (a) in an arbitration with three arbitrators, each party shall appoint one arbitrator, and the two arbitrators thus appointed shall appoint the third arbitrator; if a party fails to appoint the arbitrator within thirty days of receipt of a request to do so from the other party, or if the two arbitrators fail to agree on the third arbitrator within thirty days of their appointment, the appointment shall be made, upon request of a party, by the court or other authority specified in article 6;
    (b) in an arbitration with a sole arbitrator, if the parties are unable to agree on the arbitrator, he shall be appointed, upon request of a party, by the court or other authority specified in article 6.
4. Where, under an appointment procedure agreed upon by the parties,
    (a) a party fails to act as required under such procedure, or
    (b) the parties, or two arbitrators, are unable to reach an agreement expected of them under such procedure, or
    (c) a third party, including an institution, fails to perform any function entrusted to it under such procedure, any party may request the court or other authority specified in article 6 to take the necessary measure, unless the agreement on the appointment procedure provides other means for securing the appointment.
5. A decision on a matter entrusted by paragraph (3) and (4) of this article to the court or other authority specified in article 6 shall be subject to no appeal. The court or other authority, in appointing an arbitrator, shall have due regard to any qualifications required of the arbitrator by the agreement of the parties and to such considerations as are likely to

secure the appointment of an independent and impartial arbitrator and, in the case of a sole or third arbitrator, shall take into account as well the advisability of appointing an arbitrator of a nationality other than those of the parties.

Article 12 – Grounds for challenge

1. When a person is approached in connection with his possible appointment as an arbitrator, he shall disclose any circumstances likely to give rise to justifiable doubts as to his impartiality or independence. An arbitrator, from the time of his appointment and throughout the arbitral proceedings, shall without delay disclose any such circumstances to the parties unless they have already been informed of them by him.
2. An arbitrator may be challenged only if circumstances exist that give rise to justifiable doubts as to his impartiality or independence, or if he does not possess qualifications agreed to by the parties. A party may challenge an arbitrator appointed by him, or in whose appointment he has participated, only for reasons of which he becomes aware after the appointment has been made.

Article 13 – Challenge procedure

1. The parties are free to agree on a procedure for challenging an arbitrator, subject to the provisions of paragraph (3) of this article.
2. Failing such agreement, a party which intends to challenge an arbitrator shall, within fifteen days after becoming aware of the constitution of the arbitral tribunal or after becoming aware of any circumstance referred to in article 12 (2), send a written statement of the reasons for the challenge to the arbitral tribunal. Unless the challenged arbitrator withdraws from his office or the other party agrees to the challenge, the arbitral tribunal shall decide on the challenge.
3. If a challenge under any procedure agreed upon by the parties or under the procedure of paragraph (2) of this article is not successful, the challenging party may request, within thirty days after having received notice of the decision rejecting the challenge, the court or other authority specified in article 6 to decide on the challenge, which decision shall be subject to no appeal; while such a request is pending, the arbitral tribunal, including the challenged arbitrator, may continue the arbitral proceedings and make an award.

Article 14 – Failure or impossibility to act

1. If an arbitrator becomes de jure or de facto unable to perform his functions or for other reasons fails to act without undue delay, his mandate terminates if he withdraws from his office or if the parties agree on the termination. Otherwise, if a controversy remains concerning any of these

grounds, any party may request the court or other authority specified in article 6 to decide on the termination of the mandate, which decision shall be subject to no appeal.

2. If, under this article or article 13 (2), an arbitrator withdraws from his office or a party agrees to the termination of the mandate of an arbitrator, this does not imply acceptance of the validity of any ground referred to in this article or article 12 (2).

Article 15 – Appointment of substitute arbitrator

Where the mandate of an arbitrator terminates under article 13 or 14 or because of his withdrawal from office for any other reason or because of the revocation of his mandate by agreement of the parties or in any other case of termination of his mandate, a substitute arbitrator shall be appointed according to the rules that were applicable to the appointment of the arbitrator being replaced.

CHAPTER IV – JURISDICTION OF ARBITRAL TRIBUNAL

Article 16 – Competence of arbitral tribunal to rule on its jurisdiction

1. The arbitral tribunal may rule on its own jurisdiction, including any objections with respect to the existence or validity of the arbitration agreement. For that purpose, an arbitration clause which forms part of a contract shall be treated as an agreement independent of the other terms of the contract. A decision by the arbitral tribunal that the contract is null and void shall not entail ipso jure the invalidity of the arbitration clause.

2. A plea that the arbitral tribunal does not have jurisdiction shall be raised not later than the submission of the statement of defence. A party is not precluded from raising such a plea by the fact that he has appointed, or participated in the appointment of, an arbitrator. A plea that the arbitral tribunal is exceeding the scope of its authority shall be raised as soon as the matter alleged to be beyond the scope of its authority is raised during the arbitral proceedings. The arbitral tribunal may, in either case, admit a later plea if it considers the delay justified.

3. The arbitral tribunal may rule on a plea referred to in paragraph (2) of this article either as a preliminary question or in an award on the merits. If the arbitral tribunal rules as a preliminary question that it has jurisdiction, any party may request, within thirty days after having received notice of that ruling, the court specified in article 6 to decide the matter, which decision shall be subject to no appeal; while such a request is pending, the arbitral tribunal may continue the arbitral proceedings and make an award.

Article 17 – Power of arbitral tribunal to order interim measures

Unless otherwise agreed by the parties, the arbitral tribunal may, at the request of a party, order any party to take such interim measure of protection as the arbitral tribunal may consider necessary in respect of the subject-matter of the dispute. The arbitral tribunal may require any party to provide appropriate security in connection with such measure.

CHAPTER V – CONDUCT OF ARBITRAL PROCEEDINGS

Article 18 – Equal treatment of parties

The parties shall be treated with equality and each party shall be given a full opportunity of presenting his case.

Article 19 – Determination of rules of procedure

1. Subject to the provisions of this Law, the parties are free to agree on the procedure to be followed by the arbitral tribunal in conducting the proceedings.
2. Failing such agreement, the arbitral tribunal may, subject to the provisions of this Law, conduct the arbitration in such manner as it considers appropriate. The power conferred upon the arbitral tribunal includes the power to determine the admissibility, relevance, materiality and weight of any evidence.

Article 20 – Place of arbitration

1. The parties are free to agree on the place of arbitration. Failing such agreement, the place of arbitration shall be determined by the arbitral tribunal having regard to the circumstances of the case, including the convenience of the parties.
2. Notwithstanding the provisions of paragraph (1) of this article, the arbitral tribunal may, unless otherwise agreed by the parties, meet at any place it considers appropriate for consultation among its members, for hearing witnesses, experts or the parties, or for inspection of goods, other property or documents.

Article 21 – Commencement of arbitral proceedings

Unless otherwise agreed by the parties, the arbitral proceedings in respect of a particular dispute commence on the date on which a request for that dispute to be referred to arbitration is received by the respondent.

Article 22 – Language

1. The parties are free to agree on the language or languages to be used in the arbitral proceedings. Failing such agreement, the arbitral tribunal

shall determine the language or languages to be used in the proceedings. This agreement or determination, unless otherwise specified therein, shall apply to any written statement by a party, any hearing and any award, decision or other communication by the arbitral tribunal.

2. The arbitral tribunal may order that any documentary evidence shall be accompanied by a translation into the language or languages agreed upon by the parties or determined by the arbitral tribunal.

Article 23 – Statements of claim and defence

1. Within the period of time agreed by the parties or determined by the arbitral tribunal, the claimant shall state the facts supporting his claim, the points at issue and the relief or remedy sought, and the respondent shall state his defence in respect of these particulars, unless the parties have otherwise agreed as to the required elements of such statements. The parties may submit with their statements all documents they consider to be relevant or may add a reference to the documents or other evidence they will submit.

2. Unless otherwise agreed by the parties, either party may amend or supplement his claim or defence during the course of the arbitral proceedings, unless the arbitral tribunal considers it inappropriate to allow such amendment having regard to the delay in making it.

Article 24 – Hearings and written proceedings

1. Subject to any contrary agreement by the parties, the arbitral tribunal shall decide whether to hold oral hearings for the presentation of evidence or for oral argument, or whether the proceedings shall be conducted on the basis of documents and other materials. However, unless the parties have agreed that no hearings shall be held, the arbitral tribunal shall hold such hearings at an appropriate stage of the proceedings, if so requested by a party.

2. The parties shall be given sufficient advance notice of any hearing and of any meeting of the arbitral tribunal for the purposes of inspection of goods, other property or documents.

3. All statements, documents or other information supplied to the arbitral tribunal by one party shall be communicated to the other party. Also any expert report or evidentiary document on which the arbitral tribunal may rely in making its decision shall be communicated to the parties.

Article 25 – Default of a party

Unless otherwise agreed by the parties, if, without showing sufficient cause,

(a) the claimant fails to communicate his statement of claim in accordance with article 23 (1), the arbitral tribunal shall terminate the proceedings;

(b) the respondent fails to communicate his statement of defence in accordance with article 23 (1), the arbitral tribunal shall continue the proceedings without treating such failure in itself as an admission of the claimant's allegations;

(c) any party fails to appear at a hearing or to produce documentary evidence, the arbitral tribunal may continue the proceedings and make the award on the evidence before it.

Article 26 – Expert appointed by arbitral tribunal
1. Unless otherwise agreed by the parties, the arbitral tribunal
   (a) may appoint one or more experts to report to it on specific issues to be determined by the arbitral tribunal;
   (b) may require a party to give the expert any relevant information or to produce, or to provide access to, any relevant documents, goods or other property for his inspection.
2. Unless otherwise agreed by the parties, if a party so requests or if the arbitral tribunal considers it necessary, the expert shall, after delivery of his written or oral report, participate in a hearing where the parties have the opportunity to put questions to him and to present expert witnesses in order to testify on the points at issue.

Article 27 – Court assistance in taking evidence
The arbitral tribunal or a party with the approval of the arbitral tribunal may request from a competent court of this State assistance in taking evidence. The court may execute the request within its competence and according to its rules on taking evidence.

CHAPTER VI – MAKING OF AWARD AND TERMINATION OF PROCEEDINGS

Article 28 – Rules applicable to substance of dispute
1. The arbitral tribunal shall decide the dispute in accordance with such rules of law as are chosen by the parties as applicable to the substance of the dispute. Any designation of the law or legal system of a given State shall be construed, unless otherwise expressed, as directly referring to the substantive law of that State and not to its conflict of laws rules.
2. Failing any designation by the parties, the arbitral tribunal shall apply the law determined by the conflict of laws rules which it considers applicable.
3. The arbitral tribunal shall decide ex aequo et bono or as amiable compositeur only if the parties have expressly authorized it to do so.
4. In all cases, the arbitral tribunal shall decide in accordance with the terms of the contract and shall take into account the usages of the trade applicable to the transaction.

Article 29 – Decision-making by panel of arbitrators

In arbitral proceedings with more than one arbitrator, any decision of the arbitral tribunal shall be made, unless otherwise agreed by the parties, by a majority of all its members. However, questions of procedure may be decided by a presiding arbitrator, if so authorized by the parties or all members of the arbitral tribunal.

Article 30 – Settlement

1. If, during arbitral proceedings, the parties settle the dispute, the arbitral tribunal shall terminate the proceedings and, if requested by the parties and not objected to by the arbitral tribunal, record the settlement in the form of an arbitral award on agreed terms.
2. An award on agreed terms shall be made in accordance with the provisions of article 31 and shall state that it is an award. Such an award has the same status and effect as any other award on the merits of the case.

Article 31 – Form and contents of award

1. The award shall be made in writing and shall be signed by the arbitrator or arbitrators. In arbitrator proceedings with more than one arbitrator, the signatures of the majority of all members of the arbitral tribunal shall suffice, provided that the reason for any omitted signature is stated.
2. The award shall state the reasons upon which it is based, unless the parties have agreed that no reasons are to be given or the award is an award on agreed terms under article 30.
3. The award shall state its date and the place of arbitration as determined in accordance with article 20 (1). The award shall be deemed to have been made at that place.
4. After the award is made, a copy signed by the arbitrators in accordance with paragraph (1) of this article shall be delivered to each party.

Article 32 – Termination of proceedings

1. The arbitral proceedings are terminated by the final award or by an order of the arbitral tribunal in accordance with paragraph (2) of this article.
2. The arbitral tribunal shall issue an order for the termination of the arbitral proceedings when:
   (a) the claimant withdraws his claim, unless the respondent objects thereto and the arbitral tribunal recognizes a legitimate interest on his part in obtaining a final settlement of the dispute;
   (b) the parties agree on the termination of the proceedings;
   (c) the arbitral tribunal finds that the continuation of the proceedings has for any other reason become unnecessary or impossible.

3. The mandate of the arbitral tribunal terminates with the termination of the arbitral proceedings, subject to the provisions of articles 33 and 34 (4).

Article 33 – Correction of interpretation of award; additional award

1. Within thirty days of receipt of the award, unless another period of time has been agreed upon by the parties:
   (a) a party, with notice to the other party, may request the arbitral tribunal to correct in the award any errors in computation, any clerical or typographical errors or any errors of similar nature;
   (b) if so agreed by the parties, a party, with notice to the other party, may request the arbitral tribunal to give an interpretation of a specific point or part of the award. If the arbitral tribunal considers the request to be justified, it shall make the correction or give the interpretation within thirty days of receipt of the request. The interpretation shall form part of the award.
2. The arbitral tribunal may correct any error of the type referred to in paragraph (1) (a) of this article on its own initiative within thirty days of the day of the award.
3. Unless otherwise agreed by the parties, a party, with notice to the other party, may request, within thirty days of receipt of the award, the arbitral tribunal to make an additional award as to claims presented in the arbitral proceedings but omitted from the award. If the arbitral tribunal considers the request to be justified, it shall make the additional award within sixty days.
4. The arbitral tribunal may extend, if necessary, the period of time within which it shall make a correction, interpretation or an additional award under paragraph (1) or (3) of this article.
5. The provisions of article 31 shall apply to a correction or interpretation of the award or to an additional award.

CHAPTER VII – RECOURSE AGAINST AWARD

Article 34 – Application for setting aside as exclusive recourse against arbitral award

1. Recourse to a court against an arbitral award may be made only by an application for setting aside in accordance with paragraphs (2) and (3) of this article.
2. An arbitral award may be set aside by the court specified in article 6 only if:
   (a) the party making the application furnishes proof that:

(i) a party to the arbitration agreement referred to in article 7 was under some incapacity; or the said agreement is not valid under the law to which the parties have subjected it or, failing any indication thereon, under the law of this State; or

(ii) the party making the application was not given proper notice of the appointment of an arbitrator or of the arbitral proceedings or was otherwise unable to present his case; or

(iii) the award deals with a dispute not contemplated by or not falling within the terms of the submission to arbitration, or contains decisions on matters beyond the scope of the submission to arbitration, provided that, if the decisions on matters submitted to arbitration can be separated from those not so submitted, only that part of the award which contains decisions on matters not submitted to arbitration may be set aside; or

(iv) the composition of the arbitral tribunal or the arbitral procedure was not in accordance with the agreement of the parties, unless such agreement was in conflict with a provision of this Law from which the parties cannot derogate, or, failing such agreement, was not in accordance with this Law; or

(b) the court finds that:

(i) the subject-matter of the dispute is not capable of settlement by arbitration under the law of this State; or

(ii) the award is in conflict with the public policy of this State.

3. An application for setting aside may not be made after three months have elapsed from the date on which the party making that application had received that award or, if a request had been made under article 33, from the date on which that request had been disposed of by the arbitral tribunal.

4. The court, when asked to set aside an award, may, where appropriate and so requested by a party, suspend the setting aside proceedings for a period of time determined by it in order to give the arbitral tribunal an opportunity to resume the arbitral proceedings or to take such other action as in the arbitral tribunal's opinion will eliminate the grounds for setting aside.

CHAPTER VIII – RECOGNITION AND ENFORCEMENT OF AWARDS

Article 35 – Recognition and enforcement

1. An arbitral award, irrespective of the country in which it was made, shall be recognized as binding and, upon application in writing to the competent court, shall be enforced subject to the provisions of this article and of article 36.

2. The party relying on an award or applying for its enforcement shall supply the duly authenticated original award or a duly certified copy thereof, and the original arbitration agreement referred to in article 7 or a duly certified copy thereof. If the award or agreement is not made in an official language of this State, the party shall supply a duly certified translation thereof into such language.

Article 36 – Grounds for refusing recognition or enforcement

1. Recognition or enforcement of an arbitral award, irrespective of the country in which it was made, may be refused only:
   (a) at the request of the party against whom it is invoked, if that party furnishes to the competent court where recognition or enforcement is sought proof that:
      (i) a party to the arbitration agreement referred to in article 7 was under some incapacity; or the said agreement is not valid under the law to which the parties have subjected it or, failing any indication thereon, under the law of the country where the award was made; or
      (ii) the party against whom the award is invoked was not given proper notice of the appointment of an arbitrator or of the arbitrator proceedings or was otherwise unable to present his case; or
      (iii) the award deals with a dispute not contemplated by or not falling within the terms of the submission to arbitration, or it contains decisions on matters beyond the scope of the submission to arbitration, provided that, if the decisions on matters submitted to arbitration can be separated from those not so submitted, that part of the award which contains decisions on matters submitted to arbitration may be recognized and enforced; or
      (iv) the composition of the arbitral tribunal or the arbitral procedure was not in accordance with the agreement of the parties or, failing such agreement, was not in accordance with the law of the country where the arbitration took place; or
      (v) the award has not yet become binding on the parties or has been set aside or suspended by a court of the country in which, or under the law of which, that award was made; or
   (b) if the court finds that:
      (i) the subject-matter of the dispute is not capable of settlement by arbitration under the law of this State; or
      (ii) the recognition or enforcement of the award would be contrary to the public policy of this State.

2. If an application for setting aside or suspension of an award has been made to a court referred to in paragraph (1) (a) (v) of this article, the court where recognition or enforcement is sought may, if it considers it proper, adjourn its decision and may also, on the application of the party claiming recognition or enforcement of the award, order the other party to provide appropriate security.

Revised Articles of the UNCITRAL Model Law on International Commercial Arbitration (2006)

Reprinted with permission of UNCITRAL

Document N° 25 / 276

A/61/17(SUPP).

[Article 1, paragraph 2]

2. The provisions of this Law, except articles 8, 9, 17 H, 17 I, 17 J, 35 and 36, apply only if the place of arbitration is in the territory of this State.

Article 2 A. International origin and general principles

1. In the interpretation of this Law, regard is to be had to its international origin and to the need to promote uniformity in its application and the observance of good faith.
2. Questions concerning matters governed by this Law which are not expressly settled in it are to be settled in conformity with the general principles on which this Law is based.

[Article 7]

OPTION I

Article 7. Definition and form of arbitration agreement

1. "Arbitration agreement" is an agreement by the parties to submit to arbitration all or certain disputes which have arisen or which may arise between them in respect of a defined legal relationship, whether contractual or not. An arbitration agreement may be in the form of an arbitration clause in a contract or in the form of a separate agreement.
2. The arbitration agreement shall be in writing.

3. An arbitration agreement is in writing if its content is recorded in any form, whether or not the arbitration agreement or contract has been concluded orally, by conduct, or by other means.
4. The requirement that an arbitration agreement be in writing is met by an electronic communication if the information contained therein is accessible so as to be useable for subsequent reference; "electronic communication" means any communication that the parties make by means of data messages; "data message" means information generated, sent, received or stored by electronic, magnetic, optical or similar means, including, but not limited to, electronic data interchange (EDI), electronic mail, telegram, telex or telecopy.
5. Furthermore, an arbitration agreement is in writing if it is contained in an exchange of statements of claim and defence in which the existence of an agreement is alleged by one party and not denied by the other.
6. The reference in a contract to any document containing an arbitration clause constitutes an arbitration agreement in writing, provided that the reference is such as to make that clause part of the contract.

OPTION II

Article 7. Definition of arbitration agreement
"Arbitration agreement" is an agreement by the parties to submit to arbitration all or certain disputes which have arisen or which may arise between them in respect of a defined legal relationship, whether contractual or not.

CHAPTER IV A. INTERIM MEASURES AND PRELIMINARY ORDERS

Section 1. Interim measures

Article 17. Power of arbitral tribunal to order interim measures
1. Unless otherwise agreed by the parties, the arbitral tribunal may, at the request of a party, grant interim measures.
2. An interim measure is any temporary measure, whether in the form of an award or in another form, by which, at any time prior to the issuance of the award by which the dispute is finally decided, the arbitral tribunal orders a party to:
   (a) Maintain or restore the status quo pending determination of the dispute;
   (b) Take action that would prevent, or refrain from taking action that is likely to cause, current or imminent harm or prejudice to the arbitral process itself;

(c) Provide a means of preserving assets out of which a subsequent award may be satisfied; or

(d) Preserve evidence that may be relevant and material to the resolution of the dispute.

Article 17 A. Conditions for granting interim measures

1. The party requesting an interim measure under article 17, paragraph 2 (a), (b) and (c) shall satisfy the arbitral tribunal that:

   (a) Harm not adequately reparable by an award of damages is likely to result if the measure is not ordered, and such harm substantially outweighs the harm that is likely to result to the party against whom the measure is directed if the measure is granted; and

   (b) There is a reasonable possibility that the requesting party will succeed on the merits of the claim. The determination on this possibility shall not affect the discretion of the arbitral tribunal in making any subsequent determination.

2. With regard to a request for an interim measure under article 17, paragraph 2 (d), the requirements in paragraph 1 (a) and (b) of this article shall apply only to the extent the arbitral tribunal considers appropriate.

Section 2. Preliminary orders

Article 17 B. Applications for preliminary orders and conditions for granting preliminary orders

1. Unless otherwise agreed by the parties, a party may, without notice to any other party, make a request for an interim measure together with an application for a preliminary order directing a party not to frustrate the purpose of the interim measure requested.

2. The arbitral tribunal may grant a preliminary order provided it considers that prior disclosure of the request for the interim measure to the party against whom it is directed risks frustrating the purpose of the measure.

3. The conditions defined under article 17 A apply to any preliminary order, provided that the harm to be assessed under article 17 A, paragraph 1 (a), is the harm likely to result from the order being granted or not.

Article 17 C. Specific regime for preliminary orders

1. Immediately after the arbitral tribunal has made a determination in respect of an application for a preliminary order, the arbitral tribunal shall give notice to all parties of the request for the interim measure, the application for the preliminary order, the preliminary order, if any, and all other communications, including by indicating the content of any oral communication, between any party and the arbitral tribunal in relation thereto.

2. At the same time, the arbitral tribunal shall give an opportunity to any party against whom a preliminary order is directed to present its case at the earliest practicable time.

3. The arbitral tribunal shall decide promptly on any objection to the preliminary order.

4. A preliminary order shall expire after twenty days from the date on which it was issued by the arbitral tribunal. However, the arbitral tribunal may issue an interim measure adopting or modifying the preliminary order, after the party against whom the preliminary order is directed has been given notice and an opportunity to present its case.

5. A preliminary order shall be binding on the parties but shall not be subject to enforcement by a court. Such a preliminary order does not constitute an award.

Section 3. Provisions applicable to interim measures and preliminary orders

Article 17 D. Modification, suspension, termination

The arbitral tribunal may modify, suspend or terminate an interim measure or a preliminary order it has granted, upon application of any party or, in exceptional circumstances and upon prior notice to the parties, on the arbitral tribunal's own initiative.

Article 17 E. Provision of security

1. The arbitral tribunal may require the party requesting an interim measure to provide appropriate security in connection with the measure.

2. The arbitral tribunal shall require the party applying for a preliminary order to provide security in connection with the order unless the arbitral tribunal considers it inappropriate or unnecessary to do so.

Article 17 F. Disclosure

1. The arbitral tribunal may require any party promptly to disclose any material change in the circumstances on the basis of which the measure was requested or granted.

2. The party applying for a preliminary order shall disclose to the arbitral tribunal all circumstances that are likely to be relevant to the arbitral tribunal's determination whether to grant or maintain the order, and such obligation shall continue until the party against whom the order has been requested has had an opportunity to present its case. Thereafter, paragraph 1 of this article shall apply.

Article 17 G. Costs and damages

The party requesting an interim measure or applying for a preliminary order shall be liable for any costs and damages caused by the measure or the order to any party if the arbitral tribunal later determines that, in the circumstances, the measure or the order should not have been granted. The arbitral tribunal may award such costs and damages at any point during the proceedings.

SECTION 4. RECOGNITION AND ENFORCEMENT OF INTERIM MEASURES

Article 17 H. Recognition and enforcement

1. An interim measure issued by an arbitral tribunal shall be recognized as binding and, unless otherwise provided by the arbitral tribunal, enforced upon application to the competent court, irrespective of the country in which it was issued, subject to the provisions of article 17 I.
2. The party who is seeking or has obtained recognition or enforcement of an interim measure shall promptly inform the court of any termination, suspension or modification of that interim measure.
3. The court of the State where recognition or enforcement is sought may, if it considers it proper, order the requesting party to provide appropriate security if the arbitral tribunal has not already made a determination with respect to security or where such a decision is necessary to protect the rights of third parties.

Article 17 I. Grounds for refusing recognition or enforcement*

1. Recognition or enforcement of an interim measure may be refused only:
   (a) At the request of the party against whom it is invoked if the court is satisfied that:
       (i) Such refusal is warranted on the grounds set forth in article 36, paragraph 1 (a)(i), (ii), (iii) or (iv); or
       (ii) The arbitral tribunal's decision with respect to the provision of security in connection with the interim measure issued by the arbitral tribunal has not been complied with; or
       (iii) The interim measure has been terminated or suspended by the arbitral tribunal or, where so empowered, by the court of the State in which the arbitration takes place or under the law of which that interim measure was granted; or
   (b) If the court finds that:
       (i) The interim measure is incompatible with the powers conferred upon the court unless the court decides to reformulate the interim measure to the extent necessary to adapt it to its own powers and

---

* The conditions set worth in 17 I are intended to limit the number of circumstances in which the court may refuse to enforce an interim measure. It would not be contrary to the level of harmonization sought to be achieved by these model provisions if a state were to adopt fewer circumstances in which enforcement may be refused.

procedures for the purposes of enforcing that interim measure and without modifying its substance; or

(ii) Any of the grounds set forth in article 36, paragraph 1 (b)(i) or (ii), apply to the recognition and enforcement of the interim measure.

2. Any determination made by the court on any ground in paragraph 1 of this article shall be effective only for the purposes of the application to recognize and enforce the interim measure. The court where recognition or enforcement is sought shall not, in making that determination, undertake a review of the substance of the interim measure.

Section 5. Court-ordered interim measures

Article 17 J. Court-ordered interim measures

A court shall have the same power of issuing an interim measure in relation to arbitration proceedings, irrespective of whether their place is in the territory of this State, as it has in relation to proceedings in courts. The court shall exercise such power in accordance with its own procedures in consideration of the specific features of international arbitration.

[Article 35, paragraph 2]

2. The party relying on an award or applying for its enforcement shall supply the original award or a copy thereof. If the award is not made in an official language of this State, the court may request the party to supply a translation thereof into such language.

UNCITRAL Recommendation Regarding the Interpretation of Article II, Paragraph 2, and Article VII, Paragraph 1, of the New York Convention

Reprinted with permission of UNCITRAL
Document N° 25 / 276
A/61/17(SUPP).

Recommendation regarding the interpretation of article II, paragraph 2, and article VII, paragraph 1, of the Convention on the Recognition and Enforcement of Foreign Arbitral Awards, done in New York, 10 June 1958, adopted by the United Nations Commission on International Trade Law on 7 July 2006 at its thirty-ninth session.

The United Nations Commission on International Trade Law,

Recalling General Assembly resolution 2205 (XXI) of 17 December 1966, which established the United Nations Commission on International Trade Law with the object of promoting the progressive harmonization and unification of the law of international trade by, inter alia, promoting ways and means of ensuring a uniform interpretation and application of international conventions and uniform laws in the field of the law of international trade,
  Conscious of the fact that the different legal, social and economic systems of the world, together with different levels of development, are represented in the Commission,
  Recalling successive resolutions of the General Assembly reaffirming the mandate of the Commission as the core legal body within the United Nations system in the field of international trade law to coordinate legal activities in this field,
  Convinced that the wide adoption of the Convention on the Recognition and Enforcement of Foreign Arbitral Awards, done in New York on 10 June

1958,[1] has been a significant achievement in the promotion of the rule of law, particularly in the field of international trade,

Recalling that the Conference of Plenipotentiaries which prepared and opened the Convention for signature adopted a resolution, which states, inter alia, that the Conference "considers that greater uniformity of national laws on arbitration would further the effectiveness of arbitration in the settlement of private law disputes,"

Bearing in mind differing interpretations of the form requirements under the Convention that result in part from differences of expression as between the five equally authentic texts of the Convention,

Taking into account article VII, paragraph 1, of the Convention, a purpose of which is to enable the enforcement of foreign arbitral awards to the greatest extent, in particular by recognizing the right of any interested party to avail itself of law or treaties of the country where the award is sought to be relied upon, including where such law or treaties offer a regime more favourable than the Convention,

Considering the wide use of electronic commerce,

Taking into account international legal instruments, such as the 1985 UNCITRAL Model Law on International Commercial Arbitration,[2] as subsequently revised, particularly with respect to article 7,[3] the UNCITRAL Model Law on Electronic Commerce,[4] the UNCITRAL Model Law on Electronic Signatures[5] and the United Nations Convention on the Use of Electronic Communications in International Contracts,[6]

Taking into account also enactments of domestic legislation, as well as case law, more favourable than the Convention in respect of form requirement governing arbitration agreements, arbitration proceedings and the enforcement of arbitral awards,

Considering that, in interpreting the Convention, regard is to be had to the need to promote recognition and enforcement of arbitral awards,

1. *Recommends* that article II, paragraph 2, of the Convention on the Recognition and Enforcement of Foreign Arbitral Awards, done in New York,

---

[1] United Nations, *Treaty Series*, vol. 330, No. 4739.
[2] *Official Records of the General Assembly, Fortieth Session, Supplement No. 17* (A/40/17), annex I, and United Nations publication, Sales No. E.95.V.18.
[3] *Ibid., Sixty-first Session, Supplement No. 17* (A/61/17), annex I.
[4] *Ibid., Fifty-first Session, Supplement No. 17* (A/51/17), annex I, and United Nations publication, Sales No. E.99.V.4, which contains also an additional article 5 bis, adopted in 1998, and the accompanying Guide to Enactment.
[5] *Ibid., Fifty-sixth Session, Supplement No. 17* and corrigendum (A/56/17 and Corr. 3), annex II, and United Nations publication, Sales No. E.02.V.8, which contains also the accompanying Guide to Enactment.
[6] General Assembly resolution 60/21, annex.

10 June 1958, be applied recognizing that the circumstances described therein are not exhaustive;

2. *Recommends also* that article VII, paragraph 1, of the Convention on the Recognition and Enforcement of Foreign Arbitral Awards, done in New York, 10 June 1958, should be applied to allow any interested party to avail itself of rights it may have, under the law or treaties of the country where an arbitration agreement is sought to be relied upon, to seek recognition of the validity of such an arbitration agreement.

IBA Rules on the Taking of Evidence in International Arbitration

The *IBA Rules on the Taking of Evidence in International Arbitration* is reproduced by kind permission of the International Bar Association, London, UK.

All Rights Reserved

© International Bar Association, 2010

IBA Rules on the Taking of Evidence in International Arbitration

Adopted by a resolution of
the IBA Council
29 May 2010
International Bar Association

the global voice of
the legal profession®

International Bar Association
10th Floor, 1 Stephen Street
London W1T 1AT
United Kingdom
Tel: +44 (0)20 7691 6868
Fax: +44 (0)20 7691 6544
www.ibanet.org

ISBN: 978 0 948711 54X

All Rights Reserved
© International Bar Association 2010

No part of the material protected by this copyright notice
may be reproduced or utilized in any form or by any
means, electronic or mechanical, including photocopying,
recording, or any information storage and retrieval system,
without written permission from the copyright owner.

Contents

the global voice of
the legal profession®

Members of the Working Party

David W Rivkin
Chair, SBL Committee D
(Arbitration and ADR)
Debevoise & Plimpton LLP,
New York, USA

Wolfgang Kühn
Former Chair,
SBL Committee D
Heuking Kühn Lüer Wojtek,
Düsseldorf, Germany

Giovanni M Ughi
Chair
Ughi e Nunziante Studio Legale,
Milan, Italy

Hans Bagner
Advokatfirman Vinge KB,
Stockholm, Sweden

John Beechey
International Chamber of Commerce,
Paris, France

Jacques Buhart
Herbert Smith LLP,
Paris, France

Peter S Caldwell
Caldwell Ltd,
Hong Kong

i

Bernardo M Cremades
B Cremades y Asociados,
Madrid, Spain

Emmanuel Gaillard
Shearman & Sterling LLP,
Paris, France

Paul A Gélinas
Gélinas & Co,
Paris, France

Hans van Houtte
Katholieke Universiteit Leuven,
Leuven, Belgium

Pierre A Karrer
Zurich, Switzerland

Jan Paulsson
Freshfields Bruckhaus Deringer LLP,
Paris, France

Hilmar Raeschke-Kessler
Rechtsanwalt beim Bundesgerichtshof,
Karlsruhe-Ettlingen, Germany

V V Veeder, QC
Essex Court Chambers,
London, England

O L O de Witt Wijnen
Nauta Dutilh,
Rotterdam, Netherlands

Members of the IBA Rules of Evidence Review Subcommittee

Richard H Kreindler
  Chair
  Review Subcommittee
  Shearman & Sterling LLP,
  Frankfurt, Germany

David Arias
  Pérez-Llorca,
  Madrid, Spain

C Mark Baker
  Fulbright & Jaworski LLP,
  Houston, Texas, USA

Pierre Bienvenu
  Co-Chair 2008-2009
  Arbitration Committee
  Ogilvy Renault LLP,
  Montréal, Canada

Amy Cohen Kläsener
  Review Subcommittee Secretary
  Shearman & Sterling LLP,
  Frankfurt, Germany

Antonias Dimolitsa
  Antonias Dimolitsa & Associates,
  Athens, Greece

iii

Paul Friedland
White & Case LLP,
New York, USA

Nicolás Gamboa
Gamboa & Chalela Abogados,
Bogotá, Colombia

Judith Gill, QC
Co-Chair 2010-2011
Arbitration Committee
Allen & Overy LLP
London, England

Peter Heckel
Hengeler Mueller Partnerschaft von Rechtsanwälten,
Frankfurt, Germany

Stephen Jagusch
Allen & Overy LLP,
London, England

Xiang Ji
Fangda Partners,
Beijing & Shanghai, China

Kap-You (Kevin) Kim
Bae, Kim & Lee LLC,
Seoul, South Korea

Toby T Landau, QC
Essex Court Chambers,
London, England

Alexis Mourre
Castaldi Mourre & Partners,
Paris, France

Hilmar Raeschke-Kessler
Rechtsanwalt beim Bundesgerichtshof,
Karlsruhe-Ettlingen, Germany

David W Rivkin
Debevoise & Plimpton LLP,
New York, USA

Georg von Segesser
Schellenberg Wittmer,
Zurich, Switzerland

Essam Al Tamimi
Al Tamimi & Company,
Dubai, UAE

Guido S Tawil
Co-Chair 2009-2010
Arbitration Committee
M & M Bomchil Abogados,
Buenos Aires, Argentina

Hiroyuki Tezuka
Nishimura & Asahi,
Tokyo, Japan

Ariel Ye
King & Wood,
Beijing, China

About the
Arbitration Committee

Established as the Committee in the International Bar Association's Legal Practice Division which focuses on the laws, practice and procedures relating to the arbitration of transnational disputes, the Arbitration Committee currently has over 2,300 members from over 90 countries, and membership is increasing steadily.

Through its publications and conferences, the Committee seeks to share information about international arbitration, promote its use and improve its effectiveness. The Committee maintains standing subcommittees and, as appropriate, establishes Task Forces to address specific issues. At the time of issuance of these revised Rules, the Committee has four subcommittees, namely the Rules of Evidence Subcommittee, the Investment Treaty Arbitration Subcommittee, the Conflicts of Interest Subcommittee, and the Recognition and Enforcement of Arbitral Awards Subcommittee; and two task forces: the Task Force on Attorney Ethics in Arbitration and the Task Force on Arbitration Agreements.

Foreword

These IBA Rules on the Taking of Evidence in International Arbitration ('IBA Rules of Evidence') are a revised version of the IBA Rules on the Taking of Evidence in International Commercial Arbitration, prepared by a Working Party of the Arbitration Committee whose members are listed on pages i and ii.

The IBA issued these Rules as a resource to parties and to arbitrators to provide an efficient, economical and fair process for the taking of evidence in international arbitration. The Rules provide mechanisms for the presentation of documents, witnesses of fact and expert witnesses, inspections, as well as the conduct of evidentiary hearings. The Rules are designed to be used in conjunction with, and adopted together with, institutional, ad hoc or other rules or procedures governing international arbitrations. The IBA Rules of Evidence reflect procedures in use in many different legal systems, and they may be particularly useful when the parties come from different legal cultures.

Since their issuance in 1999, the IBA Rules on the Taking of Evidence in International Commercial Arbitration have gained wide acceptance within the international arbitral community. In 2008, a review process was initiated at the instance of Sally Harpole and Pierre Bienvenu, the then Co-Chairs of the Arbitration Committee. The revised version of the IBA Rules of Evidence was developed by the members of the IBA Rules of Evidence Review Sub-committee, assisted by members of the 1999 Working Party. These revised Rules replace the IBA Rules on the Taking of Evidence in International Commercial Arbitration, which themselves replaced the IBA Supplementary Rules Governing the Presentation and Reception of Evidence in International Commercial Arbitration, issued in 1983.

If parties wish to adopt the IBA Rules of Evidence in their arbitration clause, it is recommended that they add the following language to the clause, selecting one of the alternatives therein provided:

'*[In addition to the institutional, ad hoc or other rules chosen by the parties,] [t]he parties agree that the arbitration shall be conducted according to the IBA Rules of Evidence as current on the date of [this agreement/the commencement of the arbitration].*'

2

In addition, parties and Arbitral Tribunals may adopt the IBA Rules of Evidence, in whole or in part, at the commencement of the arbitration, or at any time thereafter. They may also vary them or use them as guidelines in developing their own procedures.

The IBA Rules of Evidence were adopted by resolution of the IBA Council on 29 May 2010. The IBA Rules of Evidence are available in English, and translations in other languages are planned. Copies of the IBA Rules of Evidence may be ordered from the IBA, and the Rules are available to download at **http://tinyurl.com/iba-Arbitration-Guidelines.**

Guido S Tawil
Judith Gill, QC
Co-Chairs, Arbitration Committee
29 May 2010

The Rules

Preamble

1. These IBA Rules on the Taking of Evidence in International Arbitration are intended to provide an efficient, economical and fair process for the taking of evidence in international arbitrations, particularly those between Parties from different legal traditions. They are designed to supplement the legal provisions and the institutional, ad hoc or other rules that apply to the conduct of the arbitration.
2. Parties and Arbitral Tribunals may adopt the IBA Rules of Evidence, in whole or in part, to govern arbitration proceedings, or they may vary them or use them as guidelines in developing their own procedures. The Rules are not intended to limit the flexibility that is inherent in, and an advantage of, international arbitration, and Parties and Arbitral Tribunals are free to adapt them to the particular circumstances of each arbitration.
3. The taking of evidence shall be conducted on the principles that each Party shall act in good faith and be entitled to know, reasonably in advance of any Evidentiary Hearing or any fact or merits determination, the evidence on which the other Parties rely.

Definitions

In the IBA Rules of Evidence:

'*Arbitral Tribunal*' means a sole arbitrator or a panel of arbitrators;

'*Claimant*' means the Party or Parties who commenced the arbitration and any Party who, through joinder or otherwise, becomes aligned with such Party or Parties;

'*Document*' means a writing, communication, picture, drawing, program or data of any kind, whether recorded or maintained on paper or by electronic, audio, visual or any other means;

'*Evidentiary Hearing*' means any hearing, whether or not held on consecutive days, at which the Arbitral Tribunal, whether in person, by teleconference, videoconference or other method, receives oral or other evidence;

'*Expert Report*' means a written statement by a Tribunal-Appointed Expert or a Party-Appointed Expert;

'*General Rules*' mean the institutional, ad hoc or other rules that apply to the conduct of the arbitration;

'*IBA Rules of Evidence*' or '*Rules*' means these IBA Rules on the Taking of Evidence in International Arbitration, as they may be revised or amended from time to time;

'*Party*' means a party to the arbitration;

'*Party-Appointed Expert*' means a person or organisation appointed by a Party in order to report on specific issues determined by the Party;

'*Request to Produce*' means a written request by a Party that another Party produce Documents;

'*Respondent*' means the Party or Parties against whom the Claimant made its claim, and any Party who, through joinder or otherwise, becomes aligned with such Party or Parties, and includes a Respondent making a counter-claim;

'*Tribunal-Appointed Expert*' means a person or organisation appointed by the Arbitral Tribunal in order to report to it on specific issues determined by the Arbitral Tribunal; and

'*Witness Statement*' means a written statement of testimony by a witness of fact.

Article 1   Scope of Application

1. Whenever the Parties have agreed or the Arbitral Tribunal has determined to apply the IBA Rules of Evidence, the Rules shall govern the taking of evidence, except to the extent that any specific provision of them may be found to be in conflict with any mandatory provision of law determined to be applicable to the case by the Parties or by the Arbitral Tribunal.
2. Where the Parties have agreed to apply the IBA Rules of Evidence, they shall be deemed to have agreed, in the absence of a contrary indication, to the version as current on the date of such agreement.
3. In case of conflict between any provisions of the IBA Rules of Evidence and the General Rules, the Arbitral Tribunal shall apply the IBA Rules of Evidence in the manner that it determines best in order to accomplish the purposes of both the General Rules and the IBA Rules of Evidence, unless the Parties agree to the contrary.
4. In the event of any dispute regarding the meaning of the IBA Rules of Evidence, the Arbitral Tribunal shall interpret them according to their purpose and in the manner most appropriate for the particular arbitration.

5. Insofar as the IBA Rules of Evidence and the General Rules are silent on any matter concerning the taking of evidence and the Parties have not agreed otherwise, the Arbitral Tribunal shall conduct the taking of evidence as it deems appropriate, in accordance with the general principles of the IBA Rules of Evidence.

Article 2   Consultation on Evidentiary Issues

1. The Arbitral Tribunal shall consult the Parties at the earliest appropriate time in the proceedings and invite them to consult each other with a view to agreeing on an efficient, economical and fair process for the taking of evidence.
2. The consultation on evidentiary issues may address the scope, timing and manner of the taking of evidence, including:
   (a) the preparation and submission of Witness Statements and Expert Reports;
   (b) the taking of oral testimony at any Evidentiary Hearing;
   (c) the requirements, procedure and format applicable to the production of Documents;
   (d) the level of confidentiality protection to be afforded to evidence in the arbitration; and
   (e) the promotion of efficiency, economy and conservation of resources in connection with the taking of evidence.
3. The Arbitral Tribunal is encouraged to identify to the Parties, as soon as it considers it to be appropriate, any issues:
   (a) that the Arbitral Tribunal may regard as relevant to the case and material to its outcome; and/or
   (b) for which a preliminary determination may be appropriate.

Article 3   Documents

1. Within the time ordered by the Arbitral Tribunal, each Party shall submit to the Arbitral Tribunal and to the other Parties all Documents available to it on which it relies, including public Documents and those in the public domain, except for any Documents that have already been submitted by another Party.
2. Within the time ordered by the Arbitral Tribunal, any Party may submit to the Arbitral Tribunal and to the other Parties a Request to Produce.
3. A Request to Produce shall contain:
   (a) *(i)* a description of each requested Document sufficient to identify it, or

(ii) a description in sufficient detail (including subject matter) of a narrow and specific requested category of Documents that are reasonably believed to exist; in the case of Documents maintained in electronic form, the requesting Party may, or the Arbitral Tribunal may order that it shall be required to, identify specific files, search terms, individuals or other means of searching for such Documents in an efficient and economical manner;

(b) a statement as to how the Documents requested are relevant to the case and material to its outcome; and

(c) *(i)* a statement that the Documents requested are not in the possession, custody or control of the requesting Party or a statement of the reasons why it would be unreasonably burdensome for the requesting Party to produce such Documents, and

(ii) a statement of the reasons why the requesting Party assumes the Documents requested are in the possession, custody or control of another Party.

4. Within the time ordered by the Arbitral Tribunal, the Party to whom the Request to Produce is addressed shall produce to the other Parties and, if the Arbitral Tribunal so orders, to it, all the Documents requested in its possession, custody or control as to which it makes no objection.

5. If the Party to whom the Request to Produce is addressed has an objection to some or all of the Documents requested, it shall state the objection in writing to the Arbitral Tribunal and the other Parties within the time ordered by the Arbitral Tribunal. The reasons for such objection shall be any of those set forth in Article 9.2 or a failure to satisfy any of the requirements of Article 3.3.

6. Upon receipt of any such objection, the Arbitral Tribunal may invite the relevant Parties to consult with each other with a view to resolving the objection.

7. Either Party may, within the time ordered by the Arbitral Tribunal, request the Arbitral Tribunal to rule on the objection. The Arbitral Tribunal shall then, in consultation with the Parties and in timely fashion, consider the Request to Produce and the objection. The Arbitral Tribunal may order the Party to whom such Request is addressed to produce any requested Document in its possession, custody or control as to which the Arbitral Tribunal determines that *(i)* the issues that the requesting Party wishes to prove are relevant to the case and material to its outcome; *(ii)* none of the reasons for objection set forth in Article 9.2 applies; and *(iii)* the requirements of Article 3.3 have been satisfied. Any such Document shall be produced to the other Parties and, if the Arbitral Tribunal so orders, to it.

8. In exceptional circumstances, if the propriety of an objection can be determined only by review of the Document, the Arbitral Tribunal may determine that it should not review the Document. In that event, the Arbitral Tribunal may, after consultation with the Parties, appoint an independent and impartial expert, bound to confidentiality, to review any such Document and to report on the objection. To the extent that the objection is upheld by the Arbitral Tribunal, the expert shall not disclose to the Arbitral Tribunal and to the other Parties the contents of the Document reviewed.

9. If a Party wishes to obtain the production of Documents from a person or organisation who is not a Party to the arbitration and from whom the Party cannot obtain the Documents on its own, the Party may, within the time ordered by the Arbitral Tribunal, ask it to take whatever steps are legally available to obtain the requested Documents, or seek leave from the Arbitral Tribunal to take such steps itself. The Party shall submit such request to the Arbitral Tribunal and to the other Parties in writing, and the request shall contain the particulars set forth in Article 3.3, as applicable. The Arbitral Tribunal shall decide on this request and shall take, authorize the requesting Party to take, or order any other Party to take, such steps as the Arbitral Tribunal considers appropriate if, in its discretion, it determines that *(i)* the Documents would be relevant to the case and material to its outcome, *(ii)* the requirements of Article 3.3, as applicable, have been satisfied and *(iii)* none of the reasons for objection set forth in Article 9.2 applies.

10. At any time before the arbitration is concluded, the Arbitral Tribunal may *(i)* request any Party to produce Documents, *(ii)* request any Party to use its best efforts to take or *(iii)* itself take, any step that it considers appropriate to obtain Documents from any person or organisation. A Party to whom such a request for Documents is addressed may object to the request for any of the reasons set forth in Article 9.2. In such cases, Article 3.4 to Article 3.8 shall apply correspondingly.

11. Within the time ordered by the Arbitral Tribunal, the Parties may submit to the Arbitral Tribunal and to the other Parties any additional Documents on which they intend to rely or which they believe have become relevant to the case and material to its outcome as a consequence of the issues raised in Documents, Witness Statements or Expert Reports submitted or produced, or in other submissions of the Parties.

12. With respect to the form of submission or production of Documents:
    (a) copies of Documents shall conform to the originals and, at the request of the Arbitral Tribunal, any original shall be presented for inspection;

(b) Documents that a Party maintains in electronic form shall be submitted or produced in the form most convenient or economical to it that is reasonably usable by the recipients, unless the Parties agree otherwise or, in the absence of such agreement, the Arbitral Tribunal decides otherwise;

(c) a Party is not obligated to produce multiple copies of Documents which are essentially identical unless the Arbitral Tribunal decides otherwise; and

(d) translations of Documents shall be submitted together with the originals and marked as translations with the original language identified.

13. Any Document submitted or produced by a Party or non-Party in the arbitration and not otherwise in the public domain shall be kept confidential by the Arbitral Tribunal and the other Parties, and shall be used only in connection with the arbitration. This requirement shall apply except and to the extent that disclosure may be required of a Party to fulfil a legal duty, protect or pursue a legal right, or enforce or challenge an award in bona fide legal proceedings before a state court or other judicial authority. The Arbitral Tribunal may issue orders to set forth the terms of this confidentiality. This requirement shall be without prejudice to all other obligations of confidentiality in the arbitration.

14. If the arbitration is organised into separate issues or phases (such as jurisdiction, preliminary determinations, liability or damages), the Arbitral Tribunal may, after consultation with the Parties, schedule the submission of Documents and Requests to Produce separately for each issue or phase.

Article 4   Witnesses of Fact

1. Within the time ordered by the Arbitral Tribunal, each Party shall identify the witnesses on whose testimony it intends to rely and the subject matter of that testimony.

2. Any person may present evidence as a witness, including a Party or a Party's officer, employee or other representative.

3. It shall not be improper for a Party, its officers, employees, legal advisors or other representatives to interview its witnesses or potential witnesses and to discuss their prospective testimony with them.

4. The Arbitral Tribunal may order each Party to submit within a specified time to the Arbitral Tribunal and to the other Parties Witness Statements by each witness on whose testimony it intends to rely, except for those witnesses whose testimony is sought pursuant to Articles 4.9 or 4.10. If Evidentiary Hearings are organised into separate issues or phases

(such as jurisdiction, preliminary determinations, liability or damages), the Arbitral Tribunal or the Parties by agreement may schedule the submission of Witness Statements separately for each issue or phase.

5. Each Witness Statement shall contain:
   (a) the full name and address of the witness, a statement regarding his or her present and past relationship (if any) with any of the Parties, and a description of his or her background, qualifications, training and experience, if such a description may be relevant to the dispute or to the contents of the statement;
   (b) a full and detailed description of the facts, and the source of the witness's information as to those facts, sufficient to serve as that witness's evidence in the matter in dispute. Documents on which the witness relies that have not already been submitted shall be provided;
   (c) a statement as to the language in which the Witness Statement was originally prepared and the language in which the witness anticipates giving testimony at the Evidentiary Hearing;
   (d) an affirmation of the truth of the Witness Statement; and
   (e) the signature of the witness and its date and place.

6. If Witness Statements are submitted, any Party may, within the time ordered by the Arbitral Tribunal, submit to the Arbitral Tribunal and to the other Parties revised or additional Witness Statements, including statements from persons not previously named as witnesses, so long as any such revisions or additions respond only to matters contained in another Party's Witness Statements, Expert Reports or other submissions that have not been previously presented in the arbitration.

7. If a witness whose appearance has been requested pursuant to Article 8.1 fails without a valid reason to appear for testimony at an Evidentiary Hearing, the Arbitral Tribunal shall disregard any Witness Statement related to that Evidentiary Hearing by that witness unless, in exceptional circumstances, the Arbitral Tribunal decides otherwise.

8. If the appearance of a witness has not been requested pursuant to Article 8.1, none of the other Parties shall be deemed to have agreed to the correctness of the content of the Witness Statement.

9. If a Party wishes to present evidence from a person who will not appear voluntarily at its request, the Party may, within the time ordered by the Arbitral Tribunal, ask it to take whatever steps are legally available to obtain the testimony of that person, or seek leave from the Arbitral Tribunal to take such steps itself. In the case of a request to the Arbitral Tribunal, the Party shall identify the intended witness, shall describe the subjects on which the witness's testimony is sought and shall state why

such subjects are relevant to the case and material to its outcome. The Arbitral Tribunal shall decide on this request and shall take, authorize the requesting Party to take or order any other Party to take, such steps as the Arbitral Tribunal considers appropriate if, in its discretion, it determines that the testimony of that witness would be relevant to the case and material to its outcome.

10. At any time before the arbitration is concluded, the Arbitral Tribunal may order any Party to provide for, or to use its best efforts to provide for, the appearance for testimony at an Evidentiary Hearing of any person, including one whose testimony has not yet been offered. A Party to whom such a request is addressed may object for any of the reasons set forth in Article 9.2.

Article 5 Party-Appointed Experts

1. A Party may rely on a Party-Appointed Expert as a means of evidence on specific issues. Within the time ordered by the Arbitral Tribunal, (i) each Party shall identify any Party-Appointed Expert on whose testimony it intends to rely and the subject-matter of such testimony; and (ii) the Party-Appointed Expert shall submit an Expert Report.

2. The Expert Report shall contain:

   (a) the full name and address of the Party-Appointed Expert, a statement regarding his or her present and past relationship (if any) with any of the Parties, their legal advisors and the Arbitral Tribunal, and a description of his or her background, qualifications, training and experience;

   (b) a description of the instructions pursuant to which he or she is providing his or her opinions and conclusions;

   (c) a statement of his or her independence from the Parties, their legal advisors and the Arbitral Tribunal;

   (d) a statement of the facts on which he or she is basing his or her expert opinions and conclusions;

   (e) his or her expert opinions and conclusions, including a description of the methods, evidence and information used in arriving at the conclusions. Documents on which the Party-Appointed Expert relies that have not already been submitted shall be provided;

   (f) if the Expert Report has been translated, a statement as to the language in which it was originally prepared, and the language in which the Party-Appointed Expert anticipates giving testimony at the Evidentiary Hearing;

(g) an affirmation of his or her genuine belief in the opinions expressed in the Expert Report;

(h) the signature of the Party-Appointed Expert and its date and place; and

(i) if the Expert Report has been signed by more than one person, an attribution of the entirety or specific parts of the Expert Report to each author.

3. If Expert Reports are submitted, any Party may, within the time ordered by the Arbitral Tribunal, submit to the Arbitral Tribunal and to the other Parties revised or additional Expert Reports, including reports or statements from persons not previously identified as Party-Appointed Experts, so long as any such revisions or additions respond only to matters contained in another Party's Witness Statements, Expert Reports or other submissions that have not been previously presented in the arbitration.

4. The Arbitral Tribunal in its discretion may order that any Party-Appointed Experts who will submit or who have submitted Expert Reports on the same or related issues meet and confer on such issues. At such meeting, the Party-Appointed Experts shall attempt to reach agreement on the issues within the scope of their Expert Reports, and they shall record in writing any such issues on which they reach agreement, any remaining areas of disagreement and the reasons therefore.

5. If a Party-Appointed Expert whose appearance has been requested pursuant to Article 8.1 fails without a valid reason to appear for testimony at an Evidentiary Hearing, the Arbitral Tribunal shall disregard any Expert Report by that Party-Appointed Expert related to that Evidentiary Hearing unless, in exceptional circumstances, the Arbitral Tribunal decides otherwise.

6. If the appearance of a Party-Appointed Expert has not been requested pursuant to Article 8.1, none of the other Parties shall be deemed to have agreed to the correctness of the content of the Expert Report.

Article 6   Tribunal-Appointed Experts

1. The Arbitral Tribunal, after consulting with the Parties, may appoint one or more independent Tribunal-Appointed Experts to report to it on specific issues designated by the Arbitral Tribunal. The Arbitral Tribunal shall establish the terms of reference for any Tribunal-Appointed Expert Report after consulting with the Parties. A copy of the final terms of reference shall be sent by the Arbitral Tribunal to the Parties.

2. The Tribunal-Appointed Expert shall, before accepting appointment, submit to the Arbitral Tribunal and to the Parties a description of his or

her qualifications and a statement of his or her independence from the Parties, their legal advisors and the Arbitral Tribunal. Within the time ordered by the Arbitral Tribunal, the Parties shall inform the Arbitral Tribunal whether they have any objections as to the Tribunal-Appointed Expert's qualifications and independence. The Arbitral Tribunal shall decide promptly whether to accept any such objection. After the appointment of a Tribunal-Appointed Expert, a Party may object to the expert's qualifications or independence only if the objection is for reasons of which the Party becomes aware after the appointment has been made. The Arbitral Tribunal shall decide promptly what, if any, action to take.

3. Subject to the provisions of Article 9.2, the Tribunal-Appointed Expert may request a Party to provide any information or to provide access to any Documents, goods, samples, property, machinery, systems, processes or site for inspection, to the extent relevant to the case and material to its outcome. The authority of a Tribunal-Appointed Expert to request such information or access shall be the same as the authority of the Arbitral Tribunal. The Parties and their representatives shall have the right to receive any such information and to attend any such inspection. Any disagreement between a Tribunal-Appointed Expert and a Party as to the relevance, materiality or appropriateness of such a request shall be decided by the Arbitral Tribunal, in the manner provided in Articles 3.5 through 3.8. The Tribunal-Appointed Expert shall record in the Expert Report any non-compliance by a Party with an appropriate request or decision by the Arbitral Tribunal and shall describe its effects on the determination of the specific issue.

4. The Tribunal-Appointed Expert shall report in writing to the Arbitral Tribunal in an Expert Report. The Expert Report shall contain:
   (a) the full name and address of the Tribunal-Appointed Expert, and a description of his or her background, qualifications, training and experience;
   (b) a statement of the facts on which he or she is basing his or her expert opinions and conclusions;
   (c) his or her expert opinions and conclusions, including a description of the methods, evidence and information used in arriving at the conclusions. Documents on which the Tribunal-Appointed Expert relies that have not already been submitted shall be provided;
   (d) if the Expert Report has been translated, a statement as to the language in which it was originally prepared, and the language in which the Tribunal-Appointed Expert anticipates giving testimony at the Evidentiary Hearing;

(e) an affirmation of his or her genuine belief in the opinions expressed in the Expert Report;

(f) the signature of the Tribunal-Appointed Expert and its date and place; and

(g) if the Expert Report has been signed by more than one person, an attribution of the entirety or specific parts of the Expert Report to each author.

5. The Arbitral Tribunal shall send a copy of such Expert Report to the Parties. The Parties may examine any information, Documents, goods, samples, property, machinery, systems, processes or site for inspection that the Tribunal-Appointed Expert has examined and any correspondence between the Arbitral Tribunal and the Tribunal-Appointed Expert. Within the time ordered by the Arbitral Tribunal, any Party shall have the opportunity to respond to the Expert Report in a submission by the Party or through a Witness Statement or an Expert Report by a Party-Appointed Expert. The Arbitral Tribunal shall send the submission, Witness Statement or Expert Report to the Tribunal-Appointed Expert and to the other Parties.

6. At the request of a Party or of the Arbitral Tribunal, the Tribunal-Appointed Expert shall be present at an Evidentiary Hearing. The Arbitral Tribunal may question the Tribunal-Appointed Expert, and he or she may be questioned by the Parties or by any Party-Appointed Expert on issues raised in his or her Expert Report, the Parties' submissions or Witness Statement or the Expert Reports made by the Party-Appointed Experts pursuant to Article 6.5.

7. Any Expert Report made by a Tribunal-Appointed Expert and its conclusions shall be assessed by the Arbitral Tribunal with due regard to all circumstances of the case.

8. The fees and expenses of a Tribunal-Appointed Expert, to be funded in a manner determined by the Arbitral Tribunal, shall form part of the costs of the arbitration.

Article 7 Inspection

Subject to the provisions of Article 9.2, the Arbitral Tribunal may, at the request of a Party or on its own motion, inspect or require the inspection by a Tribunal-Appointed Expert or a Party-Appointed Expert of any site, property, machinery or any other goods, samples, systems, processes or Documents, as it deems appropriate. The Arbitral Tribunal shall, in consultation with the Parties, determine the timing and arrangement for the inspection.

The Parties and their representatives shall have the right to attend any such inspection.

Article 8   Evidentiary Hearing

1. Within the time ordered by the Arbitral Tribunal, each Party shall inform the Arbitral Tribunal and the other Parties of the witnesses whose appearance it requests. Each witness (which term includes, for the purposes of this Article, witnesses of fact and any experts) shall, subject to Article 8.2, appear for testimony at the Evidentiary Hearing if such person's appearance has been requested by any Party or by the Arbitral Tribunal. Each witness shall appear in person unless the Arbitral Tribunal allows the use of videoconference or similar technology with respect to a particular witness.

2. The Arbitral Tribunal shall at all times have complete control over the Evidentiary Hearing. The Arbitral Tribunal may limit or exclude any question to, answer by or appearance of a witness, if it considers such question, answer or appearance to be irrelevant, immaterial, unreasonably burdensome, duplicative or otherwise covered by a reason for objection set forth in Article 9.2. Questions to a witness during direct and re-direct testimony may not be unreasonably leading.

3. With respect to oral testimony at an Evidentiary Hearing:

   (a) the Claimant shall ordinarily first present the testimony of its witnesses, followed by the Respondent presenting the testimony of its witnesses;

   (b) following direct testimony, any other Party may question such witness, in an order to be determined by the Arbitral Tribunal. The Party who initially presented the witness shall subsequently have the opportunity to ask additional questions on the matters raised in the other Parties' questioning;

   (c) thereafter, the Claimant shall ordinarily first present the testimony of its Party-Appointed Experts, followed by the Respondent presenting the testimony of its Party-Appointed Experts. The Party who initially presented the Party-Appointed Expert shall subsequently have the opportunity to ask additional questions on the matters raised in the other Parties' questioning;

   (d) the Arbitral Tribunal may question a Tribunal-Appointed Expert, and he or she may be questioned by the Parties or by any Party-Appointed Expert, on issues raised in the Tribunal-Appointed Expert Report, in the Parties' submissions or in the Expert Reports made by the Party-Appointed Experts;

(e) if the arbitration is organised into separate issues or phases (such as jurisdiction, preliminary determinations, liability and damages), the Parties may agree or the Arbitral Tribunal may order the scheduling of testimony separately for each issue or phase;

(f) the Arbitral Tribunal, upon request of a Party or on its own motion, may vary this order of proceeding, including the arrangement of testimony by particular issues or in such a manner that witnesses be questioned at the same time and in confrontation with each other (witness conferencing);

(g) the Arbitral Tribunal may ask questions to a witness at any time.

4. A witness of fact providing testimony shall first affirm, in a manner determined appropriate by the Arbitral Tribunal, that he or she commits to tell the truth or, in the case of an expert witness, his or her genuine belief in the opinions to be expressed at the Evidentiary Hearing. If the witness has submitted a Witness Statement or an Expert Report, the witness shall confirm it. The Parties may agree or the Arbitral Tribunal may order that the Witness Statement or Expert Report shall serve as that witness's direct testimony.

5. Subject to the provisions of Article 9.2, the Arbitral Tribunal may request any person to give oral or written evidence on any issue that the Arbitral Tribunal considers to be relevant to the case and material to its outcome. Any witness called and questioned by the Arbitral Tribunal may also be questioned by the Parties.

Article 9   Admissibility and Assessment of Evidence

1. The Arbitral Tribunal shall determine the admissibility, relevance, materiality and weight of evidence.

2. The Arbitral Tribunal shall, at the request of a Party or on its own motion, exclude from evidence or production any Document, statement, oral testimony or inspection for any of the following reasons:

(a) lack of sufficient relevance to the case or materiality to its outcome;

(b) legal impediment or privilege under the legal or ethical rules determined by the Arbitral Tribunal to be applicable;

(c) unreasonable burden to produce the requested evidence;

(d) loss or destruction of the Document that has been shown with reasonable likelihood to have occurred;

(e) grounds of commercial or technical that the Arbitral Tribunal determines to be compelling;

(f) grounds of special political or institutional sensitivity (including evidence that has been classified as secret by a government or a public international institution) that the Arbitral Tribunal determines to be compelling; or

(g) considerations of procedural economy, proportionality, fairness or equality of the Parties that the Arbitral Tribunal determines to be compelling.

3. In considering issues of legal impediment or privilege under Article 9.2(b), and insofar as permitted by any mandatory legal or ethical rules that are determined by it to be applicable, the Arbitral Tribunal may take into account:

(a) any need to protect the confidentiality of a Document created or statement or oral communication made in connection with and for the purpose of providing or obtaining legal advice;

(b) any need to protect the confidentiality of a Document created or statement or oral communication made in connection with and for the purpose of settlement negotiations;

(c) the expectations of the Parties and their advisors at the time the legal impediment or privilege is said to have arisen;

(d) any possible waiver of any applicable legal impediment or privilege by virtue of consent, earlier disclosure, affirmative use of the Document, statement, oral communication or advice contained therein, or otherwise; and

(e) the need to maintain fairness and equality as between the Parties, particularly if they are subject to different legal or ethical rules.

4. The Arbitral Tribunal may, where appropriate, make necessary arrangements to permit evidence to be presented or considered subject to suitable confidentiality protection.

5. If a Party fails without satisfactory explanation to produce any Document requested in a Request to Produce to which it has not objected in due time or fails to produce any Document ordered to be produced by the Arbitral Tribunal, the Arbitral Tribunal may infer that such document would be adverse to the interests of that Party.

6. If a Party fails without satisfactory explanation to make available any other relevant evidence, including testimony, sought by one Party to which the Party to whom the request was addressed has not objected in due time or fails to make available any evidence, including testimony, ordered by the Arbitral Tribunal to be produced, the Arbitral Tribunal may infer that such evidence would be adverse to the interests of that Party.

7. If the Arbitral Tribunal determines that a Party has failed to conduct itself in good faith in the taking of evidence, the Arbitral Tribunal may, in addition to any other measures available under these Rules, take such failure into account in its assignment of the costs of the arbitration, including costs arising out of or in connection with the taking of evidence.

IBA Rules of Ethics for International Arbitrators 1987

Reprinted with permission of the International Bar Association, London.
© International Bar Association, 1987

INTRODUCTORY NOTE

International arbitrators should be impartial, independent, competent, diligent and discreet. These rules seek to establish the manner in which these abstract qualities may be assessed in practice. Rather than rigid rules, they reflect internationally acceptable guidelines developed by practising lawyers from all continents. They will attain their objectives only if they are applied in good faith.

The rules cannot be directly binding either on arbitrators, or on the parties themselves, unless they are adopted by agreement. Whilst the International Bar Association hopes that they will be taken into account in the context of challenges to arbitrators, it is emphasised that these guidelines are not intended to create grounds for the setting aside of awards by national courts.

If parties wish to adopt the rules they may add the following to their arbitration clause or arbitration agreement: "The parties agree that the rules of Ethics for International Arbitrators established by the International Bar Association, in force at the date of the commencement of any arbitration under this clause, shall be applicable to the arbitrators appointed in respect of such arbitration." The International Bar Association takes the position that (whatever may be the case in domestic arbitration) international arbitrators should in principle be granted immunity from suit under national laws, except in extreme cases of wilful or reckless disregard of their legal obligations. Accordingly, the International Bar Association wishes to make it clear that it is not the intention of these rules to create opportunities for aggrieved parties to sue international arbitrators in national courts. The normal sanction for breach of an ethical duty is removal from office, with consequent loss of entitlement to remuneration. The International Bar Association also emphasises that these rules do not affect, and are intended to be consistent with, the International Code of Ethics for lawyers, adopted at Oslo on 25th July 1956, and amended by the General Meeting of the International Bar Association at Mexico City on 24th July 1964.

RULES OF ETHICS FOR INTERNATIONAL ARBITRATORS

Article 1 Fundamental Rule
Arbitrators shall proceed diligently and efficiently to provide the parties with a just and effective resolution of their disputes, and shall be and shall remain free from bias.

Article 2 Acceptance of Appointment
2.1 A prospective arbitrator shall accept an appointment only if he is fully satisfied that he is able to discharge his duties without bias.

2.2 A prospective arbitrator shall accept an appointment only if he is fully satisfied that he is competent to determine the issues in dispute, and has an adequate knowledge of the language of the arbitration.

2.3 A prospective arbitrator should accept an appointment only if he is able to give to the arbitration the time and attention which the parties are reasonably entitled to expect.

2.4 It is inappropriate to contact parties in order to solicit appointment as arbitrator.

Article 3 Elements of Bias
3.1 The criteria for assessing questions relating to bias are impartiality and independence. Partiality arises where an arbitrator favours one of the parties, or where he is prejudiced in relation to the subject-matter of the dispute. Dependence arises from relationships between an arbitrator and one of the parties, or with someone closely connected with one of the parties.

3.2 Facts which might lead a reasonable person, not knowing the arbitrator's true state of mind, to consider that he is dependent on a party create an appearance of bias. The same is true if an arbitrator has a material interest in the outcome of the dispute, or if he has already taken a position in relation to it. The appearance of bias is best overcome by full disclosure as described in Article 4 below.

3.3 Any current direct or indirect business relationship between an arbitrator and a party, or with a person who is known to be a potentially important witness, will normally give rise to justifiable doubts as to a prospective arbitrator's impartiality or independence. He should decline to accept an appointment in such circumstances unless the parties agree in writing that he may proceed. Examples of indirect relationships are where a member of the prospective arbitrator's family, his firm, or any business partner has a business relationship with one of the parties.

3.4 Past business relationships will not operate as an absolute bar to acceptance of appointment, unless they are of such magnitude or nature as to be likely to affect a prospective arbitrator's judgment.

3.5 Continuous and substantial social or professional relationships between a prospective arbitrator and a party, or with a person who is known to be a potentially important witness in the arbitration, will normally give rise to justifiable doubts as to the impartiality or independence of a prospective arbitrator.

Article 4 Duty of Disclosure

4.1 A prospective arbitrator should disclose all facts or circumstances that may give rise to justifiable doubts as to his impartiality or independence. Failure to make such disclosure creates an appearance of bias, and may of itself be a ground for disqualification even though the non-disclosed facts or circumstances would not of themselves justify disqualification.

4.2 A prospective arbitrator should disclose:

(a) any past or present business relationship, whether direct or indirect as illustrated in Article 3.3, including prior appointment as arbitrator, with any party to the dispute, or any representative of a party, or any person known to be a potentially important witness in the arbitration. With regard to present relationships, the duty of disclosure applies irrespective of their magnitude, but with regard to past relationships only if they were of more than a trivial nature in relation to the arbitrator's professional or business affairs. Non-disclosure of an indirect relationship unknown to a prospective arbitrator will not be a ground for disqualification unless it could have been ascertained by making reasonable enquiries;

(b) the nature and duration of any substantial social relationships with any party or any person known to be likely to be an important witness in the arbitration;

(c) the nature of any previous relationship with any fellow arbitrator (including prior joint service as an arbitrator);

(d) the extent of any prior knowledge he may have of the dispute;

(e) the extent of any commitments which may affect his availability to perform his duties as arbitrator as may be reasonably anticipated.

4.3 The duty of disclosure continues throughout the arbitral proceedings as regards new facts or circumstances.

4.4 Disclosure should be made in writing and communicated to all parties and arbitrators. When an arbitrator has been appointed, any previous disclosure made to the parties should be communicated to the other arbitrators.

Article 5 Communications with Parties

5.1 When approached with a view to appointment, a prospective arbitrator should make sufficient enquiries in order to inform himself whether there may be any justifiable doubts regarding his impartiality or independence; whether he is competent to determine the issues in dispute; and whether he is able to give the arbitration the time and attention required. He may also respond to enquiries from those approaching him, provided that such enquiries are designed to determine his suitability and availability for the appointment and provided that the merits of the case are not discussed. In the event that a prospective sole arbitrator or presiding arbitrator is approached by one party alone, or be one arbitrator chosen unilaterally by a party (a "party-nominated" arbitrator), he should ascertain that the other party or parties, or the other arbitrator, has consented to the manner in which he has been approached. In such circumstances he should, in writing or orally, inform the other party or parties, or the other arbitrator, of the substance of the initial conversation.

5.2 If a party-nominated arbitrator is required to participate in the selection of a third or presiding arbitrator, it is acceptable for him (although he is not so required) to obtain the views of the party who nominated him as to the acceptability of candidates being considered.

5.3 Throughout the arbitral proceedings, an arbitrator should avoid any unilateral communications regarding the case with any party, or its representatives. If such communication should occur, the arbitrator should inform the other party or parties and arbitrators of its substance.

5.4 If an arbitrator becomes aware that a fellow arbitrator has been in improper communication with a party, he may inform the remaining arbitrators and they should together determine what action should be taken. Normally, the appropriate initial course of action is for the offending arbitrator to be requested to refrain from making any further improper communications with the party. Where the offending arbitrator fails or refuses to refrain from improper communications, the remaining arbitrators may inform the innocent party in order that he may consider what action he should take. An arbitrator may act unilaterally to inform a party of the conduct of another arbitrator in order to allow the said party to consider a challenge of the offending arbitrator only in extreme circumstances, and after communicating his intention to his fellow arbitrators in writing.

5.5 No arbitrator should accept any gift or substantial hospitality, directly or indirectly, from any party to the arbitration. Sole arbitrators and presiding arbitrators should be particularly meticulous in avoiding significant social or professional contacts with any party to the arbitration other than in the presence of the other parties.

Article 6 Fees
Unless the parties agree otherwise or a party defaults, an arbitrator shall make no unilateral arrangements for fees or expenses.

Article 7 Duty of Diligence
All arbitrators should devote such time and attention as the parties may reasonably require having regard to all the circumstances of the case, and shall do their best to conduct the arbitration in such a manner that costs do not rise to an unreasonable proportion of the interests at stake.

Article 8 Involvement in Settlement Proposals
Where the parties have so requested, or consented to a suggestion to this effect by the arbitral tribunal, the tribunal as a whole (or the presiding arbitrator where appropriate), may make proposals for settlement to both parties simultaneously, and preferably in the presence of each other. Although any procedure is possible with the agreement of the parties, the arbitral tribunal should point out to the parties that it is undesirable that any arbitrator should discuss settlement terms with a party in the absence of the other parties since this will normally have the result that any arbitrator involved in such discussions will become disqualified from any future participation in the arbitration.

Article 9 Confidentiality of the Deliberations
The deliberations of the arbitral tribunal, and the contents of the award itself, remain confidential in perpetuity unless the parties release the arbitrators from this obligation. An arbitrator should not participate in, or give any information for the purpose of assistance in, any proceedings to consider the award unless, exceptionally, he considers it his duty to disclose any material misconduct or fraud on the part of his fellow arbitrators.

IBA Guidelines on Conflicts of Interest in International Arbitration

Reprinted with permission of the International Bar Association, London.

© International Bar Association

Approved on 22 May 2004 by the Council of the International Bar Association.

INTRODUCTION

1. Problems of conflicts of interest increasingly challenge international arbitration. Arbitrators are often unsure about what facts need to be disclosed, and they may make different choices about disclosures than other arbitrators in the same situation. The growth of international business and the manner in which it is conducted, including interlocking corporate relationships and larger international law firms, have caused more disclosures and have created more difficult conflict of interest issues to determine. Reluctant parties have more opportunities to use challenges of arbitrators to delay arbitrations or to deny the opposing party the arbitrator of its choice. Disclosure of any relationship, no matter how minor or serious, has too often led to objections, challenge and withdrawal or removal of the arbitrator.

2. Thus, parties, arbitrators, institutions and courts face complex decisions about what to disclose and what standards to apply. In addition, institutions and courts face difficult decisions if an objection or a challenge is made after a disclosure. There is a tension between, on the one hand, the parties' right to disclosure of situations that may reasonably call into question an arbitrator's impartiality or independence and their right to a fair hearing and, on the other hand, the parties' right to select arbitrators of their choosing. Even though laws and arbitration rules provide some standards, there is a lack of detail in their guidance and of uniformity in

their application. As a result, quite often members of the international arbitration community apply different standards in making decisions concerning disclosure, objections and challenges.

3. It is in the interest of everyone in the international arbitration community that international arbitration proceedings not be hindered by these growing conflicts of interest issues. The Committee on Arbitration and ADR of the International Bar Association appointed a Working Group of 19 experts[1] in international arbitration from 14 countries to study, with the intent of helping this decision-making process, national laws, judicial decisions, arbitration rules and practical considerations and applications regarding impartiality and independence and disclosure in international arbitration. The Working Group has determined that existing standards lack sufficient clarity and uniformity in their application. It has therefore prepared these Guidelines, which set forth some General Standards and Explanatory Notes on the Standards. Moreover, the Working Group believes that greater consistency and fewer unnecessary challenges and arbitrator withdrawals and removals could be achieved by providing lists of specific situations that, in the view of the Working Group, do or do not warrant disclosure or disqualification of an arbitrator. Such lists – designated Red, Orange and Green (the "Application Lists") – appear at the end of these Guidelines.

4. The Guidelines reflect the Working Group's understanding of the best current international practice firmly rooted in the principles expressed in the General Standards. The Working Group has based the General Standards and the Application Lists upon statutes and case law in jurisdictions and upon the judgment and experience of members of the Working Group and others involved in international commercial arbitration. The Working Group has attempted to balance the various interests of parties, representatives, arbitrators and arbitration institutions, all of whom have a responsibility for ensuring the integrity, reputation and efficiency of international commercial arbitration. In particular, the Working Group has sought and considered the views of many leading arbitration institutions, as well as corporate counsel and other persons involved in international arbitration. The Working Group also published drafts of the

---

[1] The members of the Working Group are: (1) Henri Alvarez, Canada; (2) John Beechey, England; (3) Jim Carter, United States; (4) Emmanuel Gaillard, France; (5) Emilio Gonzales de Castilla, Mexico; (6) Bernard Hanotiau, Belgium; (7) Michael Hwang, Singapore; (8) Albert Jan van den Berg, Belgium; (9) Doug Jones, Australia; (10) Gabrielle Kaufmann-Kohler, Switzerland; (11) Arthur Marriott, England; (12) Tore Wiwen Nilsson, Sweden; (13) Hilmar Raeschke-Kessler, Germany; (14) David W. Rivkin, United States; (15) Klaus Sachs, Germany; (16) Nathalie Voser, Switzerland (Rapporteur); (17) David Williams, New Zealand; (18) Des Williams, South Africa; (19); Otto de Witt Wijnen, The Netherlands (Chair).

Guidelines and sought comments at two annual meetings of the International Bar Association and other meetings of arbitrators. While the comments received by the Working Group varied, and included some points of criticisms, the arbitration community generally supported and encouraged these efforts to help reduce the growing problems of conflicts of interests. The Working Group has studied all the comments received and has adopted many of the proposals that it has received. The Working Group is very grateful indeed for the serious considerations given to its proposals by so many institutions and individuals all over the globe and for the comments and proposals received.

5. Originally, the Working Group developed the Guidelines for international commercial arbitration. However, in the light of comments received, it realized that the Guidelines should equally apply to other types of arbitration, such as investment arbitrations (insofar as these may not be considered as commercial arbitrations).[2]

6. These Guidelines are not legal provisions and do not override any applicable national law or arbitral rules chosen by the parties. However, the Working Group hopes that these Guidelines will find general acceptance within the international arbitration community (as was the case with the IBA Rules on the Taking of Evidence in International Commercial Arbitration) and that they thus will help parties, practitioners, arbitrators, institutions and the courts in their decision-making process on these very important questions of impartiality, independence, disclosure, objections and challenges made in that connection. The Working Group trusts that the Guidelines will be applied with robust common sense and without pedantic and unduly formalistic interpretation. The Working Group is also publishing a Background and History, which describes the studies made by the Working Group and may be helpful in interpreting the Guidelines.

7. The IBA and the Working Group view these Guidelines as a beginning, rather than an end, of the process. The Application Lists cover many of the varied situations that commonly arise in practice, but they do not purport to be comprehensive, nor could they be. Nevertheless, the Working Group is confident that the Application Lists provide better concrete guidance than the General Standards (and certainly more than existing standards). The IBA and the Working Group seek comments on the actual use of the Guidelines, and they plan to supplement, revise and refine the Guidelines based on that practical experience.

---

[2] Similarly, the Working Group is of the opinion that these Guidelines should apply by analogy to civil servants and government officers who are appointed as arbitrators by States or State entities that are parties to arbitration proceedings.

8. In 1987, the IBA published Rules of Ethics for International Arbitrators.[3] Those Rules cover more topics than these Guidelines, and they remain in effect as to subjects that are not discussed in the Guidelines. The Guidelines supersede the Rules of Ethics as to the matters treated here.

PART I. GENERAL STANDARDS REGARDING IMPARTIALITY, INDEPENDENCE AND DISCLOSURE

1. General Principle
Every arbitrator shall be impartial and independent of the parties at the time of accepting an appointment to serve and shall remain so during the entire arbitration proceeding until the final award has been rendered or the proceeding has otherwise finally terminated.

Explanation to General Standard 1
The Working Group is guided by the fundamental principle in international arbitration that each arbitrator must be impartial and independent of the parties at the time he or she accepts an appointment to act as arbitrator and must remain so during the entire course of the arbitration proceedings. The Working Group considered whether this obligation should extend even during the period that the award may be challenged but has decided against this. The Working Group takes the view that the arbitrator's duty ends when the Arbitral Tribunal has rendered the final award or the proceedings have otherwise been finally terminated (e.g., because of a settlement). If, after setting aside or other proceedings, the dispute is referred back to the same arbitrator, a fresh round of disclosure may be necessary.

2. Conflicts of Interest
(a) An arbitrator shall decline to accept an appointment or, if the arbitration has already been commenced, refuse to continue to act as an arbitrator if he or she has any doubts as to his or her ability to be impartial or independent.
(b) The same principle applies if facts or circumstances exist, or have arisen since the appointment, that, from a reasonable third person's point of view having knowledge of the relevant facts, give rise to justifiable doubts as to the arbitrator's impartiality or independence, unless the parties have accepted the arbitrator in accordance with the requirements set out in General Standard.

---

[3] Note General Editor. The IBA Rules of Ethics for International Arbitrators are published in Yearbook XII (1987), pp. 199–202.

(c) Doubts are justifiable if a reasonable and informed third party would reach the conclusion that there was a likelihood that the arbitrator may be influenced by factors other than the merits of the case as presented by the parties in reaching his or her decision.

(d) Justifiable doubts necessarily exist as to the arbitrator's impartiality or independence if there is an identity between a party and the arbitrator, if the arbitrator is a legal representative of a legal entity that is a party in the arbitration, or if the arbitrator has a significant financial or personal interest in the matter at stake.

Explanation to General Standard 2

(a) It is the main ethical guiding principle of every arbitrator that actual bias from the arbitrator's own point of view must lead to that arbitrator declining his or her appointment. This standard should apply regardless of the stage of the proceedings. This principle is so self-evident that many national laws do not explicitly say so. See, e.g., Article 12, UNCITRAL Model Law. The Working Group, however, has included it in the General Standards because explicit expression in these Guidelines helps to avoid confusion and to create confidence in procedures before arbitral tribunals. In addition, the Working Group believes that the broad standard of "any doubts as to an ability to be impartial and independent" should lead to the arbitrator declining the appointment.

(b) In order for standards to be applied as consistently as possible, the Working Group believes that the test for disqualification should be an objective one. The Working Group uses the wording "impartiality or independence" derived from the broadly adopted Article 12 of the UNCITRAL Model Law, and the use of an appearance test, based on justifiable doubts as to the impartiality or independence of the arbitrator, as provided in Article 12(2) of the UNCITRAL Model Law, to be applied objectively (a "reasonable third person test"). As described in the Explanation to General Standard 3(d), this standard should apply regardless of the stage of the proceedings.

(c) Most laws and rules that apply the standard of justifiable doubts do not further define that standard. The Working Group believes that this General Standard provides some context for making this determination.

(d) The Working Group supports the view that no one is allowed to be his or her own judge; i.e., there cannot be identity between an arbitrator and a party. The Working Group believes that this situation cannot be waived by the parties. The same principle should apply to persons who are legal representatives of a legal entity that is a party in the arbitration, like board members, or who have a significant economic interest in the matter at stake. Because of the importance of this principle, this non-waivable situation is made a General Standard, and examples are provided in the non-waivable Red List.

The General Standard purposely uses the terms "identity" and "legal representatives." In the light of comments received, the Working Group considered whether these terms should be extended or further defined, but decided against doing so. It realizes that there are situations in which an employee of a party or a civil servant can be in a position similar, if not identical, to the position of an official legal representative. The Working Group decided that it should suffice to state the principle.

3. Disclosure by the Arbitrator

(a) If facts or circumstances exist that may, in the eyes of the parties, give rise to doubts as to the arbitrator's impartiality or independence, the arbitrator shall disclose such facts or circumstances to the parties, the arbitration institution or other appointing authority (if any, and if so required by the applicable institutional rules) and to the co-arbitrators, if any, prior to accepting his or her appointment or, if thereafter, as soon as he or she learns about them.

(b) It follows from General Standards 1 and 2(a) that an arbitrator who has made a disclosure considers himself or herself to be impartial and independent of the parties despite the disclosed facts and therefore capable of performing his or her duties as arbitrator. Otherwise, he or she would have declined the nomination or appointment at the outset or resigned.

(c) Any doubt as to whether an arbitrator should disclose certain facts or circumstances should be resolved in favour of disclosure.

(d) When considering whether or not facts or circumstances exist that should be disclosed, the arbitrator shall not take into account whether the arbitration proceeding is at the beginning or at a later stage.

Explanation to General Standard 3

(a) General Standard 2(b) above sets out an objective test for disqualification of an arbitrator. However, because of varying considerations with respect to disclosure, the proper standard for disclosure may be different. A purely objective test for disclosure exists in the majority of the jurisdictions analyzed and in the UNCITRAL Model Law. Nevertheless, the Working Group recognizes that the parties have an interest in being fully informed about any circumstances that may be relevant in their view. Because of the strongly held views of many arbitration institutions (as reflected in their rules and as stated to the Working Group) that the disclosure test should reflect the perspectives of the parties, the Working Group in principle accepted, after much debate, a subjective approach for disclosure. The Working Group has adapted the language of Article 7(2) of the ICC Rules for this standard.

However, the Working Group believes that this principle should not be applied without limitations. Because some situations should never lead to disqualification under the objective test, such situations need not be disclosed, regardless of the parties' perspective. These limitations to the subjective test are reflected in the Green List, which lists some situations in which disclosure is not required.

Similarly, the Working Group emphasizes that the two tests (objective test for disqualification and subjective test for disclosure) are clearly distinct from each other, and that a disclosure shall not automatically lead to disqualification, as reflected in General Standard 3(b).

In determining what facts should be disclosed, an arbitrator should take into account all circumstances known to him or her, including to the extent known the culture and the customs of the country of which the parties are domiciled or nationals.

(b) Disclosure is not an admission of a conflict of interest. An arbitrator who has made a disclosure to the parties considers himself or herself to be impartial and independent of the parties, despite the disclosed facts, or else he or she would have declined the nomination or resigned. An arbitrator making disclosure thus feels capable of performing his or her duties. It is the purpose of disclosure to allow the parties to judge whether or not they agree with the evaluation of the arbitrator and, if they so wish, to explore the situation further. The Working Group hopes that the promulgation of this General Standard will eliminate the misunderstanding that disclosure demonstrates doubts sufficient to disqualify the arbitrator. Instead, any challenge should be successful only if an objective test, as set forth above, is met.

(c) Unnecessary disclosure sometimes raises an incorrect implication in the minds of the parties that the disclosed circumstances would affect his or her impartiality or independence. Excessive disclosures thus unnecessarily undermine the parties' confidence in the process. Nevertheless, after some debate, the Working Group believes it important to provide expressly in the General Standards that in case of doubt the arbitrator should disclose. If the arbitrator feels that he or she should disclose but that professional secrecy rules or other rules of practice prevent such disclosure, he or she should not accept the appointment or should resign.

(d) The Working Group has concluded that disclosure or disqualification (as set out in General Standard 2) should not depend on the particular stage of the arbitration. In order to determine whether the arbitrator should disclose, decline the appointment or refuse to continue to act or whether a challenge by a party should be successful, the facts and circumstances alone are relevant and not the current stage of the procedure or the consequences of the withdrawal. As a practical matter, institutions make a distinction between the commencement of an arbitration proceeding and a later stage. Also, courts tend to apply different standards. Nevertheless, the Working Group believes it important to clarify that no distinction should be made regarding the stage of the arbitral procedure. While there are practical concerns if an arbitrator must withdraw after an arbitration has commenced, a distinction based on the stage of arbitration would be inconsistent with the General Standards.

4. Waiver by the Parties

(a) If, within 30 days after the receipt of any disclosure by the arbitrator or after a party learns of facts or circumstances that could constitute a potential conflict of interest for an arbitrator, a party does not raise an express objection with regard to that arbitrator, subject to paragraphs (b) and (c) of this General Standard, the party is deemed to have waived any potential conflict of interest by the arbitrator based on such facts or circumstances and may not raise any objection to such facts or circumstances at a later stage.

(b) However, if facts or circumstances exist as described in General Standard 2(d), any waiver by a party or any agreement by the parties to have such a person serve as arbitrator shall be regarded as invalid.

(c) A person should not serve as an arbitrator when a conflict of interest, such as those exemplified in the waivable Red List, exists. Nevertheless, such a person may accept appointment as arbitrator or continue to act as an arbitrator, if the following conditions are met:

  (i) All parties, all arbitrators and the arbitration institution or other appointing authority (if any) must have full knowledge of the conflict of interest; and

  (ii) All parties must expressly agree that such person may serve as arbitrator despite the conflict of interest.

(d) An arbitrator may assist the parties in reaching a settlement of the dispute at any stage of the proceedings. However, before doing so, the arbitrator should receive an express agreement by the parties that acting in such a manner shall not disqualify the arbitrator from continuing to serve as arbitrator. Such express agreement shall be considered to be an effective waiver of any potential conflict of interest that may arise from the arbitrator's participation in such process or from information that the arbitrator may learn in the process. If the assistance by the arbitrator does not lead to final settlement of the case, the parties remain bound by their waiver. However, consistent with General Standard 2(a) and notwithstanding such agreement, the arbitrator shall resign if, as a consequence of his or her involvement in the settlement process, the arbitrator develops doubts as to his or her ability to remain impartial or independent in the future course of the arbitration proceedings.

Explanation to General Standard 4

(a) The Working Group suggests a requirement of an explicit objection by the parties within a certain time limit. In the view of the Working Group, this time limit should also apply to a party who refuses to be involved.

(b) This General Standard is included to make General Standard 4(a) consistent with the non-waivable provisions of General Standard 2(d). Examples of such circumstances are described in the non-waivable Red List.

(c) In a serious conflict of interest, such as those that are described by way of example in the waivable Red List, the parties may nevertheless wish to use such a person as an arbitrator. Here, party autonomy and the desire to have only impartial and independent arbitrators must be balanced. The Working Group believes persons with such a serious conflict of interests may serve as arbitrators only if the parties make fully informed, explicit waivers.

(d) The concept of the Arbitral Tribunal assisting the parties in reaching a settlement of their dispute in the course of the arbitration proceedings is well established in some jurisdictions but not in others. Informed consent by the parties to such a process prior to its beginning should be regarded as effective waiver of a potential conflict of interest. Express consent is generally sufficient, as opposed to a consent made in writing which in certain jurisdictions requires signature. In practice, the requirement of an express waiver allows such consent to be made in the minutes or transcript of a hearing. In addition, in order to avoid parties using an arbitrator as mediator as a means of disqualifying the arbitrator, the General Standard makes clear that the waiver should remain effective if the mediation is unsuccessful. Thus, parties assume the risk of what the arbitrator may learn in the settlement process. In giving their express consent, the parties should realize the consequences of the arbitrator assisting the parties in a settlement process and agree on regulating this special position further where appropriate.

5. Scope

These Guidelines apply equally to tribunal chairs, sole arbitrators and party-appointed arbitrators. These Guidelines do not apply to non-neutral arbitrators, who do not have an obligation to be independent and impartial, as may be permitted by some arbitration rules or national laws.

Explanation to General Standard 5

Because each member of an Arbitral Tribunal has an obligation to be impartial and independent, the General Standards should not distinguish among sole arbitrators, party-appointed arbitrators and tribunal chairs. With regard to secretaries of Arbitral Tribunals, the Working Group takes the view that it is the responsibility of the arbitrator to ensure that the secretary is and remains impartial and independent.Some arbitration rules and domestic laws permit party-appointed arbitrators to be non-neutral. When an arbitrator is serving in such a role, these Guidelines should not apply to him or her, since their purpose is to protect impartiality and independence.

6. Relationships

(a) When considering the relevance of facts or circumstances to determine whether a potential conflict of interest exists or whether disclosure should be made, the activities of an arbitrator's law firm, if any, should be reasonably considered in each individual case. Therefore, the fact that the activities of the arbitrator's firm involve one of the parties shall not automatically constitute a source of such conflict or a reason for disclosure.

(b) Similarly, if one of the parties is a legal entity which is a member of a group with which the arbitrator's firm has an involvement, such facts or circumstances should be reasonably considered in each individual case. Therefore, this fact alone shall not automatically constitute a source of a conflict of interest or a reason for disclosure.

(c) If one of the parties is a legal entity, the managers, directors and members of a supervisory board of such legal entity and any person having a similar controlling influence on the legal entity shall be considered to be the equivalent of the legal entity.

Explanation to General Standard 6

(a) The growing size of law firms should be taken into account as part of today's reality in international arbitration. There is a need to balance the interests of a party to use the arbitrator of its choice and the importance of maintaining confidence in the impartiality and independence of international arbitration. In the opinion of the Working Group, the arbitrator must in principle be considered as identical to his or her law firm, but nevertheless the activities of the arbitrator's firm should not automatically constitute a conflict of interest. The relevance of such activities, such as the nature, timing and scope of the work by the law firm, should be reasonably considered in each individual case. The Working Group uses the term "involvement" rather than "acting for" because a law firm's relevant connections with a party may include activities other than representation on a legal matter.

(b) When a party to an arbitration is a member of a group of companies, special questions regarding conflict of interest arise. As in the prior paragraph, the Working Group believes that because individual corporate structure arrangements vary so widely an automatic rule is not appropriate. Instead, the particular circumstances of an affiliation with another entity within the same group of companies should be reasonably considered in each individual case.

(c) The party in international arbitration is usually a legal entity. Therefore, this General Standard clarifies which individuals should be considered effectively to be that party.

7. Duty of Arbitrator and Parties

(a) A party shall inform an arbitrator, the Arbitral Tribunal, the other parties and the arbitration institution or other appointing authority (if any) about any direct or indirect relationship between it (or another company of the same group of companies) and the arbitrator. The party shall do so on its own initiative before the beginning of the proceeding or as soon as it becomes aware of such relationship.

(b) In order to comply with General Standard 7(a), a party shall provide any information already available to it and shall perform a reasonable search of publicly available information.

(c) An arbitrator is under a duty to make reasonable enquiries to investigate any potential conflict of interest, as well as any facts or circumstances that may cause his or her impartiality or independence to be questioned. Failure to disclose a potential conflict is not excused by lack of knowledge if the arbitrator makes no reasonable attempt to investigate.

Explanation to General Standard 7

To reduce the risk of abuse by unmeritorious challenge of an arbitrator's impartiality or independence, it is necessary that the parties disclose any relevant relationship with the arbitrator. In addition, any party or potential party to an arbitration is, at the outset, required to make a reasonable effort to ascertain and to disclose publicly available information that, applying the general standard, might affect the arbitrator's impartiality and independence. It is the arbitrator or putative arbitrator's obligation to make similar enquiries and to disclose any information that may cause his or her impartiality or independence to be called into question.

PART II. PRACTICAL APPLICATION OF THE GENERAL STANDARDS

1. The Working Group believes that if the Guidelines are to have an important practical influence, they should reflect situations that are likely to occur in today's arbitration practice. The Guidelines should provide specific guidance to arbitrators, parties, institutions and courts as to what situations do or do not constitute conflicts of interest or should be disclosed.

For this purpose, the members of the Working Group analyzed their respective case law and categorized situations that can occur in the following Application Lists. These lists obviously cannot contain every situation, but they provide guidance in many circumstances, and the Working Group has sought to make them as comprehensive as possible. In all cases, the General Standards should control.

2. The Red List consists of two parts: "a non-waivable Red List" (see General Standards 2(c) and 4(b)) and "a waivable Red List" (see General Standard 4(c)). These lists are a non-exhaustive enumeration of specific situations which, depending on the facts of a given case, give rise to justifiable doubts as to the arbitrator's impartiality and independence; i.e., in these circumstances an objective conflict of interest exists from the point of view of a reasonable third person having knowledge of the relevant facts (see General Standard 2(b)). The non-waivable Red List includes situations deriving from the overriding principle that no person can be his or her own judge. Therefore, disclosure of such a situation cannot cure the conflict. The waivable Red List encompasses situations that are serious but not as severe. Because of their seriousness, unlike circumstances described in the Orange List, these situations should be considered waivable only if and when the parties, being aware of the conflict of interest situation, nevertheless expressly state their willingness to have such a person act as arbitrator, as set forth in General Standard 4(c).

3. The Orange List is a non-exhaustive enumeration of specific situations which (depending on the facts of a given case) in the eyes of the parties may give rise to justifiable doubts as to the arbitrator's impartiality or independence. The Orange List thus reflects situations that would fall under General Standard 3(a), so that the arbitrator has a duty to disclose such situations. In all these situations, the parties are deemed to have accepted the arbitrator if, after disclosure, no timely objection is made. (General Standard 4(a)).

4. It should be stressed that, as stated above, such disclosure should not automatically result in a disqualification of the arbitrator; no presumption regarding disqualification should arise from a disclosure. The purpose of the disclosure is to inform the parties of a situation that they may wish to explore further in order to determine whether objectively – i.e., from a reasonable third person's point of view having knowledge of the relevant facts – there is a justifiable doubt as to the arbitrator's impartiality or independence. If the conclusion is that there is no justifiable doubt, the arbitrator can act. He or she can also act if there is no timely objection by the parties or, in situations covered by the waivable Red List, a specific acceptance by the parties in accordance with General

Standard 4(c). Of course, if a party challenges the appointment of the arbitrator, he or she can nevertheless act if the authority that has to rule on the challenge decides that the challenge does not meet the objective test for disqualification.

5. In addition, a later challenge based on the fact that an arbitrator did not disclose such facts or circumstances should not result automatically in either non-appointment, later disqualification or a successful challenge to any award. In the view of the Working Group, non-disclosure cannot make an arbitrator partial or lacking independence; only the facts or circumstances that he or she did not disclose can do so.

6. The Green List contains a non-exhaustive enumeration of specific situations where no appearance of, and no actual, conflict of interest exists from the relevant objective point of view. Thus, the arbitrator has no duty to disclose situations falling within the Green List. In the opinion of the Working Group, as already expressed in the Explanation to General Standard 3(a), there should be a limit to disclosure, based on reasonableness; in some situations, an objective test should prevail over the purely subjective test of "the eyes of the parties."

7. Situations falling outside the time limit used in some of the Orange List situations should generally be considered as falling in the Green List, even though they are not specifically stated. An arbitrator may nevertheless wish to make disclosure if, under the General Standards, he or she believes it to be appropriate. While there has been much debate with respect to the time limits used in the Lists, the Working Group has concluded that the limits indicated are appropriate and provide guidance where none exists now. For example, the three-year period in Orange List 3.1 may be too long in certain circumstances and too short in others, but the Working Group believes that the period is an appropriate general criterion, subject to the special circumstances of any case.

8. The borderline between the situations indicated is often thin. It can be debated whether a certain situation should be on one List of instead of another. Also, the Lists contain, for various situations, open norms like "significant". The Working Group has extensively and repeatedly discussed both of these issues, in the light of comments received. It believes that the decisions reflected in the Lists reflect international principles to the best extent possible and that further definition of the norms, which should be interpreted reasonably in light of the facts and circumstances in each case, would be counter-productive.

9. There has been much debate as to whether there should be a Green List at all and also, with respect to the Red List, whether the situations on the Non-Waivable Red List should be waivable in light of party autonomy. With respect to the first question, the Working Group has maintained its decision that the subjective test for disclosure should not be the absolute criterion but that some objective thresholds should be added. With respect

to the second question, the conclusion of the Working Group was that party autonomy, in this respect, has its limits.

1. Non-Waivable Red List

1.1. There is an identity between a party and the arbitrator, or the arbitrator is a legal representative of an entity that is a party in the arbitration.

1.2. The arbitrator is a manager, director or member of the supervisory board, or has a similar controlling influence in one of the parties.

1.3. The arbitrator has a significant financial interest in one of the parties or the outcome of the case.

1.4. The arbitrator regularly advises the appointing party or an affiliate of the appointing party, and the arbitrator or his or her firm derives a significant financial income therefrom.

2. Waivable Red List

2.1. Relationship of the arbitrator to the dispute

2.1.1 The arbitrator has given legal advice or provided an expert opinion on the dispute to a party or an affiliate of one of the parties.

2.1.2 The arbitrator has previous involvement in the case.

2.2. Arbitrator's direct or indirect interest in the dispute

2.2.1 The arbitrator holds shares, either directly or indirectly, in one of the parties or an affiliate of one of the parties that is privately held.

2.2.2 A close family member[4] of the arbitrator has a significant financial interest in the outcome of the dispute.

2.2.3 The arbitrator or a close family member of the arbitrator has a close relationship with a third party who may be liable to recourse on the part of the unsuccessful party in the dispute.

2.3. Arbitrator's relationship with the parties or counsel

2.3.1 The arbitrator currently represents or advises one of the parties or an affiliate of one of the parties.

2.3.2 The arbitrator currently represents the lawyer or law firm acting as counsel for one of the parties.

2.3.3 The arbitrator is a lawyer in the same law firm as the counsel to one of the parties.

2.3.4 The arbitrator is a manager, director or member of the supervisory board, or has a similar controlling influence, in an affiliate[5] of one of the parties if the affiliate is directly involved in the matters in dispute in the arbitration.

---

[4] Throughout the Application Lists, the term "close family member" refers to a spouse, sibling, child, parent or life partner.

[5] Throughout the Application Lists, the term "affiliate" encompasses all companies in one group of companies including the parent company.

2.3.5 The arbitrator's law firm had a previous but terminated involvement in the case without the arbitrator being involved himself or herself.

2.3.6 The arbitrator's law firm currently has a significant commercial relationship with one of the parties or an affiliate of one of the parties.

2.3.7 The arbitrator regularly advises the appointing party or an affiliate of the appointing party, but neither the arbitrator nor his or her firm derives a significant financial income therefrom.

2.3.8 The arbitrator has a close family relationship with one of the parties or with a manager, director or member of the supervisory board or any person having a similar controlling influence in one of the parties or an affiliate of one of the parties or with a counsel representing a party.

2.3.9 A close family member of the arbitrator has a significant financial interest in one of the parties or an affiliate of one of the parties.

3. Orange List

3.1. Previous services for one of the parties or other involvement in the case

3.1.1 The arbitrator has within the past three years served as counsel for one of the parties or an affiliate of one of the parties or has previously advised or been consulted by the party or an affiliate of the party making the appointment in an unrelated matter, but the arbitrator and the party or the affiliate of the party have no ongoing relationship.

3.1.2 The arbitrator has within the past three years served as counsel against one of the parties or an affiliate of one of the parties in an unrelated matter.

3.1.3 The arbitrator has within the past three years been appointed as arbitrator on two or more occasions by one of the parties or an affiliate of one of the parties.[6]

3.1.4 The arbitrator's law firm has within the past three years acted for one of the parties or an affiliate of one of the parties in an unrelated matter without the involvement of the arbitrator.

3.1.5 The arbitrator currently serves, or has served within the past three years, as arbitrator in another arbitration on a related issue involving one of the parties or an affiliate of one of the parties.

---

[6] It may be the practice in certain specific kinds of arbitration, such as maritime or commodities arbitration, to draw arbitrators from a small, specialized pool. If in such fields it is the custom and practice for parties frequently to appoint the same arbitrator in different cases, no disclosure of this fact is required where all parties in the arbitration should be familiar with such custom and practice.

3.2. Current services for one of the parties

    3.2.1 The arbitrator's law firm is currently rendering services to one of the parties or to an affiliate of one of the parties without creating a significant commercial relationship and without the involvement of the arbitrator.

    3.2.2 A law firm that shares revenues or fees with the arbitrator's law firm renders services to one of the parties or an affiliate of one of the parties before the arbitral tribunal.

    3.2.3 The arbitrator or his or her firm represents a party or an affiliate to the arbitration on a regular basis but is not involved in the current dispute.

3.3. Relationship between an arbitrator and another arbitrator or counsel.

    3.3.1 The arbitrator and another arbitrator are lawyers in the same law firm.

    3.3.2 The arbitrator and another arbitrator or the counsel for one of the parties are members of the same barristers' chambers.[7]

    3.3.3 The arbitrator was within the past three years a partner of, or otherwise affiliated with, another arbitrator or any of the counsel in the same arbitration.

    3.3.4 A lawyer in the arbitrator's law firm is an arbitrator in another dispute involving the same party or parties or an affiliate of one of the parties.

    3.3.5 A close family member of the arbitrator is a partner or employee of the law firm representing one of the parties, but is not assisting with the dispute.

    3.3.6 A close personal friendship exists between an arbitrator and a counsel of one party, as demonstrated by the fact that the arbitrator and the counsel regularly spend considerable time together unrelated to professional work commitments or the activities of professional associations or social organizations.

    3.3.7 The arbitrator has within the past three years received more than three appointments by the same counsel or the same law firm.

3.4. Relationship between arbitrator and party and others involved in the arbitration

    3.4.1 The arbitrator's law firm is currently acting adverse to one of the parties or an affiliate of one of the parties.

    3.4.2 The arbitrator had been associated within the past three years with a party or an affiliate of one of the parties in a professional capacity, such as a former employee or partner.

---

[7] Issues concerning special considerations involving barristers in England are discussed in the Background Information issued by the Working Group.

3.4.3 A close personal friendship exists between an arbitrator and a manager or director or a member of the supervisory board or any person having a similar controlling influence in one of the parties or an affiliate of one of the parties or a witness or expert, as demonstrated by the fact that the arbitrator and such director, manager, other person, witness or expert regularly spend considerable time together unrelated to professional work commitments or the activities of professional associations or social organizations.

3.4.4 If the arbitrator is a former judge, he or she has within the past three years heard a significant case involving one of the parties.

3.5. Other circumstances

3.5.1 The arbitrator holds shares, either directly or indirectly, which by reason of number or denomination constitute a material holding in one of the parties or an affiliate of one of the parties that is publicly listed.

3.5.2 The arbitrator has publicly advocated a specific position regarding the case that is being arbitrated, whether in a published paper or speech or otherwise.

3.5.3 The arbitrator holds one position in an arbitration institution with appointing authority over the dispute.

3.5.4 The arbitrator is a manager, director or member of the supervisory board, or has a similar controlling influence, in an affiliate of one of the parties, where the affiliate is not directly involved in the matters in dispute in the arbitration.

4. Green List

4.1. Previously expressed legal opinions

4.1.1 The arbitrator has previously published a general opinion (such as in a law review article or public lecture) concerning an issue which also arises in the arbitration (but this opinion is not focused on the case that is being arbitrated).

4.2. Previous services against one party

4.2.1 The arbitrator's law firm has acted against one of the parties or an affiliate of one of the parties in an unrelated matter without the involvement of the arbitrator.

4.3. Current services for one of the parties

4.3.1 A firm in association or in alliance with the arbitrator's law firm, but which does not share fees or other revenues with the arbitrator's law firm, renders services to one of the parties or an affiliate of one of the parties in an unrelated matter.

4.4. Contacts with another arbitrator or with counsel for one of the parties

4.4.1 The arbitrator has a relationship with another arbitrator or with the counsel for one of the parties through membership in the same professional association or social organization.

4.4.2 The arbitrator and counsel for one of the parties or another arbitrator have previously served together as arbitrators or as co-counsel.

4.5. Contacts between the arbitrator and one of the parties

4.5.1 The arbitrator has had an initial contact with the appointing party or an affiliate of the appointing party (or the respective counsels) prior to appointment, if this contact is limited to the arbitrator's availability and qualifications to serve or to the names of possible candidates for a chairperson and did not address the merits or procedural aspects of the dispute.

4.5.2 The arbitrator holds an insignificant amount of shares in one of the parties or an affiliate of one of the parties, which is publicly listed.

4.5.3 The arbitrator and a manager, director or member of the supervisory board, or any person having a similar controlling influence, in one of the parties or an affiliate of one of the parties, have worked together as joint experts or in another professional capacity, including as arbitrators in the same case.

The AAA–ABA Code of Ethics for Arbitrators in Commercial Disputes

Effective March 1, 2004

The Code of Ethics for Arbitrators in Commercial Disputes was originally prepared in 1977 by a joint committee consisting of a special committee of the American Arbitration Association and a special committee of the American Bar Association.

The Code was revised in 2003 by an ABA

Task Force and special committee of the AAA.

PREAMBLE

The use of arbitration to resolve a wide variety of disputes has grown extensively and forms a significant part of the system of justice on which our society relies for a fair determination of legal rights. Persons who act as arbitrators therefore undertake serious responsibilities to the public, as well as to the parties. Those responsibilities include important ethical obligations.

Few cases of unethical behavior by commercial arbitrators have arisen. Nevertheless, this Code sets forth generally accepted standards of ethical conduct for the guidance of arbitrators and parties in commercial disputes, in the hope of contributing to the maintenance of high standards and continued confidence in the process of arbitration.

This Code provides ethical guidelines for many types of arbitration but does not apply to labor arbitration, which is generally conducted under the Code of Professional Responsibility for Arbitrators of Labor-Management Disputes.

There are many different types of commercial arbitration. Some proceedings are conducted under arbitration rules established by various organizations and trade associations, while others are conducted without such rules. Although most proceedings are arbitrated pursuant to voluntary agreement of the parties, certain types of disputes are submitted to arbitration by reason of particular laws. This Code is intended to apply to all such proceedings in which disputes or claims are submitted for decision to one or more arbitrators appointed in a manner provided by an agreement of the parties, by applicable arbitration rules, or by law. In all such cases, the persons who have the power to decide should observe fundamental standards of ethical conduct. In this Code, all such persons are called "arbitrators," although in some types of proceeding they might be called "umpires," "referees," "neutrals," or have some other title.

Arbitrators, like judges, have the power to decide cases. However, unlike full-time judges, arbitrators are usually engaged in other occupations before, during, and after the time that they serve as arbitrators. Often, arbitrators are purposely chosen from the same trade or industry as the parties in order to bring special knowledge to the task of deciding. This Code recognizes these fundamental differences between arbitrators and judges. In those instances where this Code has been approved and recommended by organizations that provide, coordinate, or administer services of arbitrators, it provides ethical standards for the members of their respective panels of arbitrators. However, this Code does not form a part of the arbitration rules of any such organization unless its rules so provide.

NOTE ON NEUTRALITY

In some types of commercial arbitration, the parties or the administering institution provide for three or more arbitrators. In some such proceedings, it is the practice for each party, acting alone, to appoint one arbitrator (a "party-appointed arbitrator") and for one additional arbitrator to be designated by the party-appointed arbitrators, or by the parties, or by an independent institution or individual. The sponsors of this Code believe that it is preferable for all arbitrators including any party-appointed arbitrators to be neutral, that is, independent and impartial, and to comply with the same ethical standards. This expectation generally is essential in arbitrations where the parties, the nature of the dispute, or the enforcement of any resulting award may have international aspects. However, parties in certain domestic arbitrations in the United States may prefer that party-appointed arbitrators be non-neutral and governed by special ethical considerations. These special ethical considerations appear in Canon X of this Code. This Code establishes a presumption of neutrality for all arbitrators, including party-appointed arbitrators, which applies unless the parties' agreement, the arbitration rules agreed to by the parties or applicable laws provide otherwise. This Code requires all party-appointed arbitrators, whether neutral or not, to make pre-appointment disclosures of any facts which might affect their neutrality, independence, or impartiality. This Code also requires all party-appointed arbitrators to ascertain and disclose as soon as practicable whether the parties intended for them to serve as neutral or not. If any doubt or uncertainty exists, the party-appointed arbitrators should serve as neutrals unless and until such doubt or uncertainty is resolved in accordance with Canon IX. This Code expects all arbitrators, including those serving under Canon X, to preserve the integrity and fairness of the process.

Various aspects of the conduct of arbitrators, including some matters covered by this Code, may also be governed by agreements of the parties, arbitration rules to which the parties have agreed, applicable law, or other applicable ethics rules, all of which should be consulted by the arbitrators. This Code does not take the place of or supersede such laws, agreements, or arbitration rules to which the parties have agreed and should be read in conjunction with other rules of ethics. It does not establish new or additional grounds for judicial review of arbitration awards.

All provisions of this Code should therefore be read as subject to contrary provisions of applicable law and arbitration rules. They should also be read as subject to contrary agreements of the parties. Nevertheless, this Code imposes no obligation on any arbitrator to act in a manner inconsistent with the arbitrator's fundamental duty to preserve the integrity and fairness of the arbitral process.

Canons I through VIII of this Code apply to all arbitrators. Canon IX applies to all party-appointed arbitrators, except that certain party-appointed arbitrators are exempted by Canon X from compliance with certain provisions of Canons I–IX related to impartiality and independence, as specified in Canon X.

CANON I: AN ARBITRATOR SHOULD UPHOLD THE INTEGRITY AND FAIRNESS OF THE ARBITRATION PROCESS

A. An arbitrator has a responsibility not only to the parties but also to the process of arbitration itself, and must observe high standards of conduct so that the integrity and fairness of the process will be preserved. Accordingly, an arbitrator should recognize a responsibility to the public, to the parties whose rights will be decided, and to all other participants in the proceeding. This responsibility may include pro bono service as an arbitrator where appropriate.

B. One should accept appointment as an arbitrator only if fully satisfied:
  (1) that he or she can serve impartially;
  (2) that he or she can serve independently from the parties, potential witnesses, and the other arbitrators;
  (3) that he or she is competent to serve; and

(4) that he or she can be available to commence the arbitration in accordance with the requirements of the proceeding and thereafter to devote the time and attention to its completion that the parties are reasonably entitled to expect.

C. After accepting appointment and while serving as an arbitrator, a person should avoid entering into any business, professional, or personal relationship, or acquiring any financial or personal interest, which is likely to affect impartiality or which might reasonably create the appearance of partiality. For a reasonable period of time after the decision of a case, persons who have served as arbitrators should avoid entering into any such relationship, or acquiring any such interest, in circumstances which might reasonably create the appearance that they had been influenced in the arbitration by the anticipation or expectation of the relationship or interest. Existence of any of the matters or circumstances described in this paragraph C does not render it unethical for one to serve as an arbitrator where the parties have consented to the arbitrator's appointment or continued services following full disclosure of the relevant facts in accordance with Canon II.

D. Arbitrators should conduct themselves in a way that is fair to all parties and should not be swayed by outside pressure, public clamor, and fear of criticism or self-interest. They should avoid conduct and statements that give the appearance of partiality toward or against any party.

E. When an arbitrator's authority is derived from the agreement of the parties, an arbitrator should neither exceed that authority nor do less than is required to exercise that authority completely. Where the agreement of the parties sets forth procedures to be followed in conducting the arbitration or refers to rules to be followed, it is the obligation of the arbitrator to comply with such procedures or rules. An arbitrator has no ethical obligation to comply with any agreement, procedures or rules that are unlawful or that, in the arbitrator's judgment, would be inconsistent with this Code.

F. An arbitrator should conduct the arbitration process so as to advance the fair and efficient resolution of the matters submitted for decision. An arbitrator should make all reasonable efforts to prevent delaying tactics, harassment of parties or other participants, or other abuse or disruption of the arbitration process.

G. The ethical obligations of an arbitrator begin upon acceptance of the appointment and continue throughout all stages of the proceeding. In addition, as set forth in this Code, certain ethical obligations begin as soon as a person is requested to serve as an arbitrator and certain ethical obligations continue after the decision in the proceeding has been given to the parties.

H. Once an arbitrator has accepted an appointment, the arbitrator should not withdraw or abandon the appointment unless compelled to do so by unanticipated circumstances that would render it impossible or impracticable to continue. When an arbitrator is to be compensated for his or her services, the arbitrator may withdraw if the parties fail or refuse to provide for payment of the compensation as agreed.

I. An arbitrator who withdraws prior to the completion of the arbitration, whether upon the arbitrator's initiative or upon the request of one or more of the parties, should take reasonable steps to protect the interests of the parties in the arbitration, including return of evidentiary materials and protection of confidentiality.

Comment to Canon I

A prospective arbitrator is not necessarily partial or prejudiced by having acquired knowledge of the parties, the applicable law or the customs and practices of the business involved. Arbitrators may also have special experience or expertise in the areas of business, commerce, or technology which are involved in the arbitration. Arbitrators do not contravene this Canon if, by virtue of such experience or expertise, they have views on certain general issues likely to arise in the arbitration, but an arbitrator may not have prejudged any of the specific factual or legal determinations to be addressed during the arbitration. During an arbitration, the arbitrator may engage in discourse with the parties or their counsel, draw out arguments or contentions, comment on the law or evidence, make interim rulings, and otherwise control or direct the arbitration. These activities are integral parts of an arbitration. Paragraph D of Canon I is not intended to preclude or limit either full discussion of the issues during the course of the arbitration or the arbitrator's management of the proceeding.

CANON II: AN ARBITRATOR SHOULD DISCLOSE ANY INTEREST OR RELATIONSHIP LIKELY TO AFFECT IMPARTIALITY OR WHICH MIGHT CREATE AN APPEARANCE OF PARTIALITY

A. Persons who are requested to serve as arbitrators should, before accepting, disclose:

(1) any known direct or indirect financial or personal interest in the outcome of the arbitration;

(2) any known existing or past financial, business, professional or personal relationships which might reasonably affect impartiality or lack of independence in the eyes of any of the parties. For example, prospective arbitrators should disclose any such relationships which they personally have with any party or its lawyer, with any

co-arbitrator, or with any individual whom they have been told will be a witness. They should also disclose any such relationships involving their families or household members or their current employers, partners, or professional or business associates that can be ascertained by reasonable efforts;

(3) the nature and extent of any prior knowledge they may have of the dispute; and

(4) any other matters, relationships, or interests which they are obligated to disclose by the agreement of the parties, the rules or practices of an institution, or applicable law regulating arbitrator disclosure.

B. Persons who are requested to accept appointment as arbitrators should make a reasonable effort to inform themselves of any interests or relationships described in paragraph A.

C. The obligation to disclose interests or relationships described in paragraph A is a continuing duty which requires a person who accepts appointment as an arbitrator to disclose, as soon as practicable, at any stage of the arbitration, any such interests or relationships which may arise, or which are recalled or discovered.

D. Any doubt as to whether or not disclosure is to be made should be resolved in favor of disclosure.

E. Disclosure should be made to all parties unless other procedures for disclosure are provided in the agreement of the parties, applicable rules or practices of an institution, or by law. Where more than one arbitrator has been appointed, each should inform the others of all matters disclosed.

F. When parties, with knowledge of a person's interests and relationships, nevertheless desire that person to serve as an arbitrator, that person may properly serve.

G. If an arbitrator is requested by all parties to withdraw, the arbitrator must do so. If an arbitrator is requested to withdraw by less than all of the parties because of alleged partiality, the arbitrator should withdraw unless either of the following circumstances exists:

(1) An agreement of the parties, or arbitration rules agreed to by the parties, or applicable law establishes procedures for determining challenges to arbitrators, in which case those procedures should be followed; or

(2) In the absence of applicable procedures, if the arbitrator, after carefully considering the matter, determines that the reason for the challenge is not substantial, and that he or she can nevertheless act and decide the case impartially and fairly.

H. If compliance by a prospective arbitrator with any provision of this Code would require disclosure of confidential or privileged information, the prospective arbitrator should either:

(1) Secure the consent to the disclosure from the person who furnished the information or the holder of the privilege; or

(2) Withdraw.

CANON III: AN ARBITRATOR SHOULD AVOID IMPROPRIETY OR THE APPEARANCE OF IMPROPRIETY IN COMMUNICATING WITH PARTIES

A. If an agreement of the parties or applicable arbitration rules establishes the manner or content of communications between the arbitrator and the parties, the arbitrator should follow those procedures notwithstanding any contrary provision of paragraphs B and C.

B. An arbitrator or prospective arbitrator should not discuss a proceeding with any party in the absence of any other party, except in any of the following circumstances:

(1) When the appointment of a prospective arbitrator is being considered, the prospective arbitrator:

(a) may ask about the identities of the parties, counsel, or witnesses and the general nature of the case; and

(b) may respond to inquiries from a party or its counsel designed to determine his or her suitability and availability for the appointment. In any such dialogue, the prospective arbitrator may receive information from a party or its counsel disclosing the general nature of the dispute but should not permit them to discuss the merits of the case.

(2) In an arbitration in which the two party-appointed arbitrators are expected to appoint the third arbitrator, each party-appointed arbitrator may consult with the party who appointed the arbitrator concerning the choice of the third arbitrator;

(3) In an arbitration involving party-appointed arbitrators, each party-appointed arbitrator may consult with the party who appointed the arbitrator concerning arrangements for any compensation to be paid to the party-appointed arbitrator. Submission of routine written requests for payment of compensation and expenses in accordance with such arrangements and written communications pertaining solely to such requests need not be sent to the other party;

(4) In an arbitration involving party-appointed arbitrators, each party-appointed arbitrator may consult with the party who appointed the arbitrator concerning the status of the arbitrator (i.e., neutral or non-neutral), as contemplated by paragraph C of Canon IX;

(5) Discussions may be had with a party concerning such logistical matters as setting the time and place of hearings or making other arrangements for the conduct of the proceedings. However, the

arbitrator should promptly inform each other party of the discussion and should not make any final determination concerning the matter discussed before giving each absent party an opportunity to express the party's views; or

(6) If a party fails to be present at a hearing after having been given due notice, or if all parties expressly consent, the arbitrator may discuss the case with any party who is present.

C. Unless otherwise provided in this Canon, in applicable arbitration rules or in an agreement of the parties, whenever an arbitrator communicates in writing with one party, the arbitrator should at the same time send a copy of the communication to every other party, and whenever the arbitrator receives any written communication concerning the case from one party which has not already been sent to every other party, the arbitrator should send or cause it to be sent to the other parties.

CANON IV: AN ARBITRATOR SHOULD CONDUCT THE PROCEEDINGS FAIRLY AND DILIGENTLY

A. An arbitrator should conduct the proceedings in an even-handed manner. The arbitrator should be patient and courteous to the parties, their representatives, and the witnesses and should encourage similar conduct by all participants.

B. The arbitrator should afford to all parties the right to be heard and due notice of the time and place of any hearing. The arbitrator should allow each party a fair opportunity to present its evidence and arguments.

C. The arbitrator should not deny any party the opportunity to be represented by counsel or by any other person chosen by the party.

D. If a party fails to appear after due notice, the arbitrator should proceed with the arbitration when authorized to do so, but only after receiving assurance that appropriate notice has been given to the absent party.

E. When the arbitrator determines that more information than has been presented by the parties is required to decide the case, it is not improper for the arbitrator to ask questions, call witnesses, and request documents or other evidence, including expert testimony.

F. Although it is not improper for an arbitrator to suggest to the parties that they discuss the possibility of settlement or the use of mediation, or other dispute resolution processes, an arbitrator should not exert pressure on any party to settle or to utilize other dispute resolution processes. An arbitrator should not be present or otherwise participate in settlement discussions or act as a mediator unless requested to do so by all parties.

G. Co-arbitrators should afford each other full opportunity to participate in all aspects of the proceedings.

Comment to paragraph G

Paragraph G of Canon IV is not intended to preclude one arbitrator from acting in limited circumstances (e.g., ruling on discovery issues) where authorized by the agreement of the parties, applicable rules or law, nor does it preclude a majority of the arbitrators from proceeding with any aspect of the arbitration if an arbitrator is unable or unwilling to participate and such action is authorized by the agreement of the parties or applicable rules or law. It also does not preclude ex parte requests for interim relief.

CANON V: AN ARBITRATOR SHOULD MAKE DECISIONS IN A JUST, INDEPENDENT AND DELIBERATE MANNER

A. The arbitrator should, after careful deliberation, decide all issues submitted for determination. An arbitrator should decide no other issues.
B. An arbitrator should decide all matters justly, exercising independent judgment, and should not permit outside pressure to affect the decision.
C. An arbitrator should not delegate the duty to decide to any other person.
D. In the event that all parties agree upon a settlement of issues in dispute and request the arbitrator to embody that agreement in an award, the arbitrator may do so, but is not required to do so unless satisfied with the propriety of the terms of settlement. Whenever an arbitrator embodies a settlement by the parties in an award, the arbitrator should state in the award that it is based on an agreement of the parties.

CANON VI: AN ARBITRATOR SHOULD BE FAITHFUL TO THE RELATIONSHIP OF TRUST AND CONFIDENTIALITY INHERENT IN THAT OFFICE

A. An arbitrator is in a relationship of trust to the parties and should not, at any time, use confidential information acquired during the arbitration proceeding to gain personal advantage or advantage for others, or to affect adversely the interest of another.
B. The arbitrator should keep confidential all matters relating to the arbitration proceedings and decision. An arbitrator may obtain help from an associate, a research assistant or other persons in connection with reaching his or her decision if the arbitrator informs the parties of the use of such assistance and such persons agree to be bound by the provisions of this Canon.
C. It is not proper at any time for an arbitrator to inform anyone of any decision in advance of the time it is given to all parties. In a proceeding in which there is more than one arbitrator, it is not proper at any time for an arbitrator to inform anyone about the substance of the deliberations

of the arbitrators. After an arbitration award has been made, it is not proper for an arbitrator to assist in proceedings to enforce or challenge the award.

D. Unless the parties so request, an arbitrator should not appoint himself or herself to a separate office related to the subject matter of the dispute, such as receiver or trustee, nor should a panel of arbitrators appoint one of their number to such an office.

CANON VII: AN ARBITRATOR SHOULD ADHERE TO STANDARDS OF INTEGRITY AND FAIRNESS WHEN MAKING ARRANGEMENTS FOR COMPENSATION AND REIMBURSEMENT OF EXPENSES

A. Arbitrators who are to be compensated for their services or reimbursed for their expenses shall adhere to standards of integrity and fairness in making arrangements for such payments.

B. Certain practices relating to payments are generally recognized as tending to preserve the integrity and fairness of the arbitration process. These practices include:

(1) Before the arbitrator finally accepts appointment, the basis of payment, including any cancellation fee, compensation in the event of withdrawal and compensation for study and preparation time, and all other charges, should be established. Except for arrangements for the compensation of party-appointed arbitrators, all parties should be informed in writing of the terms established;

(2) In proceedings conducted under the rules or administration of an institution that is available to assist in making arrangements for payments, communication related to compensation should be made through the institution. In proceedings where no institution has been engaged by the parties to administer the arbitration, any communication with arbitrators (other than party appointed arbitrators) concerning payments should be in the presence of all parties; and

(3) Arbitrators should not, absent extraordinary circumstances, request increases in the basis of their compensation during the course of a proceeding.

CANON VIII: AN ARBITRATOR MAY ENGAGE IN ADVERTISING OR PROMOTION OF ARBITRAL SERVICES WHICH IS TRUTHFUL AND ACCURATE

Advertising or promotion of an individual's willingness or availability to serve as an arbitrator must be accurate and unlikely to mislead. Any statements about the quality of the arbitrator's work or the success of the arbitrator's practice must be truthful.

Advertising and promotion must not imply any willingness to accept an appointment otherwise than in accordance with this Code.

Comment to Canon VIII

This Canon does not preclude an arbitrator from printing, publishing, or disseminating advertisements conforming to these standards in any electronic or print medium, from making personal presentations to prospective users of arbitral services conforming to such standards or from responding to inquiries concerning the arbitrator's availability, qualifications, experience, or fee arrangements.

CANON IX: ARBITRATORS APPOINTED BY ONE PARTY HAVE A DUTY TO DETERMINE AND DISCLOSE THEIR STATUS AND TO COMPLY WITH THIS CODE, EXCEPT AS EXEMPTED BY CANON X

A. In some types of arbitration in which there are three arbitrators, it is customary for each party, acting alone, to appoint one arbitrator. The third arbitrator is then appointed by agreement either of the parties or of the two arbitrators, or failing such agreement, by an independent institution or individual. In tripartite arbitrations to which this Code applies, all three arbitrators are presumed to be neutral and are expected to observe the same standards as the third arbitrator.

B. Notwithstanding this presumption, there are certain types of tripartite arbitration in which it is expected by all parties that the two arbitrators appointed by the parties may be predisposed toward the party appointing them. Those arbitrators, referred to in this Code as "Canon X arbitrators," are not to be held to the standards of neutrality and independence applicable to other arbitrators. Canon X describes the special ethical obligations of party-appointed arbitrators who are not expected to meet the standard of neutrality.

C. A party-appointed arbitrator has an obligation to ascertain, as early as possible but not later than the first meeting of the arbitrators and parties, whether the parties have agreed that the party-appointed arbitrators will serve as neutrals or whether they shall be subject to Canon X, and to provide a timely report of their conclusions to the parties and other arbitrators:

(1) Party-appointed arbitrators should review the agreement of the parties, the applicable rules and any applicable law bearing upon arbitrator neutrality. In reviewing the agreement of the parties, party-appointed arbitrators should consult any relevant express terms of

the written or oral arbitration agreement. It may also be appropriate for them to inquire into agreements that have not been expressly set forth, but which may be implied from an established course of dealings of the parties or well-recognized custom and usage in their trade or profession;

(2) Where party-appointed arbitrators conclude that the parties intended for the party-appointed arbitrators not to serve as neutrals, they should so inform the parties and the other arbitrators. The arbitrators may then act as provided in Canon X unless or until a different determination of their status is made by the parties, any administering institution or the arbitral panel; and

(3) Until party-appointed arbitrators conclude that the party-appointed arbitrators were not intended by the parties to serve as neutrals, or if the party-appointed arbitrators are unable to form a reasonable belief of their status from the foregoing sources and no decision in this regard has yet been made by the parties, any administering institution, or the arbitral panel, they should observe all of the obligations of neutral arbitrators set forth in this Code.

D. Party-appointed arbitrators not governed by Canon X shall observe all of the obligations of Canons I through VIII unless otherwise required by agreement of the parties, any applicable rules, or applicable law.

CANON X: EXEMPTIONS FOR ARBITRATORS APPOINTED BY ONE PARTY WHO ARE NOT SUBJECT TO RULES OF NEUTRALITY

Canon X arbitrators are expected to observe all of the ethical obligations prescribed by this Code except those from which they are specifically excused by Canon X.

A. Obligations under Canon I

Canon X arbitrators should observe all of the obligations of Canon I subject only to the following provisions:

(1) Canon X arbitrators may be predisposed toward the party who appointed them but in all other respects are obligated to act in good faith and with integrity and fairness. For example, Canon X arbitrators should not engage in delaying tactics or harassment of any party or witness and should not knowingly make untrue or misleading statements to the other arbitrators; and

(2) The provisions of subparagraphs B(1), B(2), and paragraphs C and D of Canon I, insofar as they relate to partiality, relationships, and interests are not applicable to Canon X arbitrators.

B. Obligations under Canon II

(1) Canon X arbitrators should disclose to all parties, and to the other arbitrators, all interests and relationships which Canon II requires be disclosed. Disclosure as required by Canon II is for the benefit not only of the party who appointed the arbitrator, but also for the benefit of the other parties and arbitrators so that they may know of any partiality which may exist or appear to exist; and

(2) Canon X arbitrators are not obliged to withdraw under paragraph G of Canon II if requested to do so only by the party who did not appoint them.

C. Obligations under Canon III

Canon X arbitrators should observe all of the obligations of Canon III subject only to the following provisions:

(1) Like neutral party-appointed arbitrators, Canon X arbitrators may consult with the party who appointed them to the extent permitted in paragraph B of Canon III;

(2) Canon X arbitrators shall, at the earliest practicable time, disclose to the other arbitrators and to the parties whether or not they intend to communicate with their appointing parties. If they have disclosed the intention to engage in such communications, they may thereafter communicate with their appointing parties concerning any other aspect of the case, except as provided in paragraph (3);

(3) If such communication occurred prior to the time they were appointed as arbitrators, or prior to the first hearing or other meeting of the parties with the arbitrators, the Canon X arbitrator should, at or before the first hearing or meeting of the arbitrators with the parties, disclose the fact that such communication has taken place. In complying with the provisions of this subparagraph, it is sufficient that there be disclosure of the fact that such communication has occurred without disclosing the content of the communication. A single timely disclosure of the Canon X arbitrator's intention to participate in such communications in the future is sufficient;

(4) Canon X arbitrators may not at any time during the arbitration:

(a) disclose any deliberations by the arbitrators on any matter or issue submitted to them for decision;

(b) communicate with the parties that appointed them concerning any matter or issue taken under consideration by the panel after the record is closed or such matter or issue has been submitted for decision; or

(c) disclose any final decision or interim decision in advance of the time that it is disclosed to all parties.

(5) Unless otherwise agreed by the arbitrators and the parties, a Canon X arbitrator may not communicate orally with the neutral

arbitrator concerning any matter or issue arising or expected to arise in the arbitration in the absence of the other Canon X arbitrator. If a Canon X arbitrator communicates in writing with the neutral arbitrator, he or she shall simultaneously provide a copy of the written communication to the other Canon X arbitrator;

(6) When Canon X arbitrators communicate orally with the parties that appointed them concerning any matter on which communication is permitted under this Code, they are not obligated to disclose the contents of such oral communications to any other party or arbitrator; and

(7) When Canon X arbitrators communicate in writing with the party who appointed them concerning any matter on which communication is permitted under this Code, they are not required to send copies of any such written communication to any other party or arbitrator.

D. Obligations under Canon IV
Canon X arbitrators should observe all of the obligations of Canon IV.

E. Obligations under Canon V
Canon X arbitrators should observe all of the obligations of Canon V, except that they may be predisposed toward deciding in favor of the party who appointed them.

F. Obligations under Canon VI
Canon X arbitrators should observe all of the obligations of Canon VI.

G. Obligations Under Canon VII
Canon X arbitrators should observe all of the obligations of Canon VII.

H. Obligations Under Canon VIII
Canon X arbitrators should observe all of the obligations of Canon VIII.

I. Obligations Under Canon IX
The provisions of paragraph D of Canon IX are inapplicable to Canon X arbitrators, except insofar as the obligations are also set forth in this Canon.

Model Clauses

ICC (INTERNATIONAL CHAMBER OF COMMERCE)

All disputes arising out of or in connection with the present contract shall be finally settled under the Rules of Arbitration of the International Chamber of Commerce by one or more arbitrators appointed in accordance with the said Rules.

LCIA (LONDON COURT OF INTERNATIONAL ARBITRATION)

Future disputes

Any dispute arising out of or in connection with this contract, including any question regarding its existence, validity or termination, shall be referred to and finally resolved by arbitration under the LCIA Rules, which Rules are deemed to be incorporated by reference into this clause.

The number of arbitrators shall be [one/three].
The seat, or legal place, of arbitration shall be [City and/or Country].
The language to be used in the arbitral proceedings shall be [ ].
The governing law of the contract shall be the substantive law of [ ].

Existing disputes

A dispute having arisen between the parties concerning [ ], the parties hereby agree that the dispute shall be referred to and finally resolved by arbitration under the LCIA Rules.

The number of arbitrators shall be [one/three].
The seat, or legal place, of arbitration shall be [City and/or Country].
The language to be used in the arbitral proceedings shall be [ ].
The governing law of the contract [is/shall be] the substantive law of [ ].

ICDR (INTERNATIONAL CENTRE FOR DISPUTE RESOLUTION OF THE AMERICAN ARBITRATION ASSOCIATION)

Any controversy or claim arising out of or relating to this contract, or the breach thereof, shall be determined by arbitration administered by the International Centre for Dispute Resolution in accordance with its International Arbitration Rules;

or

Any controversy or claim arising out of or relating to this contract, or the breach thereof, shall be determined by arbitration administered by the American Arbitration Association in accordance with its International Arbitration Rules.

The parties may wish to consider adding:

(a) The number of arbitrators shall be . . . (one or three);
(b) The place of arbitration shall be . . . (city and/or country);
(c) The language(s) of the arbitration shall be_____.

UNCITRAL (UNITED NATIONS COMMISSION ON INTERNATIONAL TRADE LAW)

Any dispute, controversy or claim arising out of or relating to this contract, or the breach, termination or invalidity thereof, shall be settled by arbitration in accordance with the UNCITRAL Arbitration Rules as at present in force.

Note – Parties may wish to consider adding:

(a) The appointing authority shall be . . . (name of institution or person);
(b) The number of arbitrators shall be . . . (one or three);
(c) The place of arbitration shall be . . . (town or country);
(d) The language(s) to be used in the arbitral proceedings shall be . . .

SCC (ARBITRATION INSTITUTE OF THE STOCKHOLM CHAMBER OF COMMERCE)

Any dispute, controversy or claim arising out of or in connection with this contract, or the breach, termination or invalidity thereof, shall be finally settled by arbitration in accordance with the Arbitration Rules of the Arbitration Institute of the Stockholm Chamber of Commerce.

The parties are advised to make the following additions to the arbitration clause, as required:

> The arbitral tribunal shall be composed of.........arbitrators (a sole arbitrator).
> The seat of arbitration shall be....................................
> The language to be used in the arbitral proceedings shall be..........

CIETAC (CHINA INTERNATIONAL ECONOMIC AND TRADE ARBITRATION COMMISSION)

Any dispute arising from or in connection with this Contract shall be submitted to the China International Economic and Trade Arbitration Commission for arbitration which shall be conducted in accordance with the Commission's arbitration rules in effect at the time of applying for arbitration. The arbitral award is final and binding upon both parties.

GERMAN INSTITUTION OF ARBITRATION (DEUTSCHE INSTITUTION FÜR SCHIEDSGERICHTSBARKEIT e.V. (DIS))

All disputes arising in connection with this contract or its validity shall be finally settled in accordance with the Arbitration Rules of the German Institution of Arbitration (DIS) without recourse to the ordinary courts of law.

The following points should be considered:

- The place of arbitration is ...
- The number of arbitrators is ...
- The language of the arbitral proceedings is ...
- The applicable substantive law is ...

Useful Arbitration Websites

	A	B
	International Conventions	Website
1	The United Nations Convention on the Recognition and Enforcement of Foreign Arbitral Awards (The New York Convention)	http://www.uncitral.org/pdf/english/texts/arbitration/NY-conv/XXII_1_e.pdf
2	The Inter-American Convention on International Commercial Arbitration (The Panama Convention)	http://www.sice.oas.org/dispute/comarb/iacac/iacac2e.asp
3	European Convention on International Commercial Arbitration	www.jurisint.org/doc/html/ins/en/2002/2002jiinsen6.html
4	Washington Convention on the Settlement of Investment Disputes between States and Nationals of Other States (ICSID Convention or Washington Convention)	http://icsid.worldbank.org/ICSID/StaticFiles/basicdoc/CRR_English-final.pdf
5	The Inter-American Convention on the Law Applicable to International Contracts ("Mexico City Convention")	http://www.oas.org/juridico/English/treaties/b-56.html

(*continued*)

	A	B
6	UN Convention on Contracts for the International Sale of Goods (CISG)	http://www.uncitral.org/pdf/english/texts/sales/cisg/CISG.pdf
7	Convention on the Law Applicable to Contractual Obligations ("Rome Convention")	http://eur-lex.europa.eu/LexUriServ/LexUriServ.do?uri=OJ:L:1980:266:0001:0010:EN:PDF

National Laws

1	Australian International Arbitration Act of 1974	http://www.austlii.edu.au/au/legis/cth/consol_act/iaa1974276/
2	Brazil Arbitration Law	http://www.jus.uio.no/lm/brazil.arbitration.law.no.9.307.1996/
3	English Arbitration Act of 1996	http://www.legislation.gov.uk/ukpga/1996/23/contents
4	French Arbitration Law	http://www.iaiparis.com/pdf/FRENCH_LAW_ON_ARBITRATION.pdf
5	German Arbitration Act of 1998	http://www.dis-arb.de/en/51/materials/german-arbitration-law-98-id3
6	Japan Arbitration Law of 2003	http://www.kantei.go.jp/foreign/policy/sihou/arbitrationlaw.pdf
7	Netherlands Arbitration Act	http://www.jus.uio.no/lm/netherlands.arbitration.act.1986/
8	People's Republic of China Arbitration Law	http://www.dis-arb.de/en/51/materials/german-arbitration-law-98-id3
9	Swedish Arbitration Act	http://www.chamber.se/?id=23746
10	Swiss Private International Law Act	http://www.umbricht.ch/pdf/SwissPIL.pdf
11	UNCITRAL Model Law (as adopted in most Model Law States)	http://www.uncitral.org/pdf/english/texts/arbitration/ml-arb/06–54671–Ebook.pdf
12	Revised articles of the UNCITRAL Model Law	http://www.uncitral.org/pdf/english/texts/arbitration/ml-arb/A1E.pdf
13	US Federal Arbitration Act	http://www.adr.org/sp.asp?id=29568

	A	B
	Arbitration Rules	
1	American Arbitration Association/International Center for Dispute Resolution (ICDR)	http://www.adr.org/si.asp?id=6447
2	Arbitration Institute of the Stockholm Chamber of Commerce (SCC)	http://www.sccinstitute.com/ filearchive/3/35894/ K4_Skiljedomsregler%20eng% 20ARB%20TRYCK_1_100927.pdf
3	Australian Centre for International Commercial Arbitration	http://acica.org.au/acica-services/ acica-arbitration-rules
4	Cairo Regional Centre for International Commercial Arbitration	http://www.crcica.org.eg/ publication/arbitration_rules/pdf/ English/CRCICA_arbitration_ rules_en.pdf
5	Chamber of Arbitration of Milan	http://www.camera-arbitrale.it/ Documenti/cam_arbitration-rules_ 2010.pdf
6	China International Economic Trade and Arbitration Commission (CIETAC)	http://cn.cietac.org/Rules/rules.pdf
7	The Court of International Commercial Arbitration (attached to the Chamber of Commerce and Industry of Romania)	http://arbitration.ccir.ro/engleza/ rulesarb.htm
8	European Court of Arbitration	http://cour-europe-arbitrage.org/ archivos/descargas/17.pdf
9	German Institution of Arbitration (DIS)	http://www.dis-arb.de/en/16/rules/ dis-arbitration-rules-98-id10
10	International Chamber of Commerce (ICC)	http://www.iccwbo.org/ uploadedFiles/Court/Arbitration/ other/rules_arb_english.pdf
11	London Court of International Arbitration (LCIA)	http://www.lcia.org/Dispute_ Resolution_Services/LCIA_ Arbitration_Rules.aspx

(continued)

	A	B
12	Netherlands Arbitration Institute (NAI) Arbitration Rules	http://www.nai-nl.org/en/form.asp?id=14
13	Swiss Rules of International Arbitration	https://www.sccam.org/sa/download/SRIA_english.pdf
14	UNCITRAL Arbitration Rules	http://www.uncitral.org/pdf/english/texts/arbitration/arb-rules/arb-rules.pdf
15	ICSID Arbitration Rules	http://icsid.worldbank.org/ICSID/StaticFiles/basicdoc/CRR_English-final.pdf
16	World Intellectual Property Organization (WIPO)	http://www.wipo.int/amc/en/arbitration/rules/

Model Clauses

	A	B
1	Abu Dhabi Commercial Conciliation & Arbitration Center (ADCCAC)	http://www.jurisint.org/doc/html/cla/en/2005/2005jiclaen60.html
2	American Arbitration Association/International Center for Dispute Resolution (ICDR)	http://www.adr.org/si.asp?id=6447
3	Australian Centre for International Commercial Arbitration (ACICA)	http://acica.org.au/acica-services/arbitration-clauses
4	Arbitration Institute of the Stockholm Chamber of Commerce	http://www.sccinstitute.com/english-14.aspx
5	Cairo Regional Centre for International Commercial Arbitration (CRCICA)	http://www.crcica.org.eg/English_Rules.pdf (found as a footnote to Section I, Introductory Rules)
6	Chamber of Arbitration of Milan	http://www.camera-arbitrale.it/risolvi.php?sez_id=63&lng_id=14
7	Chicago International Dispute Resolution Association (CIDRA)	http://www.cidra.org/modelarb
8	China International Economic Trade and Arbitration Commission (CIETAC)	http://arbitration.practicallaw.com/9-381-9852

	A	B
9	German Institution of Arbitration (DIS)	http://www.dis-arb.de/en/17/clause/dis-arbitration-clause-98-id3
10	Hong Kong International Arbitration Center (HKIAC)	http://www.hkiac.org/show_content.php?article_id=381
11	International Chamber of Commerce (ICC)	http://www.iccwbo.org/court/english/arbitration/word_documents/model_clause/mc_arb_english.txt
12	International Centre for Settlement of Investment Disputes (ICSID)	http://icsid.worldbank.org/ICSID/StaticFiles/model-clauses-en/main-eng.htm
13	London Court of International Arbitration (LCIA)	http://www.lcia.org/Dispute_Resolution_Services/LCIA_Recommended_Clauses.aspx
14	Singapore International Arbitration Centre (SIAC)	http://www.siac.org.sg/index.php?option=com_content&view=article&id=67&Itemid=88

Codes & Guidelines

	A	B
1	AAA/ABA Code of Ethics for Arbitrators	http://www.adr.org/si.asp?id=4582
2	IBA Guidelines on Conflicts of Interest in International Arbitration	http://www.int-bar.org/images/downloads/guidelines%20text.pdf
3	IBA Rules on Ethics for Arbitrators	http://www.int-bar.org/images/downloads/pubs/Ethics_arbitrators.pdf
4	IBA Rules on the Taking of Evidence in International Arbitration	http://www.ibanet.org/Publications/publications_IBA_guides_and_free_materials.aspx#takingevidence
5	UNCITRAL Notes on Organizing Arbitral Proceedings	http://www.uncitral.org/pdf/english/texts/arbitration/arb-notes/arb-notes-e.pdf

International Arbitration Organizations

	A	B
1	American Arbitration Association/International) Centre for Dispute Resolution (ICDR)	http://www.adr.org/
2	Arbitration Institute of the Stockholm Chamber of Commerce (SCC)	http://www.sccinstitute.com

(*continued*)

	A	B	
3	Australian Centre for International Commercial Arbitration (ACICA)	http://cour-europe-arbitrage.org/index.php	
4	Cairo Regional Centre for International Commercial arbitration	http://www.crcica.org.eg/	
5	Chamber of Arbitration of Milan	http://www.camera-arbitrale.it/index.php?lng_id=14	
6	Chicago International Dispute Resolution Association (CIDRA)	http://www.cidra.org/	
7	China International Economic Trade and Arbitration Commission (CIETAC)	http://www.cietac.org/index.cms	
8	Court of Arbitration for Sport	http://www.tas-cas.org/	
9	European Court of Arbitration (Strasbourg, France)	http://cour-europe-arbitrage.org/index.php	
10	German Institution of Arbitration (DIS)	http://www.dis-arb.de/	
11	Hong Kong International Arbitration Center (HKIAC)	http://www.tas-cas.org/	
12	International Centre for Settlement of Investment Disputes (ICSID)	http://www.tas-cas.org/	
13	International Chamber of Commerce (ICC)	http://www.iccwbo.org/court	
14	International Institute for Conflict Prevention and Resolution (CPR)	http://cpradr.org	
15	Iran-United States Claims Tribunal	http://www.iusct.org/index-english.html	Note – free registration required to access database
16	JAMS, Inc.	http://www.jamsadr.com	
17	London Court of International Arbitration	http://www.tas-cas.org/	

	A	B
18	Netherlands Arbitration Institute (NAI)	http://www.nai-nl.org/english/
19	Singapore International Arbitration Centre (SIAC)	http://www.siac.org.sg
20	Swiss Arbitration Association	http://www.arbitration-ch.org/index.php
21	World Intellectual Property Organization (WIPO)	http://www.wipo.int/amc/en/
	Useful links (for research, etc.)	
1	International Arbitration – Locating the Resources	http://www.llrx.com/features/arbitration.htm
2	Baker & McKenzie	http://www.bakermckenzie.com/disputeresolution/internationalarbitration/publications/
3	British and Irish Legal Information Institute	http://www.bailii.org
4	Electronic Information System for International Law	www.eisil.org
5	EUR-Lex (Access to European Union Law)	http://eur-lex.europa.eu/en/index.htm
6	European Court of Justice	http://curia.europa.eu/
7	Collection Juris International	http://www.jurisint.org
8	French Code of Civil Procedure	http://www.lexinter.net/ENGLISH/code_of_civil_procedure.htm
9	German Code of Civil Procedure *(in German)*	http://www.gesetze-im-internet.de/zpo/index.html
10	Google Webpage Language translator	http://www.google.com/language_tools?hl=en
11	IBA Arbitration webpage	http://www.ibanet.org/legalpractice/Arbitration.cfm
12	Italian Code of Civil Procedure *(in English; this link goes to the section pertaining to arbitration)*	http://www.jus.uio.no/lm/italy.arbitration/doc.html

(*continued*)

	A	B
13	Mayer Brown International Arbitration resource site	http://www.mayerbrown.com/internationalarbitration/
14	New York Convention party map	http://www.uncitral.org/uncitral/en/uncitral_texts/arbitration/NYConvention.html
15	Supreme Court of India	http://www.supremecourtofindia.nic.in/
16	United Kingdom (U.K.) Court Service (Her Majesty's Court Service)	http://www.hmcourts-service.gov.uk/
17	U.K. Parliament – House of Lords judgments	http://www.publications.parliament.uk/pa/ld/ldjudgmt.htm
18	U.K. Statute database	http://www.legislation.gov.uk/
19	U.S. Code	http://uscode.house.gov/
20	World Legal Information Institute	http://www.worldlii.org/

Index